Findings and Keepings:
Analects for an Autobiography

Books by Lewis Mumford

LEWIS MUMFORD, Aet. 30

DRAWING BY HUGO GELLERT, 1925.

LEWIS MUMFORD

Findings and Keepings

Analects for an Autobiography

HARCOURT BRACE JOVANOVICH

NEW YORK AND LONDON

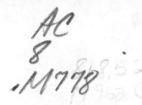

Of the articles in this collection, those beginning on the following respective pages appeared originally in *The New Yorker*: 325, 326 (last paragraph), 327, 332, 334, 335, 346, 349, 351, 360, and 369. Excerpts from letters written to Van Wyck Brooks are from *The Van Wyck Brooks Lewis Mumford Letters*, edited by Robert E. Spiller, copyright © 1970 by E. P. Dutton & Co., Inc., and are reprinted with their permission. Excerpts from Lewis Mumford's *Sticks and Stones*, 1955, are reprinted with the permission of Dover Publications, Inc. Articles that orginally appeared in the New York *Herald Tribune* are used by permission.

CAUTION: All rights in the play, "The Builders of the Bridge," including professional, amateur, motion picture, dramatic, recitation, lecturing, public reading, radio broadcasting, and television, are strictly reserved to Lewis Mumford. Inquiries on these particular rights should be addressed to Lewis Mumford in care of Harcourt Brace Jovanovich, Inc., 757 Third Avenue, New York, N.Y. 10017.

Library of Congress Cataloging in Publication Data

Mumford, Lewis, 1895-
   Findings and keepings, 1914-1936.

   Includes index.
   I. Title.
AC8.M778   818'.5'209   75-17607
ISBN 0-15-130984-1

First edition

B C D E

TO SOPHIA
The best of my 'Findings,'
the most enduring of my 'Keepings.'

Contents

POSTLUDE

Prologue to Our Time: 1895-1975

Part One

1914-1919

Concerning Analects

I will buy the suppressed part
of the author's mind—you are
welcome to all he published.
—Emerson: The Journals, 1853

This book is mainly a culling from the midden heap of my unpublished, or bashfully published, writings. The earliest writings date back to 1914, when a short story of mine came out in 'The Forum,' then a kind of adventurous variant of 'The Atlantic Monthly.' And I will thank no one for ransacking our Amenia attic for my more juvenile effusions in 'Modern Electrics' or my High School monthly. The contents of this volume are somewhat like the preliminary probings that a conscientious biographer might make, hoping to find a few nuggets in the gravel and muck.

But why, the reader may well ask, do I now choose to publish this formless Miscellany? Have I not already confessed to writing the first half of my Autobiography, in which the main events of my open and private life are being sorted out and presented in an intelligible thematic sequence, from which something like a coherent pattern should emerge? The answer is that I am not, in the current academic fashion, a conscientious biographer; for I know that only a small part of this data could be emptied into the running stream of my past experiences without muddying and impeding its flow. At one time I even thought that 'Flotsam and Jetsam' might be the right title for the present book, knowing that many significant if seemingly trivial events, caught in the eddies and backwaters of one's life might nevertheless be worth fishing out even if they never entered the mainstream.

When I began my autobiography, as far back as 1956, I hardly glanced at these 'findings and keepings': I drew almost as freely on my spontaneous memories as William Butler Yeats did in his early memoir. But before the first volume was even half written I discovered, when I was prompted to verify some of my hazier recollections, what a great difference there is between an authentic, first-hand account of events, and the residue that is left in the mind. Again and again I found, to my humiliation, that my memory proved heavily colored—and was sometimes unconsciously falsified—by later experience. Though I have duly noted those various corrections, what will finally come forth in my more formal story must be trued up in the light of the unsullied evidence in this book. In a sense, these artless items have more final authority than the finished account.

Not that 'Findings and Keepings' has been put together in a hit-or-miss fashion: it is as selective, indeed as highly organized, as any of my other books, but on a different principle. This is a deliberate effort to juxtapose in the order of their actual appearance, a multitude of ideas, feelings, emotions, experiences, dreams, observations, which will reappear in a quite different order in the autobiography, or sometimes drop entirely out of sight. For long I was skeptical of the importance of Jung's principle of synchronicity, yet in choosing these contents I began to understand how seemingly unconnected events that occurred at the same time might in fact reveal vital aspects of the inner life, if not of the operations of a mythic Unconscious.

The basic authenticity of these 'Findings' comes from the fact that, apart from already published work, there are many private revelations that I would never have committed to a letter or a journal if my eye had been even obliquely fixed on posterity. With a bare fistful of exceptions I kept no carbon copies of my letters: those that are quoted here were returned to me by their addressees, sometimes during their lifetime. My 'Random Notes' and my earliest manuscripts likewise were written on the cheapest manilla paper, many sheets by now so brittle they could hardly stay together long enough to be copied. Publication, however remote, was not in my mind.

But these notes often performed a therapeutic function. In periods of personal crisis some of the most intimate self-revelations helped me to uncover my own emotional confusions and moral contradictions: so I have not hesitated to draw on them, since they served me, as others have been served by an orthodox psychanalysis. Such candor is not always congenial to one's friends or admirers. In reserves, Melville says in 'Pierre,' men build up imposing reputations. Perhaps not the least merit of this book is that I have been ready, on occasion, to flout my private censor and have broken through my normal reserves—not to titillate or shock the reader, but in an effort to be honest with myself: honest, naked, and shameless, except when the private affairs of still living people are involved. But to a generation wallowing in pornography, these little sidelights have nothing whatever to say.

The order I have followed in putting this material together is mainly that of the calendar. But for the sake of clarifying a theme, I have sometimes departed from this order with a relevant item written years later, and have allowed these periods to be blurred a little at the edges. If there has been any guiding principle in this jumble it is that the individual items should throw some light on my 'life and times,' and should if possible be interesting in their own right—though I have not hesitated at times to dig up observations which will be boring to nine people out of ten, for the sake of some sudden illumination the tenth will get.

4

(Wise readers know when to skip.) Deliberate randomness is of course a contradiction in terms. But what I have done, I see now, is similar to what goes on in the mind in actual waking life. Was this not perhaps James Joyce's most original contribution when he wrote 'Ulysses'—though he had little to teach the author of 'Hamlet' or 'King Lear.'

The term 'analects' which I have used in the subtitle gives an accurate description of this book: for the Greek root means things 'picked up,' and my English dictionary translates this as 'crumbs,' 'literary gleanings'—a definition that wipes out any seemingly pretentious reference to Confucius. But an even more accurate word for this book would be the modern painter's *collage*, for this would emphasize the difference in size, shape, texture, color, substance of the individual items, and suggest that, despite my sometimes disconcerting juxtapositions of the old and the new, the trivial and the precious, the accidental and the purposeful, the nonsensical and the significant, the intimate and the public, what lies within this frame forms an intelligible picture.

I would not, however, overstress the biographical element in this selection, except in so far as every expression of an author's mind is in fact an essential part, often the most essential part, of his biography. For it is not merely the personal experience, but the lives of one's contemporaries, the opportunities and pressures of one's period and one's milieu, that form the living whole: so along with more purely private concerns I have taken pains to single out certain essays which, even if unpublished at the time, throw some light on the whole period: more so now, perhaps, than if they had met more timely publication.

Certainly it is important for anyone who seeks to understand my development to know that as early as 1919, 'The Marriage of Museums' struck the essential chord of the rest of my intellectual life, taken up, amplified, intensified, in book after book. Though this line of development seems clear, I have readily let slip into oblivion other tentative sallies and experiments that pointed sometimes in contrary directions, as one might throw away clothes one had tried on but never felt at home in or wanted to keep as part of one's daily wardrobe, still less wished to pass on to some ill-clothed unfortunate in a later generation. The Pauline injunction, Prove all things and hold fast to what is good, applies here, too. In this context 'good' means consistent with the whole life, or relevant to its nature.

Random Notes

I have begun these notes, partly in imitation of Samuel Butler, and partly because I stand aghast at the fund of gristy material I have wasted in the past. At best one's most vivid memories are only memories; they are flighty, unaccountable, and never around when you are really in need of them. And then, they are ever so much more pallid than the real materials of sense that you wish to recover. I would give anything for a ten reel moving picture of my life during the last four years, with copious inserts to register the ever-changing succession of mental states, philosophies, dreams, desires, plans, aspirations, and what not. It might grieve me, of course, to learn how pitifully foolish a young man can be; but it would give my present self a more solid foundation. On the other hand, I am not sure whether too great a degree of self-consciousness might not overbalance the worth of such a record. To be neither completely self-conscious, nor completely unconscious is the trick. My last three years have been wasted if I have not acquired it.   —RN. 1914 *

I think every person of sensibility feels that he has been born "out of his due time." Athens during the early sixth century B.C. would have been more to my liking than New York in the twentieth century after Christ. It is true, this would have cut me off from Socrates, who lived in the disappointing period that followed. But then, I might have been Socrates.   —RN. 1915

You may speak of Plato (if you know anything about him) as a conservative, but at any rate he was a hearty feminist, and one of the first who urged woman to leave her dolls, just as Ibsen later urged her to leave her Doll's House. His plan for having girls and women exercize naked along with the men and boys, is about the only sensible proposal I am aware of for bringing the sexual reflexes under control: as it undoubtedly would. What is especially alluring about a beautiful woman is not her beauty, but the veils you wish to remove. Once they

* Hereafter RN. refers to Random Notes.

7

are gone you have the chance of developing people who appreciate physical passion without being obsessed by it. And if you can't develop such people you must give the race over to the prudes and the prostitutes: those who avoid sex completely, and those who avoid everything but sex.   —RN. 1915

FIRST AND LAST THINGS.   Every religion and every philosophy is an attempt to make sense out of this seemingly nonsensical spectacle of life: this Shakesperian tragedy with a porter who says funny things before a doomed man's crime gets found out.

Every religion is a brave guess at the authorship of Hamlet. Yet, as far as the play goes does it make any difference whether Shakespeare or Bacon wrote it? Would it make any difference to the actors if their parts happened out of nothingness, if they found themselves acting on the stage because of some gross and unpardonable accident? Would it make any difference if the playwright gave them the lines or whether they composed them themselves, so long as the lines were properly spoken? Would it make any difference to the characters if 'A Midsummer Night's Dream' was really a dream? Would it make any difference if it could be proved with mathematical exactitude that happiness was not dealt out 'Measure for Measure'?

Is not our problem in life to say our lines properly, and 'to suit the action to the word and the word to the action'? Why should we bother whether our performance is reported in silly newspapers for the benefit of posterity. In the language of the stage, let us have art for art's sake. Or, as I would put it let us live life for life's sake. Does it really make any difference whether we get our salary on the next payday or whether there isn't any money in the box office—or any box office? —RN. 1915

JUVENILIA.   At times your oldtime pupil may forget his promises, but he will not forget you. And this, I think, is an especially fitting moment to remember you, for it is connected with Bernard Shaw. You did it! *You* advised me to study him. Of course, there was some supposition that I was to study his drama (we were dreadfully interested in Drama once, you'll remember). But I went a step further: I studied his ideas. Monstrous! In one year I was changed from a weak-kneed conservative (with no philosophy and hardly any opinions) to a rather

8

wild young man with a brick in my right hand and a red flag in my buttonhole. I might add parenthetically: with a tough philosophy (William James) and a prejudice against all opinions. . . . Well, then, in the November 'Metropolitan' G.B.S. sprang into print with a long-winded speech on 'The Case for Equality.' It was well advertized. [A prize of $500 was offered for the best reply.] At first the affair did not interest me at all. Then an intuition puddled around in my consciousness; finally it became an idea. And the idea was this: Bernard Shaw is no longer a radical; Bernard Shaw is a conservative. I am really farther in the vanguard than Shaw is. "The old order changeth, yielding place to new." Well! I was sure that I was more radical than Shaw was, but I had my doubts whether I could express my radicalism in words—the letter killeth. Nevertheless I tried. After putting the work off day after day I at length had a thousand words written, which though rather faulty in style, almost expressed my thoughts. With no palpitation or eagerness I mailed my letter to the 'Metropolitan.' (Business of mailing a letter). . . .

On the twentieth of January—well, on the twentieth of January I found that I had not won the prize (which I had expected); but also I found that my reply had been printed (which I had not expected). There was my little essay, black as type; and there was my name, brazen as Buddha. That night I regret to say it took me nearly an hour to go to sleep. For the safety of my soul I sorrowfully admit that I was more elated over the eighty-six dollars I received next morning than I was over the honor which had fallen to me. But then—I must have postage stamps!

Do not fear, Mr. Bates (what I usually fear); that I may get a "swell-head." The Fates prevent such a disaster. On January twenty-first I received precisely five rejection slips.

—Letter to Thomas Bates. January 23, 1914.

Note: There is more than one reason for exposing this perfect museum specimen of adolescent bumptiousness. Bates was my teacher of Freshman English at Stuyvesant and the faculty adviser of our junior dramatic society, The Boar's Head. Incited by him, three of us wrote a silly rural farce, Dr. Bilby's Aeroplane, painted the scenery for it, and mounted it before the School: the abortive beginning of my equally aborted dramatic career. But this letter throws an even more significant light upon the 'progress' of technology. For less than three months passed between the magazine publication of Shaw's article and the appearance of Lincoln Steffen's and my replies. What speedy decision-making and printing!

KENNERLEY ON THE NEW REPUBLICANS.   Today I met Mitchell Kennerley for the first time; and I found him cordial, kindly, humorous, and live-witted. He explained that he had taken over a new venture, and was accordingly quite busy, for the sake of being able to publish a few more volumes of poetry. This reassured me right away, and I had no further doubts about the subimpudent letter I'd written him. He asked me whether I had tried 'The New Republic.' "You belong there," he assured me. I told him I had sent them articles again and again and again, and had even been told that my last article was under consideration, only to be disappointed at long last. "I'm afraid your article had an opinion in it," said Kennerley solemnly. "It's a journal of opinion, you know, and they don't like to publish other peoples' . . ." Then he went on to say that they needed somebody with a sense of humor; and accordingly, if I had no objections, he would send Lippmann a copy of 'The Classicist' (which they had rejected) and would try to press my merits upon him. I murmured my thanks, and left him not a little elated.   —August 29, 1916

THEME FOR A PLAY: THE COUNCIL OF SUPERMEN.   Invitations are mysteriously sent to a number of Supermen, who are requested to join in a conference for their present self-protection and for the ultimate extinction of the rest of the human race. Thirty or forty of them meet in a lonely wood; hundreds more promise to come; even at the end of the play they are arriving—clamantly. Little men, big men, athletic men, puny men, scientists, artists, ignoramuses, earnest second-rate persons, poseurs, and so forth. They discuss their respective merits and grievances, and they can agree upon nothing, each claiming for himself undeniable superiority and dismissing the rest as *'of the herd.'* They finally break into a quarrel and become a hawking mob, in the midst of whose shouting Kelley, their chairman (an ex-Tammany contractor) announces that he is the conceiver of the meeting and that it is simply a gigantic hoax. *Kelley himself is the only Superman.* A couple of physicians convince themselves that he is suffering from delusions of grandeur, bind him up, and lead him away. Meanwhile the influx of Supermen does not let up.   —RN. 1918

MISSED OPPORTUNITIES.   I have no small opinion of my keenness and pertinacity, until I find myself missing the sort of opportunity I missed last Sunday. I had gone into a crowded restaurant on Broadway

10

and had seated myself adjacent to a shriveling, white-haired, hazel-eyed man whose rural aspect showed him to be remote, either in time or in place, from contemporary Manhattan. He was silent and contained: I was silent and contained: the dinners which we respectively ordered passed silently into the regions where they could be most efficiently contained. But at the very close of the meal a minor catastrophe brought us together. The revolving entrance door, with which we were in direct line, got jammed and the opening of the emergency door let in a stiff March gale. So we warmed each other with reproaches against the weather. The winter reminded him of an extraordinary frost in 1857, when the North River was deviously crossed at Communipaw—and from this he went on to discuss the panic of that year, the panic of seventy-three, the present banking system, farm tenancy in the pioneer Middle West, and the like. Among other things, he had been sent out West in the seventies, because the doctors said he had consumption, and he told me with a confident smile which I mirrored sympathetically, that he had been consuming ever since, and was none the worse for it. Then it came out that he had been a member of the old Ninth Ward. I say a member because the ward was more than a place of residence, it was a club. At this point a particularly chilly draft blew the menus off the tablecloth and fear into my soul; and with a slight exchange of compliments, I departed.

Five minutes later the depth and grandeur of my obtuseness dawned upon me. Here was an actively intelligent participant in the period about which I was writing, and yet I had done no more than tolerate negligently the revelations he was ready to make to me about that life: had done nothing to make him expand and develop his memories: had treated him as I might treat any casual stranger who had something tedious to say about the affairs of last week. Useless to blame it on my sore throat and my chills and my consequent haste to get away from the drafts. I should have sat stubbornly at table and have rapaciously commanded him to disgorge every memory, until I had at my feet a vision of the city, of the way he entered his vocation, of the movement of population, of the ideas that afflicted the young before the Civil War, of a thousand and one trifles which one either has the rare luck to get directly from a living being, or which one does without altogether. Such criminal apathy will certainly never get hold of me again; but what I am also afraid of is that I will never again get the opportunity to prove this. The older generation is elusive: and an incisive memory is not to be picked up in a restaurant every day in the year.   —RN. 1918

Fruit: A Story

Regularly after breakfast every morning Mrs. Jarvis would say: "Wilbur, that garden is a Perfect Sight. When will you *ever* get at it?" And Jarvis would answer with sublime patience: "Presently, my dear. Don't you see that these lessons keep me everlastingly busy?" Then he would resume his grim preparation of questions for an incipient quiz.

But this morning was different. In college the night before Jarvis had had a distressing argument with one of his students; and he was not sure he had come off victorious. Throughout his journey home little demons of doubt had thrust themselves out of the background of his mind; they had made his slumber uneven, and they jaundiced the golden glare of the morning sun.

"I must try to smooth myself out," Jarvis told himself, as he swallowed an extra cup of coffee. And he formally resolved to drink Postum.

He had gone a little too far, it occurred to him, as he dawdled over the afternoon's lessons; tried to load on too much. One couldn't keep up day *and* night the enervating mental stress of teaching Latin. Had his wife not assured him at the beginning of the semester that little Junius Jarvis was positively in rags, he would most assuredly have avoided teaching in the evening session. It did not seem quite orthodox to attend college after sundown—in spite of that fine phrase about burning the midnight oil. The very words used by the evening session's director should have warned Jarvis; for he had intimated that the professor of Latin was about to open the Gates of Centuries to mature men, and that consequently discipline might to a large extent be dropped. . . .

Jarvis's mouth had tightened very firmly at the possibility of dropping discipline. . . .

There were certain principles which he (as a Sane Conservative) always and forever stood for; which principles could most readily be summed up in the word *discipline*. In his very college—by some called a dungeon of conservatism—there had been alarming signs which portended that the reign of discipline, and even of the Disciplines, was coming to an end. Jarvis was wont to lament at faculty conferences that there was a "tendency fraught with the greatest danger" to allow un-trained youths to elect their studies—none of which ever, by any chance, proved to be a Discipline. He knew with awful certainty that the absence of discipline caused nations to become soft (like the Teutons); increased the discontent of the masses; was a source of sundry evils in our Public Life; and perhaps in some measure could be connected with the disgraceful sophomore beer-drinking contest.

In short, the outcome of undisciplined study was Instability—and the Red Flag!

The sovereign method Jarvis advocated for the restoration of law in the land was the restoration of Livy in the schools. He had even written a copious and well-annotated treatise on 'The Uses of the Genitive Case in Livy,' with the object of increasing the waning interest in that great historian. But he had his qualms as to whether this was not unduly catering to Popular Sentiment. . . .

For twenty years Jarvis had taught Latin with a full recognition of the immense value of himself and his subject, and of the important part both played in creating a Stable Commonwealth. Generally he prefaced the studies of each new class with the profound observation that not only was Latin a Cultural Subject, ever worthy to be studied as an example of a Noble Civilization which far surpassed these Sadly Shifting Times, but Latin was also undoubtedly an excellent training for the Intellect, especially for the Logical Faculty, being in this respect not inferior to the Higher Mathematics, and that it had afforded for many generations in the past, and would continue to afford for many generations in the future, that finely rigorous mental training which is so necessary a part of the education of a Gentleman. (Full pause.)

Occasionally Jarvis would read attacks upon classical studies in the more shallow educational periodicals; but it took considerably more than these trifling sallies to agitate the sturdy brain of Jarvis, whose nervous system was buried in the splendid dust of Rome. Nevertheless, he once took pains to establish the fact that those students who had taken Latin throughout their collegiate course, were, at graduation, superior to the rest of the human race. (*Jarvis demonstrated this most satisfactorily by means of term averages.*) But he never was sufficiently perturbed by these attacks to proceed with the matter further; and he ridiculed the need for following the Disciplined Ones into their later careers. . . .

His wife had said: "Will you *ever* get at the garden, Wilbur?" And this morning he was sure he would not. . . .

For two months all that personality of his which was rooted in 'Jarvis's Latin for Beginners' had been engaged in a frightful struggle with an idea. In the wan hours of the night that was gone this idea had lain like an incubus on his bosom; it had oppressed him unutterably; and in the lucid consciousness of dawn it had taken form for the hundredth time. *"What use is this Latin of mine?"*

For so long had Jarvis lived in an atmosphere of sanctified stupidity, with students he could awe into submission, or with colleagues whom he could ignore, that he found his night students extraordinary to the point of being monstrous. By a queer twist of fate Jarvis had elected to teach a group of men who were singularly of one mind; and what a peculiar sort of mind that was! Always questioning, always urging, always disturbing. Theirs was such an *infringing* attitude toward life! . . .

Contrary to long-encrusted precedent, they delighted to linger after the period and discuss the "value of all this." To Jarvis these sessions speedily got to be very trying. He found that when he praised Latin authors whom he had long ceased to read with any degree of pleasure, he was on unsound ground; for at least two of his students had actually read most of the works in English, and were able to discuss them far more intelligently than Jarvis himself. And when Jarvis fell back on the stupendous mental training which a study of the language afforded (not inferior to the Higher Mathematics), he was assailed by quotations from obviously biased psychologists.

"Conjugating a Latin verb gives the kind of mental training necessary for a postal clerk who has to learn to put things quickly in the right pigeonholes," said one student.

"Or for the kind of person that always has at his fingertips a thousand and one hard, dull, and uncorrelated facts, and uses them on every occasion to make a bore of himself. . . ."

Then the night before the climax had been capped. An aggressive little fellow had informed Jarvis, with an irritating confidence, that *he* was a Vitalist, and he wanted to know how Latin aided Life? He appealed fiercely to Jarvis to answer whether the energy wasted on the Humanities of yesterday could not better be spent on the Humanity of today. To which Jarvis had very sagely replied (as he thought at the moment) that he was afraid the young man was a socialist. . . .

Crossing and re-crossing the panorama of Jarvis's consciousness as he sat squirming over his papers, were all those doubts and questionings, conceived in the months past, and born during the night. Oh, that argument came back to him as particularly cutting and painful,—and he had slept wretchedly. Perhaps (my God, the heresy!) perhaps Latin was useless! Ah, Jarvis knew that he could never again face his classes with that oldtime smug assurance; he could never again so remorselessly grind the eighty-one rules of syntax into those once defenceless heads. Gone was discipline! Perhaps Latin was useless! (The awful doubt!) Perhaps then he was useless too. . . .

14

Jarvis roused himself. He stumbled to the porch; he seized a spade; and he went forth into the garden and began to dig. . . .

—The Forum. December 1914

Note: The publication of this sketch kept my courage up during the next four years, when every offering of mine was turned down by editors. But I have lived to repent my rebellion against Latin and my failure to acquire even a smattering of Greek.

Random Notes

THE SURVIVAL OF THE FITTEST: SETTING FOR A PLAY

MAGNI, *a philosopher*
TELNO, *an inventor*
GRAULA, *an idiot*
PORTSMOTH, *a politician—or one who would be, at any rate, if there were any politics*
SENIAN, *a revolutionist*
MAARI, *a girl*
VIVIA, *a matron*
LAVINIAS, *mother of Maari*
MASTERLING
WORDENSOUL } *Men about Town*

Night. Interior of the communal sitting room. Everything in perfect taste: chairs comfortable, buff walls simply decorated with border, floors bare. Every object has a utilitarian value—simplicity run riot. There are no windows; the room is lighted with what looks to be a Moore vapor lamp—the light is yellow, soft, and very pleasant. In the background a set of parallel tubes throwing out a warm, red glow, occupy what used to be the fireplace. The table which is in the center is a box-like affair of mysterious design. Over the electro-grate and directly back of the table is a white space on the wall, about eight by ten feet square.

Conspicuously absent are rugs, curtains, pictures, ornamental bric-a-brac and gew-gaws. The room is so unendurably neat that (were it not for the presence of a most un-angelic old man) one might imagine the place to be paradise.

This man is Magni, the philosopher. He looks his part: noble forehead, keen, well-preserved old face, fringed by a beard obviously used for decorative purposes since it is not sufficiently luxuriant to serve as protection against the weather. It is doubtful, anyway, if there is any weather in this year of our Lord 870,007.

As for the garment which envelops his still-supple body: it is reminiscent of the Greek period before decadence necessitated the ornamental use of clothes. His sandals are an improvement over more ancient design, being carpeted with some Utopian material. He seems, according to our standards, to be about sixty years old. Actually, he is about one hundred thirty, and a trifle proud of it.

He is seated at the electro-grate, gazing solemnly into the glow. Raising his eyes to the white space above, he notes the words which have just appeared upon the screen: *Twelfth hour of the first day of the first month, Anno Superhomini 5000 . . .* according to our sentimental reckoning: New Year's Day.

Magni rises, goes over to the far side of the table, and adjusts some kind of mechanism. The room darkens slightly, and the following is thrown upon the screen. *Superhumans leave planet amid mingled tears and rejoicing. Submerged tenth left behind sure to be extinguished within next 500 years says scientist Windar. Noisebox, Provisional President of the Earth, declares that politics of noted predecessor will be pursued. Rumor that physical inspection of humans to be made only once a week. Authorities deny this. Last Superhuman leaves Earth.* (There follows a moving picture of a naked man, superbly proportioned, walking along some trestle-work high in the air; in the distance a large body of people are reclining on a moving platform. The Superhuman turns around and waves his hand.)   —1914 or 1915

PRE-1970 ECOLOGY.   The great task of the Superman is to prevent the human race from committing suicide. And it must be admitted that the task is becoming more difficult every day. The number of methods of doing away with life has been extended by leaps and bounds; while life itself is being reproduced with greater fecundity than ever before imagined. From this it follows that life is becoming less precious; that the disrespect for life is increasing; and that unless we look very sharply after our industrial and military systems they will between them reduce life to such a low ebb that it is doubtful if even the Superman will be able to maintain himself in a world of such diminished vitality. The preservation of life is the most urgent business of the human race; without the lives of our domestic animals, our wild animals, our insects, our plants, even of our bacteria, humanity—with all its magnificent pretensions in the realm of synthetic chemistry—would perish. And just as the human race is dependent upon all these lesser forms, it is probably also necessary for the Supermen, who do not yet exist in sufficient quantities to propagate their stock, to keep Homo faber from shooting himself, starving himself, asphyxiating himself, and innoculating himself with disease: in short, from by one means or another committing suicide.   —RN. December 4, 1915

THE FUNCTION OF THE PHILOSOPHIC MIND.   Faith and
the Word are the two prime foundations of philosophy; no philosopher
can begin to cogitate intelligibly without words, and he cannot open
his mouth without believing that the sounds he utters have that peculiar
quality called meaning. So it might be more accurate to say, not that
faith and the word are the foundations of philosophy, but that faith *in*
the word is the foundation. Without the word this universe presents
itself to us as what William James called a booming, buzzing confusion;
but with that modicum of faith in the word which a child needs in
beginning to talk, it soon becomes an orderly, regular, and on the whole
comfortable place to live in. We must admire the deep metaphysic insight of the Greek who began the gospel according to St. John with
the declaration: In the beginning was the Word. . . .

The universe that man exists in (as distinct from the universe which
cows or bumblebees live in) has been built up in small increments by
our faith in the word. When at night I look up at the blue dome of
space all I can see are myriad points of light. All I *know* about that
blue dome of space is that occasionally after it has gotten dark (as we
say) these tiny twinkling patches begin to appear; that they are sometimes very numerous; and that they always seem to dissolve as soon as
a light begins to break in the east. Yet were a child to ask me about
these ethereal illuminations he would find me in confident possession of
an amazing amount of information, which I would impart to him without scruple. I would tell him that these light-spots were planets and
stars; that they were worlds, some of which were bigger and some
smaller than our world; that they were all except our moon, many
millions of miles away; that the darkness which brought them into
view was caused by the fact that *our* planet (in its daily revolution) had
so far revolved that our particular portion of it was now turned away
from the sun; and that this sun (which seemed in the morning to pop
out of the housetops on the East River, and which in the evening
seemed to drop down behind the Palisades) was in reality a center
about which this earth of ours was moving.

But if the child was so staggered by this information that he asked
me how I knew all these amazing facts to be so, I should either have
to tell him foolishly to stop asking sensible questions, or else admit that
he would have to take all these facts from me on the same assurance
that I took them from other people; namely, on faith. And then, if this
precocious youngster wanted to know whether these assumptions were
true or not, I should be compelled (in a further riot of frankness) to
assure him that I was incompetent then, and probably always would
be incompetent to decide for myself on the subject. Having granted
this much, I should advise him to accept the universe which has been
constructed about these points of light without further ado, until he

finds that such a belief is impractical or perturbing; at which time he could try to make head or tail out of it by himself.

Were he a nasty, rationalist infant, he would smile pityingly and ask me: "Then this wonderful universe, with its stars and planets and comets describing their different courses, has in fact so little foundation as far as you are concerned that its very existence rested on an act of faith, without which those little points of light would be not stars but only little points of light?" To this I would of course firmly answer "Yes." And if then he added maliciously: "What would happen to this silly universe if your faith in other people were to vanish, and other people's faith in their logarithms and telescopes and spectroscopes, were to vanish likewise?" I could only shudder and say: "God only knows. Without faith the human race would die, and the beasts of the field and the fowls of the air likewise, and there would be left no one on what we call the earth to bother his head about philosophy."

For as far as I have been able to plumb the matter rightly this precious world of ours is literally almost a castle in air, created by and thru man's crude vocalisms. Our science and philosophy is a system of credit resting on capital that most of us have neither seen, heard, tasted, smelt, nor touched; and accordingly our science and philosophy (which give us the universe man lives in, as distinct from the universe which cows or bumblebees live in) would collapse as swiftly as would our monetary system, were our constantly reiterated faith in it somehow to be shattered.

Since such an abundance of faith is needed before one can get the most simple grasp of his position in the world, his antecedents, and his probable destination, it is not surprising that this faith has amounted very often to pure gullibility. Hence the business of the philosophic mind is to examine with such critical resources as it commands, all the most dubious articles of man's faith. The old articles (such as a belief in the necessity of eating and mating) which have been so long tried and so well remembered that we call them instincts can well be neglected: the person who has any serious doubts on the subject will have them speedily pacified in the dissolution of death. The new articles of faith, however, under which head come most of our religious, philosophic, scientific and esthetic beliefs, have again and again to be examined, and re-corrected on the basis of new evidence. This is the function of the philosophic mind.   —RN. 1916

ADOLESCENT REFLECTIONS ON MY FIRST LOVE AFFAIR IN VERMONT, AET. 11.   Bertha and I exchanged exactly seven kisses before I departed for New York! The last took place early in the morning, before seven o'clock. The rest of the house was hardly roused, and for a few minutes Annie, the cook, was absent from the kitchen. It was there, in the end as in the beginning, that with a last kiss I bade Bertha formal good-bye. We promised to be friends forever, and write ever so often. . . .

All that gritty railroad journey home from Vermont my thoughts dwelt on Bertha. Next morning, which was Sunday, before anyone was stirring, I wrote a hot, impassioned letter to Bertha. I sentimentally informed her why I should consider seven my lucky number. Maybe I told her something about my plans [for our future]. I sneaked downstairs to mail it. Lucky for me I was in the habit of rising early and my stealthy deed passed unnoticed.

The letter was never answered, and I have often wondered what happened to it—did Bertha actually get it, or was it intercepted or lost? Would the course of my life have been changed if she *had* answered it? Well, she didn't. And suddenly, overcome by shame and disgust, I ceased to think about the chestnut haired girl in Vermont. Study *is* an excellent antidote for what crass-minded elders are wont to call puppy love. But always she lingered in the back of my mind, for the time as a lofty ideal; and then she became involved in furtive dreams. . . .

Again up in Bethel. A gawky, awkward youth of fourteen—nearly fifteen—just descending into 'longies.' I was but slightly troubled as to how I should behave when I met Bertha, for strangely the meeting didn't seem possible—I didn't dare ask anyone whether she was still living in the township. And I neglected to prepare a conversation!

I was standing in front of a hitching post on the main 'street,' in the glare of an August morning. In front of me was Moody's grocery store, to my left a sprawling tumbledown, yellow painted hotel, with a drugstore under the porch. I was engaged in the slow but eminently useful occupation of killing the flies that settled on Pedro's back out of reach of his tail. It was in the days before the 'swat the fly' movement so my task was merely pleasurable. Then a plump little woman in long skirts approached me and held out her hand engagingly. It was Bertha.

"Why—why I haven't seen you for a long time!" I gasped. She nodded pleasantly, with the same old gray eyes and asked me if I was still staying with Mrs. French up at the farm?

"My it's been a long time since I saw you!" I managed to utter.

"I'm just going to the druggists," she informed me, "won't you come along?"

The suggestion was outrageous.

"Augie's going to be back in a second," I stumbled, "and he's in a hurry. Besides he—he said I got to mind the wagon."

Then she shook hands frankly with a queer little smile about the mouth and went into the drugstore.   —RN. 1915

20

PORTRAIT OF THE ARTIST AS A YOUNG MAN   *The living room on the second floor of a certain brownstone dwelling on the upper West Side: a sombre reminder of the architectural crimes that were rampant in the middle eighties. The furniture is essentially modern, of the better Grand Rapids type, altho here and there remain vestiges of the days that chafed the tender soul of Oscar Wilde. With one's back toward the windows that face the street one has on the right a fumed oak typewriter desk, a swivel chair, and a set of Century Encyclopedias. (The books have been used.) Between the bookstand and the hall door in the rear is a window which opens on the court of an apartment house; it embraces a cozy, leather cushioned window seat. On the left a flowered sofa, and the stony crayon portrait of a Deceased Male, mar the esthetic victory gained by the few harmonious rugs, the hardwood floor, and the warm, tan-tinted walls. All the chairs are comfortable beyond the dreams of laziness.*

Regius is a thin, slightly stooped youth of nineteen or twenty, with a full forehead, a Napoleonic nose, and persistent, anxious eyes. He is a product of his mother's tender care, his aunt's devotion, his nurse's solicitude, his teacher's coddling, his schoolfellows' toleration, and the protection from any vital contact with the world that has been provided by an ample bourgeois income. Measured by the standards of the society he lives in, he has been excellently brought up: or, as his aunt would probably say, "He has been given every advantage." This means that ever since he learned his ABC's he has been exposed to the most vicious institution of present-day civilization: our so-called educational system. The barrenly intellectualized training he has been given in that system has ingrained in him the habit of living at second-hand; with the result that though he has apparently a vast knowledge about art, industry, science, love, friendship and so forth, he has never had the least acquaintance with any of these things. He is emotionally starved, and volitionally frustrate, while intellectually he is prodigious. A modern college president would think him a very promising young man: but according to the ideals of an Athenian in the age of Pericles, he is a hopeless idiot; a nuisance to himself; a burden to his family; and a total loss in manhood to the state.

Setting of a one-act play, 'The Invalids,' written in 1916, and accepted by The Baltimore Players in 1918, but never staged: perhaps because the company disbanded during the war.

The greatest artificiality is to seek to do away with artificialities; the unnatural thing is to seek to return to 'nature.'   —RN. 1915?

Nothing that exists is unnatural. Superstitions, creeds, conventions, cruelties, vices, morbidities—all these are characteristic of man: they are 'natural' to him. A person too rational to be superstitious, too free to observe conventions, too humane to practice cruelty, too healthy to relapse into viciousness, would be a person who could result only from an arduous system of culture, and in one sense would be as unnatural as it is possible for a man to be. But mind culture is as natural to man as 'primitivism,' and this last statement is therefore utterly false. —RN. 1916

Death was one of the great inventions life discovered for keeping itself lively.   —RN. n.d.

Only fools are afraid to make fools of themselves.   —RN. n.d.

Modern industrial civilization releases woman for work and then gives her no work to do. Automatically she becomes a consumption machine.   —RN. n.d.

Education is not *one* of man's activities: it comprises all of them; it is man singing, painting, wondering, feeling, dreaming, working, loving in that terrible comedy we call life. It is man experimenting with fire, in the stone age, or at the kitchen stove; it is man carving the first hieroglyphics, or writing his first ABC's, man wondering at the stars, or plotting them and forecasting their returns; man cackling in the treetops, or spreading the good word through the printed page. —RN. 1915

Religion in the Middle Ages was a dominant factor in determining men's views; today politics plays the same part. May not sex be the determinant tomorrow? May not the lineup—tory or liberal—be over the amount of latitude observed in the sex-relations—or something of the sort?   —RN. 1917

Literary or artistic success rests chiefly with the ability to secure useful letters of introduction.   —RN. 1915

[Note: 1973. A lot I knew about it! Never did a letter help me.]

Knowledge does not consist in knowing the things you know: it consists in knowing the things you don't know.   —RN. 1915

To be moral is to conform to other people's habits of acting; to be immoral is to obey your own impulses when they conflict with the accustomed. The thoroly moral man is a humbug: the thoroly immoral man is a fool.* And the way to avoid being one or the other is courageously to decide on being a great deal of both.   —n.d.

The attempt to describe life in chemico-physical terms is like an attempt to describe da Vinci's 'The Last Supper' by publishing the chemical formulae of every square inch of pigment; and the first gives no greater understanding of life than the second does of the picture. Each is an organic synthesis, about which the material composition is, in view of the artist's purpose, the least significant part.   —RN. 1916

The danger of a mechanized industrial regime is not that the population will press upon the supply of food (for energized agriculture has not yet sighted the limits of food-production): the danger is that population will press upon the supply of intelligence. And it holds good, alike with food or with Vision, that without it the people perish.
—RN. 1916

*From 1915 until I became an editor of 'The Dial' I practiced 'simplified spelling,' as advocated by Theodore Roosevelt and Brander Matthews.

Urban Notes

LOWER EAST SIDE: 1918.   The district from the Brooklyn Bridge upward, and from Avenue A westward I know pretty well through repeated visits to Granich's flat on Chrystie Street by night and day, and yet it presents such a complexity of nationalities and traditions and living conditions that it defies a sociological judgement. The tenements are unmitigatedly bad, in spite of the fact that many were built after the 'model' law of 1901. Eighty-one Chrystie Street [where Irwin Granich's family lived] * has, for example, fireproof stairs and walls, but the passage is dark and cramped and the greater part of the rooms face a dark alley. Sanitary conditions are precarious: the bedbugs swarm so disgustingly on the walls in the summertime that most of the inmates take to the roof or the fire-escape, and the pathogenic bacteria breed royally in the warm, dark halls. Coal stoves are pretty generally used in the kitchen, and the figure of an old man bent under a sack of coal is no unusual sight. Legitimately the kitchen is used during the winter as living room, and in families affluent enough to boast also a dining room one regrets that the two cubicles have not been thrown together so as to provide one decent-size chamber. Sleeping conditions I know nothing about, they vary from family to family and pocketbook to pocketbook. The dietary of the Jewish families is probably the most favorable part of the Ghetto regime; for it is necessarily simple and vegetarian, with great stress laid upon fish and beans, chocolate and nuts, fruit and fresh vegetables; but any careful appraisal must take likewise into account the enormous amount of putrid pickled articles, decayed fruit, dyed candies and unwholesome sodawaters that is consumed. Bananas and apples and onions appear usually first rate, and may be placed in the positive column. Against these you must place the bruised alligator pears and winter melons by means of which the push-cart dealers place on the tables of Lazarus the offal of Dives' grocer. This last fact is typical of a great many others: Rivington Street does not differ in kind from Riverside Drive, but in the quality that is acceptable within the kind. The essential similarities are closer than either class thinks.

* On holing in in Mexico in 1918 Irwin Granich changed his name to Michael Gold, best known perhaps for his autobiography 'Jews without Money.'

SOUTH BROOKLYN: 1916.   The city-hall nearby, the library, the building of the Long Island Historical Society, the Long Island Hospital, Arbuckle Institute, and innumerable churches of which Beecher's Plymouth Church is most famous give this neighborhood most of the essential institutions of a city. . . . As a contrast between the aspirations and artistic ideals of two periods an old M.E. church rebuilt in 1889 and an old Presbyterian Church rebuilt in 1846 are suggestive. The second is a sound, well-proportioned, simply designed structure of red sandstone (hewn, so the cartetaker told me, out of the quarries at Belleville, N. J.); the other is a hideous jumble of turrets, arches, and gratuitous elaborations, a building that carries Victorian gothic and romanesque down to its last degrading level. The older church, by the bye, had no cellar: just an excavation in the ground for its heating plant: and its extra-clerical activities are thus somewhat curtailed. "I suppose you're a little crowded now?" I asked the caretaker. "Well, not *crowded*, I wouldn't say crowded: but we're holding our own."

Beyond Atlantic Avenue this district falls into dilapidation: and as one goes south into the poorer section all evidences of renascence disappear. At Joralemon Street I was reminded of the model tenements that had been erected in the eighties by a philanthropic five per center.

These Riverside buildings [the first model tenements] were erected in 1896 after a successful experiment at Hicks and Baltic Streets. They are five stories high, much shallower than the ordinary tenement, and they form a quadrangle. Tho built of red brick they are curiously well-done in a sober, restrained way. The inner space was plotted into spaces for grass trees and shrubs and for clothes-drying. The verdant patches were all-too-well fenced, and the amount of space given up for children's plays was too little. This was the first criticism that entered my mind. The second criticism had also to do with this inner space: its immensity has resulted in an undue overcrowding of apartments and a smallness of rooms, and this may be too high a price to pay for such a big private park. Granting the wisdom of creating such a park it must nevertheless be urged that it must not be on a scale so grand as to do away with the internal amenities of domestic life . . .

Furman Street has on the West warehouses, refrigerating establishments, the marginal ways, and the docks: on the East a wall some twenty feet high, under which are occasional saloons, shacks and hovels, and above which are the gardens and backyards of the old aristocratic district I've been describing. An evil looking thorofare, this Furman Street, frequented by lowering men, gruff special policemen, and prostitutes in the last stages of bedraggled drunkenness. (I saw a hideous, mud-stained thing snoring in a doorway.) The impression is quite different from New York's sunny, spacious west waterfront. There were dank passageways under overhanging buildings; and the prevalent odor was urinous, disgusting. My survey ended with the

Fulton Ferry.   [This checks closely with Ernest Poole's 'The Harbor,' a book that stirred me, published in 1915.]

The vertical effects that most architects have striven for and attained in apartment house building have done away with such features as balconies, which for any large use require horizontal lines. Yet the conviction that human habitations should have direct access to light and air remains in a vestigial state in those stone and iron eyebrows which, pasted at intervals on the sheer side of a building, are supposed to serve as ornaments.   —RN. 1916

URBAN ANTICIPATIONS.   To alert minds it is becoming plain that the art of planning cities is to no little extent the art of doing away with cities. The amorphous, shapeless, bloated, unbounded, ever-spreading Mass City that we know so well today seems destined to go the way of those saurian monsters which once encumbered the earth; and that part of mankind which makes pretences to possessing a civilization will live in communities that do not, in their bleak streets, their mean dwellings, their limited outlooks and their reeking atmospheres, do violence to the very name of civilization. The statistician who figures that the population of New York fifty years from now will be 20 million, or the population of Boston 10 million has conned the figures of the census reports, but he has not read the handwriting on the wall. The glibness of his predictions proves that he knows nothing of that movement toward decentralization which is not only carrying manufactures away from the old centers of population but is also (through garden city projects) drawing families along with them.   —RN. 1916 or 1917

Introduction to an unpublished essay, printed for the first time in 'Town and Country Planning' (March 1955) and entitled: 'Garden Civilizations: Preparing for a New Epoch.'

I see a dung-heap in the foreground of every beautiful vista in America: the skeleton of dissipation at the feast of riches. Houses of stately design and sumptuous appointment as here in Newport: and on the road that approaches them, broken-down fences, tin cans, disorderly shrubbery, and abandoned instruments of labor. There is not in this the harmony even of a consistently lowly or retrograde state. Hence the loveliest notes get lost in the jangle of noises, or rather, may be said to contribute to the local ugliness of it in no little degree.

—RN. 1918

26

The materials for education are much like those by means of which a plant grows: the arts and sciences may be compared to earth, air and water. But whereas it is now commonly held that the materials themselves are the education, so that a person who has stored up certain facts and ideas is thereby educated, the truth is that they are no more the education than the air and earth and water are the growth of the plant. The analogy between plant nourishment and what we call education would hold if plants could store up large chemical supplies while remaining shriveled, wizened, small, undeveloped: a thing unknown in botany. We must realize that education is a process of growth, lasting thruout life and coeval with life. If we are wise we shall not try to force it or hasten it. We will give up the whole medal-awarding, diploma-bestowing, scholarship-granting, pupil-pushing rigmarole: and we will direct our efforts toward seeing that the environment is so ordered that the natural processes may be carried on in the most favorable way.   —RN. 1916

A man's education is tested not by what he knows but by what he is capable of learning from and using.   —RN. n.d.

Men who get tired of struggling with reality commit suicide: nations that get tired go to war.   —RN. 1918

All matter and energy is a gift. No one has created it, no one has earned it, no one 'deserves' it, and no one therefore should be allowed to appropriate it selfishly. Man's economic function is simply to wrap this gift in convenient parcels for distribution. His own ability to do this cleverly and effectively and the tradition of doing this cleverly and effectively, is also a gift. To assert that the producer or the manager or the inventor has a major part in this process is like saying that the cock which heralds the dawn has made the sun rise.   —RN. 1918

It is impossible to examine the biographies of the leaders in Victorian science and art without coming to the conclusion that they owed some part of their vigor and originality to the fact that they escaped a formal education. Tyndall, Mill, Spencer, Dalton, Faraday, Dickens, and Shaw were none of them university bred. For that matter neither were Plato or Aristotle!   —RN. 1918

Almost any achievement of man, from the stone ax of neolithic times to the planing machine of the twentieth century may well be characterized as the attainment of the impossible by means of the inadequate. Every goal seems to be demonstrably unattainable until it has been demonstrably attained.   —RN. 1919

Humor is our way of defending ourselves from life's absurdities by thinking absurdly about them. It is a mild antitoxin of the same nature as the disease it seeks to combat. Occasionally it gets the upper hand and becomes the disease itself.   —RN. 1919

The man who would be stupid enough to defend the present economic order would be ass enough to do it for nothing.   —RN. n.d.

Disorderly thinking should be as unwelcome in polite society as disorderly conduct. In fact, it *is* disorderly conduct.   —RN. n.d.

Vital interests are interests men have in common, and for not attending to which they die.   —RN. n.d.

He whom the gods dislike they overload with gifts.   —RN. n.d.

On the sands of Ogunquit I saw a sandpiper, one of whose legs was lamed, rest on its wings as a man would on a pair of crutches.
—RN. 1915

The Marriage of Museums

There is something symbolic in the proposal, possibly soon to be effected, to join by a direct path the museums of art and natural history in Manhattan; for it points to a new kinship between these two institutions that lies much deeper than their supposedly common purpose in fostering learning and spreading culture. Were the tie of education the only one that bound them together there would be no greater fitness in the plan for a connecting walk through Central Park than there would be in one for cutting a driveway between New York University and the American Geographical Society. It is not the aims of the two museums being alike, but their becoming complementary, that gives the proposal a significance. The physical connection will serve to emphasize a cultural borrowing which has at once introduced the presentiments of graphic art into the nature museum, and the organic conception of life into the art museum: with the result in certain galleries that the absent-minded visitor will be at loss to recall which museum he is making an inspection of.

The transformation which is taking place in our museums may be roughly described as that from storehouse to powerhouse. The healthy disorder one finds in these institutions today gives evidence of a conflict of traditions which marks this change from a passive "showing off" to an active education, from the uninformed miserly tradition of an earlier day to the directed socialized spirit of the opening age. On the one hand the museum bears all too plainly the stamp of its primitive origin. It is either the robber's cave, the receptacle for princely loot, or the hunter's cache, the respository for animal skins and bleached bones. In both of these capacities it is the function of the museum to acquire as much loot as possible, or as many bones, and to display as great an amount of these in its halls, hit or miss, as space and time will allow. In general, this subordinates esthetic values to those of cash, and scientific values to those of sportsmanlike interest: and to follow this tradition is not so much to promote science and art as to add renown to the hunter and the warrior, as they existed in their past nakedness or in the various thin disguises of today: commercialist and art collector, country gentleman and explorer.

Nominally instituted to further science and art, the museums have been at the mercy of every rich ignoramus who has cared to perpetuate his name to posterity through a respectable interest in cultural activities; and while this handicap has not worked grievously in the domain of natural science, it has spelt disaster in the arts, where such bequests as the Stewart Gallery in the Public Library and the biblical supplement gallery in the Brooklyn Institute swamp those of our Altmans and Morgans in the ratio of about three to one. We may laugh at the savage for burying the trophies of chase alongside the deceased hunter; but on closer inspection the savage has the advantage over us. He at least buries the trophies. We can only remove the dead, whilst, through the operation of legal processes, we allow the trophies an ascendancy over us we would never permit the living to enjoy.

Now the museums can not slough off the trophy-collecting convention by overtly refusing gifts, especially when these are accompanied by funds, and when the slightest hint of aversion would withdraw the support of some pillar of society; but they can nullify the effects of indiscriminate collection by reconstituting the very ends, and therewith the methods, of museum exhibition, so that no object need be kept on view for purely honorific reasons. *It is possible to avoid invidious selection by creating a certain environment within the museum and then trusting to the processes of natural selection to weed out objects which are exotic to the environment.* I do not say that this is what the museum authorities are at present consciously attempting; but I do say that their efforts come practically to this conclusion. And it is the tendency to abandon the traditions of the warehouse and the treasure vault, and to make the museum a concrete theater of history, as one follows life from region to region and from period to period, which has given it a new social orientation, and which promises that in pursuing the same goal the two museums will tend to approach within hailing distance of each other. Given a common social basis, collection and presentation will have a common social end: for it is chiefly owing to the absence of any serious purposes that the art and nature museums have seemed to be at cross purposes. Once it is granted that both seek to enrich the meaning of contemporary life by showing men, in colloquial phrase, where they are at, in relation to ages past and present, and lands far and near, and ancestors, living and dead: once this is granted, the museum is equipped with a criterion of selection to supplement (and in many cases reinforce) the criterion of beauty which prevails in one place, or that of truth-furtherance which holds in the other.

While the natural history museum has always nominally kept in mind the conception of a *habitat*, the idea of art's being presented in its social background was for long quite foreign to museum authorities. Art was something apart; by its nature divorced from this world of shadows and at home only in the heaven of platonic ideals; and the museum existed solely to conserve and consecrate objects of art so that men might commune with them within its walls as their fathers in an earlier age communed with God. There was no notion here of the arts being as closely bound to life as the shell to the snail: not to be severed without causing death to the creature or making futile the thing it had erected for its comfort and delight. Rather, it was felt that snails could not only live without shells, but that roundworms could by careful imitation create shells like those snails had once deposited. This attitude toward art, baldly put in metaphor, was the outcome, not of any real break between art and life (for they are joined even in dissolution) but of a divorce between life and those who patronized art; and until a very late date, when the old teachings of Ruskin and Morris began to take effect, the idea of art's being irrelevant to its environment was reflected in the museums. The showcase or the gallery was the exhibition unit; the aim was to admire art as a thing in itself; the subsidiary instruments for satisfying historical curiosity were the guidebook and the professional treatise.

Unfortunately this detached view of art defeated the very aim it thought to serve. There is indeed something to be said for not hedging the esthetic mood with all sorts of secondary intellectual interests, and on the surface the introduction of the social background might seem to provoke a discordance; but this no more holds in reality than (as I shall show) the contrary practise in the museum of natural history. Putting objects of art into what is approximately the environment out of which they have been plucked actually heightens the savor of the art itself, the esthetic note being only fully sounded when every object in the vicinity takes up the note and vibrates in sympathy with it. This is what is done in the Swiss, the Georgian, and the Queen Anne rooms in the Metropolitan Museum. Were the gallery tradition followed each bed, picture, mirror, or table in these rooms would have been presented, so to say, in severalty: and had the museum been able to put seven four-posters side by side, or a dozen consoles, the supposition would be that the museum was so much the richer. And this would be true from a mercenary and miserly point of view; but it would be a banal distortion from the standpoint of art. Three double beds by Robert Adam in the same room would give the impression that the Walpole ministry had a housing problem in Portland Square; a dozen mantels in one dining room would give currency to the notion that everyone used to "eat off the mantelpiece." A plethora of discrete objects, especially when they are the same or similar objects, prevents one from seeing a single object: when the eye is overwhelmed with a horde of creditors crying for attention, it despairs of meeting any demand at all and goes bankrupt. Hence the wisdom of putting art in its proper setting, which means putting it in its place. It is the scientific, environmental presentation that meets all the demands of art. For only when the proper surroundings have been established to provoke the esthetic mood will the esthetic mood lift the observer out of his surroundings.

Plainly this naturalist treatment of the arts, at once historic and esthetic, is but yet in its infancy; and the museum has still many a dusty corner to sweep away before every art collection will have its environment. Certain periods, it goes without saying, can never be done minutely in the grand style, with rooms to illustrate amply phase after phase of significant social life: this would be the true pinnacle of attainment, and a "consummation devoutly to be wished"; but to accomplish so colossal a work of reconstruction at present staggers the imagination, and as a compromise the miniature period stage, as indicated in the models that the Metropolitan is acquiring, enters with an air of importance.

Models have long played no little part in museum exhibition. Those of the Parthenon and of Notre Dame at the Metropolitan are especially well known; and because of their solidity and four-squareness they have a place in the study of architecture that could never be completely usurped by pictures and working drawings. But the new use of models is theatric; it aims at embodying a whole period in a scene. The model-maker takes the scattered materials that have survived the ages, here a chair and there a table and yon a wall, and he reconstructs in little the details of the society whose relics have been gathered, bringing together on his stage elements that have been widely scattered and showing in concrete, relations which would otherwise have only been dimly perceived. This art, or rather its fresh bias, is not yet sufficiently familiar to permit a final word to be pronounced upon its possibilities: its present status is due to the fine craftsmanship of a single man, Mr. Dwight Franklin. But one cannot study the already attained successes with lighting and vividly depicted action without coming to the conclusion that the mimetic representation of past epochs will annex for itself a wide territory in the reconstituted museum, and that the time may come when people, plain and sophisticated, will have opportunity for a glimpse of ancient art and manners (and therewith of social history) through the direct medium of the vision, without being forced to rely solely upon the attenuated descriptions of the printed word. Not as substitutes for the "real thing," but as a method of making real things less strange will models like those foreshadowed in the English Hall or the entrance to St. Sophia's finally be made for every period of significance. Their appearance in this Museum of Art is surely a token of that nascent social interest to which reference has been made. They introduce the notion of the arts as a natural flowering of healthy societies, rather than as a mysterious irruption that somehow, despite a popular love for the false, the vile, and the hideous, intrudes itself upon a society.

To see the arts in their proper setting is to restore the organic conception of the arts, and the organic conception is that of natural history.

But if the art museum is espousing the methods of science with its emphasis upon the continuity of living things, and the relation of organism to environment, and craftsman to period, it is no less true that the science museum is taking advantage of the synthetic vision of the artist. So far from being occupied with the purely cognitive aspects of the natural sciences, the American Museum has been increasingly eager to develop their emotional aspects and to further their application to the arts. This has been done in three ways. In the first place, art workers have been encouraged to make use of the primitive patterns created by the indigenous American craftsmen of the loom and the potter's wheel. The result of this has been to lengthen our historical perspective and to detach the workers from a perhaps too close apprenticeship to European models. These borrowings from a more primitive culture break down the ancient Greek antithesis between nature and art by means of the arts created by the so-called nature-peoples; and by bridging the gap between the two separate fields it has brought the museums that represent these fields into a closer working community.

The second phase of the museum's artistic activity has been in the reconstruction, first in drawings and then in single cases and now in whole galleries, of the natural habitat of the wild creatures whose lives are to be portrayed. No mention of this return to nature in the study of nature could be made without reference to the work of Mr. Charles Knight. Combining scientific penetration and artistic insight in a remarkable degree he has in his drawings, from the first water-color sketches of our saurian ancestors, divined from the meager evidence of a rag, a bone, and a hank of hair, to the last sweeping mural of the hairy mammoth, effaced by the synthesis of his own personality the ill-conceived antagonism between science and art that was handed down from an earlier age. That without the love and the beauty of nature there can be no geography or no nature study worthy of the name has already been urged by the eminent botanist, and art critic likewise, Patrick Geddes. But conventional practise sterilized this love and made abortive this beauty by isolating art in a peculiar building, as though it were a contagious disease, at the same time that it reduced nature study to a mere grind of names. From this paralyzing practise the artist-scientist is cutting loose. He places his art at the service of science, and he uses his science as a frame for his art: and he has thus to no little extent given back to the artist the opportunity for public service which disappeared with the decline of the Middle Ages and the usurpation by the leisure classes of the artist's talent for the gratification of idiotic whimsies.

The decoration of nature backgrounds for animal groups is but the recovery for the new cosmogony of those religious interpretations which have a hallowed place in medieval churches. And the fact that the interest in nature *per se* is contemporary with the development of landscape painting (due in both cases to the arousal of a new, non-invidious curiosity in things) is perhaps an indication of the essential reasonableness in calling in the landscape painter as an aid to the naturalist. This is a new field of the artist of realist tendencies: it opens the way for an escape from "gallery art," while it gives the *photographer* of contemporary esthetic derision a fresh raison d'être and a refurbished purpose in life. Here is also at last a place for those academics and scholiasts who in the teaching of art insist upon truth values, those of anatomical perfection and fidelity to exterior form, as the salvation from slackness, laziness, meretriciousness and the like. Losing their foothold inch by inch in the art galleries, they may at least find refuge without compromise in our museums of natural history. I do not point out this possibility in irony. The classicists in art have still a place left for them in society, as the creators of decorations that aim to establish a moral, a civic, or a scientific truth through the medium of art. And it is only within the very narrow sanctuary of pure esthetic being that the incense they offer on the altar of truth pours upward in a heavy fume that conceals all the delicate beauties of the little temple. In the museum of natural history their craft is not to be despised; for the technique of naturalism is largely an objective technique; and its logic is the single one that will accommodate itself to values extraneous to those demanded by an absolute esthetic response. Despite the difficulties offered by walls whose surface is marred with uesless windows and by galleries which were never meant to serve the ends of esthetic contemplation, the artist has much in the nature museum to spur as well as hinder his technique. And beyond doubt the new additions to this Natural History Museum will be planned in full recognition of the artist's coeval interest with the scientist in the most effective display of a collection in its manifold aspects.

The third manner in which the museum has utilized the artist is by employing him to render models in plaster and wax of animals, man for one, that defy the most adept efforts of the taxidermist. Here is a province that the sculptor of highest rank need not disdain to tread. Consider the opportunities offered by one of the life-sized or slightly reduced groups of peoples engaged in their native occupations; such a group as that of the Pueblo dwellers, for example. In many ways the ethnic casts made by the museum workers are beyond reproach: they are faithful in all the minutiæ which patience and manual skill can take care of, and they appear against such ably conceived backgrounds that it is not easy to detect wherein they fall short of the highest. Examining with more critical eye the figures themselves, however, one gets the sense of a lost opportunity, and one feels that in order to measure up to the scientific accuracy of the setting as a whole the figures should have been done by as skilled a hand as knows how to use modeling tools—that here is a subject which might tempt the genius of Phidias or Praxiteles or which might in our own day have enlisted the hand of such a many-faceted master as Rodin himself. Is it too much to expect that the museum of the future will include along with its numerous and capable artists of the brush an array of naturalist sculptors whose quality will be little, if any, below the finest offerings of their contemporaries?

The interest of the age is above all scientific: why then should it not use art creatively for its purposes? The great statues of Greece and Rome were found in the baths and gymnasia and theaters; for there the cultured life of the time was centered, and the artist was called upon to enrich the meaning of that life by transfiguring its quality in marble. Today we have not lost these interests, but we have added to them the impassioned curiosities of science; and the Milesian Venuses and Indian Bacchuses of another day have a niche awaiting them in our museums of natural history. Who but the sculptor with undisputed mastery should perpetuate for us the subtly molded human figure, differing as it does from race to race and climate to climate. The present figure groups in the museum are but a beginning. They do no more than represent the grosser divisions of the human race, as between Bushman and Kaffir, between Chinamen and European. And even here, in lieu of a robuster ideal of art, there is a perpetual baffling of the scientific interest by differentiating not between men as animals, but between men as the lay figures of civilization, a Chinese farmer being placed alongside a Norwegian matron, each in the regalia of daily life, as though the sculptor had been dismayed by his deficiencies and had thought to conceal them under the obvious camouflage of clothes. Further than this naïve revelation of types the museum must soon go; but it can obviously not travel far until the highest range of artistry is incorporated in its staff. This is not to disparage present achievements: it is rather to acknowledge their worth by showing to what heights they draw the imagination. Once let the scientific impulse get hold of the sculptor (who is an anatomist by current practise anyway) and a new horizon of possibility will open up for both science and art.

In the statuary exhibited last year by Mr. Charles Knight there is a hint of how deep the communion of purpose may be when once it is realized that knowing and feeling are not warring "faculties" of the mind, but diverse attitudes which men assume at appropriate times in their endeavor to have commerce with the things that lie about them. Any emphasis of antagonism is more than banal: it is ignorant. Both science and art are means of opening that oyster, which is the world; and if the one seeks chiefly to dissect the bivalve while the other loses itself in contemplation of the pearl, this should not obscure the fact that they must open the same oyster, and that they may well, for the attainment

35

of this mutual end, take hold of the same instrument and use their forces jointly. It is this truth that is coming to be recognized in our museums as they abandon their primitive reasons for existence and seek to justify their further extension by activities which harmonize with the democratic sympathies of the present order. Hence the environmental treatment of the arts in the art museum; hence the artistic presentation of nature in the nature museum; hence the shift in accent, but not in aim, as one passes from one museum to the other. This perception of a common and complementary purpose indicates, I believe, something like a marriage between the two kinds of museum; a union which might well be sanctified by civic authority in a connecting pathway.

—The Scientific Monthly. September 1918

"The Escort of Friends"

At some point in this narrative I must give an account of my early friendships; and on that topic I know neither where to begin nor where to end. For me, as for the ancient Greeks, friendship is one of the ultimate rewards of life; and friendship with members of one's own sex was immune in my generation and my circle from the delusions and magnifications and inordinate imperatives of erotic love: so that there never lurked behind it the suspicion that one was deviously seeking, or perhaps anxiously evading, another, more sexual kind of intimacy. I have been friends, yes, and close friends, with the widest variety of people, men and women; but none of my early friendships persevered till I encountered the group I came to know at the Evening Session of the City College. Some of these friends weave in and out of the picture: but others, who played an equal part in my life, will not be relevant to the themes I am picking up and embroidering. So now perhaps is the moment when I should talk about my early friends.

Until I was twelve, the nearest approach I had to a friend who counted more than my other playmates was Paul Brown, who lived on the same block. He loved to draw horses and became, I suspect, the artist whose sporting prints were once famous in the sports world —and even beyond. He was followed by a rather handsome, slightly older, sleepy-faced lad who lived up the block on Ninety-fourth Street, who helped to persuade me that Stuyvesant was the High School I wanted to go to. About this time, a somewhat older lad, named Will Robertson, attracted me: English born, with red hair and a hot but well-controlled temper, his speech was full of crisp consonants our slovenly New Yorkese softened or spoiled, while his sense of humor, enlivened by a literary background that included Kipling and the Bab Ballads, was adequate to every occasion, and kept him unruffled when his soft, somewhat overweight body and his polite ways made other youngsters at the Tennis Courts, the only place we met, set him down as sissy.

But I had no close friend until I met John Tucker: a lean, narrow-shouldered, freckled, sandy-faced young man, always bespectacled, who was already studying to be an engineer at Stevens Institute and who, though I was a good three years younger than he, used to seek my company, increasingly, as my own studies in philosophy led us into long arguments in the best Scots style: for his father was English and his mother a Scot, and John himself was as dogmatic in his skepticisms and his rejections as a Scots dominie would have been about Predestination and Eternal Damnation, though it was Pearson's 'The Grammar of Science' and Mach's logical positivism he was advancing as science's last demolishing word on philosophy.

He served for me as an abrasive stone on which I could sharpen my own ideas; and he used to regard me as an endless source of amusement, marked by loud guffaws of appreciation, because of all the ways in which my reactions to life were different from his own and from those around him. We had two girl friends in common—Beryl and Sarita—and though we kept such friendships in private compartments, we enjoyed comparing notes on their views and their conduct. Beneath his scientifically immaculate mind, devoted to the rational, the calculable, the observable, was a much more emotional personality that never manifested itself except in a stilted, somewhat embarrassed form. Our typical intercourse was full of calculated insults and disparagements: his didacticism—"Well, you see, Fish, *it's like this*"—was in itself somewhat insulting. But we both learned from each other; and one day I even won his respect by my irreproachable answer to a question he posed about Einstein's first relativity theory: a subject that the scientifically educated young were already discussing *circa* 1916.

At Tucker's invitation I went to the Bureau of Standards Laboratory in Pittsburgh in 1917, as a temporary laboratory helper without Civil Service status, in his own cement testing laboratory. We lived in the same boarding house on North Craig Street and usually walked back and forth to work together. Though our friendship never became closer, and our wives never met, we exchanged jibes, wisecracks, and insults by letter, along with occasional meetings, to within a few years of his untimely death after a gallant struggle against his arthritically immobile limbs.

Of all the other friendships of those early days, the two that sustained me most were those of Herbert Feis and Jerome Lachenbruch: the first was almost entirely epistolary, when he was studying at Harvard, and it hardly outlasted our student days. Feis, with his natural talents and his well-disciplined mind, had at an early moment achieved a place within intellectual circles, like that of 'The New Republic,' where I lingered hungrily on the outside; he was even, as economist, an assistant to Ordway Tead, on a Joint Dress and Waist investigation where, in 1916, I worked for two months as a lowly investigator. Herbert early became an ensign in the Navy, on active service, whereas I remained on shore, training as a mere radio operator, and an inactive one at that. But he was a generous spirit, full of irrepressible gaiety in actual life, a gaiety that sometimes gave way to thoughtful, sobering admonitions in his letters to me, for I often distressed him by letting my own gaiety and spontaneity break forth in those affairs of the mind that he looked upon as too sacred for such levity. I can still feel, in retrospect, the touch of his steadying hand.

As for Jerome Lachenbruch, he too was older than I by seven years or so: a sensitive, thoughtful, earnest young man, sober beyond his years because he had taken on the burden of earning a living without the college preparation his younger brothers were to have. We must have been in some of the same classes at City College—except for Advanced German we both have forgotten which ones—and with our common literary interests, our common German background, there was much that we could take for granted. We even went together to the German theater in Yorkville to see 'Alma Wo Wohnst Du?' He was both a friend and a badly needed older brother, aware of the inner tensions that accompanied my sexual immaturity, properly critical of the effects of this upon my stories and plays: but full of good hope and cautious counsel, in letters that often sounded the very depths of my situation. In all my life I have received just two letters that were to have a profound effect upon my literary and intellectual development, and one of them was written by Lachenbruch.

Most of the casual friendships I made in the Navy vanished quickly, but the crowded barracks at Newport brought me close to another one of the few friends who, like Lachenbruch, seasoned with me into old age: David Liebovitz. His career as a playwright and a novelist was never rounded out with the success it deserved—perhaps because his first, and most successful book, a picaresque novel called 'Youth Dares All,' was published anonymously. Accident brought us together: Liebovitz by height was in the same tall squad as I, and by alphabetic order his cot was near mine. My hacking cough in fact used to ruin his sleep, but he conquered his irritation when he found that we both took literature seriously. Though we parted when he went in for an ensignship, we had lived actually within half a dozen blocks of each other in Manhattan, and came together again when the war was over. His emotional intensity and unsparing critical honesty accompanied me through his last forty-five years, sometimes close, sometimes distant: yet always there.

The degree of intimacy under which a friendship prospers and the degree of influence it exercizes has little to do with time or the possibility of regular meetings: both these friendships flourished at a distance, with only occasional meetings: though Lachenbruch and I have seen each other only at intervals of ten years or more, none of the old sense of our closeness has disappeared. With the other great friendship of my early manhood the same rule holds. Geroid Robinson and I met as rivals for the same post on the fortnightly 'The Dial': instead of fighting for primacy we shared the job and drew closer together; and though we had hoped to continue this relation on 'The Freeman,' it was he who, perhaps because his sober literary style or his turn of mind pleased Nock, the principal editor, more, got that coveted post. For a time we were neighbors on Brooklyn Heights; for another while, neighbors again in Leedsville. But our friendship was so tightly cemented at the beginning that neither closeness nor distance affected it—until our acute differences over the Vietnam holocaust made that name unutterable, *at his earnest request*, even in our letters. Each of us had a private life he felt no need to share with the other: yet each of us knew—at least until this final breach!—that, came a moment of personal crisis or anguish, the other would be there.

Out of this gathering of early friends I have lifted these five as representative samples: but I am sad to leave out all the others who played a part in my life before I was thirty: Beryl Morse, Agnes Tait, Clarence Britten, Gladys Mayer, Walter Pach, Delilah Loch, Dorothy Thomas, Avrahm Yarmolinsky, Babette Deutsch, Eva Goldbeck, as well as those, like Van Wyck Brooks, Joel Spingarn, Clarence Stein, Henry Wright, Benton MacKaye, Paul Rosenfeld, Waldo Frank, of whom I have already said something in print. My life would have been poor and empty without these people.

—Deleted fragment from my autobiography. 1963

Part Two

1920-1925

New York in the Twenties

The Greenwich Village of my early manhood was such a different place from the spotty, murky, dingily sophisticated, glossily upper-class quarter of the city that now goes by that name, that it is worth a paragraph or two, if only to avoid confusion. Along with Brooklyn Heights it was the one part of New York that still had a vital underlayer of the early provincial town—provincial, not 'Colonial'—that Herman Melville knew, and that Albert Pinkham Ryder, on the West Fourteenth Street boundary of the neighborhood, also knew. Except for the North River docks and the Harlem River Railroad that ran along Hudson Street, Greenwich Village—the old Ninth Ward—remained a backwater, unaffected by the tides of traffic. After the Civil War the city swirled around it; and though the Ninth and the Sixth Avenue elevated railroads cut through it, they actually carried people to the more fashionable areas beyond: so the little red-brick houses, only two rooms deep, not three like the later gawky, unhygienic brownstones, remained intact, but for an insolent tenement house that occasionally, in the seventies, shouldered into the block to take advantage of the low property values.

My friend Agnes Tait had spent her girlhood in one of those old houses: it still had the most rudimentary sanitary facilities, with toilets in the backyard and a common pump in the middle of the open area; and later she had a studio on King Street, before the Seventh Avenue Extensions had wiped out whole rows of admirable houses on King and Varick streets: the fine woodwork of the Georgian doorways with their delicate fanlights, was carried through in the interiors. The cheapness of this rundown but comely neighborhood naturally drew artists to these quarters: they lived side by side with the Irish to the west or the Italians to the south: eating free lunch in the many saloons, such as that John Masefield worked in, or dining sumptuously, on occasion, in an Italian table d'hôte like Bertolotti's, or on oysters and steak at a chop house like Broad's, with its old-fashioned sawdust-covered floor—all comparably cheap.

The great feature of Greenwich Village, apart from its architectural character and its modestly priced dwellings and eating places, was the variety of its social resources: almost everything one needed for companionship, for friendship, for intellectual or esthetic stimulus, was within walking distance; and such institutions as theaters, and museums, though farther away, were easily reached by bus and streetcar and subway—and even by walking, for in those days people still walked. So it was in essence a real urban community, not the sprawling time-wasting nonentity that causes people to dissipate no small part of their free time in senseless travel. Social facilities were once just around the corner, available at any moment of the day. Only those who have enjoyed the conveniences of a compact urban community can even guess how much has been lost in endless clotted motorized wastelands, like metropolitan New York or Philadelphia or Boston.

In the twenties, some of the old blocks in the Village were being rehabilitated by turning the houses into apartments and grouping the once fenced-in backyards into a common garden. If this movement had only taken hold in other parts of the city, large areas might have undergone timely improvement instead of falling into utter confusion and dilapidation. But even where, around Washington Square, there had been a greedy preemption of good space for expensive residential apartments in the eighties, in the first flurry of fashion over high buildings with elevators—French Flats as they were called—the place had an esthetic charm derived only partly from the architecture: the bright intelligent faces, the amorous young couples, were part of it.

What characters flourished here! What varieties of national and personal culture proliferated in every street and alley! There was a sloppy upstairs restaurant off Sixth Avenue, called Romany Marie's, where the poet Maxwell Bodenheim used to sport a black velvet jacket and a red tie, and go from table to table, selling, sometimes stuttering out, his poems. There was Polly's, a place kept by one of the old Provincetown group, who had a talent for cooking, where people in summer sat in the open under a canopy at long tables, almost as in an old-fashioned boarding house; and there was Three Steps Down, where Emily Strunsky, she with the violet eyes, was worth going to look at even if the food had not been so reasonable; while on the edge of the Village, not far away, on or near Second Avenue, the Hungarian and Russian restaurants drew an equivalent Bohemian-bourgeois crowd from another group of nationalities. This was the Greenwich Village, too, of Joe Gould, the cultivated Harvard tramp, who lived at the Mills Hotel in Bleecker Street: a gnomelike figure with a ratty beard, the first of the beatniks, who kept an endless journal, an 'Oral History,' of contemporary life that might have furnished the materials for a dozen Ph.D. theses and professorial careers, had its sole copy—if it ever really existed! —not been destroyed. The banality of its one published fragment suggests that this was a happy, if not premeditated, ending. That was a neighborhood where one knew people by sight or could guess at them easily: Max Eastman, Michael Gold, Hugo Gellert, Walter Pach, John

Sloan, Kenneth Hayes Miller, Thomas Hart Benton, Art Young, Clarence Britten, to say nothing of the swarms of writers, from Harold Stearns to Llewelyn Powys or Conrad Aiken. Even the publishers were here, at first: B. W. Huebsch, and especially the audacious Boni Brothers, whose fresh ideas, like the Modern Library, and whose first soft cover books, were to lay the foundations of other people's fortunes.

In all that concerns the cultural life, Greenwich Village, between 1900 and 1930, had more of the throb of a city than had all the rest of New York taken as a whole; and the years that Sophia and I lived and worked there, along with the many contacts that I kept up during this whole period, taught me what a city could and should be, as much as the time I spent in London or Paris. Since 1945 the degradation of Greenwich Village has gone on rapidly; but that began well before this with the tearing down of the old houses on the north and then on the south sides of Washington Square, and the building of expensive apartments for those who wished to buy a little of the glamor of the Village, to set them off from their merely expensive Park Avenue.

Some of the fierce neighborhood loyalty of the old Ninth Ward has nevertheless survived; and in reaction against the sort of callous urban renewal that drives away the poor, so that the upper-income groups may live in their hygienic high-rise slums, people like Jane Jacobs have in an excess of sentimental piety, sought to preserve and even intensify the physical congestion and the disorder that came in when Greenwich Village proper first started to decay. But I am glad to have known the serener Village of an earlier day: the neighborhood that Melville skirted, when he walked to his customs' shed on Little Gansevoort Street, the Village that Albert Pinkham Ryder prowled through at night, in days when I still might, with luck, have beheld him in the flesh. A generation later, on my visits to New York, I used to stay in the red-brick house of my in-laws, Philip and Ruth Wittenberg, on Tenth Street, in a top floor rear room that overlooked an intensely cultivated little garden; and if I owned such a house, and lived in a city composed mainly on this pattern, not yet wracked by violence, I would certainly not be willing to exchange its advantages for anything the best suburb could offer me. My almost comic quarrel with F. J. Osborn over desirable urban residential densities rests on our different evaluations of urban space and human contiguity. Like the classic differences between Sergeant Cuff and the gardener in 'The Moonstone'!   —RN. 1963–1974

Notes of a Young Man in Love

Now Beryl got my verses first:
She taught me how to write;
And bound my metre's crippled feet
And cheered my muse's flight.

She held me half a dozen years
We smiled at parting—through our tears!

To Phyllis went a single sheaf
(I worshipped from afar)
And sent my poems *sans* my name:
Good Lord! That started war.

The vixen sank her claws in me
For hiding my identity.

My next verse came more easily
For I was Elsie's poet.
I sent her some of Beryl's stuff—
Don't tell! She'll never know it!

Well, Elsie liked my efforts. I
Liked Elsie's salads, tea, and pie.

A Titian blonde who loved Rossetti,
Agnes I tried with sonnets:
Her reading sounded like a wail
Stifled in woolen bonnets.

Her pictures had more life than she,
More power, lust, diversity.

When Sophie asked for comic verse
I met the challenge like a jay
And butchered all my erstwhile loves
To make a sophic holiday.

Beware! Some dark philosophy
Lurks behind this treachery.

Sophia had complained that none of her admirers had ever yet written a poem to her; and so, mockingly, though already more than dimly aware I was falling in love with her, I wrote this jingle. —1919

Confound Sophie: I am falling in love with her, and the only satisfaction I get out of this fact is the fun of watching the spectacle. Love is a sort of local anesthetic that gets one ready for the ordeal of marriage: and marriage in my present position is such a remote and unimaginable condition that the anesthetic is almost as terrifying as the operation. It is not that I am altogether losing my wits: Sophie does not appear to me in a rosy blur. In fact, I can look upon her in a steady mood of lucid aloofness and watch every movement of her mind and body through a lens of crystalline dispassionateness.* But for all that I can not get rid of an intense biological conviction that someday we will be thrown into each other's arms as mates. I feel that there is a wonderful completeness in Sophie that I have never encountered before in any other girl, as though she were an embodiment of the three graces and each were dancing in vital unison. A sort of Sophie reverie pervades what would otherwise be vacant moments—a sure sign of the divine madness! And I wonder, in a baffled, irritated way what she is thinking about me. . . .

What an incriminating folly this business of falling in love is. I ought to read Pycraft's courtship among the animals in order to restore my sense of humor. When I am not keeping close watch I find myself ruffling my feathers and strutting on parade. Does the game cock or the young buck find a challenging familiarity and invitation in his mate's eyes? . . . It occurs to me that there is some truth in Graham Wallas's belief that the dissociation of the biological man from the spiritual man is a dominant and quite modern trait. Marie tells the story of a doctor she knows. This girl had attended a medical lecture on a certain disease of the heart, and she returned home from the theater at night accompanied by a male friend of hers, who kissed her and embraced her in good Southern fashion at parting. In the midst of the embrace she diagnosed his heart palpitation as indicative of the very disease she had been studying. "Honey," she said, "you have a systolic murmur," and she told him for farewell that he must consult a physician immediately. . . .   —RN. 1919

* Oh! Can you? [Author: 1974]

. . . We both prided ourselves on our common sense, and yet we can see how easy it is to lose hold of it. My original fear that it would spoil altogether the possibilities of any intimate relations between us was absurdly wide of the mark: how easy it was for me, for example, to abandon my common sense convictions about the impossibility of marriage, and that sort of thing. The danger, as anyone but a conceited prig like myself ought have known, lay just the other way: for rationality and common sense and all those kindred instruments of sweetness and light are in constant danger of being dazed and diverted by more primitive impulses, and one shortly discovers, as does Regius' mother in 'The Invalids,' that having a level head is of no use at all when you have lost it. I think I lost mine rather more completely than you did, for your doubts were probably nothing more nor less than a symptom of a reluctantly dissipated rationality.   —Letter to S.W. May 1920

. . . Last night I was walking with James Henderson along the South Bank of the Thames opposite the Houses of Parliament. We had had supper together in a very good little restaurant, The Ship's Grill, one of the best that I have found, all things considered, in Whitehall, and we were watching the towers of Westminster change in color and aspect against the clear sunset sky. It was about nine o'clock. Suddenly I seized Henderson by the shoulders and looked into his rather heavy, good-humored face. "My dear Henderson," I exclaimed, "I should be perfectly happy this moment if instead of walking with you I was walking here with Sophie." "I often have such thoughts," Henderson replied mildly, "b-b-b-ut I never have the nerve to express them." —Letter to S.W. June 10, 1920

. . . Branford is trying to arrange a conference with Geddes and Farquharson down at New Milton next Sunday, and since I have not been invited I gather that I am to be the principal subject of discussion. [But Geddes did not come to England that summer.] Indeed Farquharson said as much. Sooner or later at any rate such a conference will be held and I shall cable you the results as soon as possible. The future of the Sociological Society, Farquharson said yesterday to Miss Loch, depends upon whether we have enough money to buy Mr. Mumford. I am glad I put my price up reasonably high and made a three years' stay the limit, because to tell the truth Sophie I don't want to be bought. If I am to get the work and study done that it is in me to do during the next three years I ought to stick to literature, pure literature, and shun anything that looks like a sufficient and lucrative job. This may mean something like a starvation diet at first; it does not *necessarily* mean that, but I am sure that it is the condition of my doing any permanently respectable work. I hate like the devil to go back to the parsimonious habit of life that I cultivated in the days of my early apprenticeship: but short of doing this I don't see any way of escaping a mechanical routine as editor, literary hack, or what not that will stunt my development during a period in which I am still capable of growing. I don't mean by this that I have any visions of living in a garret. (Of course that is where I live now!) I mean only that I shan't attempt to make more than the minimum, say

48

twelve hundred dollars a year, [too low?] which will enable me to keep going by myself. This assumes, then, Soph, that should we live together during the next three or four years we would do so independently, except for the matter of helping each other out, like two good chums, as occasion demanded. After that I shall be prepared, I'm pretty sure (if we are agreed) to make decently heroic efforts to provide for any children you may care to have . . .

—Letter to S.W. July 4, 1920

Sophie: I like you better and better each time I see the way you behave in a crisis. Your letter of June 28 wasn't an easy one to write: indeed it wasn't an easy one to read: but if you had any notion that it was going to wreck our comradeship you are damned well mistaken. I shouldn't be able to think passionately of comradeship (or love or marriage or anything else for that matter) with you if you didn't see each occasion so clearly and rise to it so bravely: you *are an equal*, Sophie, and if we never met again in our lives I should feel that somehow the whole adventure of existence was justified by my having met you. God help the rest of us if you are low and common and vulgar. I like you, Sophie, and I will be comrades with you as long as we have anything to share. I love you and I will be your mate if affection ever deepens enough between us to make our mating happy. But one or the other, as mate or comrade, I count on you: and if ever I find you falling away from our comradeship and sinking into triviality I shall jolly well up and wring your silly neck before you have the opportunity to degrade either of us . . .

—Letter to S.W. July 10, 1920

. . . Misunderstandings rarely arise from the things you say; they arise from what you've neglected to say. Keeping things back is a form of lying, and much more than any other form it hurts the person who does it. I'm not a pattern of heavenly virtues, goodness knows, but at any rate you've had opportunities in my letters to take peeks at moods and emotions that wouldn't always reveal themselves even in the closest daily intercourse, since they come out of the inner life and don't play about obviously on the surface. I've only had one or two peeks at your inner life: but each time I was happy and satisfied: and even though at the time you thought you were hurting me (and you were) they made me feel nearer to you and more deeply in love with you than you could have made me feel by exercizing the utmost care. Like the Norseman in Chesterton's fine poem I get as much keen joy out of disdain as other people do out of their sweetheart's complaisance. You aren't distant when you explain how distant you feel, Soph: you're only genuinely distant when you don't explain it. It isn't pain that makes life unbearable but the absence of sensation: it's better to be tortured than to be ignored.   —Letter to S.W. September 1, 1920

. . . I don't see why we shouldn't talk as unreservedly as is necessary about sexual matters, since if we are going to be mates (and even if we aren't) it is only by knowing the ins and outs of ourselves that we shall be able to get through life without hurting each other and everyone around us. Thank heaven you conquered your priggishness (or thank heaven the mailboat sailed on the morrow!) and didn't tear up your last letter in order to write about "politer matters." At any rate, though our letters crossed at sea, I gave you the lead last Monday, and if you hadn't had the good sense and the candor to talk about your most intimate desires you might be shocked to find out what a nonchalant scalpel I was using on your interior being.

Do you know, Soph, what the thought was that kept on sobering me and forcing me to see straight each time I read over your letter. Knowing how violent my own sexual desires are, in spite of the fact that my conduct would pass for A-1 in a Y.M.C.A. secretary, and knowing that those of a normal girl may be even deeper and more overwhelming, I wondered what chance I would have had of remaining in the state of virginity if someone had been wooing *me*. Precious little! My outward impeccability is simply a reflex of the sheltered and solitary life I've so long been leading, and though this had made deep channels of habit which in a sense "protect" me, I simply wouldn't give tuppence for the sort of chastity and purity this signifies. The only period since early adolescence when I've had any real sexual balance or health was curiously enough during my service in the navy: the sort of monastic discipline and communal solidarity that prevailed in the barracks squeezed sex out of existence without one's even noticing it. I know that this is a different version of barracks life than that which you generally hear; but this wasn't my own experience alone; and the viciousness of barracks life, about which there is no doubt, is the product of an idleness and boredom which during our training we never had time to suffer from.

Now, Sophie, I crave a full life just as passionately as you do: half the savor has been taken out of my trip over here because I hadn't you to share it with, and half the impulse to venture and roam and explore was dissipated because it made me so irritable to have to absorb all the joy of this by myself. In postponing Geddes's offer until we at least had had the *chance* to mate I did not feel that I was giving up one career for another: it seemed to me simply that two equally desirable activities conflicted for the moment and that I was choosing to give preference, while the conflict lasted, to that which most vitally mattered. Think of all the crippled, neurotic people in the world: people who have made all manner of mess and meanness out of their lives because they would not face the facts of their sex or because they would not act in terms of their deepest desires and preferred money or security or fame or what not instead of success in life *in terms of life.*   —Letter to S.W. September 10, 1920

Glimpses of England

ABOARD THE S. S. ADRIATIC.   I have been listening to the insular chatter of three Britishers next to me who have been explaining at great length among themselves what is wrong with America and what is particularly right with the Old Country. Confound their silly prejudices: they dislike our genuine virtues! The lack of pro-per discipline. The absence of do-mestic affection. And so on, *ad mal de mer*. . . . Fuller, indeed, warned me about the British Islander. He emphasized particularly his shyness and reticence. Until this morning I had not discovered much of it, albeit my companions on deck and at mess, are all John Bullish in one degree or another. Yesterday a spare old gentleman, an engineer, in tweeds, with a white Vandyke and a soft meticulous voice, wasted a whole morning which I had intended to devote to sweet, silent reflection in telling me all the weaknesses and ineptitudes he had discovered in America; as for example, item one, how altogether improper it was for the Americans to depart from the elegant orthodoxy of the true mother tongue; item two, what incomprehensible perversity it was for Americans to call the letter zed a zee; item three, what bad taste it was to permit negro railway porters and waiters to greet one familiarly instead of following the genuine British fashion of making niggers mind their place and keep their distance . . .

. . . My first example of Fuller's Englishman was the radio operator. I hung around his shack for a few minutes this morning, examining his instruments and waiting for him to say a civil word. After a few minutes he looked at me. "Do you want anything?" I replied affably that I was just an old radio man who was interested in the works for old time's sake. "Aouw!" he exclaimed, and turned his back on me. I don't know whether to label this British phlegm or British impudence or British shyness: but I am sure it is British. An American would at least have explained to me that his set was the best piece of apparatus in the Mercantile Marine, and before we had been five minutes together he would have clapped his receivers over my ears to prove it. I was not tempted to stay five minutes with this frigid Britisher. (The Britishers on my left have just begun to praise the climate of the British Isles. They have proved to their satisfaction, for the fifth time,

that it is incomparably superior to the American climate. Its very dampness keeps the grass from being burned away in the summer time, you know: and that is why English meadows are so green and English lanes so lovely. And so on, in large expressive spatters.)
—Letter to S.W. May 1920

. . . When I hear the way the rest of the American Horde is rushing around, seeing this Nabob and interviewing that Sultan, I feel altogether out of it: it doesn't give me the faintest pleasure to meet a big Nobody or a little Somebody and hold my head passively under a drenching of platitudes for half an hour; and I had much rather sit in the gutter and shy stones at them and .stick out my tongue than have to go through the painful ritual of taking them seriously. As for the real somebodies (Old Bob Smillie for example) I feel toward them the way that Walt Whitman felt toward Lincoln: he wished that their circumstances would bring them a little closer together but he was amply content to get just a bare friendly nod from Lincoln as he passed by on horseback. I hate to go after people. If one comes upon them by accident, well and good: and if one doesn't come upon them at all, well and good also: all the richest experiences of life, from birth onward, come by chance, and if they come more deliberately they are rarely worth the pains of seizing. . . .
—Letter to S.W. July 1920

POLICE MORALITY.   One of the particularly pleasing things in a London park is the shamelessness of young lovers. In the long twilight of the summer's evening one may encounter scores of couples tenderly discovering each other, with no fear of being leered at by the passers by, for the spectacle is too common to provoke even wretches who leer, or of being rudely jostled out of their ecstasy by some dogged brute in a blue coat.

The great disability of the American policeman is that he has become a censor of morals, and in our parks and at our bathing beaches he exhibits a sense of delicacy which would make the very angels in heaven seem prurient. I hesitate to think how many arrests would be made, and incidentally, how many recalcitrant heads would be broken, were a New York policeman let loose in a London park with the instructions and moral predilections that we now operate under. At tea time in Kensington Gardens a patrol wagon would back up under the trees around the tea-house, to make away with all the ladies who were shamelessly smoking cigarettes in the open air, and on its way toward

Bow Street it would doubtless stop along the banks of the Serpentine to pick up a batch of urchins that had stripped in public view and were taking an afternoon swim. (I am not quite sure whether the London County Council permits children to bathe in the Serpentine during the more exposed hours of the day; but I have seen them do so more than once; and nobody thought it worth while to protest.) Contrast this with the experience of a young lady of my acquaintance who happened to stop before the fountain in Washington Square to see some jolly and almost naked children splashing around in the water, and was told to move on by a policeman who asked her if "she didn't have no shame."   —RN. 1921

A VISIT TO LORD BRYCE.   Today I spent the greater part of my time interviewing respectable or eminent persons. The first one was Lord Bryce. Branford and I went around to his apartment shortly after breakfast, in order to solicit his blessing for our project for an international cooperation in sociology, and we found him living in a large and seedy apartment overlooking Buckingham Palace and Green Park. The furnishings of the big room into which we were shown were mid and late Victorian: the walls were plastered with watercolors and there was miscellaneous china on the mantel and rows of yellowed nineteenth century books housed in intermittent bookcases. Bryce entered: a solid-boned, athletic looking youngster of eighty-two, with more energy in carriage and conversation than either Branford or myself. His face was curtained in white hair, and even the patch of nose which protruded from the bushy whiteness was not innocent of a number of white hair stalks which my eyes simply couldn't leave, not even when Bryce was firing questions at me with the astuteness of a lawyer in a criminal court and making me feel like a mouse trying to get away from the paw of a very resolute and dexterous cat. I found that he knew 'Harvey Robinson,' and that this was safe ground: but he also liked 'Murray Butler,' and *that* was dangerous ground. Also, like a good British Islander, he was suspicious of theories and formulae, and as a good Victorian, he thought sociology had something to do with slum expeditions. I felt that there were enormous gulfs between us, in spite of his sprightly way of carrying his eighty-two years, and I perceived that the fact that he knew Harold Laski, who corresponded with him, did not so much bring him nearer to me as put Laski further away. For all that, of course, he was a man of great sageness and discernment; with an experience and record of scholarship that are both to be envied. In other words, he blessed our project. . . .   —Letter to S.W. July 21, 1920

YESTERDAY AFTERNOON IN WESTMINSTER ABBEY.   The Housing Congress delegates had a section allotted them and I knew that I would feel a little less like a lost sheep that had accidentally strayed into the fold if I sat among them. It was ten years since I had been inside a religious edifice: good Lord! ten years. I must have been about fifteen then, I remember, and I had abandoned all devout observances for a whole year, and I was lured into the house of God not out of piety but out of a pathetic desire to be in Beryl's company. She used to entice young men into church with her every Sunday; she liked the atmosphere of it and said it was better than tramping around the streets on a cold Sunday afternoon, but that was the first and last time that she inveigled me into the thickets of religious orthodoxy. And I remember going back with her to the dingy little apartment in which she and her mother lived on Eighth Avenue and 113 Street, and reading her one of my first short stories, the very first, I think, that was based on my own experience of life. Ten years! What have I learned in the interval? Many things, no doubt; some beyond antici-pation. What equipment I had I've developed to perhaps sixty percent efficiency, and as far as observation goes this is a relatively high level. Where I've failed vitally is in this: that I haven't been able to add a single element to my equipment. Hence my disastrous ineptitude as an animal; hence my lack of a mate. Beryl admired me and respected me, I know: she said so repeatedly and for once I could believe her. Damn you, Soph, I suppose you admire and respect me too—but am I a piece of statuary? Hath not a man ears, eyes, nose, dimensions? —Letter to S.W. June 7, 1920

. . . My philosophy doesn't have any place for the idea of trying to live in a Paradise where "falls not hail nor rain nor any snow, nor ever wind blows loudly." And since I object to the best of Paradises it is obvious that I detest fool's paradises most of all.
                                 —Letter to S.W. September 29, 1920

[On Sophie's birthday] . . . The usual wishes for happiness are always a little banal, because people do not know what they mean when they talk about happiness; they think it is pleasure, or comfort, or 'having all you want in the world,' and they are disappointed when they find that these things have as much capacity for producing misery as for creating anything else. When I say that I wish you happiness, I mean that I hope as you grow older you will become more intensely alive. —Letter to S.W. London, October 8, 1920

COFFEE WITH A. R. ORAGE.   The afternoon was sacred to
the presence and person of Orage, the editor of 'The New Age.'
After a search for the passageway that leads to his office, and an inter-
view with a young man lodged therein who welcomed me with true
British effusiveness (irony) I found Orage seated with another man
in the cellar of the Kardomah Cafe, a coffee house in which real
coffee is served at tuppence a cup. Major Douglas came in later, and
a couple of other Americans; and I listened for three hours to a steady
stream of conversation from Orage and Douglas, three quarters of
which was a dull and frequently metaphysical discussion of the social
credit proposals which 'The New Age' is fostering and the remainder
of which was the weirdest nonsense (coming from Orage) on the
world contest now taking place between the bureaucracy of Jesuitism,
acting through the League of Nations, and the financial manipulations
of the Jews, acting through the banking system. Orage spoke of this
as the two party system in world politics, and he intimated that the
general election which should decide the issue between the two parties was still being held. If Orage were alone in uttering this gibberish
I should have promptly sent for a padded ambulance at the first outbreak: but this sort of thing is as virulent here as spiritualism and
theosophy and astrology, and the contagion has spread through the
whole community. . . .   —Letter to S.W. June 1920

A WALK IN THE CHILTERNS.   . . . Yesterday was a sad disappointing day for most British Islanders: a holiday drenched in rain.
But the weather couldn't take the edge off the appetite for life which
this amazingly lovely little town stimulates in me five minutes after
I've set foot in it. It rained buckets all through the afternoon, but
for all that I set out for a tramp around five o'clock with a new
acquaintance I had struck up slowly during the past week at High
Wycombe, a highly reputed old dog of a London surgeon named
Parker. . . . Parker proved to be a remarkable specimen of the best
sort of Briton. Shrewd, kindly, rational, goodhumored. He is about
the finest that his country and his profession can offer. He embodies
a type: the radical doctor, the same sort of doctor that Meredith
pictures in 'Beauchamp's Career.' He is intimate with the local trade
union leaders, is a secretary of the local branch of the Workers Educational Association, publicly advocates the establishment of a Preventive Public Health Service (to the consternation of his colleagues
on Harley Street) and spends his evenings and holidays as a quiet,
unpretentious citizen in an unfashionable little town. He traces his
ancestors back on his father's side to the keeper of one of the King's

parks in the early Middle Ages, and he has a fund of interesting stories to tell about some of them. One, for example, was a New England colonist, and as a youth led a rebellion in Harvard College against the faculty in the days before that institution was called Harvard. Another, who lived in the early eighteenth century, was a woman who had married a drunken husband and who bequeathed to posterity a remarkably minute and faithful picture of her times, embalmed in a diary. Parker told me some of the things she recorded. As for example, in illustration of the hygienic standard of the time, this: "My dear son Robert is going to be married tomorrow, and this evening, in preparation, he bathed his whole body." Apparently the only time a bath was thought necessary was immediately after birth and immediately before marriage. . . .   —Letter to S.W. August 5, 1920

A VERY ROYAL ACADEMY.   Just before tea time every day the Summer Exhibition of the British Royal Academy at Burlington House is thronged with visitors. The scene is impressive by contrast with the American Academy's display. The primary distinction between the official art of the two countries lies in the fact that in America it is only the opening which can be called in newspaper slang a social event, whereas the whole season at Burlington House preserves a titillation of popular interest. This does not mean, I hasten to add, that there is a higher level of esthetic appreciation in England. Apart from the small independent exhibitions, and the folk who welcome and understand the work of the independents, the state of the fine arts in this island seems to be appreciably lower than in America. Esthetics have simply nothing to do with the popularity of Burlington House. The British Academy is at bottom a delicate social barometer.

A tour of Burlington House gives happy evidence that the British Empire is back on the old stand of business as usual. There was a period during the war when we were assured that this relapse into the slovenly habits of the Victorian peace was impossible. With a little pain one may recall the time when the world was so uncalloused to murder and starvation as to think that the war must inevitably compensate its filthy necessities by effecting splendid social transformations. We were assured on every side that the world could never, never be the same again. Society was going to be—oh! so different, and in anticipation of this happy issue the young imperialists of the Round Table school began to talk with sanguine rationality about the future of the British Commonwealth.

The British Academy of 1920 has a different story to tell. The war

is over, and the war itself intrudes in the galleries with just a few pictures of audacious puerility. The dominant feature of the exhibition is a monster portrait of their Royal Majesties, attended by a couple of clerical dignitaries. The subjects indicate by their modest and affable pose, and the help of a few corroborative words kindly limned by the artist, that the success of British arms had been achieved not by their Majesties—as had been fondly supposed—but by God. As a painting this particular achievement is a masterpiece of ineptitude; but more serious interest attaches to the fact that it is shown without the faintest note of dubiety or apology. A community which had achieved an esthetic revolution would no doubt have kept such a picture from being painted: but a State that was on the verge of a social revolution would, in order to reduce the provocation to riot, keep this massive tablet from ever being hung. The mere presence of this picture is profoundly relevant to the political observer, for it gives the mood of the whole exhibition and demonstrates what its visitors are thinking. Other countries have been raked by war and riddled by famine; other countries have lost territories, principalities, and potentates; other countries have slowly subsided into a condition of barbarism. In the British Islands nothing has changed but the prices. Hard by Burlington House, in Trafalgar Square, the veteran beggars, and the beggared veterans, swarm as thickly as ever they did in the post-African War days. The world has been made a little safer for bureaucracy.
—The Freeman. June 16, 1920

My present interest in life is the exploration and documentation of cities. I am as much interested in the mechanism of man's cultural ascent as Darwin was in the mechanism of his biological descent.

—RN. 1919

Victories are of use only to demonstrate their futility.   —RN. 1921

Men are for the hunt; women are for the meal: that is the root difference in their attitudes toward sex.   —RN. 1921

There is a great deal of art that is no more significant than the clippings of hair that must be swept up in a barber shop. We must grow hair, heaven knows, because that is our nature, and we must clip it in order to be comfortable: but the mere fact that *we* have grown it—that it expresses our physiological selves—does not make it a bit more worthy of preservation.   —RN. 1922

58

People who are thwarted by failure are fortunate enough not to know how it is possible to be thwarted by success.   —RN. 1922

In school vocational subjects must be taught liberally—not for what you can make out of them, but for what they can make out of you.   —RN. 1922

In me, Athens and Corinth are perpetually at war; and the intellectual life and the sexual life dominate by turns: they have not yet been able to adjust their difficulties and live harmoniously. To achieve a "peace without victory" is my problem.   —RN. 1922

PERSONALIA.   The moral honesty of Sophie: I vow this makes up for all the bitterness and all the sadness of my part of our relationship. Last night was, I think, the most painful evening I ever spent in her company, and I have the memory of some pretty painful evenings, like the Sunday before my departure for London; and yet, with Sophie's essential frankness and decency I can bear the pain of such encounters as bravely as a soldier carries an honourable wound. There is a temptation even to prize the wound on account of the calibre of the person who inflicted it.

In some manner or other our talk had wound around to a point where, with no little reluctance, I told Sophie how the poignant cause of my unhappiness during the past couple of weeks was the thought that, in her new developments and experiments, she might drift apart from me in the same way that Beryl had drifted. (I recollect now how I came to make this confession: Sophie had said that perhaps one of the reasons for her reluctance to enter marriage was her dissatisfaction with the state of most of the family relationships she had experienced or observed.)

I pointed out that she was not being "free" by refusing to go along my road, she was simply making the choice of another kind of road; she wasn't merely escaping my set of influences. She agreed to this and said—wisely enough—that she couldn't tell what kind of person she was until she at least experimented in another direction. Her old life had not been a satisfactory one: the new one she was playing with had made her a good deal happier, and if that was the sort of nature she had she was bound to develop in that direction. "I don't think I am spoiled by admiration," she said, "but I like it and want it. I am level-headed enough and it won't make me do anything I don't want to do. I think my case is something like Lou's: I am going through a second adolescence. Perhaps I wouldn't want all these things now if I had had them when I was younger. I am just inclined to let things take their course now and see how they turn out. Sometimes I hope that I won't keep going this way, that I'll return somehow to my old self. But I don't know. I was wondering whether you would understand. I had thought myself that maybe I was repeating the same course Beryl had taken and wondered whether you would see it."   —RN. November 8, 1920

Were the last three months wasted? My thoughts again and again come back to that question. I cannot answer. Has my whole life been wasted? Without doubt the greater part of it has, half my potentialities undeveloped, half my opportunities missed, half my energies frittered away. The business of finding a mate, and of achieving success in life in terms of philosophy, is doubtless as important as any of the things I have missed in pursuing it; but of course this leaves unanswered the question as to whether I have found my mate, and time and chance and experiment will alone tell me that.   —RN. 1920

After I have spent an evening with Sophie my sleep is filled with dreams of Beryl. What is the Freudian significance of this? Do I want to escape Sophie? Do I seek recompense for all that I missed with Beryl? Is Sophie Beryl in continuation? I find myself occasionally behaving toward Sophie the way Beryl would have liked me to behave toward her: I exaggerate politenesses and formalities and conventions which in the old days I spent most of my time in contentiously resisting. Beryl used to correct my lack of convention, Sophie slices away an overplus: both of them taming me and making me something different.   —RN. 1920

The Collapse of Tomorrow

Much of the work in a civilized community rests upon the assumption that the show is good for a long run. The drama of the present tends to move in a given direction only when it receives the double impact of the past and the future; and if the past be too frightful for remembrance or the future too cloudy for anticipation, the present ceases to move in any particular direction, and teeters fitfully about from point to point.

If this seems a rather too abstract way of expressing the part that is played by the assurance of continuity in our lives, let the reader consider some concrete examples of its absence. Almost any country that has acutely felt the effects of the war would furnish instances of the empty inconsecutiveness of a present that is divorced from a past and a future. Trustworthy observers who have been abroad during the last two years bring back disheartening reports to the effect that science, art, and scholarship among the younger generation have been steadily on the wane. Perhaps a little too much has been made of the fact that in many parts of Europe artists and students are literally starving; and it is possible that we have not taken sufficiently into account the condition of uncertainty which is making the younger generation turn aside from work the benefits of which may not be immediately realized in order to spend their energies on trifles that promise a speedy return—even if it be only a day's respite from hunger or a night of forgetfulness.

Eat, drink, and be merry, for tomorrow we die, is what the last seven years of 'preserving civilization' has written on the wall. Doubtless Mr. Bernard Shaw's 'Back to Methuselah' owes something to his observations of the attitude of his contemporaries toward wars and rumors of wars. Human life, says Mr. Shaw, must be vastly lengthened before people will have the grace to take it seriously. In that century of fitful peace which followed the Napoleonic Wars the expectation of life for a healthy European male was small enough in all conscience; but today the expectation is so precarious, with armaments piling up and diplomacy festering and home-guards drilling and privilege-hunting rampant, that one cannot even count upon continuity in the life of any particular community, to say nothing of any particular individual. As a result, all work that depends for its sustenance upon a heritage from the past, and is lured forward, through swamp and thicket and jungle, by the gleam of the future, is failing and dying.

The day that does not carry the seed of tomorrow in its womb is sterile and fit only for eating and drinking: the measured, disciplined, purposeful life depends upon the promise of continuity. Is it any wonder, then, that the holocaust in Europe has not merely decreased the amount of arable ground under cultivation but has also, for similar reasons, diminished the area of cultured and civilized life? Art, literature, and science are almost meaningless if their development promises to cease with the life of the particular persons for whom they have a meaning. If there is to be no future there can be no way of differentiating between one kind of activity and another—for the ultimate basis of differentiation must rest upon the capacity for producing a "life more abundant"—and one might equally well, on Bentham's advice, play pushpins instead of writing poetry.

Those of the older generation who have survived the years of the war and the peace will carry on their work, out of habit, as the bees build their honeycombs with no thought for the bee-keeper who will some day pillage their communities; but the younger people whose habits of work have been disrupted by war, who have never tasted the life of plain living and high thinking, who have never given themselves up to any consecutive purpose except that of "defending their country"—what can one expect of these young people except that they will seek out whatever directly promises to give them enjoyment and satisfaction? Scarcely anyone will take the trouble to be an artist or scientist when he may so speedily cease to be even a man.

Does not this account a little for the lassitude, the febrility, the spurious gaiety that a good many competent observers have noted in Europe today? What we call the future is in a sense always an illusion, and the greatest disillusion that Europe possibly suffers from is the loss of something that never existed outside the minds of those who moulded their activities in terms of it—the loss of a tomorrow. Statesmen who talk in a loud, guilty way about preserving the fabric of civilization might pause long enough in their clamour to realize that they are talking about something that actually exists. Civilization is the magic instrument by which men live in a world of time that has three dimensions: the past, the present, and the future. When neither security of life nor continuity of works is maintained, civilization must necessarily collapse. It has done so before; and it has taken hundreds of years to weave a new fabric; and it may do so again. A pretty prospect for the encouragement and discipline of adolescents!

—The Freeman. July 13, 1921

ENVIRONMENTAL DEGRADATION: 1921.   Some memory of
old times drew me over to Staten Island the other day. The shore that
I sought was the only one in my recollection which was at once within
easy reach of the city, spacious, and set with its face toward the open
sea. Presently, after passing through a waste of slum-villages, I found
myself on a beach. I remembered it of old as consisting of a little
'amusement-park' with a sprinkling of rickety bath-houses, separated
from a similar park by a long strip of virgin sand. On the landward side,
in the old days, stretched a wide sweep of salt marsh, more or less
inundated by a tidal river that broke one's passage along the sea-front,
except at low tide. The amusement-park I found had not ceased to
exist; on the contrary, in the course of some half-dozen years it had
solidly entrenched itself in the landscape; and its length now seemed
interminable. Where the Japanese ball games and the bath-houses and
the refreshment-palaces came to an end, a new kind of architectural
obscenity, the beach-bungalow, had come into existence, and the view
of the salt marsh was cut off by rows and rows, sometimes two or three
deep, of what looked like Brobdingnagian rabbit-hutches.

What had happened to the open beach I used to know? A thousand
people who liked sunlight and salt air had purchased building-sites and
had put up bungalows; and thousands more were drawn to their vicinity
every week, in search of surcease from the daily round and trivial task.
Finding, however, neither salt air nor shelter nor sunlight nor solitude
altogether to their taste, these people—visitors or residents—drifted into
the scenic railways and dance-halls, ate frankfurters, and generally com-
ported themselves in the attitudes that are popularly supposed by our
citizenry to induce happiness and good cheer. What a travesty, not
merely of the good life, but of the patent joys, of mere animality! Sadly
I turned away from this picture of teeming decay to the hard, narrow
margin of the beach, but alas! the sands seemed as wretched as the rest
of the landscape: the flotsam and jetsam washed up by the waves spoke
less of the sea and its mysteries than of the dump-heap.

There is a beach I know on the Coast of Maine, a long, noble
beach that, with the ocean, forms one of the pillars upon which the
great arch of the sky is supported; and the wreckage one finds on that
shore after a storm—perhaps a shark driven up by the breakers, or a
school of hake—seems only to be sweetened by the wind and the sunlight, and never to decay. The island strand upon which I was walking
was once that kind of a beach; but it was so no longer. I picked my
way among blackened grapefruit and bananas; here a leg of putrid salt
beef; there a dead sea-bird with a long beak and dirty, bedraggled feathers; and, of course, everywhere piles and piles of driftwood. I warped
my steps toward the trolley-track which spans the two amusement-
parks. Here there were no disappointments. The trolley was the same
old trolley that has long subsisted by collecting a feudal revenue from

people who wish to cross the tidal stream and cannot do so except by riding in the car over a precarious trestle. The same old trestle and the same old car that I had known so many years ago! Privilege, at least, seemed to know the secret of self-preservation.

Wrapped in a double thickness of solitude, I sat down on a bench by the trolley-track, but in spite of myself I shortly found myself in conversation with a vacant-faced young man who affected brazen hair and sunburned, khaki clothes. This idle individual added a few more items to my list of environmental casualties; first, by remarking that he had decided not to swim because the water was too dirty and thick with oil; second, by correlating this defilement with the disappearance of weakfish and bluefish in the Bay; and third—well, he began to drivel, in a sort of shorthand, about the diminution, in contrast with previous years, of erotic encounters along the beach on recent Saturdays and Sundays and the probable diversion of the traffic to Coney Island. This sickly lout, with his dull chatter of obscenity, put a final touch to the unhappy spectacle of waste and dreariness and decay.

This devastated strip of beach, these disastrous bungalows, these dismal amusement-parks, this dreary youth and the sweethearts he gabbled about; these things and people are not part of a settled, cultivated community; they are the offal of a civilization which is perpetually 'on the make,' and therefore perpetually 'on the move': a civilization which is as impermanent as that of the pioneer, though lacking the pioneer's excuse for existence. Puritanism indeed! The word that describes the crudeness of the greater part of our civilization is not 'puritanism,' but 'barbarism'; and it is a barbarism of which even the Australian aborigine should be ashamed.   —The Freeman. 1921

How far this generation has travelled from the dirty prudery of the last century. Sophie was telling me about an operation that one of her friends had undergone and she said that the surgeons feared at first that the ovaries had been infected. Twenty years ago Sophie's prototype would have had the sense of having committed an awful shocker to have mentioned even the ovaries of a fish in a conversation with a young man, and fifty years ago Sophie probably would not have known that ovaries existed. The world is moving along very nicely thank you: we shall soon be so healthy minded and so unrepressed then that we will look back to the age of smut with the sort of bewilderment with which a New York City plumber would greet a Constantinople latrine. What the devil will happen to the risky farce when that day arrives? What will happen to the underdrawer school of humor? [P.S. 1974. We know now!]   —RN. 1921

64

What we call "the World" has always implied a relationship between man and the world—it was so much of the hypothetical totality as man, with his necessities and urgencies, had found useful to himself. To call this world "the" world and to assume none other exists is a human provincialism—the world that the swallow sees as it darts after insects in the sunset sky is quite another thing. What is the ultimate reality of all these worlds? Perhaps there is none. What we call eternal verities may be merely shadows passing over the face of some enigmatic deity—and by the very words in which I speak of the verities it is obvious that my deity, with his enigmatic face, is a very human fellow, perhaps not very different from myself. . . .   —RN. 1921

IMPRESSIONS.   I wish I could trust this deceitful brain of mine to store up accurately all the impressions I have been receiving during the last six months. That of Jacques Loeb, a benign, sallow-faced German, in a long frock coat, in his study at the Rockefeller Institute overlooking the East River one late afternoon in January, and his mingled arrogance and sweetness. The gaping forehead and distorted mouth of Franz Boas in a room looking north from the School of Journalism over the campus; the bulging eye that seemed to focus upon one like a magnifying glass. Albert Jay Nock, at lunch with me in the Lafayette; an averted profile with a hand playing uneasily over his teeth; Walter Fuller, bursting into the Old Chelsea tearoom, expressing beatification and apologies in words that ran together like drops of mercury. Clarence Britten and I, very assured, very quiet, very genial, very sophisticated, in the dining room of the Hotel Seymour; good napery and silver, excellent service, serenity; and a long walk through Central Park with the moonlight shining over the snowy meadows and frosted trees, Clarence limping a little and answering my questions about Chicago. With Robby [Geroid Robinson] in a cafeteria near Columbia, batting the world back and forth between us to the clatter of unseemly crockery and the vapid suggestions of lukewarm tea. The gathering in Harold Stearns's basement room, with Jesus Christ [Ernest Boyd] in a brown suit and baritone voice talking atheism above the whispers of this or that clique. Around Washington Square with Sophie—but Sophie is worth a whole note for herself, and even then I shan't recapture all the separate impressions that keep on drifting into composites.

—RN. 1921

SUCCESS. Almost everything I've written during the past year has been printed. Am I elated? Not a bit of it: all my essays and miscellanies count for no better than a bull's eye when one is on top of the target: there was much more hope in my work, and incidentally much more exhilaration, when I was so far away from the target that my arrows never hit. Then, at least, I had the pleasure of using all my strength to pull a long bow, and even the misses did not lower my self-respect. Now—but what's the use of clawing through the stale garbage heap of ineptitudes which constitutes my present? The mere smell of it nauseates me, and I dare not remove the cover. . . .   —RN. 1921

To be happy one must be indifferent; but to be indifferent means indifferent to happiness; hence one might as well give it up as a bad job and take life as it comes.   —RN. 1921

THE EMPTINESS OF PLENTY.   Perhaps one of the reasons that rich people get so little fun out of "playing the game" is that they find it so easy to change the rules; and are always making use of this privilege. They get no more pleasure therefore than the football player who, in William James's illustration, would win the game by carrying the ball to the goal alone on a dark night . . .   —RN. 1921

AN ARTIST'S WIFE   . . . This afternoon I had tea with Mrs. S. K., and I came away with the pleasant feeling that if I had looked forward to the meeting with any vague illusions they were still intact at the end of it. Have I told you about her little book, 'The Cost of Living,' which I plucked out of the discard heap and reviewed sympathetically. It was a criticism of the pernicious, unchristian habit of providing for a tomorrow which may never come if we refuse to act bravely and generously in the day that is here. Well, I was about the only intelligent being out of the hundred Mrs. K. sent her book to who not merely read her argument but who was prepared to give it a practical sanction; and she was so amazed at my audacity that she wrote me a grateful letter and during the past couple of months we have corresponded from time to time. She had come down from New Haven yesterday, and today we met for the first time. She is the wife of a distinguished artist, whose methods and ideals I incidentally abominate, and she was herself an artist when she married him. She has a sort of

66

shrewish sense of humor of which her book does not show a chemical trace, and along with that the sort of stabbing candor which a woman of forty-eight is sometimes sufficiently disillusioned to adopt. She hinted, for example, that her own capabilities in art were more distinguished than her husband's, and by that hint I gathered the tragedy that her marriage must have caused at the same time that it threw over it the shadow of concealment. By aptitude and capacity she should doubtless have been the breadwinner. Instead she served as a model for her husband, and since the pictures he painted of her were inevitably more successful than those she could paint of him (for she was perhaps once a beautiful woman) it fell to her lot to continue to pose in his studio and to keep his house and to bear his children, while her own talents shriveled away and left her with no other capability for her older life than that of teaching the art she might have practiced. How long are women going to stand for that sort of thing, I wonder? How long will they be content to remain the butt of a biological joke? and how far is that sort of sacrifice biologically or morally justified? I wonder . . .   —Letter to S. W. May 1, 1920

On Our Marriage

You will remember Sophie as the beautiful dark-haired secretary that used to have the adjacent office to mine at 'The Dial,' and by a deliberate act of the imagination you will try to conceive a young female person who is my opposite in almost every quality: musical where I am deaf, slow where I am quick, hard where I am soft, and yet beneath all these oppositions and antitheses thoroughly genial and sympathetic. In short, a good companion, a sensible comrade, and (I should fancy) a jolly mate. Here the encomium ends and we descend with a bump to the ground floor of existence. In spite of my display of a splendid romantic folly (of which I had long thought myself incapable) Sophie is not nearly so much in love with me as I am with her. . . . We are not married, and as things go now have little prospect of being married.
—Letter to J.L. May 1920

. . . Well was it said that a man's worst enemies shall be those of his own household. It is just like you and Jerry to decide that I am a sociologist, and not one of the fifty-seven other things that I want to be. So Leonardo's friends all doubtless used to say that he had the bent and the skill of an engineer and a geologist, but as for painting pictures . . . ! I think what I object to most of all is not the epithet sociologist but the use of it as a means of pigeonholing me and duly separating me from that holy circle of Larpoorlarers that swing about 'The Dial.' (Can't the lad conceal his envy? He exposes it most vulgarly.) I insist that I am not so far from being the artist as they are distant from being fully developed and completely sentient men. It is only an illusion to think that you increase a person's artistic capacities by limiting the rest of his life; what happens is simply ocular magnification. . . .
—Letter to S.W. July 25, 1921

Tonight, our housewarming. Two rooms that defy the northern exposure with warm browns, yellows, and dull oranges; and on the edge of these hospitable chambers, like the tattered edge of a modern city, are the kitchen, bathroom, and storeroom. The minima of creature comforts are scattered about, and as one looks about the rooms one sees the modern equivalent, in a vile and dilapidated tenement, of the earlier beauties of medieval architecture and decoration. It is the best that we could do with our means; and the best is not so bad; indeed it is much to my liking, for I relish the stripped clean, athletic style and the sort of life that goes with it. I hate luxury, not because I am tempted by it, but because it tempts other people out of my society. . . . Tonight, I say, our housewarming. How long will the fires stay lighted? Who knows? Will I get burned? Yes. Will it be worth it? Yes. What of the wound? Where the blood flows there is life.   —RN. October 27, 1921

Belated Confession.   How profoundly my views of sexual relations have changed during the last year—not that my conduct has been altered very greatly—and yet I have scarcely written a line which would show the gap between my confident and dogmatic earlier self and the quizzical person who is now in the saddle. For the last year Sophie has been the most profound influence in my life—and has shaken and twisted me to the very foundations—and yet no one who read my notes on our relation would begin to suspect what she has meant.

—RN. April 1, 1921

. . . Dr. Schapiro's letter today pleased me because he sees in me something that everybody else neglects and affronts and hoity-toitily passes by, to my great chagrin. But as Carlyle says, with a single adherent to one's beliefs one can hold one's own against the world, and so the world, including you, dearie, had better beware. What Schapiro said was this: "I think you were wise in not specializing in any field. If you had done so, you would today be active as head of a Bronx League of Progressive Citizens, agitating for a new sewer system. Given your temperament and your abilities"—mark this, O best beloved—"given your temperament and your abilities, the only thing that you should specialize in is beauty." But, Lewis, you *are* a sociologist! . . .

SILENCE Woman! Hereafter I pray that you consider me as much a devotee of what Irwin Granich used to call Larpoorlar as any damned 'Dial' critic. As for specializing in beauty, have I not been doing that the last two years, and is not the upshot of it that we are mated? I take back the first sentence, or rather, the second, in this paragraph, down to critic. Larpoorlar be switched. I have specialized in the art of being alive, and "art" is only one of the manifestations of life, and all the other things that the Larpoorlarers neglect in their cribbed and cabined estheticism are just as fascinating and exciting, in their own fashion, as the things that the sociologists, and their ilk, neglect. The result of this attitude is, of course, that I am an Ishmael in both camps, and am about as popular as a corpse that has lain too long in no man's land between the trenches.   —Letter to S.W. August 4, 1921

. . . Dinner at Robbie's last night. Helen Marot was there, and an anonymous girl, and we discussed mother complexes and the significance of prostitution and the infantilism of the human race in a manner which, I am afraid, made Robbie and Clemens, bland hosts though they were, a little irritated. Helen resents the way in which many men treat their wives as mothers, and then run away to find their sweethearts in other women, all the while protesting that they love their wives dearly and irrevocably; and she wants women to stop permitting their maternal instinct to get the better of them and so undermine their love relationships. In fact, she wants me to write a play about the theme: she says it is what every woman ought to know. Helen's leading idea now is that people must make a conscious attempt to control their relationships; they must learn to thrash out their difficulties in conference, instead of attempting to make an individual one-sided adjustment . . . We talked about jealousy, too, and I asked Helen how the devil we were going to get rid of that. She said that it rested on misunderstanding, and that one must tackle it from that point of view. I protested; because I have found that jealousy is a curiously physical phenomenon which operates in the very teeth of knowledge and reason; and when I began to describe the boiling inside and the thumping of one's heart and the red curtain that falls in front of one's eyes, she was moved to cry, "Enough," for she knew the experience herself.

—Letter to S.W. April 25, 1921

Last night we were tired and wan and solemn. We discussed the aches and futilities of married life, and Sophie wept—a little. There were moments when she thought that some of our difficulties were due to shallownesses in her, to shallownesses which her more enjoyable contacts with other men during the last couple of years had emphasized. Still, she wanted something more than frivolity, and realized that frivolity alone would leave her quite as cold and dissatisfied as her present life. We were tender and sympathetic; we were very sorry for each other; and in the realization of all the gaps that lay between us we felt oddly drawn together and at one.   —RN. February 6, 1922

MARITAL RECKONINGS.   I have been weighing from time to time the last few days how much marriage has tied me down and how much it has released me; and I see clearly that it has done both in great measure; but, on the whole, it has permitted me to do more work than I had ever been able to do before; so that, by marriage, I have gained a little and lost nothing, in the final balance. This is a crude calculation, of course; for one marries, as one comes into the world, because one must; because, given oneself and the dear other self that fate brings within hailing distance, the desire for more or less permanent association and intercourse scores itself on every fibre of one's being.

Our first year and our second year have been as different as if they were transmigrations into another world or metamorphoses into another kind of being. During the first year we were inexperienced, blind, unimaginative, cruel; and I myself added to all these quarrels and dissidences by being evilly jealous and by being perpetually stimulated to jealousy, partly by the rivalry of other people and partly by my own sense of incapacity. During this second year I've acquired a little skill in the art of love, and a very firm and decided sense of capacity; so all my old fears and frustrations and self-reproaches have vanished; and for this reason our relations have been much more easy and intimate, and, in every sense of the word, broad; and at quite frequent times they reach the very pitch of sensuous ecstasy and love.

With this has gone a large measure of kindliness and understanding on both our parts. . . . We had a vast and almost overwhelming breach last January, when the earth seemed in travail and the streets seemed to tremble and gape beneath our feet; but after lasting a fortnight it vanished as quickly as it came, and except for very short periods of coldness, indifference, or boredom our life together has been a smooth sailing under a steady wind, always within hailing distance, if not actually beam to beam.

Our circle of acquaintances is a little narrow; and chance and decision have to some extent cut Sophie off from old acquaintances; so that I really do not know whether my serenity and lack of foreboding is due to the firmness of my mind and our relations, or to the infirmness of Sophie's other relations; and if Sophie should be drawn toward someone else it may be that we should find ourselves roasting and sputtering on the fires of a new little hell. The disintegration and frustration that oppressed me so keenly last year have almost completely vanished; I have a sense of a personal life which does not depend upon the success or failure of my relations with Sophie; and although a break with Sophie would cause a terrible wound, I have a feeling that this time it would not be a septic one, for there would not be an inferiority complex to fester in it, beyond the mild one of having another person preferred to oneself, and this would have its antidote in my easy conviction now of being able to attract and conquer someone else! Now that the basis of our relations seems pretty well settled, now that there are no deep undercurrents of resentment and antagonism, we shall each of us, perhaps, be able to develop a deeper sense of individuality without the constant fearing of breaking the tenuous thread of hope that once upon a time was all that held us together.   —RN. June 1923

Early Letters to Patrick Geddes

PRELIMINARY QUANDARIES   . . . Do you remember that walk we had together up in Richmond, Delilah, when I confessed to you that I felt that I was not primarily a sociologist but after all another kind of animal? During the last year that feeling has been growing upon me, and it accounts to some extent, I think, for my difficulty in writing to Geddes at present. . . . I should be much more enthusiastic about writing a biography of Geddes than I am about cooperating with him on the Opus. I have enough knowledge about the Opus to write a good biography, and I could not have obtained this without drinking long at the fountain from which things Geddesian flow; but the biography attracts me as a piece of creative work, in which one might by good fortune sum up and crystallize all that was good and permanent in Geddes' philosophy, (that which is best and most permanent being, I believe, Geddes's life itself) whilst putting together the Opus has no more fascination for me than the articulation of a skeleton—the poor remnants of a body which once had life. This last sentence of course does not quite do justice to my respect for Geddes's work apart from the man; but it does show where my essential interests lie. . . .
—Letter to D.C.L. May 13, 1921

RESPECTFUL DISSENT.   . . . There have been times when I have thought that Branford spent a little too much time, perhaps, in laying the pieces on the board and neglected the opportunity of opening the game, and in particular, of encouraging younger men, and specialists in particular fields, to make their own moves. It seems to me much more important that particular researches and lines of investigation should be *infused* with the sound sociological method, and illumined by the general outlook that you have developed, than that they should begin literally with an acceptance of the entire schemata. A great many people, who have neither the experience nor the background nor the mental bent for taking over the system as it stands, are nevertheless sympathetic enough to do valuable work along the right lines if they were once put on the right track. Instead of searching for a general preliminary agreement among sociologists as to scope, method, aim, and so forth, it seems to me more expedient to center attention upon getting work done in particular fields—following the broad lines that you have laid down—and then trust to obtaining a general agreement after the efficacy of the Endinburgh school had been demonstrated. . . . —May 12, 1921

ENTER THE RADIO . . . There is little real news about America, except that we are now in the throes of another huge technological jump. The success of the radio-telephone in long distance communication has now reached a point where it is a distinct rival to radio-telegraphy: and as a result thousands of people are buying radio-receiving sets, from twenty dollars to two hundred in cost, for the purpose of getting the weather reports, sermons, lectures, health advice, stock market reports, and what not that are broadcasted by central stations in Newark, Pittsburgh, Chicago, etc. The whole countryside is now in direct communication with the city: even in the remotest districts it will soon be possible for the farmer to get storm warnings at much shorter notice than the present service. Will not this probably give a new turn to rural life? . . . —March 29, 1922

THE STORY OF UTOPIAS . . . Among other things I have discovered a remarkable Utopia by J. V. Andreae, a friend of Comenius, which I think ranks much higher for sociological insight and constructive criticism than the work of either Bacon or Campanella. This 'Christianopolis' was exhumed from Latin by a young American Ph.D. in 1916, and it is about time that it was more widely noticed. Andreae seems to have been responsible, through his correspondence with Samuel Hartbib, for the founding of the Royal Society; and it is interesting that he warned his colleagues against the dissociation of literature from science, a warning which the hard-headed English physicists alas! failed to heed.

In the treatment of Coketown and the Country House I am going to suggest that each great historic period has a real, and to a certain extent, a realized Utopia, implicit in its habits and its institutions and its experiments; a Utopia which is, so to say, the pure form of its actual institutions, and which may therefore be abstracted from them and examined by itself. To write a history of these pragmatic Utopias would be to present the historical "world-within" and thus supplement the conventional historian's account of the world-without. Until psychanalysis claimed the field we did not sufficiently realize the importance of the world-within; or at any rate, we did not see that it had a directive function. (I realize that *you did* see this; what I mean is that psychanalysis gave us the tools to explore this field more fully.) So it comes about that a great many of our Utopias are infantile, in that they seek to entrench what Freud calls the pleasure-principle, and deny the reality-principle: the Utopia of the Country House, with all its comforts and luxuries, is an ideal whose wider fulfillment means a distinct loss of vitality. This is just the briefest hint of some of the trails that are opening. . . .   —March 29, 1922

RIEHL AS FORERUNNER   . . . My chief intellectual experience these last few months has been the finding of Wilhelm Heinrich Riehl, the German historian. Gooch mentions him in his 'History and the Historians of the Nineteenth Century' as one of the main culture historians; and his 'Natural History of the German People,' written in the forties and fifties, is a masterly application of the regional method to History. Treitschke once dismissed Riehl as a "historian of the salon," and the reason is plain, for with Riehl the place, the people, the work, the home, the industries, the arts, the folk-music, and so forth are in the foreground, and the political organization enters no more into his history than it does in the life of anyone who is not a functionary of the State. . . . As early as 1850 Riehl saw that the effect of the railroad was to join city to city, and to depress the countryside by draining it into the railway capitals, whereas the old system of roads enabled the city to get out into the country, and preserved an economic balance. He also predicted that freedom would be gone in America when the forests were destroyed; and the beginnings of imperialism here do indeed date from the passing of the frontier, in 1890, and the exhaustion of the Appalachian forests. . . .
                                                    —February 25, 1924

CRITIQUE OF THE MASTER'S GRAPHS.   As for the IX to 9 diagram. Once it is laid out I have a difficulty in presenting it to others as a picture of the existing order and of the possibility of its antithetical alternative. The difficulty lies in the manner in which it is built up, particularly with the initial terms.

Military	Political	Mechanical
Theological	Abstractional	Physical Sc.

Comte generalized these terms from history; the ordinary student can grasp them in sequence, but fails, for the most part, to grasp their interaction and cumulative effect. Even if IX is not challenged on the grounds of failing to represent the historic process, there is a further difficulty with the 9. Are the three corresponding terms also to follow in order? Or are the general elements of the 9 to develop more or less coordinately? If we roughly date the Military Order at 1200, the Political at 1600 and the Mechanical at 1800, are we to date the Biological at 19–, the Geotechnic at 20–, and the Eupsychic at 22–: or are they all to be resolved at an indefinite point in the future? This last point has never been clear in my own mind. How would you answer it? I hold entirely with your thesis that if we could work out the *logical* antithesis we should have a key to the *pragmatic* antithesis and by *acting upon our hypothesis* would ensure its success. It is on this viewpoint however that most of our dispersed modern minds will be in rebellion; for they do not recognize any inherent connection between logical order and the world of fact. This point occurs in the initial explanation of the diagram, too. One can either say, taking one's three terms as granted, that theology reacted upon abstractionism and created the myth of the Powers; or one can say, logically, theologize your abstractions and you get a Theologized Abstraction, i.e. the Sovereign State.

Similarly one can say that the hunter's military tradition, reinforced by machine industry, causes war; or that if you mechanize the military order you get mechanized militarism, i.e. modern war. The first set of statements is historical, the second is logical. In verbal explanation you get the benefit of alternatively using one or the other, as seems more profitable; but in a rational description one cannot slip so easily from one category to another. Quite apart from this, I have only one or two suggestions to, tentatively, make. The first is that the spiritual symbol of the financial order is not $, the theory of money, but the Prospectus or Advertisements, and that the antithesis of this, under social finance, is [Social] Policy. Likewise the antithesis to the Ballot seems to me not to be the Transition, but Group-Direction. These are, of course, minor points; possibly inevitable ones, for if the prime elements are given, the values which will be substituted for their combinations will be different ones for different thinkers until divergent interpretations are brought together and reconciled. Thus, using Good, True, and Beautiful, I got an entirely different set of institutions and states for Good-truth, True-good, etc., than you had given. This is

obviously because Good, True, and Beautiful are only counters, or tokens, for a whole variety of things. How can this be made more rigorous? That is, I think, your capital problem. Otherwise the diagrams tend to remain as personal as the more chaotic philosophies they replace. Is this not one of the reasons you sometimes lose adherents? they are not convinced of the impersonality of the logical method: it seems neutral, *but what comes out of it is Geddes!* Some way must be found to show that there are no strings, that anyone who takes pains can manipulate the same instrument, to his own advantage!
—April 9, 1924

REGIONAL PLANNING. . . . We had an "Appalachian revival" meeting at the Hudson Guild farm in October; we danced and walked over part of the Trail and spent long hours threshing out the contents of the Regional Planning number; and again and again some memory connected with you and your visit there would fall from our lips: so you remained with us and were among us. Let me describe briefly the number as it stands—or rather, as it is projected, for only a few of the articles are ready. It is to be a special number of 'The Survey Graphic': thirty thousand words; numerous diagrams and illustrations. About ten articles.

The first one is on the Fourth Migration. Each great migration in America has spelled a new kind of opportunity: first the covering of the continent and seizing the land: second, the migration into the industrial town: third, into the financial centers, New York and the ten sub-metropolises. Now, we point out, the community is on the eve of a fourth migration. The occasion is electric power and auto transportation, which, plus the radio and the telephone, tend to equalize advantages over a great area and thus rob the centralized city of much of its "attraction." On top of this is the fact that industry, housing, transportation, and so forth, must no longer operate automatically: their automatic growth tends to pile up embarrassing conditions, so that no industry, for example, can afford to pay for the urban housing of its unskilled workers. Since planning is necessary, why should we not plan so as to reap advantages from the Fourth Migration?

The next three articles paint a picture of the impossibility of life under metropolitan conditions; show how the machine is clogged and stalled, how it is falling under its own weight. The city planning movement which attempts to rectify the conditions by treating their results has not rigorously examined the problem: regional planning means, not greater city planning, but facing the problems of the city by relating them to the regions that support it. It leads to urban conservation.

Then comes the constructive section: an article by MacKaye on recreation (he has gone far since you talked with him), an article on transportation (its progressive elimination!), on the Garden City [New Town], on education, and on social life as a whole. Here is an attempt to tie up the physical garden city, of which we know a great deal, with a program of civilization-building, in which we are, relatively, duffers. The issue is timed to come out in April: the same time as the Russell Sage report, the International Garden Cities Congress, etc. etc.

. . . Stein, by the way, has been working ever since you came over here on the Garden City, and he and Wright have just made an interesting discovery: they are quite confident of being able to plan a beautiful shell: they are completely at sea as to what sort of *community* to provide for. I quoted to them Branford's notion that the townplanner needs the aid of the poet; and they agreed; and having succeeded so far, I told them a little about regionalism in Europe, and suggested regionalism must be made the cultural motive of regional planning, if it isn't to relapse into an arid technological scheme. Stein pretty well saw the point: I had waited patiently these last three years for an opportunity to make it. I think that in one way or another I shall be able to inject a little regionalism into the Regional Planning number! That may give it a strange distinction.   —December 4, 1924

'HE' came last week.   I speak of Him in capital letters; for now that I have seen a little of him I am more convinced than ever that he is one of the Olympians. Of course *that* is the difficulty. Jove never walked among the sons of men without the sons of men getting the worst of it, and I find that all the warnings and reservations I have put into my letters have had precisely no effect upon P.G.; for he is a terrible and determined old man, and now that he is ready to set down his philosophy, he wants to make use of me to the full . . .
—Letter to D.C. L. May 12, 1923

CONFRONTATION WITH GEDDES.   . . . In one sense, I have
the feeling that we have yet to *meet*. We both have been aware of the
obstacles to meeting: but it is rather hard to climb over them, partly
because of the gap between our generations and our varieties of secular
experience, and partly because my respect for you is so great that it
reduces my mental reactions in your presence to those I used to feel
in the presence of my teacher when I was twelve years old—that is,
complete paralysis! Putting this last matter aside, there is a real barrier
to understanding between us in the fact that you grew to manhood
in a period of hope, when people looked forward with confidence to
the "great world spinning forever down the ringing grooves of time";
whereas I spent my whole adolescence in the shadow of war and
disappointment, growing up with a generation which, in large part, had
no future.

 Your pessimism about the existing state of civilization as portrayed
in IX * does not prevent you from still working eagerly at the problem
of the transition to 9 * because your own career still has a momentum
acquired under an earlier period of hope and activity; and so perhaps
you don't realize the paralyzing effect of that pessimism, which is
inherent in the situation, upon those of us whose personal careers had
not yet acquired any momentum [before 1917]. Rationally speaking,
there is as much chance of doing good work as there ever was; rationally speaking, a work that is worth doing is worth doing for itself
without regard to the possible mischances of war, famine, or what not;
rationally speaking, all the interests that we had acquired before the
war are just as important and as valuable as they ever were. True
enough: but something of the impulse has gone; whatever one's conscious mind accepts is not enough to stir the unconscious; our efforts
are no longer, as the saying is, whole-souled.

    If I found this bitter sense of futility in myself alone I should be
tempted to attribute it to an unsatisfactory personal experience; quite
the contrary, however, my own career has on the whole been a happy
and eventful one; and the forces which undermine its satisfaction are
at work in almost every intelligent and sensitive person I know between the ages of twenty-five and forty. Those who are younger
than I am differ from my generation in the sense that they are "realists" who have no hope for the morrow whatever and no faith or
interest in the polity at large; whilst those who are over forty are still
living, as it were, on the capital acquired during the days of hope, and
if their store is rapidly running out they manage to scrape on from day
to day. Our sense of a 'calling,' our sense of any one task to which we
could profoundly dedicate ourselves, is gone; and until we can recover this sense a certain intensity of devotion to our professions is the

* See earlier critique of the Master's Graphs.

only thing that prevents our lives from being altogether inconsecutive and dispersed. I have fought against this drift of things from the very moment I detected it; but it is like trying to relieve one's bosom of the pressure of the enveloping air; and I see no way of relieving the crippled psyche except by trusting to some slow and obscure process of cure. It is no use saying, be different: for we are like the sick man that Saadi mentions whose only desire was that he might be well enough to desire something.

You came over to America without, I suppose, any sufficient awareness of this change which, apart from any mere difference of age, separates a large part of the younger generation from the older: you came over, too, with a somewhat over-idealized portrait of me in your mind, as a vigorous young apprentice who might work at the same bench with you for a while, and keep on at the task when you had gone back from America. You are naturally disappointed to find me bound up with literary vocations, and to find that by natural bent and by training I am of the tribe of Euripides and Aristophanes rather than of Pythagoras and Aristotle; a trait which is, possibly, a little obscured by the fact that mere necessity and convenience oblige me to get my living, from day to day, with the Sophists of journalism. Faced with an actual me, you have naturally tried to make me over into the idealized portrait, whose aims and interests and actions were more congruent with your own; and, instinctively, I find myself resisting these frontal attacks, although my defences have again and again fallen down before unpremeditated movements on my flank! In the light of this difficult adjustment between the Ideal and the Actual, it would not be at all surprising if the original portrait had turned into a Caricature—that of a clever young hack writer, rather sullen in temperament and unamenable to conversation, who had no other interest in life than those of turning out a certain number of sheafs of copy per diem: The inability of this creature to follow your talk for more than a couple of hours at a sitting you could, in the light of caricature, attribute to a lack of interest or worse still! to a general lack of synthetic intelligence, whereas it is only the obvious reaction of another thorough visual to an auditive method of presentation. And so on.

Plainly neither the ideal nor the caricature corresponds to the real creature; and one of the things that has hindered our work together is, perhaps, that you began with one and shifted to the other, without our ever having (except in chance moments quickly forgotten) the chance to meet. If instead of thinking of me as a quack journalist you'd conceive of me rather as a young scholar who publishes his notes and lectures instead of speaking to a class: and if you'd see that I have chosen to get a living in this manner because it is for me the one means by which I can work at my own pace and keep at least a third of my time free for thinking and studying of a different sort, there

80

might still be a little exaggeration in the picture, but it would be an exaggeration toward the truth. Eutopitects build in vain unless they prepare the mind as well as the ground for the New Jerusalem; and nothing you have said has shaken in me the belief that the best part of my work must be in the first field rather than in the second, although it may be true that I shall do the first task more sanely and adroitly if I have had a little direct experience of the second; and I have so far admitted this as to go ahead with the plans of the Mohegan Colony.... —Letter to P.G. July 6, 1923

Geddesian Analects

Geddes asked me if I had seen the plans for a huge building in New York with a great dome capped on it. "It looked," he said, "as if the Devil had farted into Saint Paul's and raised the dome three hundred feet into the air." He is not afraid of these Rabelaisian touches. Harry Dana was defending himself against Geddes's strictures on Professors of Literature, by complaining that he did not perhaps have enough of the bard or poet in him to fulfill Geddes's notion of a good one, and Geddes answered: "Nonsense: let us speak with biological plainness. Every man is at least passively sexual; and in moments of passion or lust or call it what you will he knows what it is to have an erection. Well, the brain, when you look at it in section, is plainly enough an erectile tissue: there is an apparatus now that measures the amount of erection when you ask a man what six times nine is; and every brain has a poet in it or a scientist; and it can have an erection under the proper conditions: People marvel at the Darwins and the Einsteins, and talk about the biological inheritance; when to me the marvel is that everybody is not a Darwin or an Einstein. What you call genius is to me only a habit of work." Again: he was contrasting the life of the meanest peasant, with its great variety of occupations and tasks from season to season, against the life of those who work in the factories and offices. "These poor devils," he exclaimed, "spend all their lives on a nightstool, with a wastebasket alongside of them to take care of the excrement." At another time he was speaking about the public schools of England. "How the devil can anyone regard England as a pure and Christian country when it boasts of public schools where the pupils learn chiefly two things, masturbation and sodomy, and where the masters have the privilege of unlimited sadism through the system of flogging."   —RN. July 7, 1923

Geddes lectured before the Russell Sage Foundation, and he mystified and irritated the city planners like Thomas Adams by talking about New York as a second Rome. They dined him in Chinatown in the midst of the vast slums of the East Side, and pointing to the city around him Geddes asked Adams and Frank Backus Williams what they would do about planning it. They confessed that they were at a loss for a solution; whereupon Geddes said: "Plan it as if you were in the service of a Labour Government. Your problem is to provide homes for the next generation."   —RN. 1923

. . . Did I ever tell you the story of 'simultaneous thinking'? Perhaps Millie Defries tells it in her awful book, 'Geddes the Interpreter.' But I am afraid she doesn't. Geddes, when he was studying under Haeckel in Jena, lived in a boarding house, and there was a remarkable man there, brilliant, witty, intelligent, scholarly. The very ideal of the thinking man, who attracted Geddes very much. They became good friends, and one day this man took Geddes aside and told him he must tell him a secret. The truth was that he was crazy: he had spent years attempting the art of 'simultaneous thinking,' and just as he was on the point of achieving it, he had broken down. Geddes mustn't tell anyone! When Geddes finally evolved his diagrams on squared paper he remembered the talented lunatic, and saw that he, too, was engaged in simultaneous thinking. Madame Zimmern's name for it, polyphonic thinking, is even better; but perhaps one ought to call it contrapuntal or even better symphonic thinking. One ought to coin a word which would describe its opposition to linear thinking: our present day notion of coordination—which explains why nothing ever really gets coordinated—is that of keeping linear thinking in parallel rows at the same rate of movement, whereas simultaneous thinking involves reciprocal action and [timely] modifications of the whole.
                              —Letter to C.K.B. September 4, 1931

DISCIPLESHIP.   The tragedy of the relation between teacher and pupil is that every disciple who is worth his salt betrays his master. It is only the spiritual Judas who remains completely loyal to the word and form of the master's statement. This treason to the teacher is really loyalty to life, and to every part of his teaching that adequately expresses life. But it is better for the disciple to be aware of the extent of his departures and additions, and to assume the duty of facing facts freshly and re-evaluating them, than to substitute his thought for the master's without making this plain, or to repeat the formulas and words which, even if they reproduce the very letter of the Master's thought, no longer can mean to even his most loyal continuators what they meant to him, since time and experience have changed both parties since their utterance.   —RN. March 24, 1935

Every country poisons itself with its great men. Whitman declares the virtues of democracy to a country that should have read Nietzsche: Nietzsche emphasizes the bellicose brusqueness of the Prussians, who should, instead have learned a little mystic humility from Tolstoi. So England, the land of work, creates a Carlyle who preaches the gospel of work: a salutary gospel, perhaps, for the Hindu. The Master preaches the doctrine of saving opposites.   —RN. For the unwritten 'Great Testament of James McMaster' [P.G.] (February 1975)

Aesthetics: A Dialogue

The corner of a library in a country house. The panel books, the chairs and divan and table, the vase in the niche above the divan all sound the note of refined simplicity—no vulgarity, no helpless subservience to the interior decorator. The dominant colors in the room, blue, green, and yellow, are echoed by the cordials which occupy a small stand near the fireplace. With that fumbling over matches and glasses which is preliminary to settling down, the members of the group begin to distinguish themselves. They are:

> CHARLES ADAMS
>
> PERCY SCOTT
>
> EDWIN O'MALLEY
>
> ERNEST DE FIORI, *their host.*

DE FIORI—What do you say, gentlemen: shall we have a fire? The heating system in this house is excellent, but unfortunately our architect counterbalanced it by installing English casement windows, and after our walk this afternoon the November wind may feel a little raw.

ADAMS (*Politely*)—It's really quite comfortable.

SCOTT—This Alsatian quetsch is proof against November. It is the only efficient form of central heating.

O'MALLEY—It seems warm enough now; but your American methods of superheating have weakened my resistance so completely that unless I am on the verge of perspiration I begin to think I have caught cold.

DE FIORI—Well, suppose, we compromise on an—ahh—æsthetic fire: just enough to give the inner feeling of warmth, rather than the physical effect. I see that Ellen has the kindling already laid. (*He draws a few billets from the woodbox, and Scott comes forward officiously with a lighted match.*) There! I am afraid Adams will not approve of such a fire. He will say that it is impossible to enjoy the æsthetic effect without suffering the warmth.

O'MALLEY—He is more of a moralist than that: he would say that one oughtn't to enjoy the æsthetic effect without the warmth; whereas it is plainly a mark of aristocracy to keep the two things apart and to have your cake without eating it. Unless one is able to withdraw the æsthetic emotions from practical life a civilized existence is impossible.

scott—I have always wondered what Adams's æsthetic theories were. I have never been able to derive them, I confess, from your criticisms, Charles, although I enjoy your page perhaps more than anything else the 'Ancient City' prints.

adams—De Fiori has doubtless lighted the fire in order to smoke me out; but I don't think it's quite fair to fall on me so suddenly directly after dinner—especially after *such* a dinner. Besides, I really have no conscious æsthetic theory: I recognize the æsthetic interest as only one of a number of interests that are served in literature; and it doesn't seem to me the supremely important one that so many of you now make it out. My æsthetics is implicit in my criticism, as is my philosophy or my psychology. I should like to use such a single canon as you, De Fiori, enjoy in your applications of Croce; but different kinds of literature seem to me to require different standards; and it is only in the realm of pure poetry that I find Croce's canon wholly justified. To dismiss the rest of literature because it is not pure poetry seems to me absurd.

o'malley—It's all very well to keep your æsthetic from showing its bones through the flesh of your criticism: but my objection to your method, my dear Adams, is that you are not really interested in a piece of literature as such: you have always an ulterior interest in its background and you keep on asking yourself what sort of society this or that book will tend to produce. You are almost as bad as Mr. Paul Elmer More, who cannot even write about Plato without paying attention to the way in which his work may affect the Brahmins and *rentiers* of New England. The chief difference between you and More is that he has enough realism to pitch his social references toward a society which actually exists, whilst you, God forgive us, refer to an ideal community which has not yet come into existence, and in a country ruled by the *booboisie* has no chance of ever being a reality.

adams (*Unruffled*)—You object, do you not, O'Malley, to the fact that I believe that a community has a permanent self, made up of its best minds and embodied in its literature, as well as the shifting, temporary self which expresses itself in its daily actions and in the opinions of those who control it in the press and on the platform? I can't conceive what function you accord to literature, unless it is to embody that permanent self and make it visible. A work of literature as such has no value except to the bookworm or the pulping mill; it is only by association with human needs and desires that its values have any meaning.

de fiori—My dear Adams: you mustn't confuse an act in the practical world with an act in the spiritual world. The values of literature lie entirely in the spiritual realm: they are independent of the society that has produced a work of art or that may be affected by it. What is it that makes the 'Divine Comedy' the glorious piece of poetry that it is? The theology? No. The picture of contemporary life, the attempt to redress the evils of the time? A hundred times No! What has preserved the 'Divine Comedy' for us in all its freshness is its complete fusion of imagination and feeling in an absolute poetic form. To judge the 'Divine Comedy' in terms of a rationalist theology like Voltaire's, for example, would be to miss all its essential beauties. That is why we must say to the critic—deal with the æsthetic form by itself and prepare our minds to experience it: do not be confused by the ideas of the author, or by his *milieu*, or by whether his poem is likely to make us good or bad men; for in the realm of art these practical standards do not exist. A work of art is good or bad in terms of the author's own world. What was the writer's inner purpose, and how has he accomplished it?

ADAMS—Your rule of judgment is satisfactory enough, perhaps, when it applies to a poem or a novel whose position is already established. But I don't see how it enables you to distinguish between—let me take an extreme example—between the Nick Carter detective stories and the 'Divine Comedy.' Some of the youngest critics are now rolling around helplessly in this very predicament. They have taken your æsthetic counsel to heart; and they find that the author of Nick Carter perfectly fits his method to his materials, develops his theme with an unflagging logic, creates an independent world of his own, and affects them with an emotion which they call æsthetic. By your criterion, De Fiori, I don't see how you can ask more of these stories as literature: from the standpoint of Pure Form they are perhaps more perfect than the 'Odyssey.' (*De Fiori makes a gasp of protest.*) Don't you see how childish it is? The æsthetic value of literature is inseparable from its intellectual and moral value: your 'æsthetician' is as grotesque an abstraction as the Economic Man of political economy: he is a spiritual Robinson Crusoe. The little Italian boy Samuel Butler told about, who thought that "Hey diddle-diddle, the cat and the fiddle" was the most beautiful poetry he had ever heard was a prince of æstheticians; and if literature were concerned only with pattern and form Gertrude Stein would have a higher place than Sophocles.

SCOTT—Our position is not reduced to quite the absurdity you seem to think, Charles. In the universe of æsthetics there are the nebulous particles of Nick Carter and the comic strips as well as the suns and planets and fixed stars; and we only say that the qualities which make Nick Carter a good piece of work at its level are what make 'Madame Bovary' a supreme work of art on another level.

ADAMS—That is all very well; but there must be a world by which the critic measures the relative importance of these self-begotten planets and particles; and this world, it seems to me, is necessarily broader than the world of æsthetics. In the abstract universe of Pure Art, Edgar Poe might be a very great figure indeed: his cold metallic verses are like the notes of some thin brass instrument which admirably echoes the plutonian tears he drops over the graves of his impalpable maidens. Well, I respect Poe as a literary critic; but I have never read a single line of his poetry which could be put alongside Tennyson's 'Ulysses' without turning out to be mere pasteboard and tin-foil; and that is because Tennyson, for all his shaky philosophizing and moral squeamishness, had encompassed the realities of this world, he had lived imaginatively in a land where lovers are disappointed or suddenly happy, where children are begotten and men face the tragedy of growing old, whereas Poe remained always emotionally immature, and growth and decay and all they carry with them were left permanently outside his world. In painting, Albert Ryder had the same kind of imagination; but it was humanized and became great. An æsthetic which tends to place Poe above Tennyson because of the 'purity' of Poe's poetry is a new sort of bowdlerism: it has an animus against the natural smut and obscenity of life—without which no work of art has ever endured.

O'MALLEY—Before you know it, my dear Adams, you will be telling us to read Sainte-Beuve again, and will lead a popular crusade under the banner, Back to Taine! I thought all this had been settled years ago. Literature is simply one thing; and life is quite another. Civilized people prefer to live in the world they have created themselves, rather than in the 'real' world, where boobies become great statesmen, and men who cannot tell the difference between a sonneteer and a charioteer become the leaders of armies. If we must have commerce with the real world, let it be through the offices of slaves and servants; it is only on those terms that culture is possible. If De Fiori's theory compels him to accept Nick Carter, yours would force us to say a good word for Harold Bell Wright!

SCOTT (*Aside to O'Malley*)—You are the most reckless sociologist of us all, Edwin: in the act of divorcing literature and life you have proclaimed a dozen contentious principles which would weld them together. Your aristocracy is as factitious and imbecile as anything else in the world: it makes no provision for the best getting to the top.

ADAMS (*Firmly, getting back to the argument*)—I am not sure that "Back to Taine!" wouldn't serve my intentions excellently.

DE FIORI—*Really*, Adams! The race, the age, and the *milieu!!* The cumbrous analysis of the climate! the manner of eating and drinking!

the form of industry!—in short, the consideration of everything but the work of art itself! You surely don't ask us seriously to bring back all these impedimenta again?

ADAMS—Yes and no. The means by which Taine approached English literature now seem to us irrelevant, because the fashion has changed, and it isn't done any more; but my point is that Taine's judgments, his æsthetic judgments if you will, are extraordinarily just and penetrating. Moreover, I have a confidence in them that I don't at all feel with Croce when he discusses Walter Scott or Shakespeare, or, for that matter, when he discusses the work of any writers except his fellow countrymen, such as Ariosto and Dante, where his æsthetic values are ballasted by all the knowledge he unconsciously draws on about Italian manners and psychology.

DE FIORI—I protest: you don't appreciate Croce. Have you read his essay on Corneille?

ADAMS—I bow to your knowledge, but I must maintain my point. If you miss the context of a work of art you miss its overtones: you miss the things that every contemporary experiences just because he is on the spot. The core of a great piece of literature is some universal human experience; but the core is surrounded by the pulp and skin of circumstance; and if we would reach it we must penetrate these things. When either the critic or the writer aims at form alone he becomes empty and meretricious. People have criticized 'Moby-Dick' because it is formless and full of irrelevancies; but the truth is that the irrelevancies are an essential part of its form, and had Melville attempted to reduce the bounds of his universe to the scene required for a slick story of the sea, that universe would not have been the multiturinous and terrible thing he sought to create.

DE FIORI (Becoming the host in order to dissipate the slight sense of strain that has entered into the discussion)—And what do you say to all this, Scott? Have you become converted to Adams's creed?

SCOTT—Indeed, I am in a difficult position. It is a personal convenience with me, indeed almost a necessity of existence, to disengage myself from the robust tangled world that Adams tries perpetually to draw us back to. I prefer to consider æsthetics as a world apart; and my own æsthetic, with certain modifications, is akin to yours and Croce's—and perhaps O'Malley's. Yet, after all, criticism must also be judged by an æsthetic standard; and I feel that Taine and Adams have the better of us! They are much more interesting, on the whole, than, say, Gourmont and Croce, although their interest in art seems so much less single-minded—so much more, if I may use the word in a neutral sense, polluted with the things of this world. I think, of course, that an æsthetic judgment is the final judgment about a work of art: if it is bad æsthetically, its good intentions, or the amiable character of the author, or its excellent tendency, will not raise it an inch in stature. Once the judgment is formed, however, there is little to be said about a work of art; and it is too easy to rest satisfied with dialectical clichés—form, pattern, movement—which the weak critic applies indifferently to the greatest and the least. Æsthetic criticism cannot elaborate the final judgment; it can only lead up to it. Adams, it seems to me, is not averse to reaching the same goal; but he does not fasten on it consciously. Confident that he will sooner or later reach an æsthetic judgment, he concerns himself with the views he encounters on the road.

ADAMS—You are a very welcome ally, Scott. My mind does not run to dialectics, and you have put my position in a much clearer light than I had seen it in myself—and I brush away your compliments as too palpably friendly. In turn I will admit that the method I practice is full of dangers: the by-paths are numerous, and in one's forgetfulness of the goal one may sometimes get lost in the thickets of psychological analysis or in mere biography. But I see that De Fiori still has a bolt or two up his sleeve: I fear my ordeal isn't over.

DE FIORI—I feel that our minds haven't really met yet; and I find it hard to manoeuvre my own into position. You are quite right, Adams, in condemning the sort of critic who talks about style as if it were a veneer which could be laid on a work of the imagination; and I regret to say that in spite of Croce this purely practical side of literature—the mechanics, as it were, of expression—is being treated by some of the younger men as though it were the essence. An interest in style, in this sense, is as foreign to æsthetics as typography; both exist in the realm of the practical. I would also admit that the mind that is purely concerned with art rarely rises to the level of art: it is a sort of fungus which feeds upon its own substance, whereas the true artist sends his roots deep into the soil of morality, of industry, of the practical and ethical life. The artist draws on this soil for nourishment: but the work of art rises above it and is so essentially different in character that by no examination of the soil and seed could one predict the strange shape and beauty of the flower, which is art itself. The observations and concepts of the practical life may enter into the work of art; but, entering it, they cease to be observations and concepts: they become inseparably part of the poem or drama itself. People have tried to draw the maxims of political government or a view of the universe from Shakespeare's plays. But what folly! In their artistic office, these maxims and views are embodied in Hamlet, Lear, and Julius Caesar; but they are thus no longer useful as philosophy or political sagacity; if we are interested in these things we must read Aristotle and Machiavelli. This was the paradox about art that Plato could never grasp: how Homer could speak about navigation without being a sailor, or about wisdom without being a philosopher. The artist seemed to Plato a charlatan, because he pretended to discourse with authority upon a hundred actions and experiences without having a practical grasp of any of them. The explanation of this paradox, of course, is that the artist portrays the imaginative truth of navigation or war or philosophy; and this truth remains authentic and real as long as one lives with the artist in the world of æsthetic. Even Bernard Shaw, who so often has been misled by a practical interest in movements and ideas, recognizes this distinction when he puts into his prefaces the overflow of thought that has not found an æsthetic channel for itself in his plays. The goal of the artist is not to be a theologian, a social reformer, or a friend of humanity: the goal of the artist is to create a work of art, and the only question for the critic is—has he created it, and what is its æsthetic merit? Æsthetic criticism does not use the same terms to interpret the 'Æneid' as it does to describe Walter Landor's chaste Greek fables in verse; but in both cases it dwells upon the floral rather than upon the terrestrial aspects of the work, and it leaves the latter to the pedants and philologists. The Greece of Landor and the Greece of Theocritus are, in so far as Landor and Theocritus are both true poets, the same Greece—a Greece of the poetic imagination. That Landor's happens to be the result of a Greek revival, which turned English country houses into temples and resulted in some excellent translations of Plato and Aristophanes, whilst Theocritus' Greece was the fields he saw and the culture he shared— that, I say, is a practical accident, and it does not concern the critic. . . . But forgive me, gentlemen: one is never so much the pedant as when one attacks pedantry, and similarly I find that I am never so earnest as when I am doing battle with Adams! I apologize if I have turned an argument into a lecture. It is more than ten years since I was Professor De Fiori, but it is not easy to shake off the practices of one's guild.

O'MALLEY—Oh, don't apologize: you have reduced Scott and myself to the abject imbecility of pupils who have the mingled pleasure and fear of seeing one of their schoolmates flogged; and I have so long felt uneasy at having no defense against Adams's criticism of the country in which I have chosen to live, or against his covert contempt for the sort of literature in which I am interested, that I am quite content to settle back in these cushions and cry, Hear! Hear! More power to you, De Fiori: I see that I shall have to read Croce after all in order to have the pleasure of agreeing with him.

SCOTT (*Hastily turning to Adams*)—There speaks the voice of envy, Charles. Let us thank heaven, however, for the miracle that reduces O'Malley to silence, and get back to the discussion.

ADAMS—I find myself so much in agreement with what you say, De

Fiori, about art that it seems a little ungenerous and pedantic to dwell upon what you don't say; and yet this, I think, is one of the chief differences between us. To begin with, I can't accept the Crocean divorce between the practical and the æsthetic or ideal: it is a dialectical subterfuge, and its sole effect is to embarrass criticism with tautologies. Soil, seed, plant, and flower are one in life, and I would take the metaphor over bodily and say that they are one in literature: cut the flower away from the plant and it soon ceases to be a flower. Art can grow and reproduce and scatter its seeds in the hearts of men only when the conditions in what De Fiori dismisses as the practical life are favorable. The good critic is therefore a gardener who pays attention to all the conditions that environ the production of a work of art. It is only when he has secured the best possible conditions in his own community that he is free to taste and enjoy, and to lead others to this pleasure. By reducing criticism to æsthetic commentary you do not necessarily further the aim of art: you may merely further the method of dialectics. If you will forgive me for saying so, De Fiori, I find nothing in Croce except an interesting critic of criticism: his appreciation of Shakespeare is singularly barren and banal. Croce's method, perhaps, enables him to avoid the dialectic pitfalls into which Frank Harris fell headlong when he wrote his study of 'The Man Shakespeare'; but it was Harris's book, and not Croce's, that sent me back to Shakespeare with a fresh set of perceptions and appreciations which, so far from being external, added to the intrinsic enjoyment of the poetry itself. From my point of view, Harris's criticism is better than Croce's. And, as I said at the beginning, I feel that the æsthetic element in literature is over-rated. Literature, after all, is an avenue to many different experiences; and I sympathize with the English critic who complained that Mr. Leonard Woolf had praised the æsthetic success of 'A Passage to India' without once saying that it was at the same time a profound study of Indian life! The true critic, it seems to me, must concern himself with the whole life of the mind, and in life, all the qualities that go into a work of art interpenetrate and mingle.

DE FIORI—Ah! we have made a brave effort to meet, Adams: but I fear we are back again at our original positions, and are as far apart as ever. We use different words and we talk about different things. I daresay we share equally in the fault.

SCOTT (*Concealing a yawn*)—Precisely! Discussion never gets one anywhere; at most it shows more clearly where one stands. I see you have an æsthetic theory, after all, Adams: its only trouble is that it sets too low a value upon æsthetics.

92

DE FIORI—I do not mean to be abrupt: but do you realize, gentlemen, that it is three o'clock? What do you say to a night-cap of Scotch? —American Mercury. November 1924. Troutbeck Leaflets, No. 3. 1925.

Though the original dialogue took place at Troutbeck three years earlier, it is a fair recapitulation—without notes—of our discussions. De Fiori is of course, J. E. Spingarn, O'Malley is Ernest Boyd, Adams is Van Wyck Brooks, while Percy Scott is more Clarence Britten, my old Dial friend, than I, who secretly lurk behind both De Fiori's and Adam's opinions.

To Sophie, Expectant

I loved the wild and virgin stalk
That flung its youth against the sky
In arrows of unflinching green
Whose leaves were banners held on high.

I loved the all-revealing flower
That opened wide the perfumed lips
Between whose dizzy velvet walls
The amorous bee not vainly slips.

In stalk and flower was delight:
Yet more, my love, they are to me
Now that the ripening seed will fall
To make love's happy Trinity.

Lewis: Christmas 1924

Geneva Adventure

PRELUDE TO MY GENEVA LECTURES: 1925.   . . . Zimmern happily reduced the course to six lectures; so as it now stands, the first lecture will deal with the background of American culture, on which I have nothing to add to the familiar criticism, except a more detailed analysis of the breakdown of Europe. The next two lectures deal with American literature; and on looking over my first draft I am a little frightened at the fact that one is tempted to read a mission into, to give a special logical function to, our literature as a whole, which only a very few writers, perhaps only Whitman, can claim. The other danger that comes from dealing with literature before a foreign audience is that one is tempted to emphasize the importance of writers who deal with patently American themes, and to neglect those who don't fit so well in the general picture; whereas we've always had our Poes and our T. S. Eliots, who, whatever their faults and neuroses, have had as much significance as the Landors and Baudelaires in Europe.

Then comes a lecture on philosophy: its only particular virtue is that it treats John Dewey and Santayana at the same time, and indicates that something like a living synthesis of their philosophies would, for the first time perhaps, embrace the values of science and of humanism. In formulating the first lecture I found myself enormously helped by Santayana; and I think it's a mistake to consider the pragmatists the sole spokesman of the American spirit. This lecture almost looks to me as if it might have the germs of that book you suggested to me three or four years ago; but I shan't be able to tell until I'm a little more deeply saturated in it. The fifth lecture is in some ways the hardest; for it is on architecture, and it demands that I think freshly on a subject on which I've already, I think, been writing far too extensively, in proportion to my knowledge and preoccupations; but somehow, perhaps, I shall manage it; for I find, consolingly, that my standards in architecture and literature are one, so that the good life that hovers in the background has, at all events, a unity of interior and exterior. I come now to the sixth lecture; which is to deal with the prospects of American culture, with the criticism and appraisal of the last generation, and with such relevant issues as I myself can muster out of the void and make real; at present this lecture remains the sketchiest and most uncertain of the whole lot, and I can only hope that the holy spirit will descend upon me and enlighten me before I step on the platform in Geneva. . . .   —Letter to V.W.B. July 22, 1925

EN ROUTE TO GENEVA.   . . . I have for neighbor on deck a horny yellow faced man, who plainly has a large and excessively active, or inactive (which is it?) liver; he is accompanied by a yellow haired harridan who is his wife, and her sister; and in his company I become banal and youthfully cynical, and speak evil of the medical profession, of dentists, of prohibitionists, of bootleggers, of women, of the current food, and am aware that the world has very little goodness or virtue in it. He has already tested my sophistication by remarking that the fat woman, who was practicing her voice in the library, had "got the clap," when she was applauded by her kindly neighbors; and I replied to this with a leering right eye, to show how thoroughly I had assimilated this fine piece of wit; but fortunately, when he is not occupied with his women, I am with Tristram Shandy, and so I manage to escape some of his doubtless finer repartee, and may even, someday, be able to turn out two or three real good smutty jokes of my own. Yes: and there is a blowsy Englishwoman with black hair who looks as if she had stepped out of a Belcher cartoon; and there is the clean-cut young American who likes to explain his country and make large and ample comparisons with an Englishwoman and—oh, the usual menagerie. There is not even a pretty face to draw me out of myself!

–Letter to S.W.M. August 7, 1925

THOUGH THE SWISS   may be only a nation of hotel keepers; at least they know their business. My French has fallen off dreadfully, but I'm getting used to the sound of other people's; and at times I can understand whole patches of it in a lecture. Mrs. Zimmern is all worked up about my lectures; she wants me to wallop the Europeans hard; and since the new lot of students will contain many English ones, about a hundred students altogether, perhaps I shan't find it difficult. Now you know everything. I detest service, I detest tipping, I detest officialdom; and when I get back to America I won't want to leave it or you for years; why, the two days I spent at the Exposition des Arts Décoratifs have made me actually admire American architecture.

. . . I laughed like a little child when I saw the snow-capped mountains again from the train; and something inside of me has been laughing since. The Rhone rushes out of the Lake of Geneva so fast that the swans have to paddle with all their might to hold their own against it; I saw one this morning who breasted the stream and kept pecking at a bit of floating weed which clung to his bosom, whilst he was swept backward. The water near the shore shows every pebble, but as it sweeps under the bridges the green becomes as dark and rich as that we've used on our screen; and on the Embankment the sycamores are pollarded and turned into huge umbrellas.

–Letter to S.W.M. August 7, 1925

NOTES ON GENEVA.   . . . The more completely the shock of travel wears off, the more completely you are mine. What does Alfred Kreymborg say?

> "When I left you
> You were you
> But I was not
> Quite me. Now I am me
> And you are me—
> And doubly you."

I've had such an afternoon as I hope lies in front of us. It all began with a lunch at Herbert Feis's villa. I mustn't say too much about that villa: it has a garden that no one would want to leave; a garden with choruses of marigolds and asters and zinnias, singing against a background of young bamboo-trees and mossy oaks; a garden walled, and the walls covered with ripe apricots, a garden nooked and shaded and in the deepest shade the black luster of holly leaves. But that's enough. . . . Herbert is always Herbert: inscrutably merry, but no longer, in his serious intervals, so pontifical. Well, lunch ended; Herbert whizzed me away in his Ford; I sat through a lecture, and then, with one of my new acquaintances, whom I already call Alfred, a young California don, keen on puns and literature, I wandered around the courts and alleys and steep narrow streets of the old city. I wanted you there; you must do that with me, you old dear. Age hangs over the stones; the smells are unaltered since the fifteenth century; there are sudden open spaces with trees and fountains; and at the end of dank passageways the blackness heaves abruptly against a garden, such a garden as lovers must have sat in at twilight for hundreds of years, and I daresay they still do today. It took one's breath away again and again; but my breath was taken away in more than one fashion. In a second-hand shop we espied two silver globes, about the size of tennis balls, obviously old, engraved and enameled with a map of the world. We were both curious about them, and went in to find the price; and as I entered the door, thinking again of 'Littleness,' I wondered whether, if they were really silver, one mightn't pay as much as ten dollars. The price was—and I daren't put it in numerals lest you think my typewriting has gone wrong—the price was fourteen hundred dollars. Sweet smiles of embarrassment, saved a little by the fact that the shopkeeper was obviously a little proud at having stumped and flabbergasted two Americans. And so up and down and in and out, along streets where the gutters were still in the middle, as they were in the fifteenth century, until we reached the modern town again—that is, the town that dates since 1750 or thereabouts! Neither Oxford nor Innsbruck has anything quite like Geneva; although Innsbruck, I still think, is the most beautiful city. . . .

—Letter to S.W.M. August 31, 1925

A DAY IN GENEVA.   . . . I'll spend the day in the usual way, which includes a swim in the lake, two or three ices, lunch with the Zimmerns and a great galaxy of young or prominent people at the Hotel Russie, and discussion. Mrs. Zimmern is as loquacious and vivacious as ever: she spits and coughs in English as I, in my best moments, have never yet achieved in French: but, as someone said the other day, at least half the things she says are important and interesting. Music is her religion: we have musical evenings at least every other night: but she hates jazz, and as much as told a group of the students in the first term that if they wanted to live in that kind of a world they had no business here. The school is an autocracy, governed with a velvet glove: one hears rumors of discontent and reproach, but there is something to be said for the autocracy . . .

The Zimmerns are afflicted with the noble idea of rallying together an elite from all the countries, and making them conscious of each other. They've treated me, the Zimmerns, in a way that would make my head reel with immodesty, if I were younger; but the only thing that makes my head reel here is Chianti wine, and I have really mastered that by now. In the meanwhile, the Zimmerns have decided to hold my second three lectures over until the week after next; so I shan't be able to leave here, I am afraid, until the first of September. The disappointment of some of the students at my not continuing immediately is a consolation: my lectures have occasionally been jumbled, but they have had meat in them, and in some ways have taken the haughty and condescending foreigner off his feet. And whom have I met? And whom do I lecture to? A mixed group, with the English and Americans preponderating, but with Hindus, Belgians, French, Germans, Swedes, Norwegians, all mixed up, and both girls and boys—about eighty altogether. The morning after my lecture an amazing young man, Jean de Menasce, partly Jewish partly Egyptian, who speaks French as they speak it in Paris, and English as they do in Oxford, gives my lecture again in French, to those who haven't been able to understand it; and after that follows the usual discussion with Jean for interpreter. He has French elegance and Oxford superiority: I hated the combination at first; but he is really very nice. He has just translated 'The Wasteland' into French; and if he weren't so confoundedly erudite and brilliant he would probably have a great career ahead of him. . . .*

—Letter to S.W.M. August 15, 1925

* Perhaps the most luminous and beautiful spirit I have ever known—though never intimately. I hope to find words worthy of him in my Autobiography.

Vain Journeys

Why should I go travel?
Adventure lies at home:
My sweetheart is the planet
Whose surface I would roam.
She is the tangled forest
Where buried cities lie:
She is the starlit cranny
Where only eagles pry.
And when I climb her mountains
Or wander on her plain
I discover wonders
Unknown on land or main.
Her eyes are pools far deeper
Than any Alpine lake
Within her jungle balsam grows
To cure a lover's ache.
Her temple holds a secret
Not found in Thibet tome—
Why should I go travel?
Adventure lies at home.

—*Parc de Mon Repos, Geneva*
September 3, 1925

AND WHAT IS MY REAL WORK?   It has been coming over me ever since I delivered the Geneva lectures; on the steamer it crystallized more definitely, and now I am well started on it: nothing less than an attempt, of which certain parts of the Story of Utopias were only the faintest sketches, to describe what has happened to the Western European mind since the breakdown of the medieval synthesis, and to trace out the effects of this in America. Likewise my job is to pick up the one or two threads in our American writers, particularly Emerson and Whitman, which seem to me to lead toward more profitable conclusions than the work of any of the great Europeans of the nineteenth century, although the great Europeans had, individually, reached a more perfect development. A hundred people have gone over this ground before; but unless *I* am blind, they have never seen anything.

The writers who have dealt with the development of the modern mind have had a bias against Romanticism, or against Rousseau, or against Science, or in favor of the Catholic Church, or in favor of Protestantism, or in favor of Liberal Reform or the Communist Revolution. My distinction, I think, is that I am reasonably free from any sort of prepossession for or against these things: I am not a Romantic nor a Catholic nor a follower of Rousseau; but I see what these things have meant in the life of the spirit, and I know a little about their insufficiencies, too.

If we are to have a vision to live by again, it will have to be different from all these efforts; and yet, it will have to learn from them and contain them; it will have to be a synthesis, not of knowledges, for that is impossible in anything but an abstract form, but a synthesis of attitudes, which will lead out toward the knowledge and the life in which we can find satisfaction. To tell the truth, I am a little frightened when I contemplate the size of my task. If it is to be done at all, it will have to call forth every particle of energy and experience I possess; and I will have to venture forth on uncharted waters, in the teeth of an adverse gale— that is to say, in directly the opposite quarter from that of my own generation, whose more sensitive members all say that we must swallow chaos, and may never know order again. Well, I am shoving off, convinced that someone must try to make this undiscovered port. . . .
—Letter to D.C.L. December 8, 1925

WITH PATRICK GEDDES IN EDINBURGH.   Geddes drives me to tears, almost he does. I have been with him since Monday; and though I anticipated the worst, the first night and day were happy. He took me about the city, showed me the hundred improvements that he had made or initiated; waste spaces become gardens, courts tidied, tenements renovated, student hostels built, splashes of color introduced by red blinds on windows; fountains designed: a great achievement in itself, all these things. On the second day Mabel Barker came, and some other visitors arrived; and then we were back again in the old cruel mess and chaos: engagements broken, time wasted on trivial idiots, and in the interim an unceasing volume of anecdotes, suggestions, and diagrammatic soliloquy.

The weaknesses and strength, the steadfastness and the impatience, the effacement of himself and the ruthless arrogance of this great man emerged from all this with an effect upon me that is still mingled. He is perfectly lovable in his human moments; in fact he is enchanting; a portrait of him at thirty—a bad portrait but a sufficing one—showing a black-bearded rather chubby man with red cheeks, almost choked me with emotion. Here was a man I might have worked with and merged myself with. But what can I do with the man whose muffled soliloquy spreads over the hours, the man who is caught in his thinking machines, as one who had invented decimal notation might perhaps spend his life by counting all possible objects in tens: what am I to do with the pathetic old man who asks for a collaborator and wants a secretary, who mourns the apathy and neglect of a world that he flouts by his failure to emerge from his own preoccupations and to take account of other peoples'; this man who preaches activity and demands quiescence or at least acquiescence; who requires that one see the world completely through his spectacles, and share, or make a murmur as if sharing, every particular and personal reaction. *I have still to have an hour's conversation with him.*

What an affectionate, loyal relation we could have, if he would permit it to exist! How much one would get out of him if he did not try to give one so much! But he wants all or nothing, and without seeking to get more deeply into one's own life, he sets before one the thwarted ambitions and ideas of his own. Once and again he returned to the notion of my getting a *doctorat étranger* at Montpellier with a year's residence; for he wants me to be active in the universities. He would like me to be a professor, a college president; he even, amazingly, hinted something about my becoming an American ambassador like James Russell Lowell! In short, everything but what I myself, consciously and unconsciously, have been driving at. I squirmed out of his presence to get into the train: I wouldn't let him and Mabel Barker stay to see me off. The incessant soliloquy like the insistent noise of a radio I simply had to run away from. And yet I love him; I respect him; I admire him; he still for me is the most prodigious thinker in the modern world. His arrogance and his weakness have frustrated him; he lacks some internal stamina in spite of all his strength and energy; and is not merely a discouraged old man, but, as I found out from things he has dropped, he fell often into black discouragement as a young man. What is responsible for all these incomplete endeavors, all these unverified hypotheses, whose rejection irritates him and whose proof, when others have given it, does not interest him? Why is there such a streak of feebleness in that greatness? For all that, the greatness is indisputable; and if I have perhaps seen him for the last time—and how sadly incomplete these days were, how fine they might have been. —I shall retain of him, not the memory of the stern, sorrow-laden old man, interminably talking, demanding what one cannot give and forgetful of all one could; no, I shall retain the memory of the brave comrade I found too late.

—RN., Waverley Station. September 11, 1925

100

KEEPING GEDDES AU COURANT. . . . Next week I go to the University of Virginia to attend a conference on Regionalism. The Southerners, particularly the younger intellectuals, have lately become conscious of themselves as the repositories of the agricultural and regional traditions of the country: a group of them recently published a book, 'I'll Take My Stand,' to uphold these traditions against the financial and mechanical standardization of the rest of the country; and though they tend to be slightly reactionary, still dreaming of the past instead of shaping a more integrated future, they may prove valuable allies. John Gould Fletcher, whom you may have met in London, will be there: our New York group, Stein, Wright, MacKaye, are engineering it. We shall miss you.

In Oklahoma a group at the University have published these last two years a Regional Miscellany, chiefly literary, called 'Folk-Say': an interesting straw in the wind. The writer of the article on Meiklejohn's college, which I enclose, is another one of the young people who have studied you well: he did a study of the French bastides last summer, but unfortunately missed you in London, though he saw Farquharson. Your disciples are coming along now rapidly; the younger generation, that is, those now under twenty-five, are much more concrete-minded than their elders were: architecture begins to share place with literature in the critical journals: Miss Catherine Bauer, the girl who is going to write a history of the House, is a very adept pupil: she has gotten much out of your Biology. These young people are more ready for Graphics than you perhaps realize.
—Letter to P.G. June 27, 1931

PATRICK GEDDES'S INFLUENCE ON MY THOUGHT.
P.G. exemplified the basically ecological doctrine of organic unity in his manifold activities: though at the end this dynamic conception was to be frozen in a series of graphic charts that mocked both the flow of events and the essential inner act. His more pious followers memorized and mimicked these static categories, instead of living the life. P.G.'s philosophy helped save me from becoming a monocular specialist: but even better, after I had achieved competence in more than one field, it gave me the confidence to become a generalist—one who sought to bring together in a more intelligible pattern the knowledge that the specialist had, by over-strenuous concentration, sealed off in separate compartments. Not that he or I would disparage the work of the specialist—like Pierre Dansereau I accept it and seek to use it—except when it mistakes the part for the whole, or renounces any effort to understand the whole. For me, as first for Geddes, spe-

101

cialism and generalism were complementary activities and effective thought must necessarily fuse them together.

Though Geddes was fertile in vivid concrete illustrations—often extremely stimulating, not least because of his satiric, even savage wit —it was his more basic personal insights and responses that have remained with me and guided my life. I never accepted C. P. Snow's division of the 'two cultures'—though I find it ironic that even American critics who discuss this thesis never refer to various contemporaries like myself who had already dissolved that false dichotomy in practice. Just the other day, in a seminar of the Jung Institut, in Zürich, I was asked by a young man with an exceptionally high I.Q. —in fact one of the self-satisfied members of the 'Mensa' group—if I considered my work 'literature.' The question was meaningless to me: it covertly assumed that if it was literature it was not 'science'— or at least not scientifically respectable. But I consider Henri Poincaré's 'Science and Hypothesis' notable as fine writing; and I am ashamed of my own writing when it sometimes slips into technical jargon, the 'secret language' of science. Mathematicians are notoriously proud of achieving 'elegant' solutions; and in my ideal world of thought I would gladly forfeit quick results for statements that would be as esthetically satisfying and humanly as attractive as Plato's dialogues, even if it required more time and effort to achieve this result.

Geddes's living example influenced me in many other ways. But this general orientation was the most fundamental and lasting one: whereas certain other phases of his thought to which he attached great value, like his adhesion to Comte and Le Play, played only a minor part in my thinking, even in my youth, and have left only residual traces. His sociological division of a society into chiefs and people, emotionals and intellectuals, has its parallel in Jung's later division of personality types. But both schemes tacitly accept the rigidities of ancient caste societies and overlook the interplay of types, their changing roles in new situations—as when the butler, in Barrie's 'The Admirable Crichton' becomes the true leader (Chief) of the castaways. The feat of personality is to escape these fixations and transcend these categories. Jung himself saw this when he said it was necessary to reinforce and develop the weak side of the personality in the interest of balance.   —RN. June 14, 1967

The Twenties in the Arts

Even after one has taken into account all the sordid and even lethal characteristics of the twenties, one sees that it was a period of high energies and ever renewed hopes, though these hopes were no longer for a great wave of utopian social improvement, but for achievements in art and literature that would enrich our days. The new novelists, like Hemingway, wrote with a workmanlike sureness, and a delicate economy that even the best of their immediate predecessors too often lacked; and the same spirit was at work in a sculptor like Lachaise, a photographer like Strand or Weston, a poet like Aiken or Eliot—or, to mention Eliot's chief enemy in the same breath— in the biographic literary analyses of Van Wyck Brooks. No single style united all these men: the plangent rhythms and strong colors of Frank's 'Virgin Spain' were far from the staccato excitement of Dos Passos: in fact, a display of intense individuality, a nourishment of idiosyncrasies, was what precisely characterized the period, as this writer or that cast his line in waters that had never before been fished in. What Gertrude Stein and James Joyce had done experimentally with words, other writers were to do with ideas: did not Paul Rosenfeld invent a new genre of musical criticism in which he sought to translate, into rhythms of prose, the salient characteristics of the work of art he was, through and beyond that act, passing judgment upon? What generally bound together all these writers, apart from their reaction to the central experience of their generation, the First World War, was something that did indeed recall the period of Thoreau and Emerson's manhood: the discovery of their own American heritage—only for this generation it was, in fact, in Waldo Frank's title, 'The Re-discovery of America.'

Perhaps that will prove in the end the most important contribution of the nineteen-twenties: certainly, it was what united me in comradeship to Van Wyck Brooks, Waldo Frank, and Paul Rosenfeld, who incidentally was almost the first musical critic to do justice to the American composers of our century like Charles Ives as it later united me in admiration to that subtle but patient scholar in American folklore and folk arts, Constance Mayfield Rourke, whom I was first to meet in 1927, a white lily mid a flowerbed of domestic geraniums, when I lectured before a Woman's Club in her native Grand Rapids. We were the scouts and prospectors in a new enterprise: the bringing to the surface of America's buried cultural past; for the scholars who had studied American history had, in their pride over our natural endowments and our political innovations, overlooked the contributions that our ancestors had actually made to a new culture in literature, painting, architecture, and the machine crafts. They took with abashed humility Sidney Smith's withering question: Who reads an American book?—and admitted that they, too, did not. If such people took pride in our literary past, it was mainly over the imitative writers, the mediocrities, whose gift to us, if they were as good as Longfellow or Lowell, was that they had become so fully Europeanized that one could scarcely tell their difference from the genuine article.

Even those who, with a flair for a promising field, or a certain provincial self-respect, had made themselves, after a fashion, master of our contributions in literature—the almost isolated figure of Barrett Wendell of course stands out—had too often put our secondary authors in the first rank and had no place left for those whose originality deserved their studious attention: for Wendell dismissed the author of 'Moby-Dick' as a writer whose promise, in 'Typee,' had never been fulfilled; and his condescension toward the author of 'Huckleberry Finn,' a good fifteen years after the book was published, was only equalled by the smudgy cleverness of his characterization of Whitman.

The fact was that the arts in America were then an almost unexplored waste—'Bad Lands,' like those in Montana and Wyoming, that everyone admitted could not be cultivated and so were hardly worth while even exploring: though if they had known their geography better they might have suspected that in literature, too, the Grand Tetons lay beyond—worth coming all the way to see.   —Notes for my Autobiography. 1973

. . . I haven't had a chance to tell you half what I've been doing. After a very tedious winter of lecturing and hack-writing and hack-editing—all in a good cause and chiefly on architecture—I summoned up what energies remained, cleared nine full days free from all engagements, and at last wrote the play I had planned out and partly written eight years ago. It was a tremendous release, or rather, delivery; and I had some of the exhilaration that Sophie felt the day after Geddes was born. I was so amazed at my own capacities that I cackled about the prodigy all over the place; something I could only have done in the critical exhaustion of the period that followed; but in spite of the fact that I must re-write the last two acts pretty thoroughly, I think it will stand inspection, and as soon as I return and finish the revision I'd like

to have you read it. I have called it: 'Sumach and Goldenrod: An American Idyll.' Let the Sumach warn you of the poison and bitterness in it! It spans the period from 1859 to 1864; and enables me to project all our own interests and difficulties, at any rate a good part of them, through the clarifying medium of time. Unless I am quite deluded about the value of 'Sumach and Goldenrod,' and I shall not remain deluded for more than a couple of years, I shall follow it with another theme that's burning in me, a little more heroic in proportions, centering around a counterpart of the brave invalid who built the Brooklyn Bridge! Don't think that I'm writing a pageant of American history in a bad medium: the situations are psychological and dramatic, but I find that I can load them more fully, and bring out the larger lines more emphatically, by placing them a generation or two away. . . .
—Letter to V.W.B. July 22, 1925

ANTICIPATION OF 'THE RENEWAL OF LIFE' SERIES.

The aristocracies of the world have never doubted the supremacy of the home and garden and temple over all the baser mechanisms of existence, and the folk-civilizations out of which aristocracies have so often risen have never strayed far from these realities. In the Norse fables, the dwarfs are regarded as queer monsters, because they are always 'busy people' who have no pride or joy except in the work they perform and the mischief they cause.

The great heresy of the modern world is that it ceased to worship the Lords of Life, who made the rivers flow, caused the animals to mate, and brought forth the yearly miracle of vegetation: it prostrated itself, on the contrary, before the dwarfs, with their mechanical ingenuity, and the giants, with their imbecile power. Today our lives are perpetually menaced by these 'busy people'; we are surrounded by their machines, and for worship, we turn their prayer wheels of red-tape.

It will not always be so; that would be monstrous. Sooner or later we will learn to pick our way out of the débris that the dwarfs, the gnomes, and the giants have created; eventually, to use Henry Adams's figure, the sacred mother will supplant the dynamo. The prospects for our architecture are bound up with a new orientation toward the things that are symbolized in the home, the garden and the temple; for architecture sums up the civilization it enshrines, and the mass of our buildings can never be better or worse than the institutions that have shaped them.   —Envoi to 'Sticks and Stones.' 1924

The Little Testament of Bernard Martin, Aet. 30

PART ONE

Of the first five years nothing remains except goldfish spinning around a slippery jar, and the furtive light of a back-parlor window against the white faces that crept around upon the red carpet that concealed a carpet beneath a wardrobe that was really a bed: that and the figure of Bernie's Granmer grimacing in haste before a pier glass as she perched a black bonnet upon a head that had once been beautiful. Silence follows. One must be silent at play: Granmer is sick: Granmer is very sick: Granmer is not. Black ribbons and black veils and trickling eyes are all that remain of Granmer: black veils are mourning but mourning is not the beginning of day: mourning is the red rim of sunset about tired eyes. Goldfish gasp softly against the translucent boundaries of their existence. Goldfish spin eternally around a glass jar.

2

The days do not hurry: the days come slow: one peels the hours off as Nornie peels a mushroom. The days creep: the minutes clatter with emptiness: an hour with Granper in Central Park rattles like seeds in a gourd, the gourd of empty days. Pine needles do not prick: darning needles do not darn: policemen eat little boys: bugaboos do not scare policemen. Granper is a head waiter at Sherry's: he brings home detachable noses and false faces. When Granper wears a false face he is the devil: false faces and policemen are not bugaboos but they are even worse than bugaboos. Granper is foxy: and when he bunches his breasts up they are like a woman's.

3

Seven goldfish play wavy hide and seek in wavy weeds. Granper mates yellow birds with green birds: on a spring morning cinnamon birds crack through the speckled eggs. Little boys have no business in the pantry where the yellow birds and the green birds sing. When a little boy leaves the pantry door open the cat eats the goldfish as well as the yellow birds the green birds and the weeny cinnamon birds. Little boys dream of false faces and policemen. Mamadear lights the light and holds the little boy's hands. Morning comes: the cage is empty: the cat is fat. The little boy smiles. Bernie left the pantry door open: the policeman did not eat Bernie: the policeman never even rang the doorbell and asked: Have you a bad little boy named Bernie here? But the goldfish and the birdies are dead: Granmer is dead too. The eternal goldfish will never spin around any more in a glass jar.

4

The hands of the clock turn around. Tick lives: tock dies: tick lives: tock dies. Bong-bong-bong is the voice of doom. The clock never turns backwards: six says wake Bernie: seven says eat Bernie: eight says school Bernie: nine says classroom Bernie. Present: present early: late: present: present. Absent never answers for itself: present never answers for anyone else except when present is naughty. Blang goes the big bell: pling, pling, pling go the classroom bells. Home for lunch: back for school: present: present: tardy: late. The schoolyard is bare: school has begun: loitering is a crime. Little boys cry when their names are put in a black book but loitering is a crime: crimes are punished. Big boys make little boys show their penis in the lavatory: little boys go home at the end of the week with a certificate for good conduct. Five hours five days five certificates make an elementary education: there is also reading writing and arithmetic: drawing is nice but faces are not allowed. Sixty seconds make a minute: sixty minutes make an hour: six years make a little boy who knows that alcohol is bad for the health that trees are deciduous and evergreen that G.C.D. means greatest common divisor that all day suckers are poisonous unless consumed to the last layer that one hundred dollars at six per cent for one year is seven goldfish spinning around a glass jar.

5

Sally is seven: she is a jockey's daughter. Her white face has been kicked in by a horse: her distorted beauty awakens six masculine summers. She cuts up her own food in the Children's Dining Room: she rides to the races in her uncle's buggy. A word from Sally is a golden ball dancing on top of a fountain: the touch of her hand is a glass of cold seltzer at the Spa. Kiss Sally: kiss Sally: hide behind the sofa: hide and seek: spring at her: kiss the hair of Sally's pigtail. But the cuff of Sally's hand behind the sofa is the splintering of a sun into sordid stars. Six masculine years long for Sally: they play with Sally before anyone else is awake: they show everything to Sally: she shows everything to them: but she is not the real Sally with the oily pigtail and the white knuckles that stung like marble against pink jelly.

6

The smell of stale onions on Nornie's cracked fingers means winter. When Granper's frock coat opens on a gold watch chain it is spring.

110

In spring goats ramp for bock beer in front of swinging doors: behind the paving stone in the backyard parsley, pansies, geraniums, and flax-seed left over from poultices grow into flowers, green, purple, red, blue. Hot potatoes in a fire beneath mummied sunflower stalks is autumn: but marbles are always spring. Push wagons in the twilight with a cigarbox lantern are summer. Mamadear getting excited and saying: Isn't the air beautiful and what are the odds on Waterboy in the Brighton Handicap with a sip of beer at a smeary table on the lap of a boney man with yellow finger tips, Mamadear lifting her brown veil and drinking, too, is spring, is summer, is fall.

7

Tick-tock: tick-tock: tick lives: tock dies. Nornie buttons the last button and pulls the muffler higher. Mamadear says don't play with naughty boys in the lavatory. Tick-tock: man is in the nominative case, subject to the verb do: do good: do lessons: do memory work: present participle doing: doing this: doing that: doing nothing: negative particle not: not doing what one wants: not telling what one dreams: not saying what one thinks: not arguing with the teacher: not looking around in class: not throwing boardrubbers: not making spitballs: not speaking out of turn. Tick-tock: report cards: A is excellent: Bernie's A's make a pattern of the months: Bernie is a grind: Bernie is the teacher's pet. When Granper walks with Bernie along Riverside Drive he shows him the ships and the freight trains and he tells him about his life in Paris, Munich, Copenhagen: when Nornie cooks she tells Bernie about the Holy Virgin and Ireland and how the nuns made a Novena and what one found on the strand of Youghal: Mamadear lets Bernie play with her embroidery silks and when she wants some thread she sends Bernie to the store and tells him to mind the change. Granper and Nornie and Mamadear show Bernie the rudiments of geography, ethics, mathematics, art: but Bernie shames them with his school knowledge. Granper can't do fractions like Bernie and he never knew how many states are in South America.

8

Portia's plea closes the Morning Assembly: Bernie wants to be a lawyer. But Shakespeare was a very great poet: Bernie wants to be a poet, too. But electricity is more fun than anything: if one had five dollars one could get a wireless set: a tuning coil and a detector bring musical dash-dots, and if one were rich and had ten dollars one could have a loose-coupler and a variable condenser and get louder music from remoter dash-dots. Barney is Bernie's best friend: Barney and Bernie share candy: Barney will buy a wireless outfit. Bernie is poor and will make his. The dash-dots are declarations of love in a foreign language. Wire and binding posts become exciting pieces of statuary. Bernie decides to be an engineer: Barney will be an engineer, too, and manage a sugar plantation in Cuba.

9

Summer is warm in the city: summer glows on the sear green of Central Park. Bernie meets a Princess: she tells Bernie he is her sweetheart. She is a real Russian Princess with a pug nose and blonde hair. He is convinced but not ravished. Summer is warm. Granper's flabby flesh falls over grayblear mournful eyes: Granper's flabby skin droops from lean shanks where the sheet parts. Kiss me Goodbye, Bernie: be good to Mamadear: be a brave man! You will not see me again. Goodbye Granper: but I shall be back soon. And I shall go soon, says Granper. Twelve years are troubled: six times twelve are putting trouble far behind them. Bernie leaves the doubtful pleasure of a Princess's espousal to meet Betty. Betty helps with the dishes on the farm. To dry the dishes when Betty washes them is to smell the perfume of ferns in her hair and see the down on her neck fall into the hollow of a perfect back. One night Betty says: Kiss me! Jacob the smelly hired man laughs many laughs. Betty has her kiss. Granper dies whilst Betty calmly engages Bernie with more kisses. Bernie does not return till Granper is buried with his griefs and loves: Bernie still dares to dream of love that knows no grief or burial. Back in the city Bernie writes Betty fevered letters, exploding with passion like a milkweed pod in autumn. Betty never gets or never heeds them. Autumn is dank with vegetation and disappointment.

10

Russian faces: German faces: Italian faces: Jewish faces: a thousand faces cloud and scatter in the halls: smudgy faces: keen faces: blubber faces. In the lunchroom they munch and shout in Bernie's ear: Bernie eats his roll alone in the dark corridor. Faces leer at Bernie and call him sweetie: false faces: but old faces are kind faces: kind faces keep school. A patient face with a blind blue eye teaches geometry as if Pythagoras and Euclid were still alive: a black sardonic face above broad shoulders utters the words Philosophy—Descartes—cogito ergo sum. A long bearded face recites his Milton like a prayer: a pink solemn face beneath a carrot pompadour sits down with Bernard, Solomon, and Freddy to write a play. The hours do not crawl: the hours are not empty: the clock says neither tick nor tock. The moments become monuments: each monument shelters a memory. Happy faces turning wood into unbelievable chair legs that never get attached to chairs: anxious faces pouring white lead into green sand molds: blurred faces following the mystery of electrons into test-tubes placed over anode and cathode: wild faces describing elegant parabolae with basketballs: jolly faces twisting in the pageant of a Christmas dance: serious faces walking home along Fifth Avenue, talking about God: these faces made Bernard's face: they translated passive tick-tock into the imperative mood and the active voice.

I I

Engines are buckets and shovels dressed up for adults. Science is abracadabra and fie-fy-fo-fum. Electricity is interesting but not so interesting as love. Smooth binding posts are dull beside the frail throbbing fountain that leaps into the sunshine of Annabel's face: alternating currents do not reverse polarity so quickly as the heart that beholds Annabel. Engines are buckets and shovels dressed up for adults who have never known Annabel. Dynamos generate electricity: but Annabel generates the dynamo that generates the dynamo that generates the electricity.

I 2

The trees of West End Avenue drip warm steam. Annabel's body curls like a white mist against the sullen recess of an August afternoon. Thunder booms in the air: lightning darts gigantic butterflies. Annabel listlessly hovers over a book, her shoulder hunching near to Bernard's. Bernard scarcely dares to sigh on Annabel's neck: a lock of her hair on Bernard's cheek dances shivered sparks within his breast. Embraces that do not touch linger longer in the arms that do not hold: manhood shudders in mid-air on a swinging beam, swinging, swaying, slipping, sliding, edging into nothingness. The soft gloom of Annabel's passion reveals green eyes dew-honeyed with expectancy. The pavements spatter with wild rain: two bodies tremble on the verge of an apocalyptic revelation. Bernard quivers with frightened dizzy joy: the lips of Annabel are sultry with a kiss that is not taken. Like taut elastic all the tension breaks when Why are you sitting in the dark? comes from a portly gray solicitous bosom with an umbrella blocking a doorway that once held at bay a fugitive and unreal world.

I 3

The love of Bernard and Annabel evaporates into billets of white and blue paper that come every morning laden with philosophy, adoration, and reproach. Autumn lifts the leaves of West End Avenue into crackled nervous heaps. Autumn leaves Bernard with the agony of a reluctant surrender to a lackadaisical youth not keyed to hesitate before an obvious embrace. Engines are shovels and buckets dressed up for adults. Love is interesting but not so interesting as electricity. Without contact or induction electricity does not travel. When sparks jumped across the electrodes of Bernard and Annabel that August afternoon, what mysterious terror became the insulator?

14

Dreams are the color left in the water when acts are wrung out: dreams are blind arrows that never leave the bow: dreams are the remembrance of a courage that never went into battle. One ounce of distilled dreams would provide the plots of five hundred moving pictures or the reality of seven murders, eighteen rapes, fifty-five suicides, a hundred Carnegie medals, and the blushes of many bridesmaids. From a day's dreams one might stock a department store with chemises or get enough courage to quench a fire in a powder plant. The dreams of fifteen would create a menagerie and overflow the house of reptiles: a medical museum could be filled with the pre-natal reminiscences enveloped in dreams, and surgical skill could not unravel the physiological intricacy of the chimeric women known to sleeping adolescents. Dreams are the color left in the water: when life leaves dreams behind life is sad dirty white. Maturity is a white sad dirtiness without the dreams of fifteen: maturity means that the courage which quenches fires will stand by a principle: maturity means that the distillation which would produce a movie will build a home: it means that wild rapes and impossible copulations become the delicious commonplaces of connubiality. But at fifteen Dionysus has a wry neck. Dreams are the color left behind by a sad white dirty life.

PART TWO

15

Why is the city sober gray? Why are the stones white sober cold? Rocks crumble into parallelograms against a geometric sky. Black creatures run back and forth in the crevices thinking that civilization is composed of subways, traffic signals, and right angles. If right angles and subways are emblems of civilization how wonderful are the tracks of a cow and the ways of a grasshopper!

16

What will Bernard be: what will Bernard be? In Broad Street white coats clack figures on a July morning: flicker-eyes watch tickers through the sickish atmosphere of desiccated cigars. American Can at 87 is another way of saying tick-tock. Everyday Wall Street goes to

114

school at ten and is dismissed at three: Wall Street has never gotten beyond fractions and elementary arithmetic. Five certificates make a gold star: five gold stars make a tip that almost came from Mr. Morgan and almost made a fortune. Good conduct means that little boys can get to the golflinks by five: good little boys can have bad little girls in nice little flats as soon as they can afford them. Begin at the bottom and work your way up is the rule of Wall Street. But even when Bernard dreams of undies he doesn't want bad little girls. Bernard does not like being a messenger in Wall Street. What shall Bernard do? What shall Bernard do?

17

What shall Bernard be: what shall Bernard be? At three-fifteen in the morning hot cocoa with malted milk is a plausible substitute for interrupted sleep. Ferryboats sound like the snores of nightwatchmen in the green corridors of a hospital: in the Herald Building, stale paper gives dirty mop water the smell of a bad cigar in a Pullman smoking compartment. When Bernard appears the boys in the corner scoop up the cards and go down to Nelligans for a last drink. Bernard lays out eight stacks of paper, buys egg sandwiches, balances three cans of beer, sweeps up the floor around the copy desk, and listens to the tedious sagacity of Rogan the night city editor labeling the morning's columns: Neb Gov: T R: Sex Fed: Pat Murd. Old news is wood pulp macerated and rolled into new news: Ships sink: men murder: wars wax: every day ships sink: men murder: wars wax. But reporters do not always remember that the verb must agree with the subject in number; and the drama of arising at three-fifteen is belittled by the fact that the sun reveals a dozen stale faces in a dirty office. To get up at three-fifteen: to report a fire: to write a stick—oh joy! but a thousand fires: a thousand sticks is tick-tock all over again. If Bernard remains a copy boy he will become a reporter. Bernard will not become a reporter—and what shall Bernard do?

18

Buckets of gold on a chain curve over the hill on an autumn evening: in the solitude of an affected antiquity Gothic pinnacles gleam whitely into fading purple. The diminished roar of the distant El creeps out under a blanket of patchwork silence. In the distance golden beer pours from electric bottles: flash signs display cheap jewelry on the bosom of Harlem: remote lamps melt into the feebleness of foggy stars. Bernard does odd jobs by day: Bernard reads by day: at night he seeks the company of students within walls of an affected antiquity.

19

Dim graygreen corridors swerve in solemn arcs: faces beautiful with thought make thought beautiful. How shall men behave in society and on what Ionic shore did men begin to wing their way above the matted forest of their daily life into the rarefied clarity of philosophic thought? Psychology deals with human behavior. The last entrail of a dissected grasshopper increases the wonder of life. If life is a tree, let us smell the flower and dig at the roots: if Annabel is worth embracing, so is the hypothesis of evolution: the organ that pries into the body of a woman is the instrument that drives excitedly into the womb of Nature: the brain is composed of erectile tissue: every living thought is a divine orgasm.

20

Brother Schapiro wields over Politics a knife that cuts with unguents and balm: man is by nature a political animal and by ill-nature a dangerous one: monogamy is as valuable for the family as it is tedious for the parents: war is inevitable while men believe in the inevitability of war. The inarticulate passion of Selwin over a slide on the microscope beatifies the rosary of great names: Linnaeus, Buffon, Darwin, Mendel, Huxley, with a special prayer for the heretics, Oken, Goethe, Butler, Driesch, Jennings, Geddes, and nameless men who forever storm against the true Church and save it. Palmer who makes literature as familiar as the smile of a beloved mouth is a white ember of happiness: the happiness of Chaucer, Spenser, Shelley, Keats. His eyes are exhausted volcanoes peering over the winter landscape of a wistful smile. The Holy Ghost descends when Adonais beacons from his abode in Palmer's sanctuary: there is religion enough in his classroom to curse a hundred churches for their blasphemy. No word is too often profaned for Palmer to redeem it: no emotion so frail but it becomes a shaft of crystal dancing on his tongue. Palmer disturbs Bernard with the joy of elevated thoughts. Life is neither Annabels nor Dynamos: life is not was not cannot won't be more than the point of calm in the moving whirlwind of God.

21

Palmer brings Bernard to the core of the whirlwind: it is the core of Plato: it is form: it is the core of Aristotle: every living thing fulfills its inner shape: it is the core of Spinoza: the intellectual love of the Universe: it is the core of Berkeley, that man and God have begotten the same reality. When Bernard thinks about Berkeley in the moonlight the dark bulk of almost antique buildings becomes the shadow of his own thought: the solidity of the ground is the exhalation of an ancient dream. There is not was not cannot won't be more matter and bottom to man's life than the ruffle of a passing thought on the brow of God. Man is a thought: cities are a thought: Bernard is a thought: and if the thought perished, what would remain? The universe is an idiot: man is God's first gleam of an idea. The world is a step in the equation of an incalculable theorem. If God knew the answer he would not bother to work it out.

2 2

This is life! This is learning! Bernard wants to drain it dry. But by day college is tick-tock on a useless metronome. Dull faces crawl through the iniquity of tortured lessons. Massed monkeys are the sport of inane tropisms called hazing, games, and college spirit. Fill out the form: sign the dotted line: report promptly: do not live with a thought lest the thought keep you from turning over memorizable papers and acquiring insignificant marks. Do this: do that: learn this: learn that: all goes toward a degree except the active use and exploration of the outer scene, the city, or the fruitful ground within where bean sprouts of ideas put forth their radicals. Never dwell on anything for more than fifty minutes at a time if you can help it: credits are credits! White worms gnaw at Bernard's soul: this is not meditation. White worms creep through Bernard's mind: this is not learning. White worms tear at Bernard's vitals: this is not living! White worms sallow nervous too much girls or what? Fever's irritation indicates a prolonged rest. The undertaker's shop leers like a pimp at a carnival: white worms are the silent partners of black undertakers.

2 3

The hours come slowly: the day is wide: the city spreads before Bernard's feet like a gleaming map. Health is a matter of slow deliberate motions, warm baths, clean clothes, and walks along unending avenues, various with economics, sociology, biology, literature, drama, and art in the guise of people. People tell everything. The full waters of the East River are an invitation to explore brown barges with dingy good natured men. From the lower docks the bridges are plutonic fountains, meeting midway between the shores. Two months making systematic tabulations among the garment workers bring Bernard face to face with the blind drama of an industry seeking to achieve stability out of spasmodic and irrelevant enterprises that ebb and flow with fashion.

2 4

Michael Marx rises to hatred of the bourgeoisie out of a bed illegitimately soiled with bedbugs beyond the usual number: he knows the hey-nonny-nonny of finding the family furniture on the street, and in the handspring of adolescence he leaves behind I pledge allegiance to the flag and to all tick-tock at six per cent. He and Bernard stamp envelopes in a Second Avenue basement where twenty Wobblies proclaim the immediate revolution of doing bad work worse. Mike and Bernard dream of education for the masses from soapboxes. Bernard writes an ABC of economics: Mike never forgets the bedbugs nor the soapboxes nor the verbal duties of class consciousness. Mike and Bernard hate the capitalist oppressors. Bernard equally hates the workers for being oppressed. But Bernard belongs to the bourgeoisie because he has an income of four hundred dollars a year and enjoys the luxury of gentlemanly indigence. Mike writes Bernard loving letters of excommunication.

25

Patches of iridescence on dull and slimy waters: the Art Museum is a patch of iridescence: plaster casts of Greek gods are iridescent on the flats of Yorkville: the Library of spacious catalogues pointing to all necessary books is an iridescence on the smutty night of Broadway. The towers of Manhattan gleaming across the upper Bay on a summer afternoon are iridescent: the Mall is iridescent with a hundred colors on a June Sunday joyblazing brightness. The meadows in Prospect Park on a misty April day are an iridescence hedged with phantom trees: the Westchester hills in October are petrified sunsets. In May the Croton Viaduct leads into Yonkers like a carpet unrolled for a dryad's wedding. Salt odors creeping along the Hudson on an August night uncage seagulls of memory. The smell of roasting coffee in Franklin Street brings perfumes from distant bazaars. The craggy face of Carl Schurz against a lavender night is a stark finger raised against oblivion. Dull and slimy waters creep around the city. Iridescent patches hide the slimy waters. Youth is an iridescence.

26

When the guns bluster with belligerency in 1914 Bernard says: This finishes my career! Bernard does not know what his career is but feels that a great war will finish it. When the cackle of insane apologetics breaks out like the tea-table gossip of Bedlam: when Thomas Mann and Henri Bergson and H. G. Wells share honors for being speciously dishonorable Bernard says: We must keep out of it—may no one win! By 1917 Bernard still hates the war but is carried away by the paper strategy of pragmatists and New Republicans: he whoops for Woodrow Wilson till Memorial Day. . . . Then he knows for sure his world is blasted. Cackles of insanity become requisites for polite intercourse.

27

Bernard's generation goes in for Social Service. They do not particularly care what Society does so long as the technique is good and whatever is done is done efficiently with a minimum wage for hired persons, examinations for the official caste, and well-designed badges of self-righteousness for those who do the thinking and direction. Universal compulsory voluntary pacifistic military service is the sum of liberal aspirations in 1917: this shibboleth will save an autocratic world for democratic unity. The dictatorship of war brings echoes of Armageddon where people who believe in the eight-hour day and the recall of judges battle for the Lord. War is inevitable, and the more we have of it the sooner will pragmatists make wise regulations for instituting a Chatauqua of machine guns. In matters of instrumental technique, conscientious scruples about killing or doubts about the purpose for which one kills are out of place. Randolph Bourne knows better than the pragmatists; with him for rocket, the Seven Arts ascends in glory-fire. He sees that chains are chains though called Democracy and Service that Hell is Hell, though called the vestibule of Heaven. How many paper warriors have said penance to the shade of Randolph Bourne?

28

Men are fighting: men are gasping: men are dying. Bernard smiles at his doctor and answers the undertaker's leer with a wink. Bernard is dying, too, but he does not die so fast as the young men who die in Flanders or in Picardy. The dread of dying excites the pugnacity of clerks and financiers who sit on stools all day and suffer from a constipation that only fear can relieve. Prepare for ripping guts out says the soldier: prepare for safety first and steen per cent says the financier: prepare for more preparedness say the clerks: prepare for the defense of Honor say the politicians, who know of Honor by reputation. Prepare to leave your wastebaskets and your vain motions says a tired God who knows that a hundred million efforts at divinity are already much more dead than they suppose. Living wastebaskets and white tape is the deafness of never hearing life's music. War is the attempt to squelch life's music in the imitative cacophony of brutal valor. In a world that is governed by tick-tock, War is a reasonable and beautiful mode of life.

29

Bernard is not dominated by his overt convictions: Bernard wants to live. But why should Bernard live? Twenty-one is a good time to die. Bernard can remember summer afternoons paddling in the White River of Vermont with heron passing overhead and the slippery flicker of

119

trout in the shadows of aqueous stones: Bernard can remember shrews playing in the woodlot and kisses in the rose garden where Bertha sought white petals and concealment: Bernard can remember the austere divinity of a condescending Annabel, arguing about the basis of ethical conduct in a tawdry Morningside Apartment: no kisses will ever satisfy him like that chastity: no surrender will ever thrill like that aloofness! Bernard can remember walks in the Westchester Hills with Agnes whose milky skin was the nectar offered at a feast of virgins, whose red hair was the last glow of the sun on russet walls. Bernard can remember the tender intimacy of Mamadear when they talked beside an open window above the rumble of the Elevated, domestically fomented with the smell of baking bread. Bernard had known grief without irreparable bitterness and joy without tedious responsibility. Bernard dear: think well: you are twenty-one. The clerks, the preachers, the politicians, the soldiers do not realize it: but perhaps this is your opportunity: twenty-one is a good time to die. Bernard alas! is not governed by philosophic arguments and appraisals: Bernard wants to live—and why should Bernard die?

30

At six in the morning the Flatiron Building shows yellow lights against a green April sky. Sleepy recruits summoned for inspection are told to return at ten for medical examination. At sunset Mamadear and Nornie become the faceless shadows of irretrievable years and it would not matter if Annabel had as many as ten lovers. Nightmares gallop convulsively through tedious days of shorn heads, weakly brackish coffee, steam-trickling clammy naked bodies, and inspection from medical gold-stripers who could learn human decency from veterinaries that handle hydrophobic dogs. Sleep is peace if you do not get bumped out of your hammock to mount guard for two hours over unassailable quarters girdled in quarantine. Sleep is peace, and under ordinary circumstances belly inspection would be funny.

31

Gruff seadogs who spit salt aren't always hardboiled. Even the little Greek C.P.O. grows husky when he tells how a man buried at sea leaves no enemies behind and all are shipmates. The mystery of the uniform of the day is that the sun always shines on overshoes and peajackets and the wind from Narragansett Bay whips icy rain on leggins and no peajackets. Seventy men in a shack cease to be Ohio, Mississippi, Kansas, to become Jim, Bill, and Jack. A squareknot, a figure-of-eight knot, and a clove-hitch can easily be untied but nothing will untie the knot in Bernard's throat on a Sunday afternoon when he sprawls on the crest of Strawberry Hill and watches the train steam-hooting around a distant curve. Men are court-martialed and sent to the brig for little offenses everyone has committed. The Catholic priest never asks Bernard whether he has any religion but gets him the impossible dispensation of a furlough and visits him in the hospital when the measles side with the commandant against God's ministers. At the Knights of Columbus Hut and the J.W.B. you can have plenty of writing paper: at the Y.M.C.A. it is doled out piece by piece, and go-getting business men preach Sunday sermons with enthusiasm for clean guts.

32

A morning on Narragansett Bay in a whale-boat takes the sting out of the Chief's nervous oaths. Sunset over the mainland makes evening muster a stale prayer in a magnificent cathedral. An hour before dawn on a rainy night wafts the perfume of lilacs and newmown hay from the misty ledge of Jamestown. Ratlike boats creep over the water in the faint lemon bleakness of sunrise. Magnolia petals make Bernard think of Agnes's bosom. The sea that surges against the cliffs is the whisper of an old friend who says: Never mind: you and I will be here when they are gone. O World! O Life! O Time! is a good poem for sentry duty on a quiet night.

33

Jerry and Bernard become friends: Jerry works in an office in New York. When the C.P.O. says: So you're wise guys from Toid Avenoo and Toity-toid Street Jerry and Bernard look at each other and smile. Jerry has read Strindberg and Ibsen too: Jerry has gone to City College too: Jerry has been disappointed in love too: Jerry is going to be a radio operator too. Jerry and Bernard recite Dehmel and Rilke to each other: they laugh at the maudlin fevers of patriotism. They would like to talk to a Hun and find out whether anyone had taken Hauptmann's place.

34

Monday roast beef: Tuesday seagull: Wednesday sou-oup: all American mothers, we wish the same to you! Da-dit-da-da: da-da-dit-dit-dit: da-dit-dit-da. In the clamorous gloom of Austin Hall in Cambridge Bernard wonders what it would be like to hear the signal of the flagship coming from a battle formation in the North Sea. Twenty-one is a good time to die. Captains and radio operators die first. The Heinies sat on their keys and beat the Limies with their radios in the Jutland fight, and if this was a good war we'd be fighting the Limies. In Hong-kong or Guantanamo or Manila we're always fighting the Limies. Perhaps when we've finished with the Huns we'll fight the Limies, too. The Navy's been waiting a long time for a good fight. Dit-dit: dit-dit: dit-dit: stand by for a weather report, Arlington broadcasting.

35

The days become a vacancy of soft lassitude, yellowsoft in the haze of September. Nature has found a rival to poison gas: Nature has found that influenza can turn streets into trenches quicker than an army. On Harvard Field the gobs sprawl around in friendly games or stand at rest. Every once in a while someone falls in a heap and gets a free ride in the hurry-up. Harry awakes in the bunk below Bernard with a chill: Bernard gives Harry his blanket and in the morning draws his arm around Harry's tired neck and walks him to the Sick Bay. When Harry comes back the first rumor of the Armistice has turned the campus into a wild auction room where men offer ditty bags to each other and trample upon white hats hurled against a gray sky.

36

The clerks, the financiers, and the politicians have had a movement! College professors have become as important as overnight ensigns: they have worn iron mittens: at their command coal has got tangled up in the Jersey meadows. Millionaires have made the supreme sacrifice of becoming godalmighty for a dollar a year: a hundred iron ships are floating like paper boats in the Delaware. Irascible men with disordered glands have become patriots by the simple method of spying on their neighbors and selling other people's sacrifices in job-lots: woolen manufacturers, carpenters, riveters, the daughters of the best families have had their fill of money, lust, and glory. Bernard has lost his chance of dying, of dying gloriously, at any rate of dying.

37

When the grinning clerks empty wastepaper baskets and the remains of the candy the boss gave the stenographer upon the white-capped radioboys who march through State Street, Bernard remembers that the Navy was a decent place after all. When spy-hunting and witch-baiting go on after the Armistice, when patriotic people declare that little Huns should be boiled in oil, when investigators from political boobyhatches discover that Godwin's 'Political Justice,' Marx's 'Kapital' and the plays of Bernard Shaw can be bought at bookstores: when Red Flags take the place of foreign enemies and Blasto for constipation—Bernard remembers that the Navy was a good place after all. The Navy does its job without throwing moral spasms over the enemy: the Navy would like a wallop at the Limies, maybe, but everything else is part of the day's work.

38

Slush lies on the fields of Pelham Bay when Bernard checks out with his seabag and an honorable discharge. Amsterdam Avenue is a queer place to walk with a seabag. When a liberated gob marches along Eighty-third Street life is life is life is no longer a nightmare. Mamadear says: I knew you'd never have to go across after I visited you last summer in Cambridge. Nornie says: You've been gone a long time and everything's different: we eat toast instead of rolls in the morning my back hasn't gotten any better do you still wear your heavy woolen sox? Mamadear says there's been a letter here from Annabel I didn't forward. Annabel was married a fortnight ago and lives in Pittsburgh with Fred who believes in the 'Saturday Evening Post,' flaked breakfast foods and oral antiseptics. Everything is different; and we eat toast instead of rolls in the morning.

PART THREE

39

Bernard is a radio operator: if the worst comes he can try a turn at sea. Bernard can pound a typewriter fast and if the very worst comes he might become a male secretary. Bernard writes better than college graduates usually write at first: but when Bernard asks for books to review at the office of 'Chronos' he feels like a thief and a perjurer when he walks away with four of them. Reviewing books is the summit of Bernard's dreams. With the love he puts into a book review he might write three sonnets or seduce a young lady. The cordiality of Richard Velvet has the hopefulness of Micawber tinctured by worldly wisdom: when Richard Velvet says Would you care for a half-time job as editor? the white fireplace capers behind a desk in time with the unexpected eructations of Bernard's heart. If Bernard knew what swooning was, Bernard would swoon.

40

To have a desk . . . to write an article . . . to offer an opinion! To pore through piles of books! to deliver more opinions! To offer the concealed cleverness of adolescence as the spontaneous breath of maturity! Pinch yourself, Bernard, is this real? Are you real? Are Velvet, Miss Herriott, Welsh, the slim impresario Harrison Martyn real? Is the Brotherhood of Man real? Is the Triumph of Labor real? Is the Russian Revolution real? Is Universal Peace real? Yes: it is all real. The peace treaty has not been signed yet: the revolution has not been choked by military oppression yet: the socialist cause has not died of infantile paralysis and hardening of the arteries yet: you are in the Reconstruction Period, Bernard. You are undertaking the Reconstruction of the Social Order. You know a great deal about it, Bernard: you have been thinking about it for at least five years: every day you are learning more. The ashen Veblen dreams of a heaven fabricated by logical engineers: the blobby Slosson dreams of a heaven concocted by poison gases beneficently used: Miss Herriott has not so much faith in engineers or chemistry as in Shop Committees and the creative impulse: Sam McGinnis, the dour young Irishman, thinks to reach Heaven, like China, by boring through the A. F. of L. There are twenty different kinds of heaven being offered in the streets in 1919, Bernard. Each heaven is a clear, chemically pure distillation of a sample from the present hell.

41

Beer provides good amber tickles in a clean dark saloon. Velvet and Welsh discuss ladies and Dostoevsky and what Copey said to the graduating class after Lowell had abolished Eliot's fraternal keg and substituted the iniquity of compulsory Freshman dorms. The lean curves of Welsh's face are the edges of a thought that evades platitude: the slight failure of focus in Velvet's green eye is the distraction of dance-music among old men in a smoking-room. When Welsh talks about women Bernard realizes he is a very virgin: when Welsh talks about women Bernard affects the boredom of satiety. At twenty-three young men should not be virgins.

42

In November, 1919, Bernard's world goes to sudden smithereens. 'Chronos,' Reconstruction, Revolution, Socialism falter into rheumatic palpitations: youth becomes grizzled: illuminated hopes burst into bitter drops of soapy water: White Guards beat Red Guards: poverty beats revolution: safety beats adventure: doubt beats certainty: the almost goes along with the never-was: and the program of the British Labor Party no longer rises as the sound of birds in a still forest. 'Chronos' slides into oblivion, and into the same but different oblivion slides Bernard.

43

Above Bernard's oblivion something shimmers and shivers as the sun shimmers through green crystal water to a rising diver: something is Eunice: Eunice is everything: Eunice is the perfection of an April day before the edge of winter has gone: hyacinth and daffodil: the shock of lavender and sunny gold: white trickle of anemone through dead leaves:

the tinge of scarlet on the beech-boughs: a spring of many clustered possibilities is Eunice: she paints pictures: she is a girl: and the kisses of men have left her as untouched as the spring sun leaves the cold flanks of the April hills: the snow of inner chastity remains through many outer meltings. She is a tease to Bernard: she meets his earnestness with indifference and his passion with disdain. When 'Chronos' crumbles, Eunice alone is left, a phantom for a ruin, a jackalantern toward which Bernard stumbles, just to find a hot breath whispering in his ear. Eunice fills Bernard's days: she makes wan and desperate the long hours of the night: but Bernard gets no nearer to the heart of Eunice than a mote gets to the eye: lodging there, he has a place of irritation: claiming place he spoils the trifling gallantries of other men but has no larger part in her himself. Bernard lives in happy torment: Bernard is a wor-shipful-wanting ecstatic coward, hanging between the desire for Eunice and the desire to remain free: the desire to avoid tragic complexes with Mamadears and the desire to mind his own affairs. When Bernard vacillates Eunice is miles away: when Bernard becomes resolute, Eunice is still miles away.

44

Letters from Hong-kong: letters come from Calcutta: they come from Jerusalem: Cairo: Marseilles: Paris: Brussells: Amsterdam: London, the New Forest: the letters are scraps of James McMaster: when Bernard reads them he partakes of the sacrament of discipleship: one of McMas-ter's ideas thrills Bernard like the touch of Eunice's arm: an invitation to collaborate on a book with McMaster causes shivers of frightened delight to run up and down Bernard's spine: to be a spoke in McMas-ter's wheel would be a short way of traveling far. Jerusalem and Hong-kong and the Sea of Japan are but suburban boroughs in James McMaster's realm: letters are dated there but the thoughts they bear edge slantwise toward infinity: a counter-love to Eunice plays in Ber-nard: if she is a warm sun, McMaster is the whole vault of sky: letters come from Aberdeen: letters come from Bergen: a letter from Pimlico invites Bernard to become a fellow in Comte House: a letter from Pimlico is a very hard letter to resist.

45

When Bernard and Eunice trudge through a soft mist of snow on Park Avenue, he tells her: I am going to London for a year. If I were not going away so long—the snowmist becomes a fuzzy carpet—the flakes cling to red wisps of Eunice's hair, unmelted, and flicker on her lashes—if I were not going to be away so long, says Bernard . . . If and if and if, mocks Eunice. If time in buckets, and gallons and gallons of ocean were not to part us, says Bernard firmly, I'd say I love you. That is very sweet says Eunice: did it take a visit to the passport office to find this out? I love you, says Bernard stubbornly: if you will marry me I'll not go off to join McMaster. If I loved you, says Eunice, I'd have to bid you go *because* I loved you: it makes no difference: I bid you go because I don't. Don't shake me so: I am not mocking now: I don't love you, but gee oh gee: I wish I did. I'll paint your picture and keep it near to me: if I say yes to it, there's hope for you. There's something deep between us: I don't think we're going to part: but Bernard, you are very young, and I am twice as old as you already: so hurry up. My wild oats are nearly ready to be gathered: but yours are scarcely planted yet. Let's sow and reap together, cries Bernard. That's marriage, says Eunice: but marriage needs more love than I can muster for anyone: so let's be friends. I am not the girl you dream about: one never is: and you are what I want a friend to be, but nothing more. That night Bernard kisses Eunice: his warmth is far too courteous: it jeers at his illusion. The Sunday before Bernard sails is icy blank with jealous despair. Eunice's kisses have a mocking reserve, and Bernard's passion is too dispersed and fretful to convince anyone, even a virgin of eighteen. Virgins of eighteen know what love is without previous demonstration.

46

A hundred pounds a year in London is better than nothing at all a year in New York. Butter and sugar require ration cards in 1920 but Pimlico recovers from the effects of invalid soldiers by the application of paint to the gentlemanly grayness of houses that might have been friends with Colonel Newcome. Sociology was made by Comte the mistress of the sciences: but the concubines of science refuse to recognize the first wife of the Prophet. Comte House in Pimlico preaches the mistress-ship of sociology to spinsters who are looking for something useful to do as well as to the passionate souls who have watched the dawn of James McMaster's thought upon a gray world solemn with wheels, six per cent, and tick-tock.

47

Alighting from a donkey cart by a brick farmhouse whose thatched roof brightens to the gorse-gold moor at the edge of the New Forest Bernard beholds the man he has begun to call his master. Age has achieved the victory of a red beard beneath a spreading crown of silver hair. Gray eyes leap to Bernard with a friendly kiss: a knotted hand that seems a tough old root holds Bernard's hand and claps him on the shoulder: and through the beard a trickle of impatient questions runs off without an answer. The cuckoo calls across the moor. Bernard puts down his handbag. So this is he!

126

48

We do not dress for dinner says McMaster: but note the gorse Linnaeus worshiped when first he trod upon these shores: ticker fools with country estates hoard their gold in banks and turn their backs to the gorse; of course you ride? New Forest ponies are perhaps too small for your six feet: my five-foot-six still finds them helpful: do you want to wash? or shall we climb that little rise and look the country over: don't bother about toilets: cockneys pollute the rivers and deplete the land in the interest of sanitation while China keeps her civilization and her health by watching her stools: I hope you got your sea-legs quickly? a thermometer dropped into the water as Franklin did is a good way to study oceanography: did you remember? This is the common that keeps the widow's cow and some of Hampshire's yeomen independence: black days for England when enclosures brokeup old folkways and prosperity: poor moles in London libraries now laugh at Goldsmith for picturing deserted villages they might find for themselves by leaving London for a day. You found Comte House and Mrs. Long? The place is a little bleak perhaps but tidy: a fine figure of a woman: they breed well in Inverness: but ay de mi! gray London will take away her scarlet cheeks: the clear thought of us Scots has all it can to penetrate the beer and fog that cover London from dawn to closing time: our bodies suffer: Henry the first—

49

Bernard's head bobs like a groggy bottle in a mountain torrent. The perpetual energy of McMaster's mind bulges the brain itself into a forehead that becomes him like a crown. Bernard longs for the slow digestion of solitude but is relieved to find a master looking like a master. . . . Stuffed furniture and stuffy coals hem in the night. McMaster says abruptly: What have your days been like? What have you done and seen? What have you thought? What have you got for me? What can I give you? Begin at your beginning not later than your grandfather. When Bernard puts himself and all he's been before the kindly sternness of those eyes he feels like children who in manhood still take their dolls to be the proof of their fecundity. The days have been crowded with emptiness; the days are the black embers of a letter with an irretrievable message.

50

A stew of paper! is McMaster's epithet. The brief diurnal flickers of your journalism have neither light nor heat enough to shame a candle. The worming through of books experience does not season is scarcely worth a worm's life, still less yours: the poor preservative of abstention is all that's kept your life from rotting utterly. You live like clerks and academic dunces who, wound in paper cocoons, prepare to metamorphose into dead butterflies. Soldiers, though stupid, have the discipline of drill: but you have neither discipline nor the strength that can forego it. Brace up, my lad, you're twenty-four and you have scarce as yet begun to live. Now look you here—

5 1

A panic sobs in Bernard's bosom. It is true. His days bear the imprint of tick-tock: they bear the imprint of escaping tick-tock: but little else is there. In the forest of Bernard's bewilderment McMaster spreads a map that diminishes the impenetrable confusion of the landscape: each contour is a shrunken reproduction of life's explored terrain. Life active and passive, now dominating circumstance by dreams, thoughts, and inventions, now submitting like soft wax to circumstance's mold: sea-shell and house, antheap and city, tropism and full-fledged idea march into an organic unity: nothing exists as by itself, but always reacting and being reacted upon as Life's pendulum swings from not-being into being and back again. Priapic beasts and the seven gods and goddesses of Greece reveal man's biological aspiration: at every stage the ideal is but the hidden uttermost of Life's own reality.

5 2

The natural history of life and life's environment, portrayed by Kepler, Newton, Boyle and Kelvin, by Chambers, Lyell, Darwin, Pasteur, Faraday, reveals a truncated panorama in which the foreground is forgotten—which is man. Upon the empty destiny of things man flings the challenge of himself: Pythagoras married mathematics and music to make the stars dance: Plato, Buddha, the Nine Muses and Shakespeare brought forms into existence that Nature, unfulfilled by man, did not suspect. Jesus Christ is just as real as Plato's Socrates: dead, each achieved a new life in the mind more powerful than any Alexander knew on earth. How many men have followed Christ who would not recognize divinity in flesh? By idea, image, an ideal man makes new bestiaries: he dreamed himself out of some blinder shape: his thought imposes destinies and ends upon a formless world that chases its own tail. Man is the chimera and the centaur and all the devils in hell and all the gods above!

5 3

The donkeys from whose backs young Bernard had painfully unloaded their damaged wares had made of science something hostile and averse to life; and all that smelled of life became a wanton idleness and imbecility. Truth and beauty were at war among the donkeys: dead science was the counterfeit of endless externalities which might be turned to the practical account of tick-tock: literature and art were phantom faces dancing in non-existent fires. Good-truth is gospel! Truth beautiful is life's highest symmetry! But donkeys purposely kept truth in calico and curl-papers lest she be raped by ambushed admirers, whilst esthetic donkeys emptied out beauty's brains, because sawdust had been found more satisfactory for dolls. Among the tough and tender donkeys the real and the ideal could never meet: they gave each other the cold shoulder and the cut direct: the grounds for their divorce were science's frigidity, slightly aggravated by imagination's impotence.

54

Science and art were separate loads upon the backs of donkeys: but in James McMaster's thought Life had begot them both: they were the modes in which Life's rhythm, now turning ego-ward for sustenance, now turning toward the world for mastery, achieved that harmony of acts and facts and dreams and deeds without which life does not dance or leap at all but moves in palsy or droops in a paralysis, now overwhelmed by facts it cannot master or by acts its can't direct, now breaking out in wishful dreams that come from nowhere, lead to nothing, now galloping in vain achievements like the conquests of Napoleon or the misplaced ingenuity of printing presses whose precise and utmost excellence makes yellow journals spawn more easily each hour. Euclid and Plato are not at war: the reality of conic sections or electrons cannot deny the other life-reality of Goethe, Michelangelo, or Blake. Life spans all categories in its movement and reconciles all verbal contradictions: we move in spite of Zeno! Our being is what makes the difference to an indifferent universe!

55

Living, men break through all the husks that keep them safe but undeveloped: the husk of status and profession: the husk of empty creed: the husk of brainless actions and inactive brains: the husk of fixed environments and habits: the husk of righteousness that clings to well-established evils lest it meet greater ones: the husk of comfort and security. Donkeys live on husks: they gorge themselves to sleep and balkiness. Their daily diet is a bag of husks, the husk of politics and mediocre letters, the husk of invention, business, scientific inquiry directed to the greater glory of card-indexes and tick-tock: the husk of acting, moving, thinking, planning, feeling with a minimum of discomfort and disarrangement: the husk of preparing for eventualities that never arrive and discoursing at length about unimportant contingencies so that stuffed donkeys may earn glass cases in museums. . . . *Vivendo discimus!* If appetites are ready, food will follow. To be alive means clear eyes and a good digestion: a readiness to risk one's neck or lose one's sleep: a willingness to work at anything one needs for bread or knowledge from catching fish to measuring an atom's dance: the will to be incorporated with others in a family, union, shop or city, and yet to keep one's proper self intact. A life well-keyed will find its way with equal ease about a landscape or a library. To be a man at all means sharing in the modes of life that men have found a help to sheer existence or to ecstasy.

56

These were McMaster's thoughts. They broke through many husks young Bernard had built up and labeled Education, Wisdom, Culture. They robbed his idols of their forehead's jewels: Bernard Shaw became a cockney limping on a crutch whose shape denied his limb's deformity: he proclaimed the Life-Force but forgot its main activities. Old Berkeley's ego-begotten world was the mooniness of lonely nights. Dear William James seemed but a half-philosopher whose appetite for life was what alone gave life to his philosophy. Dewey kept close to acts and facts but dared not embrace dreams and deeds, lest he be smothered: his better world was generated in an experimental vacuum. The socialists were cockneys, too, who took machines to be prime-movers, and forgot the sun, and what the sun does to the leaf, and how the leaf spreads through man's life. Science used Cartesian dialectics to despise philosophy: philosophy was cowed into forgetting it had forged the weapon for its defeat. Whitman, Emerson, Wordsworth, and Plato kept their seats in Bernard's pantheon: Tolstoi and Goethe joined them: most of the rest were called upon for kitchen duty or for music at vacant intervals. Rabelais and Dickens were the chief factotums in this refurbished household; but there were others. Bernard began to worship trees, because he found in them the vital harmony McMaster sought. If men were sycamores or beeches they'd know less movement and more growth.

57

Temples are built of solid stones: idols do not fall at once. The night McMaster talks till dawn with Bernard finds Bernard shrinking into a chaos of complicated resistances, half paralyzed by worship, weariness, and fear. He shrinks chamberwise with a trickling taper and cannot find the outer door of sleep, aghast at that great pride and energy of mind which takes life for its province and falters at nothing between the astronomy of distant stars and the aspirations of religion or the physiology of our inmost cells, but has a place for all, and an appetite to

130

master more. The furious iteration of McMaster's voice, the gray eyes that look past sorrow and love into the core of the Whirlwind, become the image of the dreadful God that Gustave Doré had set up in Bernard's skies at five or seven. Eventually Bernard sleeps. Eventually Bernard awakes. Eventually the reality of his own sapless days is mixed with the memory of a conversational dream that ended in an intangible triumph. India rubber tubs chill the spine: Americans are not used to bathing in a can of hot water.

58

In London dreams evaporate and intellectual discourse is difficult after a breakfast at nine that includes oatmeal, kippers, eggs, marmalade, and toast. Men worship Mammon: but McMaster plays with him and Moloch: thrice each month he meets with financiers who build railways in remote provinces of India in order to bring the curse of Manchester's dirt to a civilization that has long enjoyed its own ordure. On other days, McMaster plans museums and cities, plows through the muck of learned discourses to seize jettisoned diamonds, exhibits ideas like specimens in cases to the willing few who make Comte House their intellectual home, throws pearls to swine and goldpieces to beggars who achieve academic respectability and a modicum of fame out of the remains of McMaster's breakfast cogitations. Bernard does not rise at five. New Yorkers bred with perpetual janitors and steam do not like to arise in a cold room at five. Bernard's day with McMaster begins when the stuff of McMaster's thinking has already shaped itself in many folded wads of paper, each teasing symbol leading to a book perhaps that's still unwritten. Sanderson shares their quarters: a grizzled cherub whose pink skin is like his own translucent thought: whose blue eyes burst in merriment over entertaining ideas. When Bernard talks with Sanderson and McMaster all ideas are entertaining. Even Bernard learns to spend a whole day in discussion without feeling that breakfast dinner supper are more important. It is a great victory for an American to forget breakfast, lunch, and dinner—but even Sanderson and McMaster remember tea!

59

Twilight hours on the Chelsea Embankment: twilight mist: the snaily creep of smoke from distant chimneys: the words of Eunice's letters that never deepen beyond the twilight of scattered friendship into firm and starry night. Red Chelsea pensioners blotted against the green twilight of remote gardens: red Chelsea houses against the purple twilight of the afterglow. Human twilight! The white twilight of Carlyle's pain: the blue twilight of Whistler's sentimental cynicism: the dusky mottled twilight of the stones that whisper ancient titles to Henry James: the greasy twilight that swims around a Crosby Hall no nearer to Eutopia than Thomas More himself was! To strain for Eunice's words through the twilight of a summer's night: to find the words no warmer and no brighter than the evening: to drop one's hopes in the muddy slime of the receding Thames: to find no rest in the creaky twilight of a deserted house. . . .

60

Verhaeren and Van Gogh went mad in London: who would not? Miles of dull streets are miles of dull streets. Where does Whitechapel Road end and has anybody ever found Tooting or tried to walk through Clapham Junction or get a drink at the Elephant and Castle? To survive a beef stew in a yellowgreasy Lyons is to earn the Order of the Iron Stomach with bars: the sound of a coster hawking fresh filberts or white heather would make harsh the faint murmur of distant winds: but the English of Oxford is worse than the French of Stratford-atte-Bowe. Innocent foreigners have been stabbed at the heart by an icy Euooh? aimed at the indecency of their candor. But a bus-conductor may be a friend in need: a weaver from Nottingham may turn a weekend labor conference at Morley College into an assembly of dignified and helpful men. Snout, Bottom, and Starveling have more humanity than the prigs, false faces, uniforms, and worldly wisemen—and the crowd always feeds the pigeons in front of St. Paul's.

61

The red fog of a September morning by Green Park successfully counterfeits Joseph William Mallord Turner. When the barges slide past the Doulton potteries on a dank afternoon, they are better than almost anything in the Tate Galleries. Saturday night market on Churton Street has a levity that finds only feeble echoes in colossal music halls—and God never made a June day for anything but a walk up the tow path from Kew Gardens to Richmond. The shade of William Morris saunters under the willows to Richmond meditating news from nowhere: Bernard and Charlotte follow the shade, two friendly people drawn into the friendly world that Morris pictured, under willow, over stile, past a grass bank, by a lock, till Richmond Bridge and many punts and picnickers close up the vista.

62

Charlotte came from Aberdeen to help fallen women before she knew exactly what fallen women were. That was seven years before she found a post in Comte House and left a posey of tulips over the fireplace in Bernard's room when he arrived. Charlotte plumbed the depths of other people's tragedies so successfully she made them forget her own was deeper: but love, despair, suicide, jealousy had singed the hem of every garment that she wore. She had watched her youngest friends go bitterly and unconvinced to death in France: she had worked with labor men and conscientious objectors in the face of a family that took comfort in the editorial certitudes of the 'Morning Post': her sweetness tartened as one side of her clutched loyalty, the other love. . . . She says: Oh dear: I thought so! when Bernard tells her about Eunice. She says: Remember to wear your evening clothes, when he almost goes to a dinner in Notting Hill Gate without a dinner coat. She says: They have Maids of Honor tarts some people call nice at Richmond: and there is an old tree in the park that was meant to shelter lovers or conversation. We have plenty to talk about she adds firmly. Charlotte dresses with the ambiguous primness of a private secretary. Her tweeds are a little too heavy and her shirtwaists not less serviceable than ugly. Her voice is a clear Northern voice. Her face and her body are a fine landscape, shorn by a November storm: her mind is a lake in the midst of the landscape, agitated but deep. When one sees her mind gleaming through a copse of hazel eyes one finds that her face is beautiful. Like a blindman, poor young Bernard plucks at the heavy tweeds and the assertiveness of metallic dress supporters, and takes a long time to discover that her face is beautiful.

63

Charlotte gently wipes clear the foggy patches in Bernard's mind. Charlotte smiles at Bernard's rages against old England: she finds the southern English funny, too, and likes the gaunt dank air of Edinburgh, drinking terror in black closes, more than the slatternly complacence of London. A Sunday spent discussing Eunice in the greenwet silence of the Chiltern beeches almost removes the thought of Eunice from Bernard's heart. When Charlotte recites patches of Chaucer from a northern Down-top near the grassy Pilgrim's Way, Bernard swoops with her to Canterbury, quite forgetting ties of Franco-German-American ancestry. The smell of marjoram and mignonette: the blush of Charlotte's prim-dancing face: almost make England a possibility if ten years and many customs did not come between their pairing. In complementary qualities, Bernard and Charlotte are well-married: but the parish register does not recognize marriages made in Heaven unless they come down to earth. Charlotte feels too tender toward Bernard to let him come down to earth. She has an uncle who was a general in Afghanistan, and her father retired from the Hong-kong Customs Service with honors: Oxford, Cambridge, Eton, or Cheltenham are the prerequisites for marriage in her family. Charlotte has five equally maiden sisters.

64

The days are wrung by the dry torture of desire: the days crawl with the slow crawl of a thirsty man over a desert. . . . The days do not bring Eunice and the days do not bring peace. Ideas are gadflies that add to the sting of unslaked thirst. When Bernard proposes to Eunice again by letter she answers tardily that she prefers to keep her pastels fresh without such fixatives. She is a little diverted by the snorting raptures of a Spanish sculptor who has asked her to be his mistress: she disdains the fetters of such minor titles, too, but likes the bulky power that would impose them. She hopes that Bernard will remain her friend in any case: she does not love Bernard yet: his portrait made her brush go mushy: she's turned it to the wall: and she is rather overpowered by the Spanish bull.

65

Five ships go back and forth across the Atlantic before Bernard is reasonably sure that the bull has not immediately succeeded. When McMaster says: Come to Palestine to plan the New Jerusalem this fall, Bernard replies: I am going back to America: I want a terrestrial girl more than I want the City of God itself. McMaster says: Ask her to join you there! Bernard fuzzes a mournful and despairing reply. Ideas and sweethearts do not mix: marriage comes first or never. McMaster says: But girls are everywhere: so why turn back? And Bernard says: Such rootlets as Americans have they must preserve. Eunice was born in Brooklyn, I in Staten Island: we both know what a walk along the Palisades is like. Having no deeper roots, I keep those that I have: I'm going back. Sometimes I think that Eunice is only America: I need America too. Tough French and Scottish roots are French and Scotch wherever they may be: but what is an American but a hope that has not taken root? Old stocks may rove: we pioneers must settle down. If you would understand it, read 'The Ordeal of Mark Twain.' You have given me all that I can take—a thousand thoughts still wait to be digested. I'll give them a sea-change and set them out in an American garden. Bear with me! And McMaster says: Marriage sometimes wrecks philosophy: but a married philosopher thinks with a double mind: one such in Athens stirred up Plato—all hail Xantippe! My thoughts must stand the biological test: if marriage brings oblivion to philosophy the fault's not marriage's. An old angler never blames the fish. Good luck! my lad. When you come back, bring Eunice with you. Don't mind if there's a bairn or two: we'll find a bit for all. Unless young folks live dangerously they'll only have skeletons for thoughts and rabbits for progeny.

66

Up and down goes the boat: back and forth ply the waves. At Tillbury Docks McMaster tosses a cheery beard that almost rivals Charlotte's coster-handkerchief. Bernard's thoughts lurch through dim corridors. Back and forth: up and down. Nothingness is just about as good as Eunice no meat thank you but a little soup and crackers. Americans that slobber over the Statue of Liberty are capable of evading customs duties and clamoring about unnecessary public expenditures upon health and education. Seagulls swoop up and down: slowsteadily the boat glides past the lower skyline. Tugs tediously nuzzle the ship into the pier; portholes snap the dinginess of grimy docks. In the dim crowd at the end of the pier Eunice's face lifts a sudden white peony out of a garden of dusky zinnias. Eunice's kiss is pertly intimate. The first five minutes are pleasant. By the time lunch is over Bernard and Eunice have quarreled. She promised ages ago to go to the opera next night with Lopez. . . . Also—there is more than one Lopez.

67

O Life: Life: Life: why do you torture Bernard: O Love: Love: Love: why do you torture Bernard. The more the tawny heifer frolics the harder the stags and bulls follow her. Moo! Moo! Moo! moans Bernard. The heifer is skittish: the Spanish bull is persistent. Bernard's pocketbook is empty: Bernard's face cracks wry smiles. The heifer and the bull dance together: the heifer and the bull drink cocktails in ostentatious restaurants: Bernard does not know how to dance: Bernard cannot pay for cocktails. Moo! Moo! moans Bernard every time he sees the tawny heifer. Can't you say anything but Moo! asks the heifer. Spanish bulls do not say Moo. When Spanish bulls ask for something they act as if they were going to get it. O Life: Life: Life: why do you torture Bernard. Moo: Moo: Moo sounds more pathetic than passionate.

68

Dying of a broken heart has been physiologically demonstrated. A smile can alter the pressure of the blood; jealousy may upset the balance of the endocrines: but if Love could be reduced to its physical basis the mystery would merely be translated into another language. When the daffodils at last come out in Thorley's window, Bernard makes his will and commits himself to a physician and a dental surgeon. The pain inflicted in ferreting around Bernard's root canals is diverting anesthetic. By the time Eunice takes Bernard on a long weekend walk and says: Let's get married: spring is here! Bernard wonders whether he has not been a damned fool all along. What on earth made him think he wanted to get married? Eunice's huffled virginity when Bernard alludes to the antithesis of having babies makes him wonder if the prowess of Spanish bulls and the wantonness of girls have not been over-rated. Eunice warmsmiles a didn't-you-know-I-loved-you-all-the-time? Bernard whispers to Bernard Doesn't life beat hell?

69

Blow hot! blow cold! blow warm breezes of spring: blow through the leaf-dimmed windows: blow away dress, camisole and shift: blow against the dusk of reticent pink marble: the marble of firm trunk and rapid flanks. Blow orange fragrance from that Hymettus where no flower has withered, where no bee has sipped: blow twilight on the kiss whose shadow hovered hawklike over Venusberg: blow hot! blow hot! . . . Blow cold! blow cold! blow cold poison of embraces that others have taken: blow poison of often indifferent kisses: blow icebergs of aimless boredom and indifference: blow northeaster of manifold disappointments: blue-coldness of inadequacy and misapprehension: gray-coldness of recessive passion. Blow cold! blow hot! blow cold! . . . The rains scud: the sun comes out: the wind shifts again and yet again. In squall or calm or in somewhat between, Bernard and Eunice share a bed together and within a month or two accept a legal durance for their love lest reproaches and hysterics should disfigure too many family meetings. Blow tepid winds of legalized reality!

PART FOUR

70

Pygmalion worshiped Galatea but found that marble was impenetrable: eager lovers do not easily unlock secrets that tired experience may disclose at a glance. When young men are too hotly eager, girls get colds and bad tempers: when the ardor of young men is dampened by colds and bad tempers, it is hard to live happily for more than a few hours at a time. Bernard's thoughts about the future of civilization become gloomy: Eunice's portraits become caricature and her still lifes are taunting and unabashed symbols of defeated fruit: nothing is more amiss than usual with civilization or vegetables, but something is deeply amiss with Eunice and Bernard. Eunice dreams of triumphant bulls and awakes with a satisfied quiver until she sees Bernard's head lying black

136

and white-wan in the next room. Bernard also dreams of triumphant bulls and awakes with a nasty temper. The winter Bernard and Eunice spend on Washington Place is a winter of quarrels about nocturnal bulls. Daylight bulls often have a date or a family to provide for but non-existent bulls are always victorious. Eunice hates Bernard when she dreams of bulls.

7 1

The cheery urgency of McMaster's letters makes Bernard want to go into a corner and howl. Bernard and Eunice buffet themselves through a succession of impasses: when spring comes again they decide to separate from a tangled past by sharing their kindred miseries in Europe. They dream of a hilltop in France where bliss may be properly consummated under the approval of a burning sun and understanding but indifferent peasants: they dream of a winter in Prague, a spring in Florence, a summer in Budapest: Bernard dreams of an obscure village in the Tyrol beyond the reach of McMaster's letters: Eunice dreams of a gala promenade at Lido and grand balls where she may dance with many men and stray from Bernard without rousing his jealousy. They compromise with their dreams: their money will take them as far as Paris if they are careful. Bernard is still Bernard: Eunice is still Eunice. His love has frayed into a jealous exacerbation: her response is tenderly indifferent. They are bound together by a common disappointment. They are bound by the fear of acknowledging their disappointment.

7 2

Footfree in Europe, Bernard and Eunice still limp upon American soil: the common ground of their dissension. He wants a closer loyalty than she can give: she wants a firmer mastery than he has taken: she'd chuck her pictures and all her claim on other men if once he'd lose the balky tone of a defeated but jealous male. She welcomes Bertha on the steamer: Bertha's tall Northern limbs, a trunk that rises like a figurehead into defiant breasts and prowlike chin, her open, forthright ways, awaken something new in Bernard: Eunice leans in friendship toward Bertha, a firmer counterpart of Bernard, and Bernard leans toward Bertha too. Bertha and Eunice discuss the inwardness of sex and what experience is: when Bernard shyly joins them they continue: within a day both Bernard and Eunice have made her common confidante of half their bed and boudoir secrets. The trio share the railway ride to Paris, and at intervals exchange their feelings over lingual diffidence and love and unaccustomed beverages through several weeks of vague exploration in the Louvre and the Musée Rodin, not forgetting their disgust over the sick smell of candied lust that haunts the Boulevards and plies about the urinals which line the stately avenues as if the dogs of Paris were constrained by regulations to avoid all doorways.

73

In London, Bernard feels his competence more keenly: the streets nudge him with memories: he shares his friends with Eunice and Bertha and marvels both at English warmth, once friendship is established, and that iron ring of time which keeps one fettered to a skeleton whose spirit only offers calcareous satisfactions. Comte House is closed for summer holidays: the dust falls in tidy layers upon disordered papers: maps, diagrams, charts, photographs, left by McMaster before another intellectual jaunt to China. Bernard walks through it as through a cemetery, noting new graves of McMaster's progeny and the faint mounds of his own dead selves. What gaps! What gaps between a tea in Bertha's maisonette in Torrington Square and lonely suppers in a chophouse, followed by dull-tossing long libidinous nights and days of agitated thought, uneasy reckonings, muffled uncertainties!

74

Bernard is restless and Bernard is without decision: if mastering Eunice is a man's business, he is almost ready to leave it to some other man. Once Bernard wanted Eunice here in London: Eunice is here: he wants his Eunice still and has her less than ever: and this is gall that lechery can only make more bitter. He wonders, too, if Eunice is his deepest want: or is that want illusion? Then what is real? To find one's work and bend one's back to it! Men leave their women for a polar desert to cross or a look at the stars; no woman ever had a soldier, a scientist, an explorer until he was too tired to go on with his work. A man says, that is over, now for the work: a girl says: that is over, now for the baby: and if no baby comes, she fashions substitutes. Now for the work, says Bernard: but what work? Tick-tock says Piccadilly: Tick-tock says Broadway: Tick-tock says the Boulevard des Italiens: tick-tock, under the present circumstances, is the best we can offer. Bernard goes back to Eunice, vexed, fretful, sad: Eunice is not very much of a comfort: but Eunice is better than tick-tock.

75

Release from amorous nettles comes unexpectedly to Bernard: he gains in age and wisdom in a single night. In Bertha's maisonette, Eunice makes excited epigrams with her eyes for the benefit of a young Dane who haunts the company to curse profoundly the Anglicanism of the English and have a taste of freedom. Bernard, broiling beefsteak in the kitchen, faces a sudden flame of interest in Bertha's face, and throws his bosom on her, like a rug, to quench the fire, only to find it catching on himself. They clasp and kiss as lovers, they who a little while before had talked of sex and love as if life were a textbook with sub-headings for each paragraph: head to head and chest to breast their strength and weakness make a unity of equals: in an instant, Bernard is unfaithful and forgetful: never can he give again to Eunice that jealous and un-swerving love that had been his to give through all their quarrels, sorties, fears, remonstrances. A spurt of flaming fat and broiling stench is all that keeps these two from being taken in adultery, platonic but complete.

76

Beneath a fog that smothers the policeman's lamp, Bernard carries Eunice off in an embrace that makes her think the port-wine stronger than it was and Bernard much more drunk—only to find in bed compfleter mastery than he had ever made her feel before. You lovely dear: where have you learned all this?—In Bertha's arms, he grimly whispers to himself.—Stop: stop: you glorious one: go on: you leave me breath-less. Damn all the Danes and Spaniards, says Bernard: I've conquered you. And I'll be yours forever says Eunice. And now: says Bernard: and now goodbye. You cannot leave me now says Eunice. I'm yours. We shall have a thousand and one days of happiness before us and a thousand and one nights. But suppose says Bernard, stabbed by both jealousy and guilt, not all the other thousand are for me!

77

In mastery Bernard feels a shock of indifference: Bernard awakes to find himself a thousand miles apart from the Bernard who married Eunice. Balloonlike, all the cords that held him to her cut, he bounces into rarer atmospheres. He triumphs with his indifference: she is jealous of Bertha: he mystifies her with his indifference: she is irritated with her-self. When Eunice dabbles in paints he writes: when, to rouse him up once more she dabbles in love, he writes more seriously: when she challenges his indifference by assuming her own indifference he takes a boat back to America and smiles at the icy flames that follow in his wake. Eunice writes that he is totally heartless and that he has wantonly destroyed a beautiful thing. Bernard answers that he hopes her purse holds out but if it doesn't she can call on him.

78

Hopeless, Bernard feeds on hopelessness: faithless, he holds to empty faith: thoughtless, he spends his days on transient journalism—that treadmill where flayed oxen turn a wheel that grinds no grain: unsociable, he feeds upon the gregarious triviality of teas and dinners where conversation is strained through the stomach and laughter is an irritation in the throat. How clever is young Bernard: how wedded to urbane existence: how easily he bears his emptiness: how complacently he plumbs his shallows for a weekly cheque or a weekend invitation! For quite six months he hides from Eunice behind this front which is not Bernard but the shriveled ghost of Bernard, the mummied wraith of what was once a vehement young man. How do live animals accept such empty days? How do they call such costiveness of spirit animation and all that makes it possible, success?

79

The girls that Bernard meets are all that make him run away from Eunice without the charm that keeps him turning back. The girls that Bernard meets are windfalls, dropped too quickly from the tree, bruised a little, mealy from lying on the ground: easy to pick up and scarcely worth the picking, the cidery smell of fermentation attending all too dankly on their scarlet charm: bruised apples, speckled apples, wormy apples, frost-bitten apples, green apples, sour apples, stunted apples, apples all, but all a little less than apples ripened on the trees. When apples lie too freely on the ground one picks them up and takes a bite and tries another and takes another bite—and tries another. The girls that Bernard meets are windfalls. He bites them gingerly.

80

Queasy with dissatisfaction, Bernard spends a summer fortnight rambling slowly through the Hudson Highlands. Too many weekends: too many girls: too many articles: too many glib opinions: too many bad dinners: too many sallow mornings: damn: damn: trees are not empty: they grow: the sun is not empty: it warms: railroad gangs are not empty: they pry with a crowbar and hammer with a sledge: mothers are not empty: they give mammalian nourishment to the young: damn: damn: damn: drifting is empty: flirtation is empty: incoherent cleverness is empty: bottles of disastrous liquor are always empty: the things that make people find you an agreeable dinner partner, or an affable lover are the emptiest things of all—denials of the fullness that might be within were it not for the emptiness that—damn! damn! damn!— occupies one without. In the midst of Bernard's damns he remembers that the fortnight is over: he must catch the next deadline of the 'Causeur' with an editorial, and Beatrice has asked him to a party the same night.

81

He who has bedded in the grass and thrown ascetic arms around a birch tree is not prepared to face Fifth Avenue in August. Fifth Avenue in August steams like a Turkish bath in haze: the breasts and flanks of maidens under a gauzy negligence of dress assault rusticated young men like an opened seraglio: the buildings swell the mood: the narrow entrances are amorous caverns: the towers are erections: the city is tumescent in the August haze: the girls walk with dangling breasts and insolent thighs: in another hour: in another minute: in another second the brief allurements of dress will be cast off: the orgy will begin.

82

Beatrice's parties are like a thousand parties that begin with sodden men who want their soberness to cease and dead girls who want their deadness to live: five dead people, with Bernard tanned and almost quick, pour a flame or two of gin upon their tired ashes: dry under-brush of food will feed the fire: wine sputters up like dripping bacon fat: more wine makes the fire sing and mount. Let us kiss, my slut: that joke, like wormy Roquefort spreads a giggle with its smell: how many lovers have you had this week? The wine is warm: the air is warmer: the light is giddy warm: in darkness outer dresses slip from languid shoulders. That is better: let us drink again: the lamplight in the street's a summer moon: ha! ha! these little moons are hidden by the thinnest cloud. Gunpowder-black shadows on candle-white faces: the cordials sting the lips like kisses: kisses pour like cordials down to the nether parts. You love me and have loved me since the day I spent five minutes in your office? How strange, says Bernard to himself, to use that word for such a mood: yes: this is hell and all of us are damned: those lips are mine: they were not mine till she was dispossessed with liquor: with that same stint of liquor any other male would do. She sinks: she sinks upon the blackened floor: that tired amorousness is scarcely fit for love: it needs bicarbonate of soda and some peppermint. If this be called a gay and merry life, a free audacious life, let me be bound and prisoned. Good gods: she sleeps: black shadows entwine upon white carcasses that writhe in sleep and nausea. Out: out: follow the pavement cracks: turn west at Thirty-fourth Street: the bleary lights will clarify in time: walk on: hell opens for the dead: the damned are damned: the living damned are damned indeed to think such frantic corpses are alive.

83

That leprous taste within the mouth must go away. Naked, Bernard lies between white sheets and loves their whiteness: through the fumes of his disgust, clearing slowly, a polar radiance enfolds his being. This is he, who was a boy and played, who grew beyond a boy's age and wandered and was vexed: who married and fled from marriage, who found no work to do that called him forth until a drunken stupor sounded desperate revolt: this is he at last: readier to starve than write of servile nothings, readier to transmute his lust in work than spend himself half-heartedly: this is he, who finds no pleasure but in the unity of deed with purpose and of purpose with life: this is the sayer of Yes who denies the maudlin affirmations of the lamed, the weary, the diseased. The leprous taste is gone: baptized in light and water, Bernard turns to Shelley, reading 'Adonais' till the white radiance of eternity shines through the sullied darkness of the night.

84

The blankness of painless blank days, the spirit healing into unity: the furore of uneasy nights: the spirit dividing into seven devils married to incompatible desires: the ebb and flow of breakfast lunch and supper: the up and down of sunrise and sunset: uneasy dark suspensions before mirrors mirroring mirrors: the listening to sounds that echo sounds: attending to memories that remember memories. Disattached from Eunice, Bernard holds a womb where Eunice grows in him beyond indifference and the blankness of painless blank days.

85

The days pass: the days pass: the lone days pass. Eunice grows within Bernard's womb and Bernard grows within Eunice. Each wonders whom the other has taken for a lover: Eunice does not know that Bernard has taken her: Bernard does not know that Eunice has softly drawn him back into her: a part of each has sought to live on parts of other lives and finds it hard to be dismembered: the wholeness of Eunice wants the wholeness of Bernard: they want the disappointment of each other as well as the gladness of each other: they want what lover cannot give to lover if haste or parting be near. When Bernard proposes that they take steps toward a divorce, he really means: I love you still: why should we live apart? When Eunice says: Of course we must: she doesn't mean, I hope we're going to separate. She adds: But I must see you first, and Bernard steels himself against her bittersweet reproaches.

86

The gravity of Eunice has the pixie awe of a little girl who has learned a lesson: Bernard's heart beats fast and loud with love whilst his words utter remembered defiance. I do not need you now, says Bernard: I have found my work and can keep going quite a while alone. I don't need you, you silly wretch, says Eunice: I have found no work worth doing and no man worth caring for beyond a day or two: but both of us might be the better for a child, I think. You've come to motherhood? mocks Bernard. Another life to breed instead of suicide? My ego was a bad, bad eggo, says Eunice: I ought to hate you but I don't. My experience was just as empty as your ignorance: it ditched us both. You've never been a mate to me: why did you leave me once you learned the art of holding me completely? Let's not recriminate says Bernard. I'm happy in my work: but you need straightening out: a baby or divorce? Let's both forget the past, says Eunice: I want a future not bounded by your you-ness or my me-ness. My Eunice! says Bernard tenderly: you cancel out my meanness: I need you too. Don't—don't pun when you embrace me! murmurs Eunice. There are no don'ts between us, answers Bernard, only do's. Let go: let go you brute: the dress unbuttons from the shoulder: besides: perhaps you want divorce? Nonsense, says Bernard: you're mine forever. Why did you put the thought of fatherhood in me?

PART FIVE

87

Safety razors make it hard to grow beards in America: America would be a better place if there were a few bearded, savage, terrible old men. The old men Bernard loves are mostly in Europe: Bernard loves McMaster, Ellis, A. E., Geddes, and Shaw: he loves the passion of Unamuno and the sweet scorn of Tagore. The good die early in America: there are few splendid and terrible old men. The old men in America have slick faces and slack skins: their wisdom consists in saying: Boys will be boys: I am an old boy, too. Bernard likes the bitter steadfastness of Stieglitz: but he does not respect most American old men: nor does he learn much from his tired contemporaries. John Miel's quick spasms of exhausted da-da are realistic photographs of chaotic metal rubbish, little better than the revolutionary catchwords of Michael Marx, whose generosity and passion exhaust themselves in exclamations that do not lead to coherent actions. American minds are slot machines waiting for a penny to disgorge them: the mumbo-jumbo of behaviorist philosophy shows how little material is necessary for a successful textbook or an American mind. Jacques Loeb was stimulated to his researches on tropisms in the infusoria by watching an American crowd perhaps. The intellectuals are also infusorians who go in for the higher esthetics of advertising or burlesque, when they are not engaged in deeply proving that a two-penny candle from Paris boulevards is the incandescence of super-Tungsten lamps. The group that wrote 'Civilization in the United States' scratched their backs before they turned over to go to sleep. There are perhaps twenty quiet fellows in the laboratories and studies who would make one sit up and think. Twenty is generous.

88

The days are empty husks: but something grows and stirs within. When wars are brutalizing, when laws are oppressing, when civilizations are decaying, when stupid men are governing, when empty heads are thinking, when tired bodies are starving, these things are sure: the trees will grow and the grass will fill up the chinks in the pavement: the sky will redden at sunset on a clear day, and in the evening the stars will shine and the clouds will march like banners or linger like smoke: animals will be happy in the sun: hens will cluck: chicks will peep: cubs will whimper for their mothers: the rain will fall and the droplets will become runnels, the runnels brooks, the brooks rivers, and the rivers will widen to the sea. Men will dig and delve and if necessary invent fish-hooks and bows-and-arrows all over again: the juncture of a man and a maid will be fruitful: the sperm and the ovum will form a blastula: the blastula will become a gastrula: the gastrula an embryo: and the embryo will become a child. The days are empty husks. One hates brutal wars, defies stupid laws, doubts civilizations, resents puny men governing and empty hearts flourishing: but the sun and the grass and man's social ingenuity and the wisdom of having babies—these things remain. Only those who prefer cemeteries to cities and burial mounds to tilled fields may doubt them.

89

Autumn days are sadglad days: the shoots of next spring are hidden in autumn. The flowers of spring are already planted. Eunice's body is proud with the pride of a baby: Eunice's eyes sing with sadglad anticipation: Eunice's cross-tender aches are the aches of a plowed field open to the sun. Winter days are full days. Eunice's body swells with a great pride. Bernard is fretful over the virgin reluctance of pregnancy, but he realizes why men once worshiped the Virgin Mother. Bernard moans to Eunice's sadglad anticipation as the windharp to the wind. Bernard hopes it will be a girl like youngest Eunice: Bernard wants Eunice's first twenty years to leap proudly out of Eunice's body. Spring days are gladglad days. The knitting together of the life in Eunice is the knitting together of Bernard-and-Eunice's life. Bernard wants to see Eunice's baby and kiss Eunice goodbye and go wandering for a year by himself over the earth. Bernard wants to have a baby begotten by Eunice. The children of the body are the pledge of the children of the spirit. The children of the spirit are the pledge of the children of the body. June days are gladglad days. Girls meant for motherhood make easy mothers.

90

The indifference of Bernard's intellectual preoccupations quivers into sudden exaltation over the exquisite ugliness just three quarters of an hour old. Sharp agony leaves a solemn face mewed in pre-natal sleep. After the dizzy irresponsibility of gas Eunice takes everything calmly. The first week in the hospital brings strained faces to the bedside daily: after a while Eunice's breasts prevail over Little James's callous regrets at embryonic lassitude. Bernard's sense of fatherhood surprises Eunice quite as much as himself. For a fortnight he clucks old-hennishly over James's bassinette. The wrench of leaving to join McMaster in Geneva drives Bernard and Eunice into an appreciation of the inevitable dearness and reality of their love. If love be not dead, parting is perhaps the tenderest form of union.

91

In the middle of the ocean Bernard has a bottle of Pommery to celebrate his thirtieth birthday with a young lady whose intense white face wears spectral glasses. Eunice radios him electric love. When the steward brings around the broth at ten-thirty Bernard regularly starts to think about life—at thirty it is now or never! At thirty one does not take deck flirtations as seriously as the old women who pretend to be asleep. At thirty the porters at Cherbourg could throw an epileptic fit without getting a double tip. At thirty La Vie Parisienne and Le Rire have nothing new to say. At thirty you cash your cheques at a little bank and keep away from the American Express Company. At thirty you do not feel singularly flattered when young ladies lean with an expression of innocuous indifference against your shoulder. At thirty you suddenly realize that you are capable of looking after yourself where porters, hotel proprietors, and girls are concerned. At thirty it is now or never. At thirty life is harmonized or hopeless.

92

The Lake of Geneva is green like the cavern of a glacier: the plane trees are clipped umbrellas throwing orderly shadows: the white swans by the Ile de Rousseau quarrel like stage beauties over morning breakfast. Geneva has the sleepy tidiness of a man who combs his hair while yet in his pyjamas. I come to Geneva, says McMaster, to redd my plans and thoughts: a city washed and swept each morning provokes the bourgeois virtues in the mind. The very weakness of the League incites reflection: it might be pitiful, were great States not far worse, mere pusbags of irritated pride, pretense, and power, ready to burst. I keep a school upon the medieval pattern: some fifty students come from every part of Europe to dust away the cobwebs I've forgotten: I stir them up to manhood's task: they keep me from a fixed senescence, fastened to garrulity. How is the bairn and Mrs. Bernard? You took a long time man: I'm glad you're back.

93

McMaster's garden drops from an old close near Calvin's house onto the rooftops of the street below. The cobbled hill raps sharply to the feet that climb it: the sudden flame of dahlias at the end of a dank passage is the burst of a beautiful solution at the end of a day's darkness. In eager knots the students talk with Sanderson, with Mrs. Sanderson, or with McMaster, or between their british-german-franco-celtic-hindu-danish selves. The French and Germans continue a battle of incompatible ideas that fight on different planes: Urdeutschland is a cobweb left on cellared bottles put down before Hans Sachs or Martin Luther: French thought is like the Place Vendôme, so lucid and correct that it seems cruel to thoughts that never find a uniform in speech. When an American from Wesleyan College says: Where is this talk getting us? let's do something! McMaster answers: thought must lead to life without short-circuits. You strive for action first, as most Americans do, because you do not like to sweat in silence: your paradise, as Bernard says, is the tick-tock of a succession of alarm-clocks. Squat on your hams in isolation for seven days: resist all food and action: you'll learn as much about the East as seven trips to India would teach, and find perhaps where you Americans fall short: you'll learn, my lad, that two and two is four. Without the fertile abstract mode of mathematics even pawnbrokers would not have customers. Thoughts that divert from action are sometimes gay: but actions that lead away from thoughts, or pluck them still unripe, are the worst form of futility and idleness.

94

Bernard sees that these young men and girls have much to learn and much to teach: the Germans talk of Fritz von Unruh, Werfel, and a medievalism much renewed: the French of Jules Romains, Drieu la Rochelle, the Cahiers of L'Esprit—a renaissance that brings to weary staleness last year's stale prophets—Gide, Maurras, the brilliant Marcel Proust: the tired men of twenty tired years that brought and fought and lived beyond the War. The sickish cleverness of Morand is Tzara's da-da for the bourgeoisie: they have a match in England: poor T. E.

146

Hulme deceased and Aldous Huxley who mocks at all he'd like to worship and worships jeeringly all that he hates. Yes: yes: says Bernard: we in Amreica have known that mawkish liquid, too. But Eugene O'Neill begins to find himself: there's meat in Sandburg, Robinson, Brooks, Fletcher, Rosenfeld, and Frank: Kreymborg can make us dance and Frost lies like November's crystals on New England's fields. Mencken and Lewis ply their whips on Main Street: the smiles of pained self-accusation shriek to heaven. There's promise in all this. I see it better here than in America. New students and new teachers may call a tune for life, once whiskey flasks give out. When youth begins to swarm to an idea, beekeepers who want honey will find that masks are not enough to keep them off. We've energy to burn: once we can give it form, we'll make machines use handkerchiefs to blow their noses, and not speak in company until they're spoken to. We'll break the shells of cities that are rotten eggs, set free the gas, and build a hundred new ones in their place. Your German Siedlungen and prudent English efforts are just beginnings, don't you think? Our architecture will hug the land and dance with color and drink the sun again, instead of making murky setback canyons like imitations of bad cubist pictures. Electric power talks of culture, not subsistence, for the worker: I smell a hundred changes once workingmen have victory in their bones. You Danish lads can give us hints of this and that: you Germans too: if there were Russians here, we'd learn from them as well. This is not all a dream. The American you dread is just as much a dream. Radium disintegrates into lead! Once tick-tock begins to disintegrate it may become a rainbow—who can tell?

95

In the Geneva sun America is beautiful: in the Geneva sun Bernard approaches America as a confident bridegroom approaches a bride: in Geneva Bernard forgets about fundamentalism, poison gas, armored money wagons, aimless miles of aimless motor cars, the clownish religion of one hundred per centers. Geneva is a good place to think about America in. Mid the vast poplars of the Parc de Mon Repos Bernard thinks about America and Eunice: he is excited about America: he is excited about Eunice. He throws a verse for Eunice to the seagulls that hover over Lake Leman in early September: he says: Bring it back to Eunice in Brooklyn Heights: ask any seagull near the Battery where Brooklyn Heights is.

96

The irony of overshoes and peajackets in the sun, and leggins and no peajackets in the rain is the recurrent mystery of life. When Bernard has spent three months in Europe he can think of nothing but Eunice:

the mornings begin with Eunice and the nights end with Eunice. When Bernard was twenty young girls were not so reckless nor himself so confident: he thirsted for adventure: but now his desire is muted in an ironic aloofness. At twenty Bernard used to wear his knuckles down beating at formidable editorial doors: at thirty he crumples polite editorial notes with a gesture that might garrot a neck, and goes about his own business. Desire and fulfillment do not synchronize: life should stand still, or dreams should gallop! The self that finally achieves the dream is not the self that dreamed it: disillusion may be the fulfillment of an illusion—five years too late. Bernard has achieved all he ever wanted to achieve—five years too late. To flout this with a grin is thirty's last achievement.

97

When Bernard faces Charlotte in a restaurant in Greek Street, Charlotte's eyes snuggle into Bernard's broad shoulders. Three years ago I knew what hell was like, says Charlotte: I'm past that now: I'm thirty-nine. But you look strong and confident. I've danced on fiery stones and had my fill of nettles too, says Bernard: my letters about Eunice and myself did not begin to tell you half of it. The baby and my being thirty have made me feel mature: having lived through a first day in the Navy, a first year of marriage, and a first hour of childbirth, I'm fit for anything. Do I look strong? You do, says Charlotte: and you, says Bernard suddenly, are beautiful: how is it that I've never kissed you yet? At thirty happy married lads, though anchored fast, begin to realize another woman's worth. I'm glad you came and glad you're going, says Charlotte. A month of seeing you might bring an ache.

98

The shuffle of water against the side of the Aquitania, hovering at slowest speed in thickest fog, accentuates the intolerable loneliness: within a fog a man has nothing but his memories and his dreams. The distant hooting of ships is the passing of days: the jog of the propeller is the incessant reminder of action: when the gong sounds for lunch tick-tock recovers. Wrapped in a cape, a blanket, and impenetrable loneliness, Bernard hovers in the Atlantic: fog abaft and fog abeam. The slush of water slapping at the sides, the noisy gape between the gusts of sound, make Bernard lean upon the rail and strain to see the ship that faintly threatens. When fog descends, the captain shares the landsman's helplessness: the passengers and the crew grow almost chummy: the lookout and the man who shines the brightwork are no farther from land than those who pay their passage. One works or dances, dines or goes to bed: but sometimes fog creeps through the portholes of the cabins and takes the crinkle out of even wavy hair. Electric lights and stars are both bedimmed with fog: it lifts—upon blank ocean and blank sky. The ship recovers speed. Voices speak easily. Thank you! I like two lumps in tea: no cookies, but a bread-and-butter sandwich. But when the steward folds the chairs back in the night, we find the sprinkled sky is but another fog, the fog of distance and eternity. Life insurance and boat drill are the mumbled security of saying one's prayers with tick-tock. When fog drops down we see the unreality of all we hold most real: even ourselves are evanescent. But fog and loneliness are not the worst. If each man had to bear a hand there mightn't be so many idiots to go to Europe! A little honest work about the ship is good for bellyaches and Weltschmerz. Perhaps our work and days are all we shipmates have: perhaps the fog will never lift completely, nor even Aquitanias get to port. It will not matter much. To feel the smart sea spray and ride the waves a while is all a sailor needs for happiness. A minute is a sample of eternity.

—Published in The Second American Caravan. New York: 1928

Part Three

1926-1931

The Sense of Myself:
1895-1925

On the brink of describing my maturity, let me try to recall the phases of my early growth, which seem to fall roughly in five or six year periods.

Behold me as a baby, some eight and a half pounds at birth, with a sufficiency of my mother's milk to get me through my first year. The photographs show a 'long-clothes' baby, chubby and bright; and, when I am two, dressed in a piqué dress and bonnet, with gold, pink-enamelled safety pins, not the blue that should have been allotted to a boy, I might be mistaken for the girl my mother had counted on, so placid and docile. Most of my memories before five are in little fleeting patches, of rooms, like the 'music room' in West Sixty-fifth Street, between the front and the back parlor, where my mother and I slept. I recall the sense of waking up early and beginning to chant, insistently, monotonously, "I want my toast and coffee." The coffee was of course warm milk with a teaspoon or so of coffee in it.

In this same room, late one afternoon, I underwent my first great transformation: my mother came home from Altman's with a sailor suit, a brown check with a red dickey that I adored. A real boy at last—with my curls cut off, too. But I have other mainly physical memories before this: eating in a high chair in the downstairs kitchen, resisting its squeezing, sometimes the pinching of the tray top as it came down over my head. With this goes the taste of the fried lamb chop and toast that used to be a standard dinner for me: also the taste of canned corn, freshly opened, which I loved to eat raw.

Tastes and smells: the smell of onions on Nana's fingers, always a constant one, and the delicate, rather sweet smell from under my mother's arm-pits, a pleasant animal odor which in sufficient dilution I have never lost my fondness for: indeed, a touch of this wild gamey quality entered later into the best moments of spontaneous sexual intercourse, giving it a special animal intensity without the more specious perfumed antisepsis that too often sacrifices on the altar of Hygeia the prerogatives of Aphrodite. (On that subject Alfred Stieglitz and I, comparing notes, had independently come to the same conclusion!)

Here, in the Sixty-fifth Street brownstone, playing on the stairs with my cousin Edwin, whose whole family for a while boarded with us, I have my first sense of myself as attached to a name, Lewis Charles, I did not altogether like. His first names were Edwin Baron; and I remember challenging him with the assertion that *my* name was Lewis Baron: the Baron, even at three, seemed to me more appropriate. Legally and physically the argument went in his favor, for he was a year older and much stronger than I, and had the grown ups' word to back him. In my rage, I remember chanting in derision: "Ed, Ed, a Great Big Bed." To which he retorted with equal felicity, "Lew, Lew, a bottle of glue." His older sister, Tessie, once experimentally shoved a piece of raw potato up my nostril. I remember that scene because of my mother's way of taking me firmly in her arms and removing the stoppage with the aid of a hairpin. But this left no traumatic effects: indeed I had a special affection for Tessie.

All too suddenly, I am five, with my hair parted on the side, and brushed in the indescribable style of the period: somewhat sober, perhaps a bit snooty, caught in a photo at my little roll-top desk, as if interrupted while writing. Now, or just a little before this, one of my mother's boarders takes me with him to the saloon not far away run by the brother of John L. Sullivan; and I shake the hand of the great prize fighter, big and portly John L. himself. But it is not his face that I remember: rather, I recall the big pictures on the walls, showing naked men and women playfully disporting themselves with an abandon that fascinated me, though somehow I suspected that my eyes were not supposed to linger too intently on these images. These naked people, particularly these naked girls, will accompany me thenceforward, usually in daydreams just after an early waking. Sometimes a girl my own age will appear and join me in ritualistic exposures of nakedness that cause my penis to stiffen, though without any other sensation than this awkward stiffness. Not until I am thirteen does this bring a tantalizing, secret reward: at once delightful and disgusting, shy-making, guilt provoking, too private for words.

Meanwhile, I have ceased to be visited by the one dream I can truly recall from infancy, a dream that was almost a nightmare, which came recurrently and yet in its familiarity was almost welcome: the sense of existing in the midst of empty space, with infinity pressing in upon me from every direction: that unbearable pressure of emptiness was distinctly part of it. This is what psychoanalysts have called, as I remember, the oceanic dream: they find in it a direct reminiscence of the prenatal life one spent surrounded by the amniotic fluid in the womb. I shall never forget this dream: yet it is only verbally that I can recapture the sensation.

My first insensate childhood fear was the fear of death: so intense that though I enjoyed the nurserybook rhyme about Cock Robin, I insisted on skipping the page which showed Cock Robin's funeral.

That fear was accompanied by an anxiety which should have given me greater insight into my children's approach to bedtime than, in my forgetfulness as an adult, I actually showed: for until I was seven or eight, I never went to sleep without an adult lying down beside me. This was not an unusual practice then. Patrick Geddes gratefully recorded the way that his father, almost two generations before, a stern but kindly old soldier, had held his hand when he, as a child, went to sleep. Even when they did not hold my hand, I made sure of their presence by calling out good night or asking what time it was. The real horrors, the well-grounded fears, that the present generation faces were not part of our waking life: we went through no air raid or atomic disaster drills. At most, partly because of the famous disappearance of Charlie Ross, we were warned against kidnappers, mysterious beings who offered candy to little children on the street and spirited them away. But when, riding my bike on the sidewalk, I was rudely pushed aside by a grim woman, I identified her, not as a witch or a kidnapper, but as a "stepmother."

Our anxieties and fears sprang out of a deeper source in the psyche that psychoanalysis has still hardly plumbed, still less exorcized. And while our own son, from infancy, had accepted the stoic discipline of going to bed by himself, after a final story and a final pat, so that my wife and I thought he was quite immune to such fears as I had experienced, we learned from him, at sixteen, that as a child he used to hide his head under the pillow, to fend off the witches that threatened him when we left. Our daughter knew those witches, too, and made magic to ward them off.

And now I am nine or ten; rather slight in build, medium height for my age, with a wide mouth, slightly twisted for the next dozen years, probably from chewing on the side of my mouth where the teeth were less decayed: eager for games, but without any stamina: with a weak, receding chin, and a low forehead, for the frontal cranium was then far from being as rounded as it became in maturity. Never ill, yet never exuberantly healthy: with a heart so sensitive, so wildly rapid, that the visiting physician at school would soothingly reassure me, after making the usual examination with his ear directly placed against my chest. No removal of clothing, no stethoscope in 1904!

By the time I was fourteen I had shot up in height to five feet seven or so—in maturity I reached five feet ten and a half inches—and was already taller than my mother or my Uncle Charley: an ugly adolescent, with a disproportionately big nose, a scrawny neck, loose limbs, stooping shoulders, face splotched with beady acne: an altogether unattractive creature, even to myself, with hardly a redeeming feature except a sense of humor always verging on the wry and cynical. Hand-me-downs, or ill-fitting clothes bought at random by my mother (usually at Altman's!) often without my presence, did not improve my general style: so my first brown tweed suit with a Norfolk jacket, at nineteen, marked a turning point in both the inward and the outward youth.

Now it is the inward youth I would like to recapture, between fourteen and twenty, with both his night dreams and day dreams intact: that strange elusive creature should tell me more about myself than I will ever be able to tell the reader. But he is almost beyond recall: the one thing I know clearly is that daydreams swarmed through his entire waking life, displaced only by books and occasional human companionship: dreams of heroism, dreams of erotic adventure badly handicapped by sheer ignorance, dreams such as James Thurber translated for all time—and why did no one do half so well before him?—in his picture of 'The Secret Life of Walter Mitty.' Wild dreams and vague frustrations, ambitions and inhibitions: paralyzing disintegration and sedulous order. Out of all this a new creature emerges, outwardly at least: vehement, almost choking with ideas, trying on new thoughts as he might try on costumes, one day a pragmatist, next a Spinozaist, now an anarchist, now a socialist, now a Ruskinian Tory, now a Shavian, now a Platonist, now a disciple of Samuel Butler, a Whitmanite, a Geddesian, or a Tolstoian.

But the scars that accompanied this growth remain: the sense of being physically unattractive to girls, with its self-protective aloofness and simulated disdain, in order to avoid the possibility of rejection.

And now I am nineteen: still under the threat of tuberculosis, with monthly checkups by the family doctor, who happily dismisses the notion of treatment in a sanatorium. Going to Ogunquit alone for a month, I get a new sense of myself: for now I am filled out, normal in weight for my size, bronzed in the sun, almost handsome, reading Plato's 'Phaedrus' and feeling very much like an ancient pagan when I stride along the beach, just behind the skittering sandpipers, or when, in my bathing suit, I practice half mile runs and shorter sprints for the joy of it.

On those lonely morning walks I give lectures on my new found subject, geography, to imaginary classes, or I work as an assistant to my newly discovered master, Geddes, or—because nothing is impossible—I am reading Bernard Hart's 'The Psychology of Insanity,' and have become a practicing psychiatrist, giving advice to a fellow boarder, a neurotic young woman, who shows symptoms of an approaching breakdown. (I tremble guiltily in retrospect over that impudence, that rashness!). Yes: nothing is impossible. Young women—but more often, alas! older young women, five or ten years too old—smile at me and make friendly advances. Part of me—I can tell it from a sheaf of notes—still is vividly aware of his recent callow past: another part is shrewdly, intently, consistently laying out a fresh territory to explore. The sense of invalidism is beginning to lift: I have already made my departure in a one-act play, called 'The Invalids,' in which the real invalid, my other self, dares to fall in love with an enchanting nurse and propose their elopement.

Except for the fact that the scarifying mortifications of the flesh (acne) are spreading from my face to my back, this new youth has no bodily embarrassments: even his nose, though it will always be big, no longer seems preposterous; and the very set of his chin has changed: some thrust of determination has modified his lower jaw. Seemingly his metabolism is unstable: every once in a while, with too heavy a diet, his face will round out into a moon, only to return, just as swiftly, to a decent leanness. With his Byronic collar and his crew cut turning to a wavy pompadour, he looks 'poetic' in an older romantic fashion: almost to the point of casting a doubt upon his masculinity. It is this image on one old snapshot that his son, twenty years later, will turn away from in disdain, as having no relation whatever to the father he knows and acknowledges.

But these soft outlines can be deceiving: underneath, a well-articulated armature of iron has been forming. By the time he is thirty-five the effect of the iron will be visible on the outward form, too: then not merely the body but its posture will bear testimony to its achievement, in all the smiling confidence of maturity. There are only a handful of such snapshots and no formal portraits to record this transformation objectively. Agnes Tait's romantic glorification of the youthful 'poet'—with a Scots plaid over his shoulders, and his parted lips full of sensual yearning—doesn't tell even half of the story; but the complementary portrait head she did very hastily twenty years later to fill out an exhibit of her paintings, is too smoothly in the same tradition to mark the inner growth. Certainly, somewhere between 1924 and 1930 the last outward traces of larval adolescent form disappeared: a tough, firm-muscled, broad-shouldered figure took over. But maturity was still to come!   —Memorandum for 'L.M.'

Fashions Change in Utopia

1760

Utopia consists of wide lawns, flanked by clipped chestnut trees; in the distance is a temple, preferably a ruined temple; near at hand are a few cows, imported from Arcadia. The common people, except when the cows have to be attended to, are in the background, out of sight; the place is inhabited by philosophers and nymphs. The philosophers have returned to Nature: the nymphs have returned to the philosophers. The days are long and lazy; banquets spread themselves as if by magic upon the cool lawns; and when one lies back in the grass there are no pebbles to rasp the neck or spine. If the gardens of Versailles would take care of themselves, so that the gardeners wouldn't always be poking their loutish feet into the scene, or showing their noses through the bushes—yes, that would be utopia.

1790

Utopia is now a street corner where middle class people can talk to their heart's content without feeling bashful or foolish. They can ride in a coach, too, if they have the courage to kick out the owners; they can also guillotine the fine rascals of both sexes who didn't pay their bills promptly. The sun looks different if you change the name of the day; the seasons are milder if you change their names; in fact, everything is transformed if you change its name. That is the great secret of the utopia of 1789: change the name, and if you believe hard enough in the power of words, everything else will change too. Just look at the classic buildings: aren't they more noble and beautiful, now that the words Liberty, Equality, and Fraternity are written across the front? And isn't life almost too wonderful—for words?

1830

Utopia is a place where iron cows bring forth golden calves. The veterinary is called industrialism. Plenty of well filled orphanages, placed near at hand to the factories, promote efficiency; little maxims that tell the young and tender that God is Love also promote efficiency; and the essence of utopia is to build more machines so that more orphans can learn more maxims about the truths of religion and the dangers of sin. The aim of this utopia is the inculcation of evangelical protestantism and the spread of invention; they are almost the same thing. When utopia is perfected, children will be born in the factory, too, thus avoiding unnecessary transport. People live in iron houses; they go to sleep in iron beds; they even add iron to wine and beef, in order to feel happier and healthier. When embryos protest against being born into this utopia—so absent are religious sentiments in the very young—they are drawn into the world by iron forceps.

1890

Utopia has at last arrived. It includes everybody; even the capitalist is put to work as a paid servant of the state. It was all so simple. After all, utopia was almost here: didn't people have more food than ever before, more inventions, more ways of obtaining culture? To achieve utopia we needed only to switch the flow of gold from the pocket of the capitalist to the pocket of the community. The corporation has shown the way: "What's good enough for Rocky is good enough for me." Instead of a little corporation, like the Standard Oil, we'll have a big one to include everybody. The State is the Big Combine that embraces all the little combines. One day, at a regular election, held in a nice respectable way under the Constitution, we will vote the Big Combine in. It is very simple. Edward Bellamy shows how it can be done. We are just waiting for the next election.

Postscript: (Thirty years later.) We are still waiting.

1910

Utopia is the star produced by the clash of two planets called the Master Class and the Proletariat. The proletarians have been going downhill for ever so long: conditions are getting worse and worse; at last—bump!—they must reach the bottom: they will see stars then, and will know that they are in a new world. What kind of a world? Well, a new world, a nice new world. Everything is new: the telegraph is new: factories are new: electricity is new. New and good mean the same thing. Utopia is unimaginable because it is very, very new. Utopia will contain the New Man; it will also contain the New Woman; they will produce the New Marriage, which must not be confused with the old liaison; they will do the New Work, and not more than four hours of it; they will enjoy the New Art; they will learn the New History; they will understand the New Science. There will be room for everything new, except the new rich (allrightniks) and 'The New Republic.'

1918

Utopia is the World War, carried on in a big way, long after the fighting is done. Everyone is registered; everyone takes intelligence tests; everyone is trained; everyone is shown his place; everyone gets food; everyone is entitled to shelter; and young females who belong to Old Families may talk to and flirt with desirable males in uniform without being suspected of performing anything besides a patriotic duty. Everyone is better off than before; because each gives his all to the country. The workman is better off than before; he gets fifteen dollars a day instead of three; the financier is better off than before: he gets fifteen millions instead of one. At the top of society is a corps of trained intellects, consisting of college professors, ex-newspaper men, pragmatic philosophers, real estate brokers and transatlantic cardsharps who see that everything is done for the greatest good of the whole. Everyone has a stake in the country; whether it is a big stake or a little one depends upon how much you love your country, and whom you know.

1923

Utopia consists of you and me, and a bottle of bootleg whiskey still slightly flavored with the original methylate. Under the influence of the whiskey, you are finally able to forget that even I exist, and I similarly manage to forget you. We have solved our social problem by eliminating society. We can now go back and begin all over again.
—The New Republic. June 16, 1926

Random Notes And Letters

SYMBOLIC ARCHITECTURE.   What hinders the development of a symbolic architecture, which will do for our own age what Chartres did for the thirteenth century, is, primarily, the fact that we live in a spiritual chaos. There are scarcely any values that a Catholic and a Ku Kluxer and an honest atheist, a scientist and a stockbroker, a Californian and a New Yorker hold together and deeply respect. For the sake of conventional agreement we have turned toward the past, particularly during this last century, in order to conceal our own spiritual barrenness and timidity; but a formal rehash of the past, without love, faith, or understanding, has not even the virtue of self-deception. And we are not in much better shape when we take the lowest common denominator of our life today, and attempt to worship the machine. We can, in a fashion, symbolize dynamos and airplanes, by structural forms that are subtle repetitions of these contraptions, but this is a crude and insufficient source of inspiration; for genuine symbolism is the translation, not of a fact, but of an idea. Eric Mendelsohn has designed a hat factory that has the outlines of a hat, and Raymond Hood has designed a Radiator Company Building which has the suggestion of a radiator; but neither of these efforts gives a hint as to how we shall build a library, a theater, or a school.

For a while, it seems to me, our real salvation will lie in the steady pursuit of a vernacular.   —The American Mercury. June 1926

For the generation that I had the honor to grow up with, W. C. Brownell was a symbol: Irving Babbitt and Paul Elmer More were also symbols. These excellent gentlemen were effigies that we dragged mercilessly through the streets, attacked with the daggers of revolt, and on occasion made a bonfire of. There was something that represented mildew in American letters, the mildew of closed parlors with lace doilies and embroidered texts, the mildew of nice sentiments and gentlemanly blandness, and, looking around for some living figures to sum up in their person all the qualities we detested, we lighted upon the critics of an older day. If we wanted to swear hard we said "Babbitt!" "More!" "Brownell!"

There was much unkindness in this practice and little sense. In

161

ignoring the writings of these critics we missed a considerable amount of criticism which was not merely good for its day, but good for any day. When I finally came to read all these writers without rancor and without any desire to protect myself against their contamination, I discovered that Mr. More, for example, was a man of extraordinary tact and resolute good judgment in every matter that pertains to literature —a Tory in politics, he made up for his opacity and harshness in this department by quite adequate sympathy for writers like Thoreau and Whitman and Samuel Butler. Within the limitations of his social prejudices no one has, since Sainte-Beuve perhaps shown a finer capacity to get to the heart of a writer and discover what is sound and permanent in his work.   —New York Herald Tribune Books. November 27, 1927

. . . My lack of a degree has become a valuable distinction in America. The Ph.D. is such an inevitable sign of mediocrity here that when the Carnegie Foundation for the Advancement of Art wanted someone to examine and report upon the various schools of art in America they tried to get hold of me—and this in the face of the fact that with their resources they had all the academic young men in the universities at their beck and call. I was lured by the prospect of touring all over the United States; and almost accepted for that reason: but I countered with an offer to write a critical history of the development of the arts and crafts in America *when I got around to it*—and at that stage we both left it . . .   —Letter to P.G. May 22, 1926

Did I mention Whitehead's 'Science and the Modern World' to you? It's a book of first rate importance. He has an ingenious solution of the problem of mechanism versus vitalism; by showing that the categories of mechanism are useless to further modern explanations in mathematico-physics, and suggesting that even the electron is modified by the properties of its environment—so that iron in a stone is one thing, and iron in the human body is quite another, although the laboratory analysis may reveal identity—i.e. identity in the laboratory. It indicates the important modification of the old physical concepts by biology; and is quite in the line of all your own thinking—unless I misunderstood both Whitehead and yourself! Do look at it.
—Letter to P.G. September 1926

I begin my daily notes again. This week marks the first *feeling* of freedom from anxiety, although the actual condition disappeared more than a fortnight ago, when I stopped writing as visiting critic for the Herald Tribune. On Monday I met, at Kenneth MacGowan's house, Eugene

162

O'Neill. A quiet, charming man, frail, diffident, a little slangy, with deep glowing eyes. I work at my essay on the Arts, and in short snatches read Melville. Today Josephine Strongin spent the afternoon with us, more sudden, wild, and fairylike than ever. "You must tell me: how does one live? How do you live, from hour to hour and minute to minute? I think I am happy. Are you happy?" I had no answer, and I felt old, decrepit, sinister, revolting.   —R.N. December 1927

As to Happiness—I don't know whether I am happy or not; or rather, I have discovered that happiness is not the thing that interests me; since the best moments, the remembered moments, the ones one can return to and make something out of, are those that were too sharp and terrible to be embraced at the time; whereas the 'nice' moments are forgotten, and almost as meaningless, as this morning's breakfast, which was nice, too, and no doubt necessary—only it doesn't mean anything. There is one kind of happiness I do prize: but it isn't happiness, it is rather a sort of physical poise, when one's hand is steady and one's eyes bright, clear, and there is nothing but wind and sunlight inside of one; but that is a physical sort of happiness, it is that of a keen animal, and it has nothing whatever to do with one's relations with other people. When they come in, one gets, not happiness, but tension—or—snap!— no tension, and then the relation is over. Balance? Equilibrium? Yes; the balance of the dancer and the equilibrium of the spinning top, which seems motionless because it is in perfect motion, one part playing off against the other in a terrific battle of equal forces. And yet sometimes balance and equilibrium come a little too easily: the old suit fits too well. Then one must deliberately break out of the cage that one fits into so perfectly, lest it become a coffin. But I think I know the mood in which you write: in the midst of it, all tangible things seem a mirage, which one forever is reaching one's hand out to grasp—and forever failing to reach. Wait: and something else will happen, too: life will become all foreground, and you will only have to put out your hand to touch your uttermost desires—and that will be tantalizing, too; and you will long for the mirage you couldn't reach. Do you want to know what I most regret about my youth? That I didn't dream more boldly and demand of myself more impossible things; for all one does in maturity is to carve in granite or porphyry the soap bubble one blew in youth! Oh to have dreamed harder! . . .
                                        —Letter to J.S. December 5, 1927

THE RELIGION WHICH VAN GOGH could not express through his ministrations in the church comes out in his pictures. It loses its mysticism and its certitudes about the after life: "No fixed idea about God, no abstractions, always on the firm ground of life itself, and only attached to that." Vincent's religion knows suffering because he has felt it in the toil and danger of the miners; it knows sacrifice because he has shared his last crust with people who habitually live on crusts; but at the bottom of it all is a simple, generous animal faith which gives up material happiness because it knows that the happiness of the artist or the thinker begins at the point where the more obvious modes of happiness are left behind. Near to simple folk, he feels in himself, no matter how brutal or petty they are, the strength of their lives: Gauguin, who is a sophisticated cockney, goes to Martinique, or to Tahiti, to discover what Van Gogh finds in his backyard.

Before Vincent can make his feelings manifest in his pictures, he has a long apprenticeship to serve: he is almost twenty-seven before he begins definitely on his new career, and although he follows it with magnificent persistence, there are obstacles enough in his way. What eventually becomes the 'style' of Van Gogh—firm, lean brush-strokes or quill strokes that are part of the design of the picture, a solidity of form, a palpable third dimension—discloses itself at the beginning only in the clumsiness that makes him inferior to the student who can copy surfaces with greater ease. Everyone doubts him; he needs a double share of courage not to doubt himself.

. . . Now what was there remarkable in Van Gogh's life and art? What was remarkable was his capacity to absorb the most devastating experiences without losing his own vitality and faith. He achieved in sorrow and discouragement and ridicule and degradation what other men sometimes achieve out of health and fine adventure: one feels in his paintings and his letters that things went well with him, no matter how badly. This natural animal faith retreats sometimes in shipwreck and disaster, when men cling to phantoms whose existence they renounce in fair weather; but in Van Gogh it steadily gained strength. "For you, too," he writes Theo, "there will come a moment that you will know *for sure* all chance of material happiness is lost, fatally and irrevocably. I feel sure of it, but also know that at the same moment there will be a certain compensation in feeling in one's self the power to work."

Vincent van Gogh was a great lover of art: he loved Rembrandt, Corot, Ruysdael, Millet, Delacroix: but he was a poor critic of art, because he loved life more, and included in his embrace men like Luke Fildes and Frank Holl because they made up for him in human compassion what they lacked in color or design. No artist of his time was more fully absorbed in the thought of his own age: he read Dickens, Hugo, Zola, Michelet, Renan, Carlyle: and no one succeeded better than he did, I think, in escaping the limitations of his time and in reaching, in thought and art, toward a new generation which would be "able to breathe more freely." He purchased his faith, not cheaply, by day-to-day living. The miner, the peasant, the weaver, the prostitute, whose lives he shared, were all outcasts in bourgeois society; and he was an outcast, too. But Van Gogh knew what honest work was; and he lived by it; and if his pictures are still most talked about in salons and art galleries that irony is not without its parallels in history. I know scarcely a single figure since St. Francis, whose life lays such a hold on the imagination. If he lived tragically, he also lived to a purpose. The moral is incommunicable perhaps; but it lies open on every page of his letters.   —New York Herald Tribune Books. November 13, 1927

There is today one universal and accepted symbol of our period in America: the skyscraper. It came to us as a practical expedient: it has remained as a monument. When a small city wishes to show that it has an active Chamber of Commerce and a well-stocked Rotary Club it builds a skyscraper: when a university wishes to show that it stands for progress and big donations, it proposes to build a skyscraper: when a business man wants to express the pride of success or to advertise his product he builds a skyscraper: when, finally, a church wants to proclaim to the world that God and Mammon have, after all, a good deal in common, and that "the Man Nobody Knows" was really a go-getter and a super-salesman, it builds a skyscraper.

—Architecture. October 1928

. . . As for Melville, I have not yet plunged into him: I feel like a diver on the edge of a high diving platform, ready for the exhilaration, but a little afraid of it. All the people who have so far touched the 'madness' of Melville have been the feeble-mad sort themselves; whereas it takes strength to feel the strength of Melville's madness, which at bottom was not madness at all, in the medical sense, but a tragic insight into a destiny without bottom. Happiness, I think, lies on the surface: it lies in the arts, in love-making, in all the sports that take one out on the sea or up into the mountains: in being a parent or a gardener and watching things grow: in feeling confidence in one's professional technique, whether it be sweeping a street or writing a sonnet: but when one plunges under the surface all these buoyant things disappear, and the farther down one gets the more cold and dark it seems: and the more oppressive space feels. Melville could not stay on top; had he been able to do this, he would have remained, very possibly, among the Typees in the South Seas; but he could not even rest happily with his wife and children; one by one he stripped all the things that make a happy man away from him, until finally he had not even his own

165

courage in adventure to buoy him up. I don't think that his was a road to follow; but it is a road that one must be aware of and reckon with.   —Letter to J.S. January 29, 1928

NOTES ON YOUNG GEDDES.*   Our boy, Geddes, who is now three years old, as the result of his mother's tactful interpretation of his dim questions and puzzlements knows more about biology than I did at twelve: he not merely knows the sequence of seed, shoot, plant, flower or fruit, and seed, by participating in the garden; but he also has bridged the gap to mammals and knows that all animals grow from seeds, and that the mammals carry the young inside of them. This is a genuine farming district; and there is no difficulty in providing the boy with illustrations and experiments. At three years, the sexual interest is awake and active, and this seems to us a much better period to establish such knowledge and relations in a plain simple way than a later time in childhood when self-consciousness and shame make the business of asking questions and answering them much more difficult, and when one may say far too much, if one does not err on the usual side and say far too little. And emphatically, this is a matter for a mother, not for a teacher; for the time to get these matters settled is when the query is dawning, not when the school schedule allots time to it.

—Letter to V.B. August 22, 1928

. . . [Geddes] was playing he was a horse this morning, and the horse was looking after the two little baby birds (Sophie and me). I said that I had never heard of a horse taking care of birds. But he answered: "Yes: this is a horse with wings: it's Pegasus." . . . He has an enormous interest in living creatures, mice, moles, fish, insects, as well as the barnyard creatures, and will spend half an hour at a time following an ant about: in short, he has a distinct bent toward following his namesake's footsteps! . . .   —Letter to P.G. August 26, 1929

* For more copious notes see 'Green Memories,' 1947. Reprint edition, 1974.

. . . I am now reading a book that I have not read since my very early childhood—when I probably only looked at the pictures—'Robinson Crusoe,' and I am entranced with it. Its limitations are honest, the prose is supple and masculine, as supple as George Moore and as masculine as Cobbett—one can't think of anybody later than Cobbett who is really masculine; and short of being able to outpass all limitations, having honest ones is next best, and I honor Defoe for the result. He is better than Fielding: there is a touch of the judicial humorist in Fielding: the ponderous trifling with the classics and with the reader: whilst Defoe has both feet on the ground. What a paean he writes to the Middle Station in Life—such a paean that from that time on every person who has got past his abc's has attempted to achieve it, lured by that plain, manly voice, with his hoarse sigh of regret of having so long bereft himself of the comforts of that middle station, and his sly pride at achieving it by his own hands on the desert island. We doubtless have Defoe to thank for running water and postage stamps and electric washing machines, all because he praised the middle station. He is the siren voice of the modern age, leading us on, on, on. But there: I am already giving you extracts from my next book plus two—'Defoe: A Study of Eighteenth Century Saws and Twentieth-Century Practices'; or some such title. Still, I confess that I am surprised at 'Robinson Crusoe.' It is quite as good as the world has always said; and I have long since given up hoping that this would be true about anything. . . .   —Letter to B.D. July 6, 1928

. . . I read long and lazily. 'The Red and the Black' has been my most extended adventure; and to speak frankly, I don't like it. Were I a Frenchman, I daresay I might see the whole history of my country embodied in it; but I'm not, and though the story carried me along with it, I felt as though I was irresistibly being conducted along a long passage which scraped my shins and shoulders, and which bruised my spirit, without offering me a single vista—or, what is worse, a single depth. It is an arid book; and it has remained for an arid age to resurrect and to find its virtues admirable. They are admirable: but they are not sufficient. I have begun to re-read 'War and Peace,' with the sensation one gets on going to Switzerland, when one passes out of the tunnel and suddenly sees the great ice peaks hanging over one in the distance. Glad to get the smoke out of my lungs and leave the tunnel behind!   —Letter to B.D. & A.Y. July 27, 1927

TIME AND BEING.   The belief in time and movement and change is a commonplace to the time-minded man: change is the one thing he thinks is unchangeable—so complete and overpowering is the convention. But the convenience of time-keeping is greatly over-rated; and the people who practice it so faithfully that they lose the capacity for appreciating the fixed and the static and the spatially related experiences cut themselves off from a good part of reality. I can conceive of a civilization, not lower in the scale of culture than the present one, in which respect for the clock and the calendar would be far this side of complaisant idolatry. In such a society, it would be looked upon as a waste of effort to bring out newspapers and magazines on recurrent dates, whether there was anything important to put in them or not; and no one would trouble to read the latest novels, copy the latest styles, or dismiss from consideration inconvenient ideas because they happened to be 'out-of-date.' One has only to outline a time-less society to see what a fine and agreeable place it would be: one can pick out, in one's own circle of friends, a few wise, serenely disposed people who conduct their existence very much on these terms—and one knows it is neither a low ideal nor an impossible one. Thoreau escaped this convention of time; so did Blake; so in their way did Dostoevsky and Tolstoi —and is this not perhaps why their writings and the characters they created all seem 'contemporary'? Do they not live within that perpetual present in which the arts [from the paleolithic caves onward] have their being?   —The New Republic. March 7, 1928

OUR AMERICA.   Every Sunday our metropolitan newspapers assure us that our civilization is a great one. In art, or in literature, or in the industrial organization of society, we are in the midst of a renaissance. These announcements are very gratifying: but one has only to look closely at our new skyscrapers to see that at least three out of five are a disgrace to the profession of architecture; one has only to follow the season's output of books to discover that among the twenty geniuses who are hailed and hallooed about in February it is doubtful if a single name will be recalled with a shrug of respect in December; while after one has read the lyrical ballads that are written about the benefits of mass-production and the reign of prosperity, it is a little discouraging to walk half a mile from the heart of any large city and come upon a sordid environment, a physical destitution, which contrasts oddly with the happy ejaculations of the economists.

From the fact that these paeans to our civilization are repeated every week, one gathers that no one is really convinced; and one has a little reason to suspect that all our grand assertions and confidences are bottomed on a doubt. Indeed, the one heartening sign of a renaissance in America is that there is a considerable body of intelligent people who realize that a new order and being do not yet exist; or, if they do exist, are still embryonic and hidden. These people gaze upon contemporary life without any comforting illusions; and, what is more important, they are not content to be overwhelmed by it, and to drift, blindly and trustingly, in its currents. . . .

—New York Herald Tribune Books. March 1929

. . . I find that after a day's work I have no better desire than to do something frivolous; and I can understand Herbert Spencer's habit of playing pool—or was it billiards? The village library hath a room in our cottage; and it is a prize, a great prize. It contains Sherlock Holmes and George Borrow and Mr. Dooley and Ouïda and Florence Barclay and Ethel M. Dell, and best of all, it contains 'The Woman Who Did,' one of a series of books, gotten out in the year I was born—wasn't it nice to be *Fin de siècle* and to hear Tarra rarra boomdeay in one's crib, Babette?—with a frontispiece by Aubrey Beardsley. Haven't you always wanted to read 'The Woman Who Did'? I have. It is a funny and pathetic book: the author was a hack named Grant Allen; and in his dedication he confesses that this is the first book he had written for his own pleasure in twenty years. The heroine renounces the iniquitous institution of marriage; and with heroism, moral courage, and blushes that no flapper could even imagine, much less imitate, she has a baby without enchaining the only too-willing-to-be-chained father. The upshot of this great pioneer step is incredible, in the light of what has actually happened in our own generation: the girl grows up, turns against her mother for not having been respectable, and says that she will never be able to marry the man she wants until her mother is dead!!! (No asterisks on my typewriter.) And the heroine, Hermione, being no amateur in the way of martyrdom, swallows a little convenient prussic acid, in one last heroic vindication of herself. But life is more astonishing than the boldest and most progressive of books: the actual sequel today would have astonished and I have no doubt outraged Grant Allen much more than the suicide. . . .

—Letter to B.D. and A.Y. June 1928

VARIATIONS ON A PSEUDO-GEDDESIAN THEME.

I. The Testament of the Four Brothers: Adam, Francis, Benedict, and James. The last three brothers weave in and out of the narrative, like The Confidence Man in Melville's story. They are never seen together, but are always referring to the absent ones. At last it becomes plain that all four are Adam.

II. The Meeting in Switzerland. The Master has been 'dead' for five years. He has left a 'book' and a will. The book is written in a strange

169

language which each disciple interprets differently. The will turns out to be a blank, except for a provision leaving all his goods to the remaining brothers as soon as they have become reconciled. Sects multiply. The brothers never get together.

III. The Shrine and the Tomb. People gather here worshipfully, with offerings of paper flowers, day after day, year after year. But the shrine is periodically defaced and covered with mocking graffiti. At last an old beggar (Adam) becomes suspect.

IV. The Concentration Camp. Here is where the reconciliation between the four brothers finally takes place.

V. The Disciple and the Deserted Wife. The disciple worships her but dares not approach. She fears he will supplant Adam, but her desire for him overcomes her loyalty to her aging husband, and so she becomes pregnant with the baby the Master had never planted in her. In betraying his Master the disciple has added what was missing in the Master's doctrine and example.

VI. The quest of power in the Master's life has crippled him. He marries in his old age—for the first time he gives himself to love, and so for the first time discovers what has been weak in his philosophy and in his relation to his family and his disciples.   —RN. 1922–1938.

Personal Note: These contradictory fragments dating back to the early twenties have mainly, perhaps only, a biographic interest. But even before I met P.G. they show that my fantasy was playing with a theme centered around him, which I was never able to develop. My best effort at presenting him imaginatively will be found in 'The Little Testament of Bernard Martin': but from the beginning I had planned to finish this off with a complementary 'Great Testament of James McMaster.' Once, on a memorable walk in Hanover, I found myself projecting a quite different scenario, in which I would bring together the events of a single day, the changing of the seasons, the historic succession of years, and the trajectory of a full human life, from birth to death. Somewhat like Rainer Maria Rilke with his 'Duino Elegies,' I waited year after year for this theme to seize hold of me and bring all my life experience into focus. But the moment of release never came, if only because my dream needed a veritable Dante to bring it to life.   —L.M. 1974

. . . The days pass; and most of them I spend with Herman Melville. Occasionally I find some strange, oblique glimpse of you in Melville: in Pierre's sister, and in Yillah, the creature that the stranded seamen wander from island to island seeking to capture, in Mardi. Yillah is,

I think, your right name: not that I know who she is, or what she means in Melville's parable: but you are she.

—Letter to J.S. December 5, 1927

In a great degree, Herman Melville's life and work were one. A biography of Melville implies criticism; and no final criticism of his work is possible that does not bring to it an understanding of his personal development. The exotic elements in Melville's experience have usually been overstressed; the fatality and completeness of his withdrawal from the contemporary scene have been exaggerated; the incidental rocks and rapids and whirlpools have diverted the critic's attention from the flow of the stream itself. It is with Herman Melville's strength and energy on the spiritual plane that I shall chiefly deal. He lives for us not because he painted South Sea rainbows, or rectified abuses in authority in the United States Navy: he lives because he grappled with certain great dilemmas in man's spiritual life, and in seeking to answer them, sounded bottom. He left the clothed and carpeted world of convention, and faced the nakedness of life, death, energy, evil, love, eternity: he drew back the cosy hangings of Victorian parlors, and disclosed the black night outside, dimly lighted with the lights of ancient stars. Had he been a romantic, he would have lived a happy life, buttering his bread with feeble dreams, and swallowing down his regrets with consolatory port: he who wishes to escape the elemental stings of existence need only grasp the outstretched hands of his contemporaries, accept the subterfuge goals they call success in business or journalism, and shrink by means of a padded physical apparatus from the thorny reality of human experience.

But Melville was a realist, in the sense that the great religious teachers are realists. He saw that horsehair stuffing did not make the universe kinder, and that the oblivion of drink did not make the thing that was forgotten more palatable. His perplexities, his defiances, his torments, his questions, even his failures, all have a meaning for us: whether we renounce the world completely, affirm a future transcendence in heaven, or, like Walt Whitman, embrace its mingled good-and-evilness, our choice cannot be called enlightened until it has faced the gritty, unassimilable substratum Melville explored. Melville left a happy and successful career behind him, and plunged into the cold black depths of the spirit, the depths of the sunless ocean, the blackness of interstellar space; and though he proved that life could not be lived under those conditions, he brought back into the petty triumphs of the age the one element that it completely lacked: the tragic sense of life: the sense that the highest human flight is sustained over an unconquered and perhaps an unconquerable abyss.

—From 'Herman Melville.' 1929

. . . You were right in your criticism of my Melville biography: there is much of me in it, but the material itself was not created by me, and I was cut out by nature and circumstances to do something other than comment upon other men's work—however able or pertinent the commentary may be. I have always known that: but I have kept this impulse patiently in check, for I plan to do something larger, more terrible, than the ordinary novel or play, and one must use a good part of one's life in the mere absorption of nourishment before one is ready for such a task. It is in this manner that you must consider the books that I have so far written, and the one or two more I may have to write, before I am ready to kick over the traces, and gallop forth in my own right, without bit or bridle. One should write poems about love while one is young, and still learning: but one can't write epics then, for an epic demands a mastery and a control large enough to manoeuvre an army or dig the Panama Canal. Now, at last, I feel that the vital years for me are approaching: and I am ready for the plunge. In five years, ten years, we shall see the results. In the meanwhile I am happy; and happy not because things are going well with me: they never went worse than this winter: but because I can stand on top of them and bear them down, whether they go well or ill. When I was a little boy my nurse used to call me Your Royal Highness, and I am afraid that such early suggestions must have fostered my pride and made it enlarge; it took me years to lose the royal habit of expecting the world to wait upon me and attend to my wishes, and now that I have become reasonable about such things, only the lure of pride, which the Romans called—how much more adequate it sounds!— *superbia*, remains. It is not altogether a lovely quality. Dante had it to the full, and he is an odious person; but a quality that is dreadful at a dinner table may be marvellous in a work of art, and it is so in 'The Divine Comedy.' What a furious and rich work that is! I am reading it at last in an adequate translation, Melville Anderson's, and though I reject the whole conception of the universe on which it is based, the marvel is that so much remains. A man: a life: a culture: they may be a tissue of defeats and failures, but so long as they have aimed at something beyond, which is full and rich and whole, they endow us with life. . . .   —Letter to J.S. March 27, 1929

Dante as a Contemporary

Dante Alighieri seems at first blush the most distant of poets. Homer's world, with its fights, quests, brazen deities, capricious doxies and strong vain men, is so near it can easily be dished up as a popular novel. Horace makes his bow in the newspaper columns; and Hamlet in modern dress might be a young man under the care of a psychoanalyst. The things that separate us from Horace's Rome or Shakespeare's London are decorative and topographical, in great part; and with one step of the imagination we surmount them.

Dante is not so easily approached, for he belongs to a different spiritual organism, and we might visit his Florence a score of times, and saturate ourselves with the physical images of his contemporaries and their buildings, without penetrating the body of which he was so typical and potent a member. His world had a dimension which even the most orthodox can now keep before himself steadily only by a rigorous effort: it had the dimension of eternity, and its rapid, brawling, turbulent life was dwarfed by the shadow of another world. Life was, at best, a dying, and death, even for the damned, was the beginning of one's essential career.

The credulous marketwomen of Verona who believed that Dante could descend at will into hell, and pointed to his smoky complexion for proof, exhibited, but scarcely exaggerated, the closeness of the natural and the supernatural during the crowning years of medieval culture. The realm toward which Dante's vision was directed in 'The Divine Comedy' had been described with the same sort of authority that now convinces us of the existence of electrons or the efficacy of germs in producing disease; and no one suspected in his time that the body of dogma upon which it was founded could be successfully assaulted, or, what is even more serious to the orthodox, could simply be ignored. Life existed, for Dante, within a vast Necropolis: to understand the Hereafter, and to portray it, was an immediate and objective task.

When one has said this much about Dante and his times one realizes that the breach between him and the modern reader is so great that the intuition of his poetry, though always the surest approach to his mind and spirit, is not enough for real comprehension. If 'The Divine

Comedy' is to mean something more definite than music, or music accompanied by pictures, we must make ourselves contemporaries of Dante. Is the effort worth making? Assuredly; not merely because we shall enlarge our enjoyment of poetry, but even more, perhaps, so that we may understand ourselves. Foreign travel gives one a perspective upon one's home; and there is no country today whose customs and modes of thought are so strange as the Eternal Realm in which Dante lived and moved.

Fortunately for us we have a Virgil to guide us through this labyrinth, a scholarly Virgil, Karl Vossler, whose monumental study of 'The Divine Comedy' has just been translated into English. The American title of his work, 'Medieval Culture,' is an accurate one, for Dante was the creative embodiment of the entire culture that preceded him, and that culture, we now perceive, had its roots deep in the ancient world, its notion of heaven and hell being derived from the Persians, its idea of the Logos, the immanent principle of order, being Greek, while its historic acceptance of a redemptive Messiah was, of course, Jewish.

How Dante came by all the materials that enriched his mind and personality is the first or proximate object of Vossler's study; what Dante made of these things in his great poem is his final goal. His discourse sweeps, with epic reach and breadth, toward these two ends. After all the weak outlines and simplifications the last decade produced, it is a great joy to embrace a work of real scholarship which is also a living synthesis. Of very few books can one say, with even a faint touch of justice, that to read them is the better part of an education, and yet this work of Vossler's deserves such a description, if any single work deserves it. The crucial problems of philosophy, religion, ethics, politics, the outlines of ancient and medieval literature, the origins of modern language and poetry, the psychological penetration of the poet's task and character, and, finally, the explication of 'The Divine Comedy' itself are brought together in an impressive unity.

Too well do we know the kind of minute scholarship which, like the mole, turns over the ground so exhaustively and raises such a prodigious molehill that the living plants under which it has burrowed are left uprooted and lifeless; that scholarship which aridly fulfills itself in the preliminaries of investigation and never by any chance reaches or appreciates or infects anyone else with a love for the work it has chosen to expound. Mr. John Jay Chapman in his ingratiating study of Dante, has wisely railed against such tedious intrusions, saying: "The truth about religion and the fine arts can only be expressed in terms of religion and the fine arts." It is such an order of truth, no barren, extraneous erudition, that Karl Vossler displays in his 'Medieval Culture.' He comes to Dante by a hundred different paths, and each of these excursions has an independent import; but the supreme interest of all is Dante and 'The Divine Comedy,' and once he reaches the poem he casts aside the impedimenta that have been so useful on the journey.

How is one to summarize the richness of Vossler's study? It begins with a comparison of Dante and Goethe, which may well be placed alongside Mr. Santayana's perspicuous essays, and goes, with apparently effortless mastery, into all the conditions and dilemmas of medieval thought, life and ideality. There is no way to convey Vossler's achievement except to say that he makes one a citizen of Dante's world; doing this, he prepares one for that tumultuous and passionate experience of life whose molten stream, not free from the scum of personal animus, was finally poured into the rigid mold of 'The Divine Comedy.' Vossler does not arbitrarily separate 'ideas' from poetry, or 'structure' from intuition; 'The Divine Comedy' becomes, under his interpretation, a resolution of all these discrete elements, Dante's life among them, into a final whole.

One cannot, however, too often repeat that the unity which the Middle Ages boasted and which Dante supremely exemplified existed in art, and only partly in the conglomerate experience of daily life. It is in the dead Middle Ages of our ignorance or obtuseness that the Realists always triumph over the Nominalists, that the Thomists uniformly defeat the Averroists, and that orthodoxy prevails over paganism and heresy. In the actual Middle Ages, even at the peak of its unity in the thirteenth century, the clash of forces was constant and relentless, and the victory of any particular set of them was more than doubtful. Men sought for a common ground in custom, action, creed; but the facts were slippery, and the very man, Dante himself, who absorbed the most diverse elements of his culture and presented us with the completest image of his age was for his contemporaries a defeated and discredited man.

The only doctrine that remained unchallenged in those troublous times was the unconscious dogma of art. Forms changed throughout this period; but the belief in form remained. It is this belief that has been attacked in modern times, partly as a result of the necessary effort to wreck and get rid of old forms which stand in the way of new achievement, partly because the new achievements themselves are so often quantitative in nature. We have lost faith in the formal powers of the mind, not, as some suppose, because our universe is too difficult to grasp, but because we lack the inner principle of order. If the author of 'The Divine Comedy' does nothing else for us, he should restore our belief in the efficacy of the mind. For his world, a world which we now enter with such difficulty, was formed by the imagination over a period of more than two thousand years, and while mountains melted away and cities sank beneath the dust that world retained its contours and its actuality. Even today, though Dante's supernaturalism is at odds with all our fundamental concepts—its necrology being the precise opposite of our biology—his universe keeps its shape: millions of people, not themselves Roman Catholics, are nearer to Dante in habit of thought than they are to Bergson, Whitehead, Geddes, Freud, Einstein.

If Dante's world was palpably not eternal, it nevertheless had a different quality from the helpless evanescence and formlessness which is the characteristic mode of thought and life today—that harried 'journalism' which threatens us as much in the laboratory and the studio as on the streets. Until the constructions of our own minds and the works of the imagination seem as valid to us as the ideal body of his life did to Dante, we will not, one may say pretty confidently, be able to impose direction upon the mere flow of life, or order upon the chaos that surrounds us. Our form cannot, of course, be Dante's; what he stands ready to give us is his faith in its existence.

We shall not appreciate Dante's triumph if we think of his period as a fabled time of harmony and unity, established in an outward world, such a period as he himself dreamed of under the Roman imperium. Dante's wholeness was not an external thing that existed as an image exists on a wood-block before it is duplicated in a print: it was rather the outcome of a long struggle of conflicting forces and beliefs. Medieval society was constituted like a great French cathedral—load, thrust, tension, counter-thrust, living, pushing, acting forces, all pitted against each other so as to produce a stable fabric. Such equilibrium as the society had was a dynamic one; it implied constant effort.

If Dante is a classical writer, as in every sense he surely is, it is not because he begins with a heavenly harmony, but because, by dint of an imperious will and a splendid talent, he finally achieves it. Let no one be deceived by current academic fatuities as to the nature of classicism: this Dante wrote in the midst of an almost paralyzing discomposure. Politically, he was at war with the Pope and his party, and on the losing side: his domestic life was bleak and probably unhappy, married as he was to a woman who belonged to a family he hated: exiled from his native city, he wandered, full of scorn and bitterness, through the minor courts of Italy, meditating too long and too often on things which were altogether of this world, and quite beyond his personal power to rectify.

Out of this strife and personal frustration, not out of serene fulfilment, his poem arose: it was from the abyss of his soul's darkness, perhaps made more keen by remorse over past sins and mistakes, that he beheld the inner illumination of his star. But, unlike minor poets and petty romanticists, his fantasy was something more than the covert elaboration of pangs and grudges. On this point I agree with Professor Vossler and not with Mr. Chapman, for whom Dante is supremely the type of Solitary Egoist, and 'The Divine Comedy' itself a *journal in-*

time, forerunner perhaps of Amiel and Maurice de Guerin. Dante poured into his poetry all those diverse streams of thought, from Plato to the Provençal troubadours, which constituted his culture, to say nothing of the warm, homely images of landscape and daily toil which he stored up on his solitary walks and journeys. So completely did he enrich his poem with the spiritual heritage of his time and his country that his spites and vanities and weaknesses are transcended by that greater Ego which he at the same time expressed.

Such a man, such a culture, may seem to be a tissue of flaws and failures; and yet because they have aimed at something full and rich and whole, they have power to endow us with life. Dante gave his age a common territory in the imagination, the true meeting ground of all our partialities and diversities. What existed, diffused and contradictory in life, became crystallized, purified, hard as a diamond, brilliant as its reflected blues and yellows. Popular fable and scholastic metaphysics, political intelligence and ideal hope, Italian patriotism and human magnanimity, all had their place in his supernatural universe; and in that universe all the warring forces of medieval Italy responded to a common emotion.

Dante left nothing out of the picture; certainly he left out no antagonisms, lusts, heresies; but, on the contrary, he used them stone by stone in his final structure. That structure itself was defined with mathematical exactness: the stanzas of three lines, the three divisions of the Hereafter, the thirty-three cantos, and the completion of each part with the final symbol of spiritual illumination, the star. With all his architectural sense of form, however, Dante made no attempt to limit the contents of his poem or to elevate his figures into barren abstractions. As in the cathedral, the gargoyles and obscene or ludicrous images are as much a part of the whole as the saints and the angels: the mud is there as well as the eternal bath of light. That is true order, for it rejects nothing; and that is true ideality, for it transmutes everything, not by glozing dogmas, but by conveying them onto the plane of the imagination.

By examining the stuff that pours into Dante's poem, we can convince ourselves that another Divine Comedy will not be produced in our own day by those who dream tepidly of such a humanism as may be achieved, without further contact or strife or effort, in the decorous isolation of a classical college. Dante the municipal ruler, Dante the technician, familiar with the construction of public works, if not the designer of them, Dante the amateur artist and friend of Giotto, Dante the diplomat, the author of 'De Monarchià,' are as necessary to the composition of this poem as the youthful follower of Cavalcanti and Folquet of Marseilles, or the student of St. Thomas Acquinas. Before the poet can create a work which will be approved by later academic critics, he may, perhaps, have to live a life from which they would shrink, smugly horrified. It was not the studious disciple of the inner check who discovered that the perfect hell for Paolo and Francesca would be an eternity of dovelike rapture: Dante must have known what a week of such a hell was like.

Vossler puts this point with admirable clearness and finality. "But for his pride and ambition, Dante would never have plunged into politics; but for his sensuousness, he would never have found Beatrice. His love, however, molded him into a religious man, his political struggle made him a moralist. Without *luxuria* and *superbia*, no 'Divine Comedy.' It is because he is a complete man that his virtues are so indissolubly linked with his vices."

The main subject of Dante's poem, the fall and redemption of mankind, as exhibited in every phase of the human personality, from utmost baseness and animality to the illumination of beatified love, would have lost its power to hold us today had Dante merely given expression to medieval theology. It is because Dante included all the varieties of human experience, natural, cultivated, deformed, transcended, that his poem is still an enrichment of human experience. The sugared supernaturalism of a minor poem like Rossetti's 'The Blessed Damozel' is as antipathetic to Dante's imagination as the raw realism, untouched by ideal relations, of some of Zola's novels of the middle period. Indeed, that breach between the empirical and the transcendental schools which marks the literature as well as the philosophy of the nineteenth century, with a few grand, germinal exceptions, resulted in illusions far grosser and essentially far more superstitious than those Dante exhibited. Dante's Inferno, Purgatory and Paradise existed, when all is said and done, in a place that is still accessible to us: the human soul. By showing us his dilemmas and picturing to us the eternal fate of his contemporaries Dante is also, by parable and example, showing us ourselves.

No: it is not alone Dante's supernaturalism that erects a barrier and embarrasses our approach to his vision. The thing that has kept his achievement remote is that, though his world was one of strife and conflict and on the brink of dissolution, it formed and embraced a whole culture; while ours, during the last three hundred years, has been split into fragments. While the Asiatic and the European now wear the same clothes as the American and ride in the same motor cars, we have no common ground in the imagination: it is only in practical methods and in the governance of materials that we are one. If Dante put a pinnacle on medieval culture, the most that the wisest can say in our own day is that they have got down to bedrock again and are exploring our rotten foundations. Contrast 'The Divine Comedy' with our characteristic works of art! 'Ulysses' and 'The Waste Land,' for example, do not gather the living elements in our culture into new organisms: they are themselves shards in the débris of a demolished building. Our most valiant efforts to build anew—and no one doubts the *valor* of Mr. Eugene O'Neill—are little better than the attempts of mimicking children to build a new temple with chance blocks, fit only to compose dolls' houses.

The completion, the perfection, which Dante attained in 'The Divine Comedy' may lie beyond our reach; but the audacious effort itself is a challenge. The poet who would resolve our chaos will be as deliberate as Dante. He will not order experience by turning away from and renouncing it, as our academic humanists advise; but, confronting it, absorbing it, dominating it, he will convert it with implacable will into the materials of art. To achieve this, even decently to fail at this, he will have to be a poet, but such a poet that men will mistake him equally for a scientist, a technician, a philosopher, a statesman. For our age will have its own culture and unity, and even now, playing over features that are in slumber, one begins to detect the mood of its dream. In such potent embryons as 'Faust,' 'Moby-Dick,' 'Leaves of Grass,' 'War and Peace,' our own imaginative synthesis begins to take form and grow. In its naturalism it will have a place for all nature, including that which is ideal and directive; and though it will show the supernatural world of Dante in reversed image, it will be nearer to his art, I think, than it will be to the lesser poetry and philosophy of our immediate past. Dante seems distant now, not because we have left him behind, but because he strides on ahead of us. Almost all the dogmas he consciously believed in have crumbled or are crumbling, but the dogma of art remains, and it is our star.

—New York Herald Tribune Books. April 7, 1929

The Task of
Modern Biography

The writing of the old-fashioned biography was a relatively simple matter. The subject was a homogeneous unit, an individual. He had been born at a certain date, had gone through this or that experience, and on dying had left behind two invaluable things: a set of papers and letters and a well-modeled clay mask called a 'character.' To sift the papers, to put the letters in order, carefully expunging words of questionable taste or opinions which were not 'in character,' and to cast a bronze effigy from the clay mask—this was the main task of the biographer. In an excess of piety he would often gild the bronze head; but it was a rare biographer who, like Froude, questioned its correctness or sought to present an image closer to life; and his contemporaries repudiated such skepticism with horror, even when, as was the case with Carlyle, they had reason to admit its truth.

The task the modern biographer has chosen is so much more complex than that of his predecessor that one does not wonder that there are timid critics who are shocked by the dangers it presents, and who loudly proclaim that the whole duty of the biographer is to verify and set down 'the facts.' What they mean by facts are such data as the old-fashioned biographer uncritically used. But this demand is a good deal like that of the simple-minded moralist who believes that all the ethical dilemmas of life are neatly solved by obeying the injunction to be good. What *is* good? What *are* 'facts'? What relation do they bear to the life that they punctuate? By what principles are the facts themselves to be selected and ordered? The hard-boiled exponent of 'facts' offers no answer to these questions, because he is not acute enough even to ask them.

Let us first dispose of the notion that the facts of a life, the recorded sequence of events, are the sole business of the biographer. The facts of any life are the sum total of its experiences in living; they comprehend all that the subject has ever seen, felt, sensed, touched, heard, remembered, or otherwise encountered. Plainly, then, no one-to-one relation can exist between a life and even the most exhaustive biography; indeed, no one has even been able to know his own life in this fashion. It would need another super-Boswell, serving as a recorder from moment to moment, to set down this experience; and at that, a good third of it, what transpired in sleep and dreams, would be pretty well lost to the observer.

The nearest approach to this complete kind of biography has been, perhaps, the autobiographical notes of a Montaigne, a Samuel Butler, an Emerson; but even here it is the conscious, intellectual life that is chiefly portrayed. In introspection and reflection our experience is inevitably foreshortened. Did not Joyce take a whole volume to describe even a day in the lives of Stephen Daedalus and Bloom? Try as we will, we cannot grasp more than a fragment of the totality of our living, for to grasp the whole would be to live the whole over again, and that would require another lifetime. By force of circumstance, then, all biography is selective; it is based, not on all the facts, but on such facts as seem, from one standpoint or another, to be significant.

But there is another difficulty that dogs biography. Like the book of evolution as Darwin once so graphically described it, most of the pages have been lost and what remains is barely decipherable. There is no necessary connection between the important elements of a life and the records of it that have been preserved in memory, in documents, in memorials, or in living testimony. The biographer must compose his life of what he has, just as the archeologist must restore his temple or his statue with such fragments as thieving time and careless men have left him; but fate often ironically leaves him a well-preserved leg and a dismembered torso, while the head, which would supply the main clue to the body, is missing. Hence, in addition to the purposive selection exercised by the subject himself and by the biographer in making use of such materials as are left, there exists a purely external selection dominated by chance, which cuts across the evidence in an arbitrary fashion. To correct for such distortions the biographer must be an anatomist of character: he must be able to restore the missing nose in plaster, even if he does not find the original marble. It will not be the authentic organ; but it will help cement the face together. To make such restorations the biographer must be a historian as well as a student of the individual; he must know, at a given moment, in a given habitat, what would be the probable color and shape of a missing part. If he have no clues, the good biographer, when he leaves such a detail out, will at least call attention to its absence.

There is, however, a favorable side to this lack of major data that so often confronts the biographer, and this is the fact that to a sufficiently perceptive eye no datum is altogether insignificant: in understanding a civilization, a rubbish heap may disclose as many important things as a palace, and the mere débris of an individual life may take one farther into the core of it than the most outstanding events. A chance letter written to a friend on the eve of a marriage may be a more significant clue to the marriage itself than all the testimony that contemporaries who observed the marriage will bring forward. This eye for the little, this fine sense for infinitesimally small quantities, this perception of the significance of the insignificant, is one of the distinguishing marks of modern science, and the minerals and vitamins in diet have their equivalent in the writing of a modern biography. Perhaps the most expert user of such data in America is Mr. Thomas Beer: his Stephen Crane and his Mark Hanna both gain in psychological richness by reason of his uncanny perception of the value of stray bits of evidence that usually remain below the threshold of most biographers' consciousness. If in part this method is derived from science, or rather has developed parallel to science, it has been reinforced and amplified by the work of such a novelist as Mrs. Virginia Woolf. It implies a respect for events that do not stand high in the conventional scale of importance.

But in addition to the essentially fragmentary nature of the data of even the most completely documented lives, there is still another difficulty in writing a modern biography. We can no longer be content with depicting the shell of outward events, with using merely those materials which were open to everyone's inspection. There is a partly independent, partly autonomous, partly unconditioned inner life that must also be examined and revealed; and much of this inner life is as obscure to the subject himself as it is to the person who seeks to understand him. Long before Freud, an able English esthetician named Dallas, in a book called 'The Gay Science,' had called attention to the importance of what he called "the hidden soul," and before him Emerson had said, Tell me what your dreams are and I will tell you what manner of man you are. But the notion that the hidden life of the unconscious, welling up in dreams, obscure impulses, secret promptings, was coeval with the more orderly forms of waking consciousness and partly conditioned them did not make its way very speedily into biography. Novelists like Meredith boldly dealt with such phenomena long before the biographer dared to handle them.

And no wonder; it complicates the biographer's task enormously. The old-fashioned individual, that creature of reason and sobriety and deliberation, was like the Newtonian universe; the 'new' individual, on the other hand, is as difficult to conceive and to explain as is the modern universe of physics. For the sake of practical convenience, the biographer, like the working engineer, is sorely tempted to limit his investigation, so to say, to Euclidean space and Newtonian motion; but to do this he must ignore the fact that his subject now, in certain relations, behaves like a moving particle, and in certain others like a wave—now he is a rational being, and now an explanation which should assume his continued rationality will throw the entire picture into the most spotty

182

kind of confusion. The new subject of biography has both surface and depth. The biographer who is not aware of this unconscious element, who does not seek to penetrate it, or, worst of all, who deliberately ignores all the special data that it heaps up, is guilty of ignorance or childish cowardice; and when he exhibits this cowardice under the cloak of sticking closely to objective facts alone, he is adding error to his original weakness, for a dream or a fantasy is as much an objective fact as a bag of gold or a blow on the head.

The courage to resort to this inner world, and to that remoter part of it, the unconscious, in order to interpret the objective facts of a career was displayed in American biography by Mr. Van Wyck Brooks in 'The Ordeal of Mark Twain.' Brooks sought in the inhibitions, the constraints, and the terrors of Mark Twain's boyhood for a key to his later mediocrity and frustration, despite the eminent talents he obviously possessed. Brooks's analysis of Mark Twain's inner development has been challenged by Bernard de Voto, who professes to find the whole clue to Mark Twain's life in the frontier environment in which Mark Twain spent his early days: but unfortunately such a broad environmental explanation does not account for the fact that the same forces which produced the amiable Mark Twain also produced the diametrically opposite and no less typical character of Ambrose Bierce. And the point is that even if in detail Brooks's psychological analysis of Mark Twain is subject to correction, the effort itself was fruitful. It is better to make mistakes in interpreting the inner life than to make the infinitely greater mistake of ignoring its existence and its import.

If the overt and conscious life were the simple expression of the hidhen and unconscious impulses, one might, without forfeiting anything except the primitive richness of experience, accept a careful exposition of the first as a sufficient symbol of the second. But unfortunately the conscious and the unconscious are only fitfully in harmony; frequently they are in conflict and elements that are unresolved in action and expression are thrown back into the unconscious and assume disguises there, or, in the reverse direction, they escape from the dark into the light, like a prisoner from jail, by being concealed under the petticoats of an apparently naïve impulse. One cannot help seeing the excessive purity of Dickens' heroes and villains as a relief from the intolerable complexity of his own moral dilemmas, caught as he was, in his relations with his wife's sister, between his own impulses and actions and the strict Victorian code upon whose observance he had built up his vast reputation as a writer of 'Household Words.' Life, as he knew it, had no such whites, no such blacks; and his novels were emotionally adolescent because he could not, in print, face the man that he was or disclose the realities of life as he knew it. Because of the importance of the hidden life in interpreting the fullness of any character, there is a natural tendency, upon the part of those who espouse this method to use men of letters for their subjects; for, unlike the statesman or industrialist, limited by external affairs he dominates, the writer projects his subjective life in letters, poems, novels, plays, and however great or elaborate the disguise, the essential materials are there.

One of the earliest, as well as one of the most daring, of all such attempts to read from the objectified fantasy, the play, or the poem back into the life that produced it was Mr. Frank Harris' study 'The Man Shakespeare.' This biography exhibited at the same time the dangers of the method, for it can be used with impunity only when the biographer's guesses and interpretations can be backed by a body of independent data, not derived from the works of art, which can serve as a means of checking up these excursions into subjective events. The complexities are baffling; the dangers are inescapable. But it is merely a prejudice of thought to believe that clearness, accuracy, and certainty have any necessary connection with truth and reality. While the biographer must aim at all these things, he must likewise acknowledge data which introduce an obscurity, a confusion, a certain number of unresolved contradictions, into his final portrait; and a biography which loses internal unity by reason of these unassimilable facts may be in closer accord with the actualities of life than a tidy narrative cut in one piece.

There has been still another outcome, for biography, of this desire to build up a four-dimensional character, in which the hidden motives and the devious passages of the inner life will be dealt with as zealously as the more obvious events. The removal of the moral mask has become one of the main tasks of the school whose most distinguished exponent was the late Lytton Strachey. In this biography the point lies in the contrast which is deliberately created with the old-fashioned biography. Strachey took a 'noble' life like Florence Nightingale's, an 'adventurous' life like Chinese Gordon's, and sought to show the essential nature of the naïve impulses that often lay sealed in the apparently consistent and harmonious envelope of the public character.

In Strachey's original essays in biography there was obviously a certain *Schadenfreude* in poking open the stuffed reputations of the Victorian deities and in applying the tiny candle of rational analysis to their waxen nobilities. But Strachey was too good a biographer to lose sight of the realities of the life itself, and in the case of Queen Victoria it is notorious that he came to scoff and remained to pray, or, at all events, to sympathize and to understand. Strachey's many imitators, unfortunately, saw in his ironic method of examination only an instrument for increasing their own self-esteem and that of their generation. Seeking to deflate—their word was "debunk"—the extravagant reputations of the past, they often completely neglected the realities upon which they were founded. Besides, they lost an important clue. The mask itself is as important an aspect of a life as the more devious tendencies it conceals. To tear off the mask and to throw it away was a little like tearing off the face of a clock on the hypothesis that if one wanted to tell time correctly one must get nearer to the works; it abandoned the very part of the instrument that recorded the action of the works.

And again, the a priori notion that all noble attitudes were false, the notion that anger was unreal if one could explain it physiologically by the release of adrenalin, or that love was imaginary if it were also related to the functions of the hormones and the glandular system, prevented the lower type of biographer from understanding the integration of a character or the development of a harmonious life out of the original welter of animal impulses, instinctive desires, projected wishes, and purposeful abnegations and controls. So that, paradoxically, the attempt to strip off the moral mask usually led, not to a clear reading of the character, but to the building-up of a sort of negative moral mask, as artificial and arbitrary as the one that it replaced—or rather more so, because the original mask was a work of art produced by the subject himself and it bore his own veritable imprint. This misconception of the task of the modern biographer is so common today that one recent biography was characterized by a professor of literature as an "old-fashioned hero-worshiping biography" merely because the author, though he had revealed unsparingly all his subject's weaknesses, had nevertheless preserved a sentiment of respect for his character and his achievement!

The biographer's task, plainly, is neither to praise nor to blame, neither to glorify nor to deflate. His business is to approach as closely as possible the life he is describing, to take advantage of the psychological distance that time and a different frame of values give him, and thus to make explicable the inner and outer events that formed the character, shaped the destiny, and made the life significant either to his own contemporaries or to us or to that timeless society which includes past, present, and future generations. The ultimate result is necessarily selective, as even the purest mirror or the most faithful photograph is selective—if only because the size of the picture and the distance from the image places a direct physical limitation upon what can be shown. But if the biographer has worked well, the biography will be a concentrated symbol of the subject's life; and even forgotten or concealed events will be implied in those that are presented.

There is one final thread that enters into the modern biography, and this is the society and the landscape in which the subject moved; for, like all forms of life, he was in part a creature of his environment, and characteristics which might seem specific and distinctive if taken alone become generic and communal if considered in relation to a particular place or tradition. The relation of the personality to the social milieu is perhaps one of the most delicate tasks set before the modern biographer; for the temptation to explain specific traits or events by references to large general influences is as often as not a disguise for laziness or psychological incompetence, and this mars the interpretations of even such a great critic as Hippolyte Taine. Even the most solitary character, a Leopardi shut up in a castle, a Hawthorne confined to a Salem house which he leaves only at night, takes in, almost out of the atmosphere, traits, attitudes, interests, and beliefs which mark him as a product of his society and his age—and of no other. One of the soundest and most effective reconstructions of a geographical and social environment was that in Carl Sandburg's description of the Prairie Years of Lincoln: he not merely explained Lincoln but gave the quick, immediate taste of his life.

To create a real character and to portray him against a mere conventional background of painted canvas and makeshift stage props borrowed from a local costumer is to falsify every word and gesture of the character himself; for what is living but the interaction of an organism with its environment? To neglect the environment is just as bad an error as to forget the organism in which its forces are momentarily concentrated. But the term "environment" must be taken in its widest sense. It means not only the soil itself, but the people living on it; not merely teachers, family, friends, but the economic class, with its special array of traditions, hopes, and prejudices; not merely the physical scene, but the social heritage of ideas, and that more diffused subjective environment which I have elsewhere called the "idolum." So that, finally, the ontogeny of the individual's becoming crosses the phylogeny of his species; and the good biographer, who wishes to seize and penetrate a particular life must also be a historian conscious of the entire fabric in which this life, no matter how great, how original, how significant, is only a minor figure in the pattern. To achieve such complete knowledge, to arrive at such an exhaustive interpretation, is to aspire toward an unattainable goal. But the modern biography will fulfil its purpose to the extent that the biographer is aware of the depth, variety, and complexity of his task, and moves forward along the various roads I have indicated.   —The English Journal. January 1934

Abstain from literary teas, being polite to commercial intruders, permitting publicity to be thrust on one, speaking or writing about topics not vitally important. Give more time and thought to the labor movement, economics, the prevention of war, and the removal of wardom. Don't be afraid to wound the feelings of friends where truth is concerned. Damn politeness!   —RN. November 1929

Benton MacKaye told me that he had gone to church one Sunday in Shirley—"just for the hell of it." His mother, as good a rationalist as himself, once went to the same Meeting House and was thrilled by the sunlight, the choir singing, the whole esthetic impression. "You would scarcely believe it," she said, "but it was really a *religious* experience!" —RN. November 1929

Painting and music and the drama isolate and intensify experiences that occur in life fitfully, weakly, or in confusion. One looks at a landscape; the soughing of the wind through the trees, the distant murmur of water, the chirp of a cricket, the hum of an airplane overhead, share and divert—but sometimes intensify—the ecstasy of the eye. One experiences both more and less of the landscape. The full reality is neither music nor picture. The painter extracts the visual element alone: from that he takes away irrelevant details and recomposes it into a design having the maximum power as pure landscape: gone are the sounds, the human associations, the fatigue of one's muscles after the walk: here is the rarefied experience itself. One cannot recover this moment in life, though one return to the same spot a hundred times: the painter himself cannot recover it as actually experienced; but out of a hundred similar experiences, aided by the conventions of his art, he can create a symbol rich enough to recall the reality.   —RN. September 1929

. . . Every once in a while some larger idea rises before me, and I walk around it quietly and look at it and say to myself: Yes, I'll return to you in a little while, and then we shall see! Patience! I am not ready for you yet. I have done a little consecutive reading, slow, at my own pace; and that is a great pleasure. The first part of 'Swann's Way' entranced me; and I said to myself, Ah! I have kept away from Proust too long; this man reincarnates one as a Frenchman, just as Tolstoi does as a Russian, and every hour one spends with him lengthens one's life by a year. True: as long as he kept to the little provincial society of Combray. But Paris and Swann left me with a brackish taste. A marvellous picture of jealousy, and even at times of love, but tedious in the way that obsessions are tedious, and beneath it one felt the sourness and boredom of French society, despite its cultivation, refinement, finesse, intelligence; that sense of perpetual *un*youthfulness which makes one say to oneself as one walks along the Boulevard des Italiens: Thank Heaven I am an American! If I had to live here, I would become a whiff of anarchy, yes, a hurricane, and blow it all away!
—Letter to J.S. June 23, 1929

The Buried Renaissance

The period after the Civil War, roughly from 1865 to 1895, is one of the most difficult to interpret in our annals; and no one has yet, I think, done full justice to it. Mark Twain's epithet, the Gilded Age, has stuck to it, for the reason that it calls attention to its most blatant and offensive characteristics, the oil-pirating, the stock-jobbing, the grafting, the desire for foolish ostentation and display: but this is not the whole story, for the murky fabric of those days is shot with threads of gold and crimson. If Colonel Mulberry Sellers was the representative business man, Mr. Thomas Bailey Aldrich was far from being the chief poet.

Unfortunately, both Sellers and Aldrich occupied the center of the stage, and it is difficult to get away from the estimates they put upon their own work and that of their contemporaries: their successes are the very things that cause us to affix the label of sordid futility to the entire period. But if one wishes to see post-bellum America truly, one must also be aware of the forces that were working under the surface; for they carried on into new departments, into painting and architecture and engineering and science, the spirit of the Golden Day. One might indeed call this period the Buried Renaissance; for, as in Whitman's terrible objurgation, it reversed every value, giving insignificant poetasters precedence over Emerson and Melville, distributing stones instead of bread, and wrapping in a shroud the newborn offspring of the mind. Yet something positive was achieved in this topsy-turvy world, and neither the wholeness of the age that preceded it, nor the material flatulence of its own dominant interests, should prevent us from recognizing and enjoying its chief creations. If this period produced the sordid model tenements that swept over New York in the eighties, it also created the Brooklyn Bridge; if it nourished sublime charlatans like Mrs. Eddy, it likewise produced Charles Peirce; if there are, with the exception of Emily Dickinson, no poets that can be placed near the earlier galaxy, there is for the first time a considerable amount of talent in painting and architecture, and even music makes a timid début.

The mass of America was undoubtedly a sour lump of material enterprise, although even here the sordid chicane of a Vanderbilt or a Cooke was occasionally offset by the work of a man of vision, like James J. Hill. Within the lump, however, a leaven was at work: Ryder and Eakins and Homer in painting, Lewis Morgan and G. P. Marsh and

W. G. Sumner and Willard Gibbs and William James in the sciences, Roebling and Eads and Richardson and Sullivan and Root and Charles Eliot, Jr., in the arts of architecture and engineering. These men did not perhaps mold the period and give it its special tone and accent, but they did something almost as important: they kept the tradition of the spirit alive through the originality and vitality of their own isolated works. Let us forget for a while the mansard roofs, the scroll-saw villas, the cast-iron Renaissance post offices; let us put behind us the timid mysticism of Elihu Vedder, the shabby leadership of Grant, and the feeble correctness of Stedman and Aldrich; these phenomena were massive, no doubt, but here and there within the crannies of this extraordinary society there lurked a man of genius; and if we ignore this fact we have no real notion of the character and the promise of the day.

One of the difficulties that lie in the way of appreciating the Buried Renaissance is the fact that the works of art it produced are frequently inaccessible, its scholarship and science have in the natural course of things been superseded or covered over by an imposing superstructure, and the creators themselves have been moldering away these many years with no one to celebrate their careers or investigate their material remains. The fate of Charles Peirce, for example, would stand for that of most of his eminent contemporaries. He is an interesting figure in his own right; the love and chance which played such a part in his conception of the universe were likewise elements in his experience. He did not share the timid decorum of his academic friends at Cambridge; his originality was as great an affront to them as his manners; and his very solid contributions to thought were shouldered to one side as the obscure products of an eccentric. Only recently have we been promised a biography of Peirce; and, alas! that will be an 'official' one, with all the limitations the adjective implies. Peirce's great accumulation of notes will doubtless be published—belatedly; but his intimate letters are still, I understand, withheld from publication. The curious commensal relation that existed between him and William James, whereby Peirce lived off James's material bounty whilst James helped himself, quite openly and honestly, to Peirce's ideas, worked out to the advantage of James's reputation rather than Peirce's. One suspects that the place these men occupied in the appraisal of their contemporaries is just the opposite of their correct valuation: how long it has taken us to find this out!

But the most tantalizing figures in this period are those of John A. Roebling and his son, Washington, whose careers make one of the great industrial sagas of America. Their chief product, the Brooklyn Bridge, is such a powerful work of the imagination that it has not merely served as subject for innumerable painters and etchers, but has become the symbolic theme of a poet like Mr. Hart Crane, to say nothing of at least two other writers whose unfinished manuscripts deal with the same subject. What do we know of these heroic figures and the drama they took part in? Alas! we know precious little; but such fragments as are available are of a sort to stir the imagination. Born in Germany three years after Emerson, Roebling studied at the University of Berlin. In addition to pursuing architecture, bridge-construction, hydraulics, and language, he took philosophy under Hegel, who, according to later testimony, avowed that John Roebling was his favorite pupil: and unlike so many of his contemporaries, Roebling did not leave philosophy behind him when he turned to the practical life.

Coming to America in 1831, to found an agricultural settlement for immigrants in western Pennsylvania, Roebling shortly turned his technical skill to account by designing the first wire cable, as a substitute for rope in the hauling of canal boats up the incline portages in the Alleghenies; and in 1855 his first cable suspension bridge over the Niagara was opened. Roebling had meanwhile not merely founded an engineering plant and constructed bridges; he had mixed with the American scene and come under the influence of Emerson; and when he died in 1869 he left behind him a thousand pages of manuscript entitled: 'Roebling's Theory of the Universe.' What would one not give for a glimpse of that work! What would one not give, too, for a full length picture of the man himself! Inquiry has failed to disclose the philosophical treatise, or even for that matter the manuscript account of Roebling's life, left by his eldest son; and unless these things still remain in the dark corners of an attic and are supplemented with a sufficient file of family letters, the story of John and Washington Roebling will never be properly told. That is a distinct loss to our history; for it leaves things out of proportion, and permits the Carnegies and Rockefellers, who reached the crest of their achievement by masterly chicane, to give the tone to the period—a tone which is to some extent modified by the activities of a much more rounded and cultured kind of industrialist, such as the original Roeblings were.

This period, then, is a buried one, buried with a vengeance. Yet the more debris one removes, the more fascinating are the treasures, broken and incomplete though they may be, that one finds under the surface. We have found the Currier and Ives prints, a naïve art often as interesting for its remarkable draughtsmanship and design as for its historic details; but it will take a tactful hand to uncover the wealth of admirable manual skill and esthetic perception that one finds in the magazine woodcuts of the seventies and eighties. The grain elevators, which rose directly out of such bold experiments in engineering as the seventies had produced, now have their admirers; but, with our refreshened sense of form, we can also see more clearly than Richardson's contemporaries the worth of his little railway stations and his cottages in New England, to say nothing of his even completer achievements in Chicago. We can perceive the latent modern esthetic in Sullivan's Auditorium Building and Root's Monadnock Building, however far they be from our present mode of construction, and however gravely they affronted the academic practitioners of their own day; and we know that there are more buildings of the same order, buried here and there about the American landscape, which will presently be replaced by something poorer, unless our uncertain modern taste at least comes abreast of the best work of the eighties. In short, if relatively little art or thought *came through* after the Civil War, there is no doubt that much was started; and that the few things which did come through, like Ryder's paintings, are supremely important.

When one compares Aldrich's patronizing criticism of Emily Dickinson's poems with Mr. Conrad Aiken's one sees how much nearer we are to the best spirits of the Buried Renaissance than their contemporaries were; and this applies all along the line. We, too, have been burked by a war; we, too, have been inundated by a muddy overflow of 'prosperity,' and so we have perhaps a right to look upon ourselves as the special contemporaries and continuators of the more adventurous and original minds of that period. In uncovering their work, we are becoming aware of our own inevitable foundations; and, more than this, we are establishing an active connecting link with our earlier robust tradition, through Eakins and Sullivan to Whitman, through Emily Dickinson to Emerson, through Ryder and Henry James to Hawthorne and Poe. To feel this continuity is to gather new strength for our own task; for we can now see that the interpretation of American civilization solely in terms of the manufacturer, the inventor, and the business man, is merely one of the vulgar myths of the Industrial Age—what an old barber I knew used to call, not inappropriately, a mirth. Even during the lowest and most unfavorable stages of our journey, the mind has played over the material facts of existence, and worked them over into new patterns whereby the human spirit was quickened and refreshed. When one brings together all the facts of American history, something more than mere matters of fact emerges: there has been an ideal and esthetic aspect to all our efforts, which we may no longer neglect or ignore, still less shamefacedly cover up. Instead of fancying that our business men are artists and our inventors poets, as the shallow utilitarians and the disciples of Spengler attempt to interpret the American effort, we may point to the fact that the ingredients for a completely human society have always existed here, even though they may temporarily have been buried under ashes. Coketown could no more exclude Mr. Sleary's circus than America, however raw, money-bent, and crudely industrialized, could exclude the men who realized that the goal of practical efforts is not further practical efforts, but the creation of fine personalities and a humane community. If we have not yet reached that goal, we still, even in our most dejected moments, have never altogether lost sight of it.   —The New Freeman. March 15, 1930

Here and There

THE WORLD AS A WORK OF ART.   We know the world we live in only as the environment of life. That there is an external universe, independent of life and indifferent to it is an assumption of Newtonian physics which is of great practical convenience: but it is an inference, and not an immediate datum, since every such datum demands the existence of an observer; that is, life. The universe as we know it implies not merely the interlinkages of organic life and all the sustaining conditions in the physical world, such as those which Professor Lawrence Henderson brilliantly demonstrated in 'The Fitness of the Environment': it also implies the developments of human history. Our thought itself, our concepts, our grammatic structure, are the products of the multitude of human beings that came before us; and the existence of human society is a much surer fact of experience than the existence of Betelgeuse, or, for that matter, the whole physical universe —all of which is derivative and inferential, since it rests on the existence of human instruments like language, mathematics, measurements.

Instead of beginning with a portentous sterile physical universe, and finally discovering man, with all his aims and values, as a pathetic, ludicrous by-product at the end of it, we begin with the human personality itself. The abstraction of an 'independent world' from the ego itself is the result of a long difficult process which begins in the cradle; and while this abstraction is a genuine aid to growth, the present convention of regarding the human personality as merely an insignificant fragment of that world is quite as false as the infant's original hallucination of creating milk or warmth out of the void merely by crying for it. We find ourselves, at the very beginning of our adventure, in a state of complicated interdependences which unite us not merely economically and spiritually with other men and societies, but to remote parts of the world and to physical conditions which were established long before human forms appeared upon the earth. Value and significance are the marks of human society: hence our task is not merely that of maintaining or reproducing the species, but of enlarging the domain of value and significance.   —Saturday Review. May 10, 1930

THE SCIENCES AND PHILOSOPHY. During the nineteenth century a curious thing happened in the world of thought: philosophy abdicated. The dominant philosophers of the century, the Comtes, the Mills, the Spencers, took their cue from science, and avoided inquiries which were not directly comprehensible in terms of science. So far as their philosophies still have significance it is chiefly because they sought to formulate the rationale of the scientific method. Science and truth were synonymous; and because philosophy was not science it ceased, according to the prevailing conception, to be truth.

During the last generation, a great change has taken place in the realm of ideas. Partly under the influence of profound scientific minds, like Clerk Maxwell, Mach, and Poincaré, the limitations of science itself have been more clearly understood; its laws are approximations, its categories are practical conveniences, rather than insights into the ultimate nature of things: and as it becomes more rigorous in method, it is forced to exclude the complex and the anomalous. In short, the scientific picture of the world is as selective as the artist's picture; and just as the painter has to ignore in his symbol the change of colors and the movements of his forms, to say nothing of matters like odor and heat, so the scientist is compelled for his purposes to limit experience to those aspects which may be quantitatively handled and repeated. "Evidence which lies outside the method," as A. N. Whitehead points out, "simply does not count."

Instead of looking upon a rigorous scientific statement as an exhaustive account of a phenomenon, we have at last come to recognize the clipped and conventional quality of such reports. As a result of this perception philosophy, beginning particularly with Bergson and Croce, has recovered a little of its own self-respect: for its claim is to deal with the totality of human experience, including the limited part of it which comes under the province of science. This change has not merely taken place among the traditional philosophers: it has been abetted by a series of scientific thinkers, who have turned the guns of science upon their own citadel: Eddington in astro-physics, Lloyd Morgan in biology, J. S. Haldane in physiology, Whitehead in philosophy, have shown the crudeness and the metaphysical dogmatism of Newtonian science—which hitherto was another name for exact truth. 'The Sciences and Philosophy' and 'The Function of Reason' are both pertinent examples of the way in which philosophy is reclaiming the place which science so confidently pre-ëmpted on the basis of its pragmatic applications.   —The New Republic. May 7, 1930

. . . What is truly living in any period is what is capable of remaining alive; and this can be established only in relation to the ages that succeed it . . . Our freedom of choice depends upon our ability to make use of the past, and when we lose this, we become slaves of the immediate, do we not? . . .   —Undated letter to A.J. Nock, 1930

There are many ways of establishing how old a person is, and one of them is to mention the name of Randolph Bourne. I had the good fortune, a little while ago, to have tea at an Eastern girls' college [Vassar] with a group of very charming and able instructors: in the first blush of acquaintance, I took all four young women to be very nearly contemporaries. When Bourne's name happened to come up, I discovered that instead we had a cross section of American society, since the beginning of the 'Aufklärung' in 1910.

The oldest instructor had known of Bourne when she was at college; she had heard him talk; his spirit was one of the encouraging emblems of her youth, and he represented for her that mingling of passionate resolve and critical inquiry which was the very spirit of youth in America in 1914. We nodded across the teacups to each other in sudden sympathy. I had grown up in that world, too, and can still remember a night of turbid clouds and distant flares in Schenley Park, Pittsburgh, when I paced back and forth pondering Bourne's prophetic words on the War in 'The Seven Arts'—words that in two brief years were to be grimly justified by actuality. The thunder boomed that night, the rain pelted down, and the lightning struck in many unexpected places. Next morning there was an uprooted tree outside my boarding house and a sewer backed up into the street: that was somewhat prophetic, too, and may heaven forgive me for projecting this private microcosm upon the public events that followed. There were portents enough that spring to have affrighted an honest Roman; why, the northern lights even appeared for once in an age over Manhattan Island in red-white-and-blue streamers!

But I am forgetting Bourne. The next instructor, Miss W., was graduated in the class of 1918; she knew Randolph Bourne only by his books, and most of these she had read in the subsequent years. She valued him, she respected him, she knew the curiously central place he had occupied, despite his youth, in those stirrings of thought in America that had given birth to 'The Seven Arts' and 'The Dial,' and had affected personalities as various and incompatible as Mr. Van Wyck Brooks and Mr. Scofield Thayer, both of whom were his friends. But it was obvious that Miss W. had never carried Bourne next to her heart, nor having been once acquainted with his work, had she been tempted to return to it again as Miss B., the first instructor, confessed to doing. The next instructor blushed a little guiltily:

her blush made me feel aged. [I was thirty-five then!] She had only heard of Bourne, had seen the backs of his books in the library, at most had opened a page or two and read no farther. She supposed that he must be very fine, but she hadn't got around to him. He had written about politics, hadn't he? Her own field was art.

Already I saw the rime on Bourne's young grave, and with a little trepidation I turned to the beautiful girl who had remained silent. She still remained silent when I raised my eyebrows in question and then, with a little self-conscious laugh she said, "I belong to the class of 1926, and the truth is I never heard of Randolph Bourne until this very hour." These four young women, roughly four years apart in their respective graduation classes at college, had, it seemed, spanned the immediate times of Randolph Bourne's immortality: from intimate worship to final ignorance. Bourne had apparently not survived even as the symbol of a decade, and yet he was surely that, that if nothing else; and if we had an active cultural tradition in America, he would at least have this particular place for many a year to come. Indeed, his importance here would become more apparent as the interest in his actual literary work diminished, became attenuated . . .

—The New Republic. September 24, 1930

Letters to A Friend

. . . I have been reading precious little since coming up here; in fact, for the first three weeks I drugged myself with manual labor: writing was like the struggle of a young child to awaken from deep sleep; and it is only for the last couple of days that I begin to realize that, despite appearances, I still have a mind, and it can be made to function if I am firm and insistent enough about it, and remember to carry about a pencil and a pad of paper! My sole spiritual nourishment, in fact, has been a single chapter of the 'Bhagavad Gita' every night, as the sun is tinting the last clouds in the West, and the swallows are darting overhead.

How little of that Scripture remains alive! The wonder and awe at the multitudinous universe: yes: that lived there as it was not fully to live again until Newton and Darwin. Also the feeling that life matters in the process, not in the result: "Counting gain or loss as one prepare for battle!" That's fine. Finally the notion—in a sense it suggests what is best in Dewey, only he sees but half of it—the notion that action and contemplation are both means of reaching ultimately the same end, and that when the mind is enfranchised and the personality enlarged, one may do almost anything and not be soiled by the action: which is true, too, although the thieves, liars, and murderers are not habitually the persons by whom this truth is vindicated. As for the rest, a curious mixture of beauty and uncouthness—especially the retention of the notion that Krishna himself, the All, is to be worshiped, propitiated, sacrificed before. How that lower side of godliness stuck! What inordinate human vanity, to require such servilities for the gods, our images! But enough: it is a good Scripture, and what meat it has is very nourishing indeed: I put it alongside the Sermon on the Mount.

What is it to be religious? I have finally come to the conclusion that it is to have the conviction that oneself is powerless: for the belief that one is almighty is the first illusion of the infant, and its abandonment is the beginning of the tight and narrow period of maturity. Hence the association of religion with fear and dread, with disease and all manner of infirmity: these are the things that lend conviction; hence too the truth of Jung's dictum, in times of grave emergency the spirit survives only by calling on the gods. When one fails to identify the universe with oneself there is but one course left: to identify oneself with the universe. This is called resignation; and I begin to see what it means. I spent thirty happy years without religion. I am still very jealous of the gods, and lay down all sorts of conditions for them: but I hear their footsteps on the hills and see their faces mirrored in the waters! . . .

—Letter to B.D. June 28, 1930

. . . May I say, before I forget it, that I like your pieces in 'The New Yorker': they have penetration without malice; and to remember to be human after one has thrust inside one's subject is almost the art of literature, if not in fact of life. This last year, or rather these last two years, have improved my own morals in this respect enormously: I have sinned as often and as copiously as a Dostoevsky hero, and I think that at last I could get to the bottom of the most forbidding sort of character and yet fish up something which, if it would not redeem him, would bring him back within the pale of humanity: so perhaps I am at last ready to write novels and plays: and I can't pretend that I have ever been before. One can do everything with the intellect—that is what makes one so proud of it—except understand another human being. Well: here I am—and I hope I haven't piqued your womanly curiosity too much by mentioning my sins in such a lordly and offhanded way: one's worst enormities remain within, and it is only one's vulgar commonplaces of error and folly that turn into murders and suicides, treasons, infidelities, and betrayals.

Sophia is here, too, much refreshed by her trip, with a serenity that reminds me of the unawakened girl I first knew on 'The Dial': very dashing and beautiful and confident of herself, too. It was a good trip and a well-timed trip; for though almost every introduction she had missed fire, and there were all sorts of minor disappointments, she achieved all that we had both hoped out of the journey; and now, perhaps, we have broken our curious streak of misfortunes: although it is too early to whistle, and wise people don't whistle anyway. She is much pleased by what has happened to our Geddes in the meanwhile, and is generous enough to admit that I had something to do with it: although the break itself was perhaps the only thing that was necessary for both of them, after their too long companionship on beds of misery: with all the harassing and bullying that goes with illness to make it worse. I enjoyed having him by myself very much: it gave us a new sense of intimacy, and even in the worst depths of my cold our relations were quite tolerable, although not without a little Spartan self-discipline on my own part. Having him so solely dependent upon me for the time, made me curiously anxious not to die at an inconvenient moment; amusingly enough, he was a little anxious about it, too, and kept on asking me who would look after him. At present we are a happy family. . . .

—Letter to B.D. August 16, 1930

. . . Amenia is more than tolerable: the hot spells are never impossible here; whereas Charlottesville was a miasmic pool of heat, and the kitchen in the University Commons gave off the horrid odors known only to cheap London fish restaurants. But the South: my brief four days there gave me a truer picture of our country, or certain aspects of it, than I'd ever had before. The buildings of the University are marvellous: Monticello is in sight and aspect beyond one's most imperial dream, although Farrington, now a country club, has the better interior. It is all Mr. Jefferson, and Mr. Jefferson was quite as great a man as Virginia thinks he was. The Ranges, as his groups of buildings on each side of the central lawn of the University are called, form the finest piece of architecture in America: and heaven knows I have no love, ordinarily, for the taste of the eighteenth century. But he had an eye! The human scale of his arcade, his admirable monastic cells for students, his equally fine buildings which were once, under his plan, professors' residences and class rooms, are unequalled in America for plan and design. The site and the scenery constantly stirred and abetted the architect: I have not had more glorious views anywhere: and if this is my enthusiasm produced by muggy smothering July days, heaven only knows into what gibbering inexpressible ecstasy I would go if I had first seen the University and the surrounding region in October.

But the Southerners themselves are still exactly like the Old Regime in Russia as portrayed by Tolstoi and Chekhov: lazy, slow-moving, torpid, imperturbable, snobbish, interbred, tolerant of dirt, incapable of making effective plans or organization. Our handsome fraternity house had dirty beds in it, dreary walls, dilapidated furniture, an insufficient supply of pillows and towels, and bugs on the upper floor— not, happily, on mine. In spite of the preparations made for our coming, the human occupants had not been effectively moved out of our rooms: they hung on a day or two past their time, making our life uncomfortable. Six weeks in this environment would turn one, in sheer desperation, into a. Connecticut Yankee. But I learned much in those four days that neither the historian nor the sociologist could tell me, things that require the immediate presence of one's eyes and nose. I will say nothing about the hospitality: it was *komisch*; but the chief point about it was that it handsomely took down the conceit of four distinguished New York visitors, who, despite their personal modesty, had still secretly half a notion that they and New York between them

were objects of some importance in the planetary scheme. Perhaps on *their* planet, my dear Babette; but certainly not in Virginia. . . .
—Letter to B.D. July 10, 1931

. . . I have at last made a contribution to the paper where you are such a familiar star: I wrote an article for 'The New Yorker' on Radio City. Oh these good editors! I respect them so deeply and they are so bothersome! They tempt one with their high rates, and by the time one has met them, debated with them, struggled with them, and come finally to a diplomatic understanding, one has spent enough time and energy to have written half a dozen articles for less competent and therefore more easily pleased editors! It has been fun, however, to see how their minds work: they really do know their business, and that is rare enough in any line of work to be enjoyed in itself. They have even asked me to do a Profile: but I have a preference for the full face, and have said No.   —Letter to B.D. June 2, 1931

Reflections on Our Present Dilemmas

There are times when one spends perhaps a whole day, vaguely conscious that one has been through all its details before. Was it in a dream, was it in the imagination, was it in activity? I have had this feeling during the last year, and upon analyzing it I find it has to do with a series of decisions and purposes that came more or less to a head about ten years ago. The deflation of the war and the deflation of our recent 'prosperity' were not altogether dissimilar events: each left behind a sinister aftermath of hunger, terrorism, disillusionment, fatal resignation.

Upon looking through some old papers the other day, I found the fragment of a novel I had begun in 1917—it was called, in pointed irony, 'A Soldier's Testament'—and discovered, certainly to my own surprise, that I had anticipated the letdown that the war was to bring, and that I sought to find some way of carrying into the later years the élan that before 1915, my generation had known. The novel is still a fragment on crumbling yellow paper; but the letdown came; and I remember well the series of watchful calculations that determined the course that I set in the dozen years that followed. Was that course a reasonable one? Can it still be pursued in 1931? Perhaps the answer is not the same to both questions; but they are closely bound up.

Let me recall the scene that I confronted in 1919. I had been in training in the regular Navy: it was, in essentials, the same Navy that Melville pictured in 'White Jacket' almost three generations before. But the Navy had, during the war, one characteristic that set it off from the mass of civilians: it was not, so far as I came into contact with it, manned by hysterical and demented people. One could admire German seamanship in the Navy without being immediately arrested as a Hun; one could refuse to subscribe to a Liberty Bond—a sturdy handful of us did!—without being written down as a traitor. So I remember with pleasure all the useful work I accomplished during that year in the Navy. I read Emerson's essays on chow line and studied 'The Republic' carefully during the influenza epidemic.

In the odd hours that were free from routine, I did a study of housing and community planning and drafted a long essay on the subject. I faced the cold bright world of February 1919 with accumulated reserves of energy, and no sense whatever that my whole generation was already painfully skidding downhill. The armistice had not been signed, and it was still possible to think, at least to hope, that the world had been 'saved for democracy.'

During the next six months, the original momentum, acquired before the war, carried us all along: but sinister habits, generated by the war or given a full rein then for the first time, rose to the surface. The Department of Justice, under A. Mitchell Palmer, kept on with that series of vindictive violations of civil liberties which, to this day, make the defenders of law and order more suspicious to decent citizens than undisguised crooks and cutthroats. The historian who seeks a clue for Mr. Wilson's loss of prestige will err greatly if he does not take into account the domestic infelicities of his war and post-war administration. In New York, in the summer of 1919, my colleagues on 'The Dial' were hailed before the Lusk Committee and examined under strict oath of secrecy about the radical activities of the paper. This same committee discovered with horror that the works of Karl Marx and Bernard Shaw could be purchased in ordinary bookstores, and that large groups of people believed that the economic and political basis of the country should be changed—as if a nation that supported Palmers, Burlesons, Archibald Stevensons, and Lusks [read McCarthys and Nixons] were not in an enviable and permanent state of perfection!

But while these depredations of law and order were going on, it was still possible to gather encouragement elsewhere. In the face of foreign opposition, the Red Armies in Russia were successfully combating the reactionaries under Denikin: the able young engineers one met [at 'The Dial'], men like Captain Otto Beyer, were in favor of shop-committees and management-sharing in the factory, as well as a more rational and equitable system of distributing the product. So, too, economists like Veblen had left the Government administration in Washington convinced that, had the war only lasted a few years longer, the superior efficiency of a socialist organization of our national resources, under the control of economists and technicians instead of financiers, would have been shown. The I.W.W.s had not yet been extirpated; their profane songs still echoed in unexpected places; and even the strong conservative unions, not yet tempted by the bait of Florida land speculation, were intellectually alive enough to listen sympathetically to such an hopeful American translation of the English guild idea as the Plumb Plan.

Thorstein Veblen was not alone, in the summer of 1919, when he looked forward to an early collapse of the financial system and to the institution of a more socialized method of production in the United States: but he was ten years ahead of his time, at least in the negative side of his prediction; and before 1919 was over it became apparent that the expectation of salvaging any positive benefit from the war was gone. The Treaty of Versailles had been signed; and our country, with a perversity that has become characteristic of its foreign policy, certainly during the last ten years, accepted the indefensible part of the treaty and renounced the one hopeful element that remained, the League of Nations.

Wilson made a gross strategic error in binding the Treaty and the Covenant together. Those of us who were against the treaty, opposed the League, too, because it seemed merely to be an instrumentality for bringing more power back of that inequitable and unworkable arrangement. The two instruments have not proved to be quite as closely bound up as Wilson would have had them be; and the League, though still feeble, and still too often merely a convenience of the big powers, has certainly turned out better than we expected. But the United States can claim no share in this development. On the contrary, our arrogance, our bad manners, our self-righteousness, and our downright imperialism make us one of the first nations that should be bound over to keep the peace.

Now the only valid reason for our entering the World War was to ensure a decent peace. We failed in this; and we failed in creating better conditions in the twelve years that have followed. Indeed, the chief boast of our present administration is a Naval conference which has sanctioned the expansion of the American fleet to a level that was undreamed of before the war: a sanction which, though only permissive, and in this sense a sop to our childish sense of prestige, has been taken by those in favor of war as mandatory. Those of us who watched the development of the Army and the Navy after the war in the United States need not be surprised at this turn. The support of the Chemical Warfare Division; the refusal to sign the League Covenant abolishing the use of poison gases in warfare; the shameless distribution of bonuses and loans to all able-bodied veterans; and finally, the use of a large air fleet to dramatize the delicious terror of an impossible invasion—a dramatization accompanied by large scale propaganda in favor of war over the radio—all these events show how little sincerity there has been in our governmental professions of good will. To stand for peace only on our own terms, to adhere to the common decisions of other nations only when they happen to coincide with our own interest or our own sense of self-esteem—these are the marks of stultifying belligerency.

We are today the most belligerent of the larger powers. That we attempt to veil this situation with fine counsels to other nations to lessen their land-armaments and to accept our tariffs and our immigration discriminations in a humble and contrite spirit only makes our offensiveness more odious. But our present development existed in the germ in 1920. It looked then as if an out-and-out militarist, General Leonard Wood, might get the nomination for the presidency: it even seemed for a moment as if this might be the stepping stone to a dictatorship: who could tell? When one was setting one's course, the likelihood of witnessing an even more ghastly war than the past one was a constant possibility.

That likelihood is still here. The situation for peace is almost as precarious today as it was in 1919; it is certainly much worse than it was in a world so comparatively unorganized for war as was that of 1914, that innocent world, without passports and visas, without compulsory military service in the United States and England, with no greater instruments of destruction than the siege gun and the rifle, with populations that were still largely unregimented and with even an unorganized and somewhat independent press—not completely tamed to organized falsehood by official propaganda! That was an innocent world indeed. *Let us not make the mistake of thinking we are still living in it.*

As it turned out, our hopes for social justice were as badly deflated as our hopes for peace. Among the things one had to reckon with ten years ago was the fact that a large social revolution, which had once, by peaceful methods, seemed so imminent, had within almost a few short months ceased to be a reality. This was not due to the wave of prosperity: it will be remembered that this did not begin until 1922; and in 1920 and 1921 the greater part of the population was in an acutely miserable state. The lack of housing accommodation in our big cities was scandalous: it was scarcely possible to obtain quarters of any kind, and what few leftovers remained were run down and expensive. In fact, it was only by letting down the salutary tenement house regulations in New York, permitting the doing over of old-fashioned dwellings into apartment houses without sufficient fire safeguards, that the situation for the middle classes was eased. No one who had been conscious of the poverty and distress and lack of amenity that attended the housing of the greater part of our population could think for a minute that it had been removed; what was gone in 1921 was the hope for a speedy remedy. We saw by the example of Russia that the ruin of the existing system, with all its inefficiency and injustice, and the building up of a more adequate substitute were two different matters.

Meanwhile, in America, the Socialist Party, which in 1916 had seemed so vigorous and formidable, suddenly melted away; some of their slogans had been taken up by the more progressive members of the conservative parties, who favored government ownership of waterpower rights or of railroads. What remained lacked force, conviction, and point: socialism had become an empty formula. The trade unions were waning, undermined by their complacent antagonism to ideas, by their distrust of the intellectual, to say nothing of mere go-getting and bribe-taking and racketeering on the part of many of the leaders. If their absence left deplorable conditions for the unskilled unorganized workers, their presence was far from a guarantee of utopia.

In our political and economic life, no pressure of ideas remained. The great abstractions of the eighteenth and nineteenth centuries suddenly became ghosts. People might still call themselves Republicans, Democrats, Socialists, Single-Taxers, Trades Unionists; but in the United States you could not, from their actions, tell them apart. The period of 'normalcy' had begun. There were oil wells to be stolen, stocks to be promoted, graft to be picked up, flimsy houses to be built, motor roads to be laid, vacuum cleaners and radio sets to be sold. In the great excitement of pursuing these concrete symbols of affluence the impoverished conditions that surrounded the mean lives of the greater part of the population were forgotten. One's contemporaries even dared talk about 'prosperity'; and toward the end of those fat seven years the 'Duty to Consume' began stridently to be preached—a premonition of the disaster that was to come.

Let me sum up the conditions I faced during the years immediately after 1918. I lived in a world committed to war, a world subjected to intermittent tremors of animosity and hatred, a world still organized into belligerent states, girdled with fortified frontiers and supported by armies and navies and air fleets: a world where the principal resources of modern industry—petroleum, rubber, lac, coal, steel, vanadium—were unequally parcelled out and sought for by nations still clinging to their outdated notions of independence and sovereignty. This was a world where every important activity was on an international scale except international organization for political control.

At any moment this latent warfare might actively break out. My master, Patrick Geddes, had characterized this posture of civilization as Wardom (not unconscious of tieing it with whoredom), and what we called war was not a new aspect but merely its old active phase. The first time that I heard a radio blare in the public square of a little European city [Geneva] I knew that another war would be accompanied by such a terrorism of the mind as was unknown in the previous one, except at moments perhaps in the trenches. One had only to combine the threat of an air attack on an unfortified city with the announcement that could be made over the radio to see that the instruments of hysteria and collective psychosis now at the disposal of governments were more dire than ever before. Our own War Department, like every other government, no doubt, had a blacklist of pacifists and radicals: on the outbreak of war they would be rounded up and imprisoned or shot. The chance of an intelligent man's surviving would be small: smaller still that he would survive with his intelligence. The machine had regimented us too well. War contracts with manufacturers were already signed; doubtless war propaganda and war lies were already manufactured, too, with a blank space left for the name of the particular enemy who was to be vilified.

Facing this kind of world, one had roughly three choices. The first and most obvious was to throw oneself into it and go with the current: forget the war that would maim one's children if not oneself, take things as they came, engross oneself in little personal ambitions and little tasks, ignore the problems of international intercourse and economic organization that had been put to one side but not solved by our political and economic leaders, and trust to bad bootleg liquor to blunt one's feelings and perceptions and destroy one's sense of reality. This only slightly caricatures the choice most Americans made during the last ten years.

The second choice was to deliberately pit oneself against the forces that have made the world what it is today. Since it is militarism that embodies all the disastrous aspects of our civilization, one could become a pacifist: one could fight against the conscription, against the militarization of our schools, against the interference with freedom of speech. In social and economic matters, if no positive course appeared open in the United States, contrary to Russia and Italy, one could at all events protest against the invasion of civil liberties, keep open the memory of the injustice dealt to Tom Mooney, fight against the class vindictiveness that executed Sacco and Vanzetti, and in international matters, one could campaign for the League of Nations and the World Court, oppose our imperialism in Haiti and Mexico and Nicaragua, vote against increasing the funds devoted to the Army and Navy. I do not disparage these activities; certainly I would not do so only because they were weak or because they were the work of anxious minorities.

But in the period of inner debate that I have been recounting, still a third course presented itself. When one searched for the roots of our present evils one found that they had not come about in a few short years, and that they were not the product of a small class or group which one could isolate and summon to justice. If it were only a matter of fighting the militarists, or dispossessing the financiers of their symbols and agents of power, that would be easy—as easy as beheading Charles the First or Louis the Sixteenth. But when one sought for the origins of Wardom, the chronic state of belligerency in which the great powers exist, one found that it went back to the origins of the national state itself: the attempt of a group of hunter-warriors to organize a relatively peaceful population for the purposes of laying and collecting annual tribute. This was abetted, from the fifteenth century on, by a slowly increasing deadliness and accuracy in mechanical technology: the machine process had been a powerful aid to warfare itself. The animus of the miner, combined with that of the hunter, had created a life-destroying mythology into which everyone was indoctrinated.

The increase of international commerce, so far from working toward peace, as the Manchester school hopefully believed, only created new situations of irritation and rivalry; and democracy, which the thinkers of the eighteenth century had erected as a check to the greed and arrogance of the privileged classes, had rather rounded out the technique of militarism by contributing the terrible notion of a 'nation in arms.' As a result war had ceased to be a restricted professional and aristocratic business: it had become a means of universal mass slaughter. The regimentation of the rising democracies by the machine process itself only increased their docility and their readiness to face death for trivial causes. By 1917 there were no draft rioters and no audible copperheads in the United States, much though the authorities, with the memories of 1863 in mind, had feared their possibility.

The very monotony and imbecility of life under modern conditions had created large city populations, living and working perpetually in an abstract world of paper notations, that needed the thrill and excitement and stress provided on such a vast scale by war. These masses could, for a time, get a second-hand catharsis from a daring flight over the Atlantic Ocean, from a visit to the South Pole, from even the mere dogged triumph of swimming the English Channel: the series of parades and celebrations of these events for their entertainment constituted no small part of the bread-and-shows budget of our Modern Rome. But the very monotony and sterility of this mass-city civilization demanded war, or at least the threat of war, as an equivalent for the farmer's and fisherman's and miner's constant tussle with the elemental conditions of life. . . .

In the light of these observations, what conclusions could one draw, what course could one plot? The conclusion that I drew for myself was that the situation demanded, not specific attacks on specific evils and specific points of danger, but a wholesale rethinking of the basis of modern life and thought, for the purpose of eventually giving a new orientation to all our institutions. In this situation, it might be more important to contribute a new philosophical idea than to prevent a battleship from being launched or oppose an effort at territorial aggrandizement: for the latter, at best, was a matter of bailing water out of a leaky boat with a spoon, while the essential need of the time was to create a more seaworthy boat than that we were afloat in. There was always the risk that any large-scale revision of purposes and institutions would be arrived at too late. In one's ears rang Schiller's ancient aphorism, "Whilst philosophers debate, hunger and love are settling the affairs of the world." In fastening on tangible, concrete objectives, in not being satisfied with purely abstract interpretations and ideal directions, the ordinary man who had taken the first choice and grasped at some positive end, however limited and little, had been right. The reason that our gas-filled idealisms had been so suddenly deflated after the war had been due to their own limitations: they either mistook the abstract compass points for actual goals that we were trying to reach, forgetful of the fact that if all one seeks to do is to travel toward the magnetic North one reaches in the end only a waste of ice; or they took some limited portion of reality, like the control of the economic system, as equivalent for the general re-orientation of life, not realizing that no alteration in the means would be significant until it was coupled with new ends and objectives.

The two countries where political ideas had not suddenly rusted away were Italy and Russia: both had been faced by concrete situations that demanded a concrete solution, even when that solution contradicted the philosophy with which the ruling group started out. In each of these countries, moreover, there had been an attempt to rethink the entire basis of life, not merely to alter some special set of institutions: religion, education, philosophy, even recreation had been affected by communism, and however much the immediate economic situation engrossed the government's efforts, communism did not lose its positive direction toward larger goals.

Why then, one may ask, did not either a fascist or a communist program appeal to me? The answer is that both these ideologies carried with them a large part of the errors and vices of the civilization which they had set out to combat. Communism, with its limitations on free intelligence, with its dogmatic adherence to Hegelio-Marxian formulas, with its distrust of pure science, with its notions of forcible indoctrination, with its apotheosis of the machine process, had powerful elements in it which were as life-denying as any in a so-called capitalist civilization: indeed, they both spring from the same common sources in the seventeenth and eighteenth centuries. Both fascism and communism tended to deify the State; both of them denied the actual autonomy and authority of other corporate groups such as the university, the city, the church, the professional association, the industrial organization; both ideologies tended to be at their maximum of effectiveness in a state of war, a fact which is supported by the curious way in which the peaceful efforts to consummate the Five Year Plan in Soviet Russia have been accompanied with devices of dramatization derived from war. Skilled and loyal workers are called 'shock troops,' and the various industries are referred to as the lumber 'front' and the steel 'front,' and the population is keyed up to a continued sacrifice of the barest decencies of life by a constant appeal to the heroic mood—alternated with threats of another kind of warfare.

Soviet Russia even in peace was what the United States had come close to being in times of war; and the reason was that the underlying ideals of both countries had been derived from the same source. It was these ideals, this mechanistic plan of life, this absolutist ideology of the Power State, that seemed to me the largest sources of our present evils. Nothing less than a complete philosophic and social reorientation would guarantee a more satisfactory social order.

The breakdown of our present system of production, the worldwide depression, the threats of war, war between the big states, war between the capitalist nations and communist Russia, the impoverishment and dire distress of vast masses of people, while wheat clogs the grain elevators and even the price of butter and eggs tumbles to new low levels—all these things increase the tension of our days, and lead to a feverish demand to "do something." Mr. Edmund Wilson, one of the ablest of our literary critics, voiced such a demand in a ringing article in 'The New Republic' last winter: an article that reached its climax, after a picture of the sordid and futile and desperate state of current society, with a demand that we "take communism away from the communists."

This article gained wide attention; it called into existence a number of earnest responses, all of which recalled, in one way or another, those hopeful expectant days of 1919; but neither the original essay nor those that served as commentary, it seemed to me, took sufficiently into account the fact that our remedies are as much under suspicion as the dire diseases we would like them to exorcise. To take communism away from the communists, or even capitalism away from the capitalists, we must have a much deeper critical grasp of the situation, and we must have a definite plan of action, capable of being worked out, step by step, in our daily personal life and our institutions. It is not merely a matter of appropriating catchwords or starting parties: it is a matter of altering the entire basis upon which our present venal and mechanistic and life-denying civilization rests. This is not a task for the next ten years, but for the next two hundred.

Meanwhile, a war may come—and any war will be a disastrous war. In that case, our efforts will be interrupted: in all probability destroyed. But I see no shorter and easier way to our goal than that which is indicated by thought, by purposeful experiment, above all by a re-orientation, in terms of a more abundant life, of personalities, groups, communities. There is no single, plainly marked path to follow. On the other hand, imaginative thinking and foresighted action need not wait for a wholesale revolution to demonstrate their effectiveness. Growing things do not resemble a cataclysm but a leaven in dough; and given the well-milled grain, an active ferment will eventually leaven the whole inert lump. It was in this fashion that the industrial revolution made its way into life: and the revolution which will supplant the partial values, the abstract and one-sided aims, the purely mechanistic modes of this revolution will be on the same scale and will, one can scarcely doubt, require a similar length of time for its fulfillment. We who have a sense of another future stand today where Campanella and Glanvill did in the seventeenth century. Like them, but even more so, we are aware that we are on the brink of a fundamental change. If our own predictions are as accurate and our own hopes prove as capable of fulfillment as theirs turned out to be, we may congratulate ourselves—and even more our descendants.

—First draft of an unpublished manuscript. 1930

THORSTEIN VEBLEN   was a humorist whom Miss Constance Rourke might well have added to her galaxy in 'American Humor,' for he had the American mechanism of the impassive face and the solemn exaggeration. His sentences were as elaborately wrought as Henry James's: his desperately accurate circumlocutions, his perfectly elephantine means of expressing a platitude in such a way as to show its fatuousness, his use of polysyllabic jargon, after the worst fashion of the young Ph.D.—all these characteristics were part of the mechanism of his humor. When he was obscure, he did not fall into obscurity by accident: it was rather the summit of a delicate effort, and he enjoyed the effect he sought to produce on the reader who must be astute enough to follow him. Veblen was careful about the last detail of his writing, being even jealous of any changes that were made in his copy to make it conform to those rules of punctuation and capitalization which most magazines—foolishly it now seems to me—insist upon. The following instance will serve for a dozen others. In one of his 'Dial' articles Veblen had characterized Samuel Gompers as the sexton beetle of the American labor movement. In preparing the ms. for the printer, one of the editors had automatically changed this over to sexton beadle, in order to make sense. Veblen was furious: his white ashen face was more ashen than ever with anger—such anger as seemed especially terrible in the mild, reticent person that Veblen always seemed. He wanted to know if the unknown dunderhead who had mutilated his copy did not realize that a sexton beetle was an insect that spent its life in storing up and covering over dead things? Besides, there was an overtone in the allusion: Gompers looked more like a beetle. (Veblen was right: I never saw Gompers after that without recalling the insect.)   —The New Republic. August 5, 1931

Technically there is no end to the possible use of glass with a modern concrete or metal frame construction. But without social control there is as little benefit in the potential openness of the glass house as there is in the potential height of the skyscraper. For glass is not an end in itself: it is a means to sunlight, pure air, pleasant vistas. If, for lack of effective community planning, these things are not secured, if the houses are badly spaced and give no privacy, if the air is polluted by motor traffic, and if instead of gardens and parks there are only cat-walks and garages, the boldest of technical innovations may be no more than waste and lost motion. In fact, we may lay it down as an axiom that every collective economy, every labor saving device, every modern material or utility, tends to become a nuisance until it is collectively controlled and integrated into a new pattern. As an abstract invention, foisted on the market for financial gain, it merely adds to the amount of chaos our civilization is capable of producing. For lack of integrated patterns, the resources of modern technology have not been adequately applied to modern architecture. If we are to live in glass houses, we must abandon many other practices besides that of throwing stones.
    —From an unpublished ms. 'Form and Civilization.' 1930–1931

When one dates the beginnings of modern architecture, not from the Crystal Palace or the Marshall Field Warehouse, or the Tacoma Building, or the Eiffel Tower, but from the Elizabethan period, one is taking into consideration the increased production of glass during this period. The result had a profound value for civilization: it not merely altered the relation of window and wall in the design of a building: it also changed the internal plans and fittings, increased the possibility of hygiene, and above all, altered the outlook of the occupants. It is scarcely an exaggeration to represent the medieval mind by a closed wall and the modern one by an open window: what we have lost in defensive solidity we have gained in exposure to light. When the medieval man looked at the world through glass, he saw his own imagery: the virgin, the saints, the blue of heaven, the red of sacramental blood. But when a modern man looks through glass, while he may magnify the object he beholds, he takes the utmost care to maintain the purity and transparency of his medium, since he values it not for its own sake but for that of the object beyond.
    —From an unpublished ms. 'Form and Civilization.' 1930–1931

210

Form in building exists, not in a static, photographic view of the structure, but in the dynamic fulfillment of all its relationships. The impression upon the eye, though constant and important, is not the only effect of good architecture. To forget movement in relation to a building is to forget the essential difference between architecture and painting, and even between architecture and sculpture: for a building, unlike sculpture, is not so much a plastic mass as an envelope: the outer effect is rhythmically related and in part determined by the inner structure: indeed, the resolution of that double relationship is the very key to a positive work of architecture. A mountain, a pyramid, an obelisk, a statue may be seen from various angles and exposures: but, unlike St. Sophia, they cannot be approached from within. One may halt at any point to take advantage of the picture presented by the building: but the building itself is not a picture. Buildings conceived as pictures should never leave the draughting board.

—From an unpublished ms. 'Form and Civilization.' 1930–1931

. . . This brings me back to an old point of mine: the economy of writing books, as compared with publication in any periodical form. For books alone are reviewed; and books alone remain in circulation long enough to be discussed by a succession of readers at different times, and so slowly gather their audience. C. K. Ogden has had an influence far out of proportion to Victor Branford or yourself, considering not merely the quality of his contributions but the amount of energy he has spent on disseminating his ideas: and this was because his main efforts have gone into a series of publications, rather than into the 'Cambridge Magazine' with which he originally started. The original idea for 'The Making of the Future' Series was a good one: but the series weakened as it progressed, because Branford's energies and money went to the Sociological Society, and instead of using the series to gather around new writers and to build up a school of thought, he let it finally peter out.

For the sake of the ideas that both you and Branford had to give to the world, I could wish that you both had either gone into a lay monastery in 1920 or been imprisoned by the civil authorities, with nothing other than pen and ink and a library to keep you company! A garden would have kept you both in good health, and instead of communicating with a few poor disciples like myself, scattered at the ends of the earth, you would presently have found yourselves surrounded by a school. Surely, it was contrary to your own teachings, to build the buildings first and then seek to attract the pupils. That is our own weak American method: the method that produces palatial buildings, and fills them with vacant minds. . . .

—Letter to P.G. May 3, 1931

211

INTERLUDE

The Builders
of the Bridge

Prefatory Note

If this play should prove a surprise to the reader, let me confess that it was even more of a surprise to me when in 1970 I read it as if for the first time forty-three years after it was written. Though I can date its writing accurately to the summer of 1927, I had until lately no memory of the notes for it I had made in 1925, though even an inexperienced critic would guess that such a broad canvas, peopled with so many diverse characters, was not a work of sudden inspiration, however swift was its actual composition.

Far back in my childhood, the Brooklyn Bridge left its imprint on my mind, beginning with my periodical visits via the Bridge to our Brooklyn relatives. And after my wife and I moved to Brooklyn Heights in 1922, walks over the Bridge, at all times of the day, from one end or the other, were one of our favorite modes of recreation. So it was natural for me not only to study the Bridge as a superb architectural monument, but to delve into its actual construction and find out all that was readily discoverable then about its builders, John A. and Washington Roebling. The pages I wrote about the Bridge in 'Sticks and Stones,' and amplified later in 'The Brown Decades,' were I suppose the first words of critical appreciation since Montgomery Schuyler's masterly essay in 1893.

As early as 1925, perhaps earlier, the Brooklyn Bridge took shape in my mind as a character in an epic drama. Though Hart Crane was living on Columbia Heights during the twenties, in the very house Washington Roebling had occupied, we did not know of each other's intentions when I gave my play the same name as the poem he was writing. In the end I gladly yielded the title to him, for as it turned out it was the builders of the bridge whose works and days, whose sacrifices and heroisms, whose frustrations and triumphs I was celebrating.

While preparing this preface I stumbled upon a series of old notes on the Bridge, the first in 1925, the last in 1929: but the notes I wrote on August eighth and ninth, 1927, with fragments of a plot and a partial cast of characters were swept aside immediately after when I began work. Almost in the wink of an eye, the preliminary sketches were superseded by the actual play, for both the characters and the

215

scenario underwent radical transformations as soon as they shifted from my unconscious to the workaday world of 'The Bridge.' From then on they worked out their own fate, with only little help from me.

In the summer of 1927 I began to compose a critical biography of Herman Melville from the vantage point of Martha's Vineyard. But I swerved aside to spend six weeks perhaps—certainly not more than two months—writing 'The Bridge.' The outward circumstances of this composition I remember clearly. Each morning I would go to a one-room shack, a hundred feet away from our cramped seaside cabin, to sit down and write; and before eleven I would toss the day's stint aside and walk half a mile over the sands to the ocean for a swim, while Sophie first finished up with the dishes and the diapers. The lifting morning fog, the radiant sky, and the muted roar of the breaking waves mingled with my imagined characters and scenes; and the play, for which I had sketched out only the briefest scenario, flowed from my fingers when I returned to it each morning, so swiftly, so steadily, so effortlessly that I became a little uneasy, feeling that something must be amiss with either the theme or with me. No work of mine, except 'The Little Testament of Bernard Martin,' had ever come to birth with so little struggle and anguish! This was too good to be true!

When finally 'The Bridge' was finished I was far from elated over it, for even the conclusion did not satisfy me: it lacked the inherent dynamism, the resonant, affirmative quality I had found in the design and construction of the great Bridge itself. Not that I was put off by any lack of verisimilitude to the actual scene and period, or by the fact that I had substituted two creatures of my imagination for the larger and sterner figures of the two Roeblings. But I was near enough to the realities of the theater to admit to myself that this almost Tolstoyan epic—I was reading 'War and Peace' that summer for the first time—made far larger demands than any American producer would have welcomed—though a few years later during the depression the Federal Arts Project could readily have commanded the large cast of actors.

In short, there were excellent practical excuses for my failure to go further with 'The Bridge.' If anything, I had produced the script for a film, but unfortunately in 1927 the motion picture still lacked the human voice. My deeper reason, however, for abandoning my play was the admonitions of my literary conscience. Every scene seemed to me to call for re-writing, if not more drastic reconstruction: so I put the play aside as 'unfinished,' waiting for some outer call or some inner prompting to return to the task I had so easily begun.

"So easily" gives the clue to this decision. I distrusted that facility! And so the manuscript lay buried in my files: indeed I never showed

216

even a fragment of it to my fellow editors of 'The American Caravan,' Paul Rosenfeld and Alfred Kreymborg, though that was the most obvious vehicle for a long but perhaps readable play. Not until Elmer Newman, engaged on a bibliography of my writings, ransacked my files in the summer of 1969, did I have the slightest impulse to look at this play, though it was the last of a series, two of which had almost been produced.

The fact that I am now ready, at long last, to publish 'The Builders of the Bridge' does not of course establish its value as an authentic work of art. On this matter the reader must judge for himself. But the play at least deserves a place in these analects, as an essential contribution to my spiritual autobiography, revealing much that a more explicit narrative of my life would leave out. To make the reader's judgement easier I have made only the most trivial corrections or additions, except in one case: the ceremonial opening of the Brooklyn Bridge. Here I have changed the farcical original version of the Orator's speech to one closer to the kind of pedestrian eloquence that actually marked the occasion. Otherwise, 'The Builders of the Bridge' remains exactly what it was in the first unrevised draft.

—L.M. 1974

CAST OF CHARACTERS *in the Order of Their Appearance*

JEFFERSON BAUMGARTEN. *Structural Engineer. A second generation American*

MARGARET MILLS BAUMGARTEN. *Jefferson's wife*

DELIA. *Maid-of-all-work and Jefferson's one-time Nurse*

ELIZABETH MILLS (BETH). *Margaret's sister, younger by three years*

MRS. BAUMGARTEN. *Wife of John Baumgarten*

JOHN BAUMGARTEN. *Father of Jefferson. German-trained Engineer. U.S. Major General. Hegelian philosopher. Designer of the Bridge*

CLARK. *A draftsman and clerk*

SHANE MAGONIGLE. *Leader of the Riveter's Union*

MIKE CASEY. *Magonigle's rival*

JIM RUSSELL. *A walking delegate*

ROBERT-OWEN BENNS. *An artist*

THOMAS FIELDING. *A Long Island Sound waterman*

MIKE AND TIMMY. *Two water-rats*

JOHN POWERS. *Jefferson's chief foreman*

WILLIAM BAXTER. *Saloon owner and Tammany boss*

IKEY. *Baxter's 'private secretary'*

LOIS MILLS (LOLO). *Margaret's youngest sister (aet. 18)*

BASTIAN. *A 'Forty-eighter,' old crony of John Baumgarten*

GOEBEL AND MRS. GOEBEL. *Bismarckian Germans*

COLONEL HICKS. *A military friend of old Baumgarten*

THE WORK GANG. *Bill the Swede. Tony the Dago. Fred, an irrepressible skylarker. Grogan, Mike and Pat, all Micks. Flanagan, a night-watchman. Murphy and Ahearn, riveters*

MIRIAM BENNS. *Robert-Owen's sister*

MACKAYE. *A Glasgow worker*

ORATOR, *at opening of the Bridge*

218

Scene One

October first, 1873, is moving day. Jefferson Baumgarten has moved, with his wife, Margaret, and his man-servant and his maid-servant, and all his chattels, to a gray-green serpentine covered house on Columbia Heights. It is around the corner from John Baumgarten's house. The move brings John Baumgarten and Son, Engineers and Builders of Bridges, nearer to the Bridge whose foundations have just been sunk.

The side of Jefferson's new house opens on a street; from his garden, or from the covered iron balcony in the rear, he has a clear command of the Harbor and of the East River. His study and library and bedroom, second story rear, covers the same sweep of waterfront through the turret-like posture of its oriel window, with sides of rounded glass, in the extravagant fashion of an age that has just discovered how to use a scroll saw and how to bend plate glass into rounded sheets.

What Jefferson's room will finally become, it is almost impossible to predict: late this October afternoon it contains two large glass-fronted bookcases, partly filled with books stacked any way; seven packing cases half emptied of books; a flat top desk in the middle of the room; a drafting board alongside it; a number of low, contorted walnut chairs, stuffed and tufted to the last degree; against the wall is a cot, without any mattress on it, covered up for the moment by a deep red plush scarf which will finally grace a mantelshelf. The wall is papered in an uncertain gray-green pattern which loses a little of its coldness in the rich light of the setting sun, framed by the oriel window over a landscape of vivid blue and gold. Even without the red-gold leaves of the Virginia creeper, one would detect October in the air. From the garden below comes a sound of carpets being beaten; the rap of a hammer comes from another part of the house; the squeaky whistle of a tugboat may at any moment announce the traffic in the Harbor below.

With his back to the window, Jefferson Baumgarten sits at his desk, quickly assorting a pile of papers. Born in Germany in 1832, he came to America at the age of five with his family; and though

219

he has gestures which recall his father, and occasionally speaks with a shade of German intonation, the new scene has already left its mark on him: he is taller by three inches than his father, is less thick and heavy set: his gestures are a little keener: there is a taint of restlessness in him which contrasts with the steady, fixed, purposeful, drive of John Baumgarten. Jefferson's chestnut hair, his firm, close-cropped beard, his steady penetrating blue eyes, his large hand and stubby fingers, leave a total impression, when he is happy, of great power and beauty. But at the moment we find him, he is not happy. The disruption of moving has put him into a fit of childish exasperation.

JEFFERSON (*getting up and pawing rapidly over the wooden boxes*): Margaret! Margaret! Where on earth is the box of office papers? They are not up here.

(*Margaret enters with a reproachful look upon her face: she is a handsome woman of thirty-five, with light sandy hair and gray-blue eyes, two features that are almost obliterated by the triumphant ugliness of a dusting cap and apron.*)

MARGARET: My dear: I can't be everywhere. Where did you put your papers last? I am sure that everything we told the movingmen to bring up here is here. Besides, you can't *work* tonight, the beds aren't put up yet.

JEFFERSON (*growling*): What the devil do I care about beds? You can all sleep on the floor.

MARGARET (*oblivious*): We can't do anything until the carpets are down, and one of the men threatens to quit before the work is through. He says the Union won't let him work more than ten hours. It's outrageous. The carpets must go down tonight. You've got to speak to him.

JEFFERSON: The carpets can go to the devil too. The granite contractors are coming around tomorrow morning with their revised estimates, and I've got to be ready for them. I must find the box of office papers. The sooner you and Delia find it . . .

MARGARET (*playfully*): The sooner I'll realize I am married to a man and not to a grousing-mousing bear! You are ridiculous: but I know what's the matter. You haven't had a bite to eat. I never saw a man so helpless over such a little matter. What was I saying—oh yes! (*She goes back inexorably to her point, with the persistence of a great organizer.*) The carpets. You must go down right away and talk to the carpet man. He just laughs at me.

JEFFERSON: Don't be an idiot. He wants you to offer him a bonus for staying.

MARGARET: I shall do nothing of the kind.

JEFFERSON: This is October first. Five thousand other people in Brooklyn want their carpets laid tonight, too. If you can't offer it, someone else will. Don't bother me with carpets. I must find that office file.

(*Delia enters with a big cup of coffee and a plate of cookies.*)

DELIA: Was it a black box?

JEFFERSON: It is a big black box.

DELIA: If it was a dog it would 'a bit you. You've been sitting on it all the time.

JEFFERSON: Nonsense I've been— (*he looks around, sees that Delia is right, becomes sheepish, and tries to cover it up by bullying her.*) It's about time you brought up that coffee. When will dinner be ready?

MARGARET (*outraged*): Dinner? You talk to us about dinner, with the carpets not laid and the beds not put up. The china isn't washed yet either, and the only thing in the house is the bag of salt and the loaf of bread your mother brought.

DELIA (*mothering Jefferson, to Margaret's annoyance*): There, there, darling: you'll get your dinner all right. Delia will see to it. But drink your coffee first. It's tired you are; you always were a frail child.

MARGARET: A frail child! I suppose you'll believe her! (*Jefferson, with the coffee warming and cheering him, breaks into a grin and nods a yes to tease Margaret.*) You're a stubborn, self-centered, inconsiderate beast. I've been running my feet off all day, and here it's only five o'clock and you're talking about dinner. (*She is about to cry but thinks better of it*). She's spoiled you.

DELIA (*oblivious, pouring a little fat into the fire by pushing a pillow between Jefferson's back and the chair into which he has sunk*): Sure: the least little thing wrong in the house upsets him. There: there: nothing's too good for His Majesty. Will ye have some more coffee?

MARGARET: You don't really want a wife. A nurse could attend to all your wants.

JEFFERSON: Nonsense, Margaret. Delia's just used to me: she knows when I need a spanking and when I need a cup of coffee. Please get me another cup. (*Suddenly remembering that he is not the center of the universe*) Perhaps Mrs. Baumgarten would like a cup, too. (*Delia leaves the room*).

MARGARET (*vindictively*): Oh, don't mind me: I'm not a poor, frail, starved little boy.

JEFFERSON: I was ill for a whole year when I was fifteen; and Delia can never be persuaded that I've gotten over it. Don't talk so waspishly, Margaret. One would think you didn't like Delia.

MARGARET (*marvelling at his blindness to the obvious*): One would, wouldn't one? (*She suddenly feels a little tender to this infantile part of him and goes over to give him a kiss. He pulls her down to him in an habitual gesture of fondness*).

JEFFERSON: Well, at last we're on the Heights. I think it's going to be a good move. I shall be able to run home occasionally for lunch; and you won't feel that the Bridge is keeping me away from you all the time.

MARGARET: Why can't you do your work like other people? Why can't you leave it behind you, at the office? One shouldn't work all the time. All work and no play . . .

JEFFERSON: Pooh: pooh. I wish I could teach you something about bridges, Margaret: perhaps now that you can watch this one growing, you'll understand a little more about it. My work is play: that's why I don't want to leave it behind me. (*Naïvely, but with conviction*) Building bridges is the nicest thing in the world!

MARGARET (*uttering an old conviction*): I positively think you're more interested in that Bridge than you are in your family or me.

JEFFERSON: Why of course! . . . No! *But don't you see?* It's quite different. I couldn't do without you, Margaret: but it would be dreadful to *live* with you twenty-four hours a day. We'd both be cranky and get on each other's nerves. Living with a thing means changing it: doing things to it. People who are in love, love each other for what they are. It's fatal to try to change the person one loves, isn't it? The Bridge is different: when I wake up in the middle of the night, I can see some detail I haven't attended to, some problem I haven't sufficiently thought out. There's so much to be done. That's living.

MARGARET (*bitterly*): That's what a man calls living, I suppose. I don't find the hours we spend together tiresome. I wish I had a little more of you.

JEFFERSON (*brightly, as if this really settled it*): Well, now you shall have me: I'll come home for lunch regularly—(*with an afterthought of reserve*) or at any rate, when I can break away.

MARGARET (*moodily, with a soft sarcasm she knows will not penetrate*): Yes dear: that will give us a great deal of each other. Besides, I am used to sharing you with Delia and the Bridge; those are the stresses and strains of our marriage. Are those the right words, dear?

JEFFERSON (*blind to the meaning, and delighted with Margaret's vocabulary*): That's right: the stress is a force, a pressure: the strain is a pull: pounding and stretching. When the two are adjusted, the result is an equilibrium of forces. People think that a bridge is just a solid, static thing: on the contrary, it is a raging battleground of

222

forces: if the bridge has been well-designed, the result is a perfect draw. That's what equilibrium is: balanced movement.

MARGARET (*resigned, but still ironic*): Yes dear, we understand each other. I am becoming a bright pupil, aren't I? Pardon me now: Delia will be along with the second cup of coffee; and I must look after the carpet man.

JEFFERSON (*unconsciously echoing Margaret's reproach*): Ach, why do you always have to go away? Just when I want to talk to you. As soon as we get really intimate— (*Margaret arches her eyebrows at Jefferson's idea of what being really intimate is*) —yes—really intimate, you always have the dinner to attend to, or have to put the children to bed.

MARGARET: Just a minute ago you were roaring for dinner and a minute before for coffee: then you were roaring about your office file. Now you have forgotten about both of them, and are roaring for me. (*Briskly*) You can roar a little longer, my darling. I mustn't let that nasty carpet man get away.

(*From the staircase outside a woman's voice says: Oohoo: Is there anyone up in this part of the house?*)

MARGARET: That sounds like Beth. It must be after five-thirty. Now you can have somebody you can be really intimate with to talk to— someone who understands you and doesn't have dinners to cook and socks to darn.

JEFFERSON (*covering up his pleasure at the prospect*): The devil: I'm busy. Elizabeth does nothing but talk.

ELIZABETH (*standing in the door*): What's that about Beth? If I'm not wanted I can go away. A girl who can earn fourteen dollars a week isn't dependent upon any man!

(*Saying which, since it is pay night, she flourishes fourteen one dollar bills in a vague triumph. She is an intellectualized version of Margaret: and while she must be at least three years younger, and is quite virginally slim, there is a sharp, nipped look about her that makes her seem even older than her married sister.*)

MARGARET (*kissing her*): Deliver anyone from moving with this man in the house. The furniture is nothing: but there are no cages big enough to keep him in. We've all been slaving since six o'clock this morning—and he wants intellectual conversation. He's yours, Beth!

(*With a swish, partly triumphant, partly indignant, she leaves her sister and Jefferson together*).

ELIZABETH (*with conviction*): Margaret is an idiot. She thinks the world revolves around you.

JEFFERSON: So it does. Margaret's world revolves around her. Your world revolves around you. Every person is in the middle of his own world, and on the periphery of everybody else's. Your and my worlds, for example—why they've never once collided.

ELIZABETH: They had better not. Go on with your work. You're busy. I've just finished my work. I drew up seven deeds today; and most of them were for irregular parcels of land, too.

JEFFERSON: You work in the office regularly now?

ELIZABETH: Regularly: eight-thirty to five-thirty with an hour for lunch. Fourteen dollars a week. Two weeks vacation a year. I've been working for the last month, and I am still alive: my virtue is intact: I haven't been insulted or disgraced.

JEFFERSON: Don't give me any of your suffrage orations. I learned all the catchwords before you did up your hair. I don't object to your working; but why don't you do something real?

ELIZABETH: For instance? . . .

JEFFERSON: Building bridges for instance. Be an engineer. Any monkey can work in an office and draw up deeds. What does that require? A parrot's memory and a donkey's docility!

ELIZABETH: Office work is the only thing that's open to women. (*Defiantly*) We do it better than men; and when engineering and medicine are open we'll do that better, too.

JEFFERSON: Come in our office. I'll teach you to be a draftsman. That's better than memorizing: "We hereby and herewith do make, covenant, and agree." If you have any talent for mathematics or physics, I'll make an engineer of you.

ELIZABETH (*wary*): I want to be an independent woman. I don't think you respect a woman's independence.

JEFFERSON: An independent woman! That's a fine sort of childishness. Am I an independent man? Is anyone an independent anything? Nonsense: the more work I do, the more responsibilities I take upon myself, the less independent I become. When a child is born into the world he is dependent upon his mother: that's as near to freedom and independence as we ever get. The older he grows the more people and the more things he is dependent upon, and the more he himself matures the more people are dependent upon him. I have a wife: I have a family to nourish, to house, to educate: I have a bridge to build: I have ten draftsmen working under me in the office, and a hundred and fifty men working on the Bridge. My time is theirs: my brains are theirs: in a pinch my life is theirs. If I wanted independence, what would I be—? An invalid. Back again to the baby state of independence, with a nurse looking after me.

ELIZABETH: If you didn't take the bit in your mouth and run away with it, you might understand what another person was driving at. I

224

want my own life on my own terms. Drafting deeds and manifolding documents gives me that. I am my own master. I don't have to live at home if I don't want to. I am free from five-thirty at night to eight-thirty in the morning. No one can tell me what I must do. (*Passionately, as if drowning something that gives it the lie*) It's worth it!

JEFFERSON: I understand, I understand. I ran away from home when I was fourteen; and I know what that sort of freedom and independence is worth. The tramp thinks he is independent of family life: but he is dependent upon the meanest slice of bread he gets from the poorest kitchen. The deserter thinks he has broken away from the discipline of the army; and he cowers at a rustle of leaves as he would never cower before his sergeant. I offer you a real job —and you are afraid I won't respect your independence. You are right. I wouldn't. *It* wouldn't. If you're going to keep yourself to yourself, you'd better embrace the smallest, meanest, driest, most shrivelled-up job there is.

ELIZABETH: I am ready to give myself completely, if the job is worth it. But I don't know that I'd like to work under you.

JEFFERSON: Ah: that's different. If you are going to choose your employer as you might choose a husband, you may have to wait a long time before you get the right sort of job. (*Suspicious*) What's wrong with me as an employer?

ELIZABETH (*quietly, with a shrewd smile*): You are a bully! (*She gives time for this to sink in: then she repeats the blow.*) You're an unscrupulous bully. You are so interested in your Bridge that you wouldn't let anything stand in the way of it. One might as well be your wife as work in your office. What you couldn't get by dictating and storming, you'd get by cajolery or flattery or "intellectual conversation." I prefer to keep a sister-in-law's privileges, Jefferson, and enjoy you just as you are. I don't envy Margaret or any of your minions at 11 Fulton Street.

JEFFERSON: It's all nonsense, Elizabeth. I am a faithful husband and an honest employer. But I like a little serious conversation with you; you are the only person that really grasps what I am talking about, and that doesn't automatically agree. I do respect your independence. Keep it. (*With malicious afterthought*) Much good will it do you!

ELIZABETH (*shaking hands with him in rather firm, manly fashion*): You'd be a nice man, Jefferson, if you hadn't been spoiled, first by Delia, then by Margaret, and more or less I suppose by everybody. You have such a nice father and mother too: one wonders how it happened.

JEFFERSON: No son can be like his father and still be a credit to his father. The General is a buffalo: all shoulder and head. The proof that he was a good father is that I don't resemble him at all. I use my eyes and avoid obstacles. He uses his shoulder and knocks them over. Together, we can build better bridges than anyone else in America, except Eads. (*Respectfully and quite naïvely*) Eads is a great engineer too!

DELIA (*entering the room, ahead of old Mrs. Baumgarten*): He's up here ma'am. The coffee boiled over and I'm after making him a new cup. He can taste the boil if only a drop of it gets too hot. Your mother has come. (*To Elizabeth*) Your sister Lolo is downstairs helping the carpet man to lay the carpets, and him working like a nigger to beat her. The missus says will you take off your things and stay to a delicatessen supper. That's all we'll be having tonight.

(*Old Mrs. Baumgarten enters: a cleanly chiselled woman of sixty: sharp gray eyes: firm but not severe mouth: she speaks the pure and precise English of perfect acquisition: she is ten years younger than her husband in years, and double that in spirit: which makes her about her son's age.*)

MRS. BAUMGARTEN: Good evening, Elizabeth! (*To Jefferson*) Congratulations on your new home. (*She kisses him.*) It will be good to have you all over here on the Heights with us. The children are staying with me this evening: so I must go back and see about their suppers. (*With slightly sentimental eyes*): May you be prosperous and healthy and happy in your new home, Jefferson. Health comes first: happiness follows.

JEFFERSON: Stay, mother: we'll all have a *Kaffeeklatsch*. It's only five o'clock.

MRS. BAUMGARTEN: What are you thinking of: it's nearly six! You're not being very nice to Margaret, my boy. She wants you to help put up the beds. . . . And by the way: your father asked if you would be sure to bring the estimates on the stonework to the office early tomorrow, so that you may both go over them together.

JEFFERSON: The damned estimates. Excuse me, mother. What have I been drivelling about? I meant to tend to them an hour ago.

ELIZABETH (*evening up on Jefferson*): The welcome burdens of responsibility, my dear brother-in-law: beds! estimates! contracts! supper! As an independent woman, I think I shall go home and read 'Madame Bovary' this evening.

JEFFERSON (*herding his mother, Delia, and Beth out of the door*): Go: go: go. (*To Beth*) Don't take Margaret's invitation to stay seriously: we'll all be cross and cranky by supper time. Read your 'Madame Bovary'! You could do that without spending nine hours in an office beforehand and dulling all your faculties! I'm sorry we can't be more hospitable tonight, mother. It's nice of you to look after the boys. Let's have a nice big *Kaffeeklatsch* next Sunday.

Tell the Chief I'll be at the office at eight o'clock tomorrow morning. Delia: where the devil are you going with that coffee. (*Out in the hall*): Be careful you don't tumble over those pictures. Bring back the coffee: I must do some work. Beds? Beds? Don't bother me with your beds! What's that Margaret? Oh, very well: where are the beds? I suppose the Bridge doesn't make any difference. . . . In the bedrooms? Of course! of course!

DELIA (*coming back into the room with the coffee*): Here's the coffee, my spalpeen. Leave Delia to tend to the beds. Just give me a little lift with the big double mahogany in the wife's room and I can do the rest myself with Mary.

JEFFERSON (*coming back and drinking the coffee*): Why didn't you say so before? By the way: did you see the office file around anywhere: a big black box?

(*Delia folds her arms in reproach at his forgetfulness and points with a stare to the box.*)

JEFFERSON: Oh damn it all: yes: there it is. Well now: clear out: I must look over those contracts!

(*Curtain*)

Scene Two

The office of John Baumgarten and Son, just below the Fulton El, two blocks from the Fulton Ferry. The building itself is of brick with a soiled yellow portico of classic dimensions whose pillars reach above the second story: there is no attic floor and the space enclosed by the gable forms a spacious barn-like room, the northern end of which, facing the El, is lighted by windows and a skylight, while, within an enclosure at the nearer end of the room are two desks, placed back to back, with a big drafting table in the center. Three draftsmen are busy with tee-square, triangle, tracing paper, and blueprints at the north end: John and Jefferson Baumgarten, on swivel chairs, are busy, each at his own desk, one with the morning mail, while Baumgarten Senior is inscribing, in a fine, minute hand, a number of items in a small black leather notebook.

John Baumgarten is a bison; but without the sense of a herd. A powerful chest, and an unusually large head, with a great upward sweep of forehead and curley gray hair, show a man who is used both to outdoors and to the study. Baumgarten has caught the rhythm of his own era, and has timed himself to it with a complete sense of fitness and accomplishment.

It is a March morning in 1879. Icicles hang from the window-ledges: and though there is a great stream of sunlight playing among the chequered shadows of the Elevated, the load of snow on the skylight prevents it from filling the office, which is therefore, in opposition to the brilliance outside, a little gray. One of the draftsmen goes over to the coal stove in the middle of the room, and throws on a small shovel of coal.

BAUMGARTEN (*without raising his head*): Mr. Clark!

CLARK (*stepping down from his stool with military alacrity*): Here, sir!

BAUMGARTEN: Please to come inside with your calculations on the footway.

CLARK: Very well, sir. Here they are.

(A seedy, sandy-haired man of forty, with a weak intelligent face, which comes with a character which is both cocky and distrustful of itself, enters through the swinging bar.)

228

BAUMGARTEN (*looking up with a kindly smile of superiority*): Mr. Clark: your calculations for the footway are seven tons heavier than the original ones. Did you reckon on using mahogany instead of yellow pine?

CLARK (*flustered*): No sir. Yellow pine. I checked the calculations carefully; and Brown confirmed them. There must have been some error in the original.

BAUMGARTEN: I made the original calculations: there was no error, my friend.

CLARK: That may be. But seven tons comes within our margin of safety. A little more or less on the footway won't count.

BAUMGARTEN: That's where you are a bad engineer, Mr. Clark. The margin of safety is just the thing we are not going to tamper with. With a mistake in the calculation here, and the beams a little heavier there, and an unexpected load in the next place—so—before you know it the margin of safety is gone. The margin of safety and the margin of error are two different things. We maintain the margin of safety: we reduce the margin of error. Come! Let's see where you have gone wrong.

CLARK (*nettled*): There's no possibility of my having gone wrong on the calculations. I'll stake my job on that.

BAUMGARTEN: Don't give up your job so quickly, Mr. Clark. If your calculations are all right, the error must lie in your original figures. If the answer is wrong, perhaps you haven't begun with the right question. Now then: footway twenty feet wide. Right?

CLARK: Right.

BAUMGARTEN: Air dried yellow pine, thoroughly seasoned. Right?

CLARK: Right.

BAUMGARTEN: Two inch boards?

CLARK: Yes, yes.

BAUMGARTEN: Three inches wide?

CLARK: Three inches wide? No: I reckoned on the basis of six inch board. That's the usual thing.

BAUMGARTEN (*triumphantly*): It doesn't pay to go according to the usual thing. This is an unusual bridge, Mr. Clark: if you follow the original specifications you'll have to waste much less time in checking. Do you realize that this bridge is going to be used?

CLARK (*chagrined*): Of course it will: and a six inch board will splinter less easily than a three inch one will.

BAUMGARTEN: You are quite right, Mr. Clark. But a three inch board gives twice as many spaces between the boards as six inch boards would. There's the factor of lightness: in a mile and a half of footway it comes to four tons. If a three inch board wears out it can be replaced without danger or interference. With bigger boards we might have to interrupt the traffic.

CLARK (*more chagrined*): I see, General.

BAUMGARTEN: Good. Please make new calculations, and send the specifications off to the bidders by tonight.

JEFFERSON (*joining in*): What's the hurry, General. It will be another year or two before the Bridge is ready for the footway; that's almost the last thing.

BAUMGARTEN (*briefly dismissing Clark before tending to his son*): Go ahead, Mr. Clark. Send the bids out tonight! (*Turning to his son*) *Du bist ein kluger Kerl*, Jefferson. We want seasoned lumber. Here nobody has time to season it. The rascals will give us green wood: I know them! We'll let it season itself.

JEFFERSON: That means tying up so much capital for two years.

BAUMGARTEN: Capital: tying up capital? Well, if it's tied up, it won't get into mischief. In the army we didn't have that sort of nonsense to deal with. The contractors were dishonest and the quartermasters were scoundrels, most of them: but when we needed guns we didn't ask whether we'd got the capital. I'm a capitalist, too: I'd like to get interest and profit all the time on my money: *das würde kollossal!* But I'm an engineer, and if I want a job done right I can't worry if some shyster banker or financier is going to get a big plum out of it, too. The Bridge will pay in the end: that's enough!

JEFFERSON: When it comes to the rewards of capital, I am a socialist. But for the moment that's our working basis, and the board of directors are kicking hard enough already about the Quincy granite. One of the directors has an interest in a Pennsylvania quarry.

BAUMGARTEN: Let us do what's necessary, Jefferson. Don't mind the board of directors. They play the same part in building a bridge or running a factory that the politicians did in the war: they are interested only for what they can get out of it—that's why they interfere. The job comes first! The Bridge is in our hands, not in theirs.

JEFFERSON: But have we any storage space for the lumber?

BAUMGARTEN: Did you see Baxter about getting that municipal property near the Bridge on a short lease?

JEFFERSON: No, the last time I dropped in the Hell-house he was drunk.

BAUMGARTEN: I'll see him tonight. I can handle a souse like that. When the treat's on me, he has to drink my kind of Schnapps, and that's better than his *verrückte* Irish whiskey. They want us to build the biggest bridge in the world without giving us any storage space. The holdup men in the City Council ought to be hung up on all the lamp-posts around Borough Hall.

JEFFERSON: Did you get permission to use that property near Sand Street?

BAUMGARTEN: Permission? No: they kept us dilly-dallying a whole month about that. I tore down the fence and gave Powers orders to

230

store all the girders there. Let them move them out now. They haven't any derricks and there's no place to move all that stuff to!

JEFFERSON (*shocked*): Look here, father: the war has been over a long time. You can't use such high-handed tactics nowadays.

BAUMGARTEN (*chuckling*): That which cannot be done *was* done! There you are, my son. The war is always on. The people who know what they want, get it. When the honest men know their minds as well, the robbers and rascals in the city will all starve. Look at Tweed. If you and I had had the courage to build boulevards and parkways, such loafers wouldn't have gotten fat.

JEFFERSON: Baxter is a rogue; but I'd rather come to an understanding with him and get hold of the land in a legal way through the Council. There's no use in setting those swine against us: they give picnics once a year to all our unskilled laborers, and they have every Mick in the hollow of their hand. They can make trouble for us.

BAUMGARTEN: Come to an understanding with Baxter? I understand him. He wants his rakeoff. He can whistle for it. I'd rather come to an understanding with Shane Magonigle.

JEFFERSON (*quietly*): Magonigle is coming this morning.

BAUMGARTEN: Hah! What does he want with us?

JEFFERSON: Half the riveters are in the Union now. They want a nine-hour day and Saturday half-holiday, and a ten per cent increase.

BAUMGARTEN: What else?

JEFFERSON: They want insurance against accident at our expense.

BAUMGARTEN: What are you going to tell him?

JEFFERSON: If we raise the wages on more men, we upset our budget: perhaps we'll be wrecked before we finish the work. There's nothing wrong in what the men are asking; but we can't afford to do it. They should have been organized before we made our contracts.

BAUMGARTEN: Good: that settles it. You tend to them!

JEFFERSON: We're working on too close a margin. The factor of financial safety was estimated a little too low. Prices are always fluctuating: but over ten years there has been a trend upward; and at the rate we are going it may take us almost ten to finish the Bridge. We've made no allowance for that.

BAUMGARTEN: *Mein Kind*: you and I are the best engineers in the country: with the exception of two or three other ones, the rest are plumbers and nightwatchmen! But we make mistakes like children: we work with half a dozen variables, and we think that if we master these we can build our bridges. In reality, there are a hundred variables; and each one we forget or don't allow for comes out in the form of a mistake. It was a mistake to let the Municipal Council pick out the site, without examining the river bottom; it was a mistake to calculate on the cost of labor without remembering that the Irish immigration may fall off if Ireland gets Home Rule: and so on: one mistake after another. The only thing that keeps us from going under—the only thing that makes us good engineers instead of bad ones—is that anyone else would have made twice the number of mistakes. (*With conviction*) We are children. You are an ignoramus. I am an old fool!

JEFFERSON: If we bothered to work out all the variables, we should never have time to begin. It's only by accepting the mistakes as a part of the work that we can do anything at all. After all, the Bridge must be built!

BAUMGARTEN (*a little sadly*): When you are young, you can think that way. When the Civil War came here in America, I didn't reckon with all the variables: I plunged in. Do you think I foresaw that Lincoln would waste two whole years before freeing the slaves, and another two years before Grant got the upper hand; and that the total result would be the wreck of the best agricultural and mineral land in the country, with a government of thieves and carpetbaggers to humiliate and ruin the conquered territories? Pfui! I don't believe so much in cutting the Gordian knots any more. In Germany we learned to think; if I had to start in again as an engineer, I should think more and build less. In warfare one hasn't time to think; the sacrifices must occur if the game is to go on, like the capture of pawns in chess: but now—if one doesn't use one's critical reason one is a pig, a sheep, a donkey—a Baxter!

JEFFERSON (*cheerfully*): I expect to eat my peck of errors before I die.

BAUMGARTEN: Yes my son: but for every error we have to swallow personally, a hundred other people will get the belly-ache. We didn't foresee the rise in prices: so we can't give the riveters a rise in wages or insurance. The result is that Mrs. X hasn't enough money to pay for the funeral, Mrs. W. has to send her children to the orphanage, Mrs. T. U. and V. don't get enough nourishment while they are carrying their babies. (*Mixing up his biblical allusion*) You eat a peck of sour grapes, and all the workers' teeth are set on edge.

JEFFERSON: You are right, General. You usually are. But you don't make it any easier for me to meet Shane Magonigle.

(*There is a knock at the door, which isn't answered by any of the draftsmen. The knock is repeated: and when Magonigle comes in, followed by three other workmen in their leisure clothes, Clark at last slips off his stool and goes over to Shane.*)

BAUMGARTEN: That's another matter. You can't do anything now. In the Church they let you repent of your sins: in real life you have to live with them, and make more of them in order to cover the first ones up. The moral is: repent of your sins before you commit them.

MAGONIGLE: We've come to see Mr. Baumgarten. He knows what it's about.

JEFFERSON (*calling over, with resolute affability*): Come right in, Magonigle. This way.

(*With an involuntary clinching of his hands to get control over himself, Magonigle leads the other two men over. He is a lean, long-necked Irishman, about forty, with a slightly irregular but handsome face: eloquent gray eyes surrounded by fine wrinkles, and a broad mouth, a little too tender for real leadership, but suitable for any oratorical occasion. One of the other men is heavy, small-eyed, stubborn, a little dour: the third is black-haired, very handsome, full of blarney: the kind that eats well, liquors easily, is a devil with the girls and popular with the men, without having a single genuine merit which will stand fire. Jefferson rises to hold out his hand. Old Baumgarten, with a brief nod of acknowledgement, turns to the papers on his desk and takes no part in the conversation.*)

JEFFERSON: Good morning, Magonigle. Good morning Casey. (*Turning to the debonair delegate*) I don't think I know . . .

MAGONIGLE: He's our new secretary. Russell: a Belfast man.

RUSSELL (*smiling*): Jim Russell.

JEFFERSON: You haven't been on our gang?

RUSSELL: No: I was in the Navy shipyard till they laid us off.

JEFFERSON: Sit down: sit down. (*Calling over to the draftsmen*): Will one of you boys bring over an extra chair? (*They all remain standing a little awkwardly until the extra chair is brought.*) Well now! (*The three men clear their throats uneasily, Casey and Russell looking to Magonigle to begin. Jefferson continues impatiently*): You boys have come to talk over the list of demands you submitted in writing last week?

CASEY: That's it.

MAGONIGLE (*glancing quickly at him to be sure he won't speak further*): We've come to you with the full authority of the Union behind us. The men held a mass meeting last Friday night, and empowered us to negotiate with you at our own discretion. I suppose you know that more than half your riveters are now with us?

JEFFERSON: Let's not begin drawing up our forces and counting heads, Magonigle. That will look as if we were going to have a fight: and before you know it we will be fighting.

RUSSELL (*grinning*): Fight was never a word to daunt an Irishman, Mr. Baumgarten.

JEFFERSON: Fighting may be your business, Russell. Building bridges is mine.

MAGONIGLE: But who builds the bridges? The workers. The sooner you learn that you can't do without us . . .

JEFFERSON (*cutting short his speech*): Nobody wants to do without you, Magonigle. What I want you to understand, before we go ahead, is my position—(*nodding over to his father*)—our position. We are between two parties. We are hired by a group of capitalists to build the Bridge. They are one side. They have the money; and as long as we have to buy steel and granite and wood with money, we are all in their power.

MAGONIGLE: In the Socialist Commonwealth . . .

JEFFERSON (*interrupting*): Let's deal with one world at a time, Magonigle: a hundred years from now it may all be different: the government will collect and manage the capital: you and I will be treated like soldiers in an army. If you threaten to strike, as you are threatening now, you will be imprisoned as a mutineer or shot as a traitor.

CASEY (*soberly*): We don't want to deal with the government. We're against the government. We want to deal with you.

JEFFERSON: All right: let us stick to that. We're engineers: we are between two groups. The capitalists give us the money: that means go ahead. We make the plans and boss the job. You do the work: you carry it out.

MAGONIGLE: Yes: we do the work. And who gets the benefit out of it: a lot of lazy gentlemen with side whiskers who don't know a pick from a crowbar, and who dress up their daughters like Astor's pet horse so that they can marry an English Duke or a Russian Count. All we ask is a little justice. We are human beings. We can't work ten hours a day, six days a week, and be decent husbands and tend to our children. You're a decent man, Mr. Baumgarten. How would you support a family of five on fifteen dollars a week?

JEFFERSON: I've hard enough work to mind my own business: I don't pretend to know how to mind yours, Magonigle. Your business this morning is to get three things out of me: a ten per cent rise in wages, an insurance against accident and disability, to do away with suits and going to law, and a Saturday half-holiday.

CASEY: Good: that's talking brass tacks.

MAGONIGLE: Those are our immediate demands: they are our minimum.

JEFFERSON (*facing the music all at once*): Minimum and maximum come to pretty much the same this morning, Magonigle. About the first demand: we can't grant the ten per cent rise. If we do it for one trade, we'll have to do it for the rest; or there'll be bad feeling and dissatisfaction. We simply haven't enough money in our budget to cover it. The people who are backing the project

234

won't advance any more capital: the Bridge already is going to cost a third more than we expected.

MAGONIGLE: That means a strike.

JEFFERSON (*going on rapidly*): Now to the second point: the insurance. That's an excellent idea.

CASEY (*shrewdly*): Maybe we can make a compromise.

MAGONIGLE: Hold your tongue, Mike. This is no time for compromise. There's many a riveter who doesn't make enough money in the summer to keep so much as a fire in his stove in the zero of winter. This means a strike, I say! Have you counted the cost of that, Mr. Baumgarten?

JEFFERSON: There were three points. The second is a good one. Under ordinary circumstances we'd be in favor of it. In a project of this scale, a certain number of accidents and deaths are bound to occur: it's a dangerous business. It needs men of guts, and their families ought to be pensioned when anything happens to them. I am for the insurance. But we can't take the financial burden of it. Our budget limits us again.

MAGONIGLE: What are you beating around the bush for! If you are going to turn down all our demands, say so. Don't pretend you are on our side. You're for the side that butters your bread thickest.

JEFFERSON: I'm on neither side, can't you understand that? We can't build the Bridge without capital: it's as necessary now as sand or mortar. (*Magonigle opens his mouth and Jefferson continues hastily*): Never mind about what it will be in the Socialist Commonwealth. In the here and now it's the thing that limits us. As the job is going through now, we haven't a penny to spare.

CASEY: Would you stand half the expense of the insurance wid us?

JEFFERSON: I hadn't thought of that. There's a possibility. Let's put that to one side. If we can, we will. Now as to the third point: there's a lot to be said against a Saturday half-holiday. How will most of the men spend it? Getting tanked up and unfit for work on Monday.

MAGONIGLE (*bitterly*): I thought you had hard enough work to mind your own business: if you don't care if the worker has to starve, why should you care if he drinks?

JEFFERSON: Good! you've got me. I agree. Therefore, we are ready to compromise. More than that, we'll reduce the hours to nine *and* give you a Saturday half-holiday.

RUSSELL: That's spoken like a gentleman.

CASEY: That's getting us somewhere.

MAGONIGLE: There's a catch in it. He wouldn't go so far if there wasn't a catch.

JEFFERSON: You're right, Magonigle. Why should you think I am looking after your interests? I am looking after my own. I've been keeping account of the number of rivets driven per man per hour. It falls off badly after four-thirty. That extra hour might as well be written off altogether.

MAGONIGLE: I said so.

CASEY: An hour is an hour. It's a victory. We can face the boys wid this.

MAGONIGLE (*to Casey*): Is this the first time a gentleman has ever shaken hands with you? If they'll give us this much, they'll give us more. After all, I'm responsible for seeing these demands through. If you won't back me up you can back out.

CASEY: I wasn't saying nothing. Let's get back to the ten per cent.

BAUMGARTEN (*without raising his head*): We can stand half and half on the insurance. The steel market is in our favor now; and we can make it up there.

JEFFERSON: We'll go in for the insurance then, fifty-fifty.

CASEY: There: what did I say?

MAGONIGLE (*conceiving a bold stroke on wages*): If you're ready to meet us we'll meet you. We'll take a five per cent raise on the wages.

JEFFERSON (*glances over to his father who nods a faint negative*): Not a damned penny.

MAGONIGLE: You'll give us insurance, which is a trifle; and you'll give us hours, which don't bring you in anything, anyway: but you won't give us any money. There's where your class consciousness comes in. Well, let me warn you, Mr. Baumgarten: the working class is becoming conscious of its power, too. We won't be tricked by your fair words and your sympathy. It's deeds that count. You're either for us or against us. We shan't stop until we have wrung every last penny and every last ounce of power out of you. Then we'll tell you what you can work at for us.

JEFFERSON (*sardonically*): That's what you call being a free man, eh?— giving somebody else orders, and grinding your heel in somebody else's face?

MAGONIGLE: The worker has been the underdog all along. It's time to exchange places.

JEFFERSON: We've offered you the best terms we can, and still carry the job through. If you had any sense of pride, you'd be happy to cooperate with us. This is a great bridge. It stands among bridges where the Parthenon stands in architecture.

MAGONIGLE: Yes: maybe. And what does the worker get out of it? I have read my history, too, Mr. Baumgarten. The Parthenon was built by slaves; and for all you care we'd be slaves, too. You are trying to gild our chains. What good does the glory do us?

JEFFERSON: But the job, man, the job! You are right: you have the

236

slave psychology. The slave wants his three meals a day and clean quarters and as little work as possible. A real man wants to do his job even if he eats slops, sleeps on the ground, and works till he is sick. When you feel that way about the Bridge you won't be whining about justice: when you feel that way, the Bridge will be yours, and you'll get your justice without whining about it.

MAGONIGLE: A man wants his family and he wants his home.

JEFFERSON (*with conviction*): The work of the world would never get done if men were really satisfied with that sort of thing. A man wants blood, wounds, privation, death!

MAGONIGLE: That's your bourgeois heroism—the buncombe that the privileged classes preach to the workers to keep them satisfied with their poverty and to make them ready to fight their wars. Let's see your blood and wounds and privation. You live in a brownstone front: we don't. You have down comforters on your beds and open plumbing and hot-air heating. We don't. You *preach* the heroism: we *do* the dirty work.

CASEY (*seeing the tangible points drifting away, wheedling*): Say five per cent, and we'll make a contract on it for three years.

JEFFERSON: Sorry, Casey: figures don't change the way one's feelings do. I've met you on every possible point.

MAGONIGLE: Then be prepared for a strike!

JEFFERSON (*quietly*): You are going to strike!

MAGONIGLE (*fiercely*): We are going to strike!

JEFFERSON (*folding his arms and facing Magonigle firmly*): Very well: I'm ready (*a pause*): Are you?

(*Magonigle looks at him steadily for a moment, then gets a little abashed, moves back a step, opens his mouth as if to say something; and then turns for consultation to the other two workers.*)

(*Curtain*)

Scene Three

The corner of the Fulton Ferry House, nearest the Bridge: the gate for vehicles, and the butting slabs of the bulkheads, stretching out into the water are all that can be seen of the House. There is a stretch of wharf, with heavy wooden stanchions at intervals; the river is slapping at the timbers, and from a barge below a gang of laborers are unloading bags of cement. Towering above all this is the unfinished eastern pier of the Bridge: the masonry reaches a little above the level of the future suspension work, blocking out in space the lower part of the arch. At this stage the stonework might be taken for either a beginning or a ruin; the fresh face of the granite is all that gives it an assurance of the first.

A hot afternoon in August, 1880: the Italians unloading the barge are working very slowly, a few of them stripped to the waist, showing knotted shoulders and arms, and glistening bronze skin. Two little gutter rats, aged thirteen and fifteen respectively, and looking to be, by evidence of height and degree of nourishment, no more than nine and twelve, are fishing from the farthest corner of the wharf. They use a line, a sinker, and a worm, and for a float have only the faith that keeps them pinned to the blistering planks in spite of the sun and the inevitable lack of even catfish in the dirty waters. The westering sun, at four o'clock, casts a friendly shadow from the Ferry House, in the relative cool of which sits, on a camp chair, Thomas Fielding. He is a sweet-faced, emaciated man with the sort of fair skin that never tans past sunburn, and white hair, which go very well with his blue shirt and darker blue overalls. Chewing tobacco and whittling a long wooden stick, as he is now doing, he is the antiquated counterpart of Whittier's barefoot boy. A little distance away, on a box, sits Robert-Owen Benns, with a sketch pad on his knee.

FIELDING: The DeWitt Clinton comes on at four-thirty for the rush. That's my boat. Reckon you ain't got much time left.

ROBERT-OWEN: Just turn your head a little to the left again, Mr. . . . Mr. Fielding. That's right. I'll be ready before then. It's just a sketch.

238

(Robert-Owen Benns has the dark eyes and the dark complexion that one finds in certain Scotch strains: his face at first glance looks saturnine; at second, it is kindly, understanding, and even a little wistful. He is compact in build; rather grave and soft-spoken in voice; there is a touch of Edinburgh and London in his accent; but the four years spent abroad have been spent mostly in Paris. He is dressed in unbleached linens, which include a vest, and around his neck is a light red scarf: like most cultivated Americans, he is slightly conscious of being a foreigner in America: but, being distinctly an American, he is equally a foreigner anywhere else.)

ROBERT-OWEN *(to make Fielding pose a little easier)*: You know the waterfront pretty well, I suppose?

FIELDING: I've a-ben on the water ever since I was kneehigh to a toadstool. I could row a rowboat before I could add three figgers. I kin remember the old hoss ferry acrost here. There used to be four of 'em between here and Atlantic Avenue, not counting all the others right up to Wallabout Basin.

ROBERT-OWEN *(abstractedly)*: You were brought up in Brooklyn, then?

FIELDING: No: I'm an old Long Islander. I was born in Whitestone Landing and bred and brung up in Little Neck. I used to bring the vegetables to market down through Hell Gate, when Hell Gate *was* Hell Gate. Anybody can get through her now: but many's the dousing I've had before they dynamited the Devil's Whirlpool.

ROBERT-OWEN: You've seen a lot of changes, then, haven't you?

FIELDING: Changes? Aye, plenty of changes. Far too many changes I'm a-thinking. I used to be an oysterman, too, but the big companies hired a lot of pirates and an honest man didn't get a living. I shipped once on a whaler from Block Island. But I don't like the deep sea. I'm a Sound man. *(Profoundly)* Long Island Sound's the finest stretch of water in the world, taking everything together.

ROBERT-OWEN *(tolerantly smiling)*: Southampton Water is fine, too, between the Needles and the Hampshire Coast. Casco Bay up in Maine is wonderful.

FIELDING *(doggedly)*: You can have your Southampton Waters and your Casco Bays. There's nothing like the Sound. Look at the vegetables: where did you ever get better potatoes or asparagus? Look at the clams and the oysters. Look at the ducks over on the South Marshes at Moriches. There's everything here: the Dutch knew what they were doing. They spread all through Long Island when there wasn't so much as a toll gate between the Bowery and White Plains. For living, you can't beat the Dutch:

for land, you can't beat Long Island; and for clean, nourishing water, you can't beat the Sound.

ROBERT-OWEN (*glancing down into the water, and wrinkling his nose*): It's nourishing, all right: but most of the nourishment is a little too old and decayed. I shouldn't call it clean any more.

FIELDING: This ain't the real Sound. This water here's all churned up and muddy. Nothing around here is right any more, since all them furriners come in. (*The Italians on the barge are having a pleasant quarrel, with many gestures and much violence of tongue.*) Look at them: a lot of Dagoes and Syrians from Siberia. They don't speak grammar: and they don't know nothin'. They live on snails and cockroaches; I see them eat them every noon; and they never tasted any proper food. Someday we'll have to clear them all out again. What did we ever want them here for in the first place? (*With great scorn*) Immigrants: that's what they are.

ROBERT-OWEN (*smiling at the shrivelled old man's pathetic arrogance*): If it wasn't for the immigrants, you and I wouldn't be here, either, I'm afraid. The Italians are very nice people, Mr. Fielding: an Italian discovered America. This is everybody's country, isn't it?

FIELDING (*with conviction*): I don't hold with you there. An American is an American. If you're here, you're an American: if you come here, you're a furriner.

ROBERT-OWEN: Well: if it weren't for the foreigners, we wouldn't have our railroads or our bridges built. Do you mind turning just a little to the right again? . . . There! (*He goes on sketching.*)

FIELDING: And what do we want with all these bridges and railroads? This was a good country before they were here. A man had plenty to eat in the old days. A day on the water would give him all the bluefish and weakfish he could eat in a month of Sundays. If the fish didn't bite he could eat clams. If the clams were scarce, he could hoe potatoes. I had my own patch of ground once. Along came the railroad and snatched it under my nose; they made me sign a paper and done me out of it, all but three hundred fifty dollars I had to divide half and half with my lawyer. And what's the result? The trains drive out the ducks and the quail; they drive out all the watermen who used to bring the vegetables by boat and charge twice as much for expressage: and wherever the railroad goes a man can't farm any more: the land is divided into building lots and eats its head off in taxes. That's what progress means. Progress means hard times and a lot of furriners and no place for an honest American to get a decent living. Here am I, nigh on to sixty-seven years, working on a steam ferry. When we hit the dock I open the gates: before we leave, I close the gates. When the morning rush is over I swab up the Ferry House. Tarnation! that ain't living. If I didn't want to be by my darter in my old age, you wouldn't see me on these waters. And now folks say the ferryboat will go soon, soon's the Bridge is up.

ROBERT-OWEN (*consoling the man's age*): That will be a little while yet, Mr. Fielding. Neither you nor I, possibly, will see it.

FIELDING (*venomously*): I don't believe them, but that's what folks say. (*Prophetically*) Mark my words sir: *that* thing is going to sink. It's on a float now; and before you know it they'll put a stone too many on that bridge and—kerplunk—it'll all go down in the water and be an obstruction to the Sound. Stands to reason: nobody ever built a bridge like that before. It's flying in the face of Providence. (*He stands up in a rage: his finger towering prophetically over his head.*) Damned furriners!

ROBERT-OWEN (*eagerly*): Just hold that for a moment, Mr. Fielding: just a moment: don't lower your arm. The voice of the prophet storming against the sins of Israel. (*He looks up puckishly, purposely mystifying Fielding*) This is a page for a modern Bible.

FIELDING: You took me up pretty short, young man. (*Becoming self-conscious, and a caricature of himself*) Is this it?

ROBERT-OWEN (*still bent over his pad*): That's all right. I've got it. I am very grateful to you for sitting for me. Would you— (*he puts his hand dubiously in his pocket, not knowing quite whether the generous thing is the tactful thing.*)

FIELDING: Don't say a word, young man. My time's my own, same's my face. You're welcome to it. I once had my pitcher taken on a tintype. Kin I see this?

ROBERT-OWEN (*holding up his pad*): I am going to make a bigger picture later on, maybe. This is just a few sketches.

(*While Fielding gazes at the sketches, with the naïve puzzlement of one who sees only pencil marks instead of the form they represent, Owen gets up and stretches. The urchins espy him for the first time; and run over.*)

TIMMY: Make me a pitcher, mister.

MIKE: Gimme a penny, mister.

TIMMY (*brilliantly*): Gimme a penny and I'll letcher take me pitcher, mister.

MIKE: He's me pal. Yeh gotta take de bot' of us. Come on, mister. (*Glibly*) My fadder's outa work and I ain't got no mudder. We got seven children, we have. Gimme a nickel mister. I'll give it straight to me mudder, mister, hones' to God I will. (*As Robert-Owen continues to look at them in cryptic silence, Mike's imagination enlarges the possibilities*): I once posed for a guy, mister, and he gimme a dime he did. I know how to pose. My mudder's a widder-woman, mister, and I bring in all de money to her. Gimme a dime. Ah gwan. Gimme a dime. You don't have to sketch me; just gimme a dime.

TIMMY: Shut up, you little bastard. He's lying, mister. Don't you believe him. I'll let yer take my pitcher for a nickel. Gimme five cents.

ROBERT-OWEN (*to Timmy*): What would you do with it?

TIMMY: I'd give it to me mudder. Honest I will.

MIKE: I'd buy an ice-cream sody . . . (*generously*) and I'll let him have half the suds.

ROBERT-OWEN: Here's a nickel for the soda. Wash your face once a week and don't tell so many lies.

MIKE (*injured*): I'm not lyin', mister. I was only fooling. (*Cajolling*) Gimme a nickel for a chocolate ice-cream sody!

ROBERT-OWEN (*aside to Fielding*): He that repents at the eleventh hour shall enter the Kingdom of Heaven, too. Here you are, lad!

FIELDING: It's wrong to abet those young scamps. (*He makes a flourish with his hands.*) Be off with you: Don't let me catch you hanging around here again. (*They leave: and in half a minute come back skulking to recover their fishing lines and bait cans.*) They spend their time thieving and lying. Honest men don't get money so easily.

ROBERT-OWEN (*seeing that the time has come to act and that he may do it safely, slips a half dollar into Fielding's hand, and covers it up with a request*): May I have your camp chair for sketching the rest of the afternoon? This box has too many splinters.

FIELDING (*almost obsequious*): Certainly sir. Glad to oblige a gentleman any time sir. Just ask for Old Tom Fielding if you want a turn done around here. When you get through with the camp stool just put it back behind the partition in the men's room.

(*Jefferson enters in rough working trousers and open-fronted shirt. Powers, his chief foreman, a thin, crusty Irishman of fifty, with a hard, puckered mouth, a short nose, and penetrating but kind eyes, follows him half a step in the rear.*)

JEFFERSON: There: just as I thought. They've been dumping the bags of cement on the wet part of the dock! It will cake through.

POWERS: The damned wops! But I can't be everywhere, sir. We've got a new timekeeper on the construction job that's been letting the men flim-flam him; and I had to stay wid him this afternoon and . . .

JEFFERSON: I know: I know. It isn't your fault. I shall have to give you an extra man as assistant. Will anyone on the gang do?

POWERS: Hey there you! (*The sheepish head of a young man raises itself above the wharf, from the barge below.*) What the hell do you mean by dumping cement on the wet floor. Have you been sleeping all afternoon? Get a gang of wheelbarrers and move them right over to the shed.

JEFFERSON: And turn the wet sacks up in the sun to let them dry! Phew! It's a hot day: what do you say to a schooner of beer, John?

POWERS (*to the man in the barge, who has muttered something under his breath*): What's that ye said? Say that again and I'll knock ye down; and I'll knock the whole goddamned gang for a gool, too.

AN ITALIAN HEAD (*appearing indignantly over the edge of the wharf*): Me no sonovabeech.

POWERS: Arrah! (*And he makes a sudden, prompt move toward the barge. The head ducks. The men on the barge come up sullenly, and file across the pier, coming back presently with wheelbarrows, which they load with the cement. Powers looks down into the barge at the foreman*): What the hell's happened to you. This ain't a Sundayschool picnic. If you can't get the work out of the men, take a wheelbarrer yerself, and I'll work ye!

JEFFERSON: Don't push them too hard, John. You think everybody can work the way you can. They can let up a little on an afternoon like this if they want to: but we can't have them wasting the cement like a lot of brainless idiots.

POWERS (*contemptuously*): A lot of yeller livered sheep that don't know what a decent day's work is. Did you say beer, Mr. Baumgarten? Beer it is!

JEFFERSON: Come on, then. (*Going over in the direction of the Ferry House he first notices Robert-Owen, who has resumed sketching, this time of Powers*): Hello, Benns!

ROBERT-OWEN: Hello, Baumgarten!

JEFFERSON: Been sketching the Bridge?

ROBERT-OWEN: No: the people.

JEFFERSON: You should see the waterfront from the top of the pier: if nothing else ever got built, we could run an elevator up to the top and turn it into an open air museum, ten cents a peep, just for the view.

ROBERT-OWEN: The men who are building your Bridge are what interest me. May I drop around to your office some slow day? I'd like to sketch you, too.

JEFFERSON: People be hanged! The Bridge is going to be a beauty.

ROBERT-OWEN: The Bridge be hanged! When a bridge can change its expression, or ripple its muscles under the skin, or move its arms and legs rhythmically, I'll be interested in bridges instead of men.

JEFFERSON: That shows you don't know what a bridge is like, Benns. (*Turning triumphantly to Powers*): Think of it, John, he doesn't know she's alive! The Bridge is always changing its expression; when the span is over the river you'll see it as quick as I do. It has its muscles and its arms and its rhythm, too. You don't see then, Benns, because you are anthropomorphic: you want a bridge or a machine to have the same kind of organs as you or me: just as an ignorant person thinks that God is a creature with a fair complexion and whiskers and a strong right hand. You want a bridge to change its expression in a second, like a man: but a bridge's life is a long life: it's taken ten years to change its expression. The engineer has to watch every change. If the bridge looks depressed, it needs a coat of paint; if it looks nervous and over-wrought, it needs a suspension of traffic and a complete rest, until we can operate on its organs and replace its wornout parts! (*Nodding toward the Bridge*) This is a healthy bridge: look at those legs! I don't expect any nervous breakdowns.

POWERS (*grimly*): It's we that'll have the breakdowns, till the dommed beauty can stand by herself and look after herself.

ROBERT-OWEN: The mischief of talking about bridges and machines as if they were alive is that it leads you naturally to talk about men and women as if they were dead. When a piece of machinery is your ideal, you have a complete contempt for mankind because they are poor and inefficient machines.

JEFFERSON: A bridge is a glimpse of perfection. You and I and Tom, Dick, and Harry are a succession of lapses, failures, and mistakes. Aren't we now? If there's going to be any kingdom of heaven on earth, it will be through bridges and not through us. (*Irrelevantly*) Helmholtz was right: the eye is an imperfect instrument: any optician would be ashamed of it. The rest of us is just as bad!

ROBERT-OWEN: You want your heaven outside of you because you've given up the hope of building it within yourself.

JEFFERSON: Yes: I have. Haven't you? If I hadn't the Bridge to build, I'd be a whining, puling, self-centered idiot with a disordered liver and a bad complexion. What's good in me comes out in the Bridge. The Bridge is a Reality.

ROBERT-OWEN (*smiling at Baumgarten's naïve assurance*): You confirm my suspicions about the Practical Man, my dear Baumgarten. He is an overgrown child; and what he calls the real and the practical is just an escape from Reality. The bridge is a toy. All your machinery is toys. What you call the practical life is just an escape from real things into the simplicity of the nursery.

JEFFERSON (*delighted with his own aptness*): Unless you be as little children you shall not enter the Kingdom of Heaven. Perhaps I am a child. Perhaps we're all children. (*Looking at Robert-Owen's sketch*) You are a child, too: what are those scratches on paper? Do they make you any happier than blowing soap bubbles in the sun? Is beauty any more solid than a soap bubble? (*He points to the Bridge*): Lay up your treasure in heaven; rain and frost will take a long time to corrupt that granite; and as long as the metal is painted regularly, no rust shall destroy it.

ROBERT-OWEN: Since when have you become a student of the Bible?

JEFFERSON: I used to read it to Delia when I was a kid.

ROBERT-OWEN: You don't think you have seriously answered me, do you?

JEFFERSON: Why of course I have.

ROBERT-OWEN: In that case, let's all have some beer. (*Putting the camp stool under his arm and turning to Powers*): Do you believe in Mr. Baumgarten's religion, Mr. Powers?

POWERS (*crossing himself*): It'll help him in this world; but it's no good in the next. I'm a Roman Catholic. He's a pagan, sir.

ROBERT-OWEN: Why do you build bridges, then, Powers?

POWERS: There's worse ways of dying than on a bridge, all but the lack of the sacrament.

JEFFERSON (*arrogantly, putting his arm affectionately through Powers'*): Nonsense, John, you enjoy it: it's a great life.

POWERS (*solemnly*): Or a great death: what's the difference? Did ye say beer, Mr. Benns?

ROBERT-OWEN: Powers is a little nearer to reality than you are, Baumgarten! He remembers death! (*Turning to Powers*) Beer it is, Powers: the treat is on me. I want to do your portrait some Sunday if you can spare me an hour. I wish we could have a little music with the beer, as they do in Munich.

(*Curtain*)

Scene Four

The back room of William Baxter's saloon at the bottom of Furman Street: a blackened, smokey, cobwebby place, the floor spattered with badly aimed tobacco-spittle, all the light coming, late this November afternoon, from a dingy little window that opens on and airshaft, opposite an unshaded gas jet, projecting from the wall. There is an old print of the Sayers-Heenan fight on the right wall, while on the wall which opens into the main bar of the saloon, where a few men are perfunctorily drinking, there is a half-hearted attempt at convivial lewdness in the form of a leering lady in tights, from Koster and Biel's, lying on a lacy bed. The door in the wall with the gas jet has a sign on it: Ladies' Parlor. It is a wet day. The men who come slogging in leave puddles of water when they stand for as long as a drink in one place. In the furnishing of the saloon proper there is an ancient attempt at elegance: mirrors with frosted designs, varieties of polished glasses for every occasion, and a great store of strange liquor bottles, some from as remote places as Peru, which somehow give an air of sophistication to the beer, gin, and whiskey which are almost the only liquors drunk. There is sawdust on the floor; and the barkeeper's assistant is pushing the dirty wet particles together in one corner with a floor brush, before putting on a new sprinkling. It is almost five-thirty; and when five-thirty comes the rush at the bar becomes violent, stormy, and compact, breaking out into little knots of men who have no railing for their feet.

William Baxter and John Baumgarten are seated at a little table in the corner of the back room. Baxter is a fat, coarse man, with spare gray hair cut with almost convict closeness, a pendulous lower lip, and tiny, pig eyes, that look greedily on food and flesh. He is a natural rogue, moral in his gambling, pimping, whoring, bribing, as other men are moral in marriage, business, or professional service. He has his standards: but knows enough of human nature not to push vice too far, so that he is sometimes found on the side of honesty in politics, or will collaborate with the priest on the side of maidenly virginity—though he can scarcely look upon a girl without mentally soiling her. He is the chief power in his ward and high up in the city councils: his authority rests on a certain sleepy shrewdness of judgement, which never entirely leaves him, even when he is fuddled with drink. As age and lapse of memory begin to overtake him, for he is now over sixty, he has taken under his wing a living memorandum pad who has no other name than Ikey. Ikey is a keen-witted, undersized Jewish boy of fifteen, dressed punctiliously in imitation of a man. He sits on a chair a little behind Baxter, all alertness.

BAXTER (*raising a finger of whiskey*): Here's looking at you!

BAUMGARTEN (*nods: they both drink. Baxter wipes his mouth with the back of his hand, and takes a quick gulp of water. Baumgarten steadily pours out another drink*): Prosit!

BAXTER: *Cheers!*

(*They drink and relapse into reflective silence. Baxter's sleepy, beady eyes are almost closed.*)

BAUMGARTEN: For warmth: one glass. For wet feet: two glasses. For wet feet and a chill: three glasses. *Noch einmal*, Baxter!

BAXTER: Willin' to keep you company this side of hell, General.

(*He pours out a third potion, and raising their glasses silently, they drink again. Baxter notices Ikey out of the corner of his eye.*)

BAXTER: You little scut: what are you shivering there for? Take a swallow, Ikey: If you're gone to be a man you got to learn to drink early. (*He pours out a small amount and pushes it gruffly in front of Ikey. He turns to Baumgarten in explanation*): That's my little Jew-boy.

BAUMGARTEN: So!

BAXTER: The ward over in Williamsburg is fillin' up with Jews. His father runs a stuss game and wants to start the kid in right. He's a great help and comfort in me old age. Did ye ever know an Irish lad that could multiply and add in his head and write Spencerian and keep his mouth shut? Just look. Ikey: what's my bank balance?

IKEY (*eagerly*): Four thousand and eighty-seven dollars even.

BAXTER (*looking significantly at Baumgarten*): How many Jews has moved into the eighteenth ward since the last election?

IKEY (*promptly*): Five forty-three.

BAXTER: How many Presidents have there been in the United States?

IKEY: Nineteen.

BAXTER: Where does Wild Katie Flynn live?

IKEY: Number 73 Sands Street.

BAXTER: Look at that! He's got a perfect memory. I haven't lost a dollar since I got that Jew-boy. When I'm drunk or having a party with the ladies, he takes charge of me pocketbook.

247

BAUMGARTEN: *Merkwürdig!*

> (*There is a silence between them again. The clink and chatter in the next room grow a little louder. Ikey plucks at Baxter's sleeve and whispers something in his ear.*)

BAXTER: There's me little memory-tickler! I was going to ask you something, General, the next time I saw you. Tonight's as good a time as any.

BAUMGARTEN: If it's business, you must wait until my son comes in. I'm getting old, Baxter, I can design bridges still; but I let my son attend to detail. When one grows old the details don't matter any more. One sees things better as a whole.

BAXTER: It ain't business, General. I was just wantin' a little favor of you. The Municipal Council has passed an order for you to vacate the Sands Street property. I guess I can bury that a while, if you'll do a little turn for me.

BAUMGARTEN: Speak up, *du alte* rascal! *Soll ich die Hände noch mit Geld schmieren?*

BAXTER (*understanding him well enough*): General, you and I are practical men. We are old timers. We understand each other. Your son is a good man; but he thinks honesty is just another way of being disagreeable. He don't like me. We don't get on well.

BAUMGARTEN: He is a fine engineer and a good executive.

BAXTER: Ah: but he ain't a politician.

BAUMGARTEN (*impatiently in German*): *Also!* . . .

BAXTER: I'm gettin' there, General: I'm gettin' around to it. This has been a hard year and lot of the boys are out of work. It ain't so easy to give them a dollar or two and a bit of whiskey and see that they vote right. I got to do better by them till the election is over. I want you to take on a hundred of 'em just for a few weeks. If we win all the wards, I can put 'em on the city payroll in the street-cleaning department. But now the Bridge is the only big job that's open, where the reformers won't raise a hell of a stink.

BAUMGARTEN: On the payroll?

BAXTER: Yes.

BAUMGARTEN: Will they work?

BAXTER: No.

BAUMGARTEN: At our expense?

BAXTER: No, General: I never ast something for nothing. Half and half. I'll pay half out of me personal pocketbook. (*Turning around to Ikey*): Make a note of that, Ikey. And I'll see that the Council's ordinance about the Sands Street property gets buried.

BAUMGARTEN: My son wouldn't say Yes to that!

BAXTER (*nodding*): Just between us, then, General.

BAUMGARTEN: I will see what I can do. When I calculated the cost of the Bridge and the length of time it would take, I only made allowances for the materials and the construction. I forgot that we had the political overhead to deal with.

BAXTER: Come, General: it's give and take. If it hadn't been for me taking Casey and putting him in a good solid municipal job one day a month, signing his own paycheck, there would have been nobody in the Union to keep off the strike. Shane Magonigle is a lily-livered temperance dude that will never see what's what or which side his bread is buttered on. With a lot of damned anarchists like Magonigle stirring up a fuss and no one here to blow it down for you, it's more than one delay you'd have had in building the Bridge.

BAUMGARTEN (*solemnly, speaking above Baxter's head and really soliloquizing*): Baxter, you are what Hegel calls the antithesis. When I was young I was a disciple of Kant. My motto was: so act that every deed could be made a universal one. On that principle, your conduct is an abomination. A world of Baxters and Caseys would sink under its own corruption.

BAXTER (*good-humoredly*): Easy there, General: we're all human. When the time comes to die, the priest'll be with us and we can all repent. I've been overfond of fornication and the lusts of the flesh, meself. (*Remembering something*): Ikey, Go and tell Lizzie I want to see her upstairs after dinner, and if Lizzie ain't there, tell the Big Baby it's her turn, with my compliments.

BAUMGARTEN (*speaking past the interruption*): Kant wishes to do away with evil. Hegel is more profound: he sees that evil is part of the World Spirit in its negative movement. So to do away with evil, we must embrace it: to embrace it firmly, we must combat it. Out of the combat comes the synthesis, that which is neither the old evil nor the old good, but something which is beyond both and which is different. You are necessary to the World Spirit, my friend Baxter!

BAXTER (*a little fuddled and taking it for a compliment, raises his glass*): Here's looking at you, General.

BAUMGARTEN: My son is necessary for the World Spirit, too: he is your antithesis. As for me, I am your opponent in the spirit, Baxter: but I cannot fight you. One must be unconscious of one's part if one is to play it well. The World Spirit will cast me aside.

BAXTER (*encouragingly*): Go on, General: you're a long way from dead. I wisht I had your health and strength.

BAUMGARTEN (*bound up in his metaphysics*): One is already dead when one loses the conviction of one's historical necessity.

BAXTER: Ye'd be a great one to talk with Father de la Salle. The Dominicans are great boys for long words: he'd match you heel and

249

heel. (*Looking through the doorway at the saloon and without changing his expression*): Ah! here's your son now. Don't let on about the payroll. We'll fix it up between us.

JEFFERSON (*entering and removing his wet coat and hat*): A fine pair of old cronies you are!

BAXTER: Pull up a chair and have a drink on the house, me boy.

JEFFERSON: Fill it up: I'm wet to the bone.

BAUMGARTEN: Have you been out on the pier?

JEFFERSON: No: I got wet walking from Fulton Street. I've been hiring an extra gang at the shed.

BAUMGARTEN: An extra gang?

JEFFERSON: Yes: we must push the masonry on before the frost and snow comes. I've taken on twenty more hod carriers and laborers.

BAUMGARTEN: When do they begin work?

JEFFERSON: Tomorrow morning.

BAXTER: Have another drink, me boy.

BAUMGARTEN (*boldly*): I have hired fifty men myself this afternoon.

JEFFERSON: Why didn't you tell me? I thought you were leaving that in my hands. When do they begin work?

BAUMGARTEN: They don't.

JEFFERSON (*looking suspiciously at Baxter*): Baxter: what have you been putting over on the old man while I was gone?

BAXTER: Just till the election is over. It's half pay and no fuss at all about the Sand Street property. They'll bury the Municipal Council's bill.

JEFFERSON: I see by tonight's paper you've just bought it yourself for a song.

BAXTER: Is that out already? The damned bastards should have kept it covered till election was over.

JEFFERSON: That property may be worth a mint of money when the Bridge is finished.

BAXTER (*coolly*): Maybe it will. Have another drink on your landlord, me friend.

BAUMGARTEN (*with conviction*): Jefferson: Baxter is a damned scoundrel. I leave you to settle with him. (*He shakes hands with Baxter.*) My friend, you are a strategist.

JEFFERSON: General, you have been defeated. This is Baxter's saloon, Baxter's ward, Baxter's city, and by God, if we don't watch out, it will be Baxter's bridge.

(*Curtain*)

Scene Five

A fourth floor apartment in the Alfred Robert Benns' Model Flats on Joralemon Street. The three rooms are the utmost constriction in space that has yet been achieved: despite ventilation front and rear, and a large plot of ground in the center of the tenement block, with trees and a drying green and a sign forbidding children to play on those premises, the Flats are a depressing improvement. In order to achieve the central court, the rooms have been shortened, and in order to maintain neatness and order, an air of rigid virtue hangs over the establishment. On this hot July night an ordinary tenement roof would be filled with improvised pads and pallets; but although swarms of tenement dwellers are finding a little comfort and coolness on the grass of Prospect Park, the dark well on which the kitchen-living room opens holds no such sign of repose. At ten o'clock at night, which it now is, there are a few people hanging out of the windows of the flats opposite, the white pillows under their arms being all that shows up against the darkened flats.

In one of the little hutches off the living room, Mary Magonigle is lying on a bed; since the door is open, the white spread and a thin, delicate arm can be seen; but the Welsbach reading lamp in the living room is shaded by a long sheet of paper that drops from the shade itself, so that the inner room is obscure and dark. There is a stove on one side of the living room, with a cupboard and a sink; on the other is a drop kitchen table with a red and blue checkered table cloth. In a wire rack over the table are stuck a large number of tintypes and photographs; on the wall on the same side as the door is a crayon portrait of Mary, made from a photograph, stiff, devoid of expression, false in every line. On the same wall is a picture of an older woman, surrounded by a wreath of purple immortels. The walls of the living room are a hideous bluish green, which, mixed with the cold white glare of the Welsbach turns the healthiest cheek into that of a corpse. The floor is covered with oilcloth; and by the table, the stove, and the sink, the oilcloth is in turn protected by strips of worn red hall carpet.

On a kitchen chair by the table Robert-Owen is seated, holding a book under the lamp, but plainly not reading. He is in his shirt-

251

sleeves, his coat being neatly folded across another chair near the stove; and his sleeves are rolled up, as if he had perhaps been attending to some manual duty. He suddenly starts, as if he heard someone calling; and then gently tiptoes over to Mary's door to hear if she has been calling. While he waits there silently, the outer door gently sways back, and Shane Magonigle, with a face almost distorted to tears, enters, his black shirt open at the front. Robert-Owen motions for him to remain quiet; and tiptoes back to the table where he sets out a chair for Magonigle. At first they talk in whispers.

SHANE: Was the doctor here yet?

ROBERT-OWEN (*nodding*): He came an hour ago. I was just waiting for you to come before going out for a nurse.

SHANE: A nurse?

ROBERT-OWEN: She was ironing all afternoon. Dr. Van Orden says that the heat and the exercize brought on a heat prostration.

SHANE: And is that all?

ROBERT-OWEN: No: she has had a miscarriage.

SHANE: Will she have to go to the hospital?

ROBERT-OWEN: He thinks not. He is coming tomorrow again; when she gets over the prostration he will attend to the rest.

SHANE: Poor Mary. She wanted the baby.

ROBERT-OWEN: Yes: she doesn't know yet.

SHANE: Isn't there anything I can do?

ROBERT-OWEN: Nothing. I sent the neighbor's child down for the medicine.

SHANE: She wanted the baby, and I wanted the baby; though God knows how we'd have managed it. (*He tiptoes over to the room to peep in at Mary; and comes back very groggily.*)

ROBERT-OWEN: You're as white as a sheet. Sit down, man, sit down. Have you any whiskey?

SHANE: I never touch it.

ROBERT-OWEN: Have you eaten anything tonight? (*Shane nods No*). Sit down in that chair and I'll give you a sandwich and some tea.

SHANE: Don't you be doing anything. You've done enough. Far too much.

ROBER-OWEN (*gently closing Mary's door to shut out the noise*): What's happened about the strike? Did you get back in time?

SHANE: Everything's gone wrong. While I was staying with Mary that Casey got hold of the meeting, and got them all to go back at the old rates. He convinced them that the time to strike was the winter, when we haven't got any work anyway. He's a traitor to his class, Casey. They're all a lot of cowards and fools. If I'd been there ten minutes earlier, I could have stopped them.

ROBERT-OWEN (*preparing the sandwich expertly, while Shane takes off his boots*): What a devilish business. Are they going back?

SHANE: They're going back. Casey is a traitor and a blackleg: but I haven't any evidence against him yet, except for the fact that he's neglected Union business, and spends most of his time in Baxter's saloon.

ROBERT-OWEN: I'll have the sandwiches ready in a second. Next time my father builds any model flats I'm going to see that he puts a gas range in them. It's impossible to boil up a cup of tea without setting that furnace working.

SHANE: Is it you father . . . ?

ROBERT-OWEN (*quickly*): Yes: Didn't you know we were related?

SHANE: I never would have thought it. Of course ye have the same name.

ROBERT-OWEN: Yes: that's about all. He's very proud of these flats. If he ever boasts about them to me I shall tell him a thing or two.

SHANE: They're clean and decent: no bugs. (*Listening suddenly*): Did she call then? (*Robert-Owen crosses to the door and listens steadily, then nods No.*)

ROBERT-OWEN: You and my father have more than one point in common, Shane.

SHANE (*automatically*): The working class has nothing in common with the master class.

ROBERT-OWEN: That's where you're mistaken. Your aims are almost identical. My father would like to give you a clean home without bugs, three square meals a day, steady work. That's exactly what you would like to take; and as long as it's a dollar more in money or an hour less in work that you're fighting for, the Caseys will beat you every time—and maybe you won't get the dollar.

SHANE (*doggedly, eating his sandwiches, forgetting his distress in the mood of argumentation*): A starving man needs something to eat first. The working class needs more money first. We are entitled to the full product of our labor. That's justice.

ROBERT-OWEN: And if you got it, what then? You might afford a bigger apartment; Mary might have an extra bonnet. The working class would become the middle class, *my* class.

SHANE: That's better than being where they are.

ROBERT-OWEN: I am not so sure of that. The Greeks were a wise and beautiful people: and essentially no one had any more physical comforts than you have here, not in private homes at any rate.

SHANE: What does that prove?

ROBERT-OWEN: The burglar who holds you up cries: Money or your life! That's a real choice; it's always being offered to us; you can't have both. You ask for money; and if you don't get it you become bitter and class-conscious: if you do, you become bourgeois and purse-conscious. Suppose you demanded life instead: suppose you asked for responsibility and power, suppose you asked for education and culture, suppose you built your own parks, playgrounds, and homes, instead of living in what my father builds for you—or in far worse!

SHANE: When the Revolution will come, all that will follow.

ROBERT-OWEN: On the contrary, that *is* the revolution. When you march toward those points and capture those positions, that will be the revolution. Unless you achieve those goals on your way, you will never achieve them at all: your revolution will be an empty uprising: the lawyers and the soldiers will talk and fight interminably: a lot of good people will be killed: the rascals will step into their places: and the uprising will be over. That's what happened in France three times. It will happen everywhere until you realize that there must be a revolution inside as well as one outside: and in order to conquer the master class you must not merely be more powerful, you must be different.

SHANE: I believe in those things as much as you do. In one way, you're right: but in a democracy the leaders must follow the men. The worker knows where the shoe pinches. When he wants bread for his family or clothes for his children, he'll fight for them; but he won't fight for education or culture.

ROBERT-OWEN: Exactly! He'll fight for what the middle class fights for. This century is possessed by the delusion that food and clothes and railroad trains and empire are the only real things that are worth fighting for. That's the bourgeois belief. They'll bring in the police, call out the national guard, and kill right and left in order to keep most of the comforts of life coming in as regularly as they have been accustomed. If that's all you are fighting for you'll never win; after a while you'll wonder what on earth you ever fought for.

SHANE: You're discouraging me. It's not fair after tonight. I'm too tired to argue.

ROBERT-OWEN: Have another sandwich. Don't talk about discouragement. I am on your side. Do you suppose I can enjoy a good dinner if the worker is starving; that I can spend my time easily at philosophy if I realize that the great mass of people have every last spark of life and interest taken out of their minds, first by the prisons we call schools, next in the prisons we call factories, and finally by marching like chained convicts, to the prison called the grave? The notion that happiness means a few dollars more or less a day is a delusion. Happiness is life. A saint can be happy while he is fasting. An artist can be happy on a crust while he is working. When the worker asks from life what the artist asks from it—and will accept it only on those terms—he will no longer be a slave and a starveling.

254

SHANE: That's all right for you to say: you don't have to earn your living.

ROBERT-OWEN: You're wrong there, I do. I've told my father to go to the devil: I haven't a penny coming in to me except what I earn. Tolstoi says that the first thing to do, when you're on some one else's back, is to get off it. Well, I am off.

SHANE: Why did you do that? One man can't do anything. It's the mass movement that counts.

ROBERT-OWEN: What one man thinks today, a thousand may think to-morrow. A mass movement merely means that an impulse which was real to one man has become equally real to nine hundred and ninety-nine others.

SHANE (*wearily*): Your intentions are good, but you don't know what it is to be a workingman. Mary spent the whole day over the iron-ing board. That's what brought this on. That's the sort of thing that happens day in and day out, every week and every month. I wish I could make things easier for her. She wants a child and she needs a child. If it weren't for all the men that are depending on me, I'd go back to my trade. I'm a pattern-maker by trade. I joined the riveters when the patternmakers wouldn't form a union.

ROBERT-OWEN: Let me help you out. I don't use my money myself; it's there for anyone who needs it.

SHANE (*gratefully*): You've done enough, Robert. Yes: and more than enough.

ROBERT-OWEN: You'd better get a little sleep. I'll go off after the nurse now. The doctor said she'd probably sleep through the night: if she wakes she's to have another dose of the digitalis for her heart.

SHANE (*a little shattered*): Oh why did it all have to come at once! If it wasn't for me having to fight Casey, I could lay off the Union a little and be a decent man to her.

ROBERT-OWEN: Won't Baumgarten meet your demands halfway?

SHANE: He's a good man, as employers go. But nothing matters to him but the Bridge. He'd give in if the strike meant that the Bridge would be halted. But there's too many blacklegs around the city now. We're not more than fifty per cent organized. I don't know what to do.

ROBERT-OWEN: I'll get the nurse then . . . (*going back to the argument*): I don't know what to do either. (*In friendly warmth*): You're doing the best you can, Shane. I was a brute to discuss things at this moment. Go on, Old Man: go on. The doctor will come to-morrow: Mary will be better. The weatherman has predicted a cool wave.

(*Curtain*)

Scene Six

Mr. and Mrs. John Baumgarten's apartment, overlooking the Bay, one of the first of the Paris flats with elevators to be built on the Heights. Through a long, narrow hall, off which branch the maid's room, the bathroom, the bedrooms, the kitchen, and the dining room, one reaches the large living room, with a bay window. A modern architect might be horrified at wasting so much space on the hall; a modern investor would not sink so much of his money into high ceilings which provide many cubic feet of air beyond the minimum requirements of the tenement house law; but in 1883, when we enter the apartment, the architect is still fumbling lazily with this new program of building, the investor is thankful to get two or three per cent for a safe investment in real estate, and the tenement house laws do not exist. The result is a sort of homely spaciousness, which bad lights and insufficient ventilation do not altogether disturb.

It is a June Sunday, John Baumgarten's birthday, and the room is filled with furniture, flowers, bricabrac, and people. The mantelshelf on the left is draped in Japanese embroidered silk; cloisonné and Sevres knick-knacks compete for place on it: in the middle of the room is a table with firm but agitated legs, of solid walnut, draped with a tasseled velvet cover; all the chairs around the room, both with and without arms, are completely covered in heavy orange-brown plush: there is a whatnot in the right-hand corner near the window, laden with souvenirs and June roses. There are two oil portraits on the facing wall; they represent Baumgarten's father and mother; and while they are bad, they are not altogether destitute of art, but are rather the thinning out, after three hundred years, of a great tradition, leaving behind a sediment of mediocrity. Standing in the hall doorway on the right, one has, on the outer wall, a large bay window, while opposite the doorway is the portiere-hung opening to a shallow room, technically called the music room, but which in this instance serves as the library.

Besides the Mills family, Margaret, Elizabeth, and Lolo, and the Baumgarten family, there are three old cronies of Baumgarten, one of them with his wife. Bastian, the oldest man, with a head a little like General Grant's, but snowy white, is a sweet idealist of the old school, dreaming of Rousseau and Ficthe and Fenimore Cooper: Goebel is a prosperous business man, much younger, and much more of a German figure, prominent in Saengerbunds, Turnvereins, and Church receptions: while Hicks, a tall, stately gentleman of the old school, with a firm back and erect head, is a Civil War comrade, proud of his record, honoring the occasion with his uniform. Margaret, Mrs. Baumgarten, Mrs. Goebel are grouped together in the corner by the window. In the 'Music room' Goebel is rather patronizingly playing a game of checkers with old Bastian. Elizabeth and Robert-Owen are talking in the nearer corner by the window. Baumgarten, in full general's uniform, is seated on the biggest chair, by the table: he is smoking a firm, mild cigar with the even deliberation of the connoisseur, whilst Lolo, on a footstool nearby, is posing in what seems to her the admirable role of the adoring younger generation. She is not interested in the General, but in her pose. She is a bundle of appetites, with a histrionic gift of concealing them under the disguises of love, charity, generosity, sympathy and any other convenient virtue which enables her to attain her end. She is as healthy as an alleycat and quite as unscrupulous: but neither she nor anybody else fully realizes it.

BAUMGARTEN: Yes: I was forty before I came to America. I have had the best of both countries. Germany gave me wisdom at twenty: America gave me youth at fifty. I was never so young as I was the day when I put on this uniform.

LOLO: You look adorable in it.

BAUMGARTEN (*patting her cheek*): You know how to flatter the old gentleman, *mein Kindchen.*

LOLO: People aren't so brave any more as they were then. Tell me some more about the battle of Gettysburg.

BAUMGARTEN (*turning to Hicks*): That's the gentleman who can tell you about Gettysburg. He was on Meade's staff. I was in the rear with the reserves. All we saw was the last hour.

HICKS: The General is a modest man, a modest man. It was the last hour that won the battle.

LOLO (*turning to Hicks and beginning to patronize him*): Tell me about it!

JEFFERSON (*interrupting*): Pooh! There's just as much heroism today as there ever was. It takes as much nerve to wind a cable over the East River as it does to charge a regiment of men. Seven men have been killed and twenty-five have been wounded since we started to build the Bridge.

LOLO (*contemptuously*): Oh, the Bridge! That isn't a battle.

BAUMGARTEN: Yes: building bridges is like fighting: fighting is like building bridges. Modern warfare is a form of engineering. What is war? War is engineering in the negative aspect: it is the wrecking department of engineering. If you know how to build a bridge, you can lead an army.

HICKS: Engineering doesn't win battles. It's men, and the faith in them.

BAUMGARTEN: Then engineering doesn't build bridges, either, my friend Hicks. What wins battles? God knows! We know how much powder it takes to burst a shell: we don't know how much it takes to break down the resistance of a man. The good general deals with the fixed quantities: materials, munitions, distances, the number of men. In every battle there is the spirit of the army. In the long run, the thing that escapes our calculations is the thing that determines them.

HICKS (*firmly*): That's it. It's the men. General McClellan knew as much about organization and tactics as Grant: but one Grant was worth fifty McClellans.

BAUMGARTEN: Every army becomes the image of its leader. When Napoleon was a young active man, with the faith of a revolutionary, he made an army of Napoleons that conquered everything. When he got fat, and wanted to spend his time eating and posing before the mirror and accumulating a great fortune, the army became that way too: it looted Moscow, instead of exterminating the Russian army in 1812.

JEFFERSON: It's the same way with the Bridge. One man like Powers can make the whole thing hum. If we had another Powers as foreman on the New York side, they might catch up with the Brooklyn gang.

BAUMGARTEN: Ach: the men are becoming old, like me, Jefferson. It's time I let you take hold of everything.

JEFFERSON (*fondly*): I am getting older with the worry of building the Bridge. You are younger every day. You take it lightly.

BAUMGARTEN: The older one gets, the more one sees that everything is *Kinderspiel*.

LOLO: What is that? I don't understand German.

JEFFERSON: Child's play.

BAUMGARTEN: No: not child's play: that would mean it is easy. I mean *Kinderspiel*: children's play. It is serious: everything is serious: but it is all make-believe. It doesn't matter. So long as we are alive and active, one kind of *Kinderspiel* is like another. I once thought philosophy alone was great. Then I thought that war alone was great. Then when I designed this Bridge I thought that engineering was great. Now I see that everything is great; and everything is—*nichts*.

ELIZABETH (*joining the conversation*): That sounds like Bazarov's doctrine in 'Fathers and Sons.' Are you a Nihilist, General Baumgarten?

BAUMGARTEN (*horrified*): No! no! no! I mean that the greatness is nothing: that is the illusion. When I was happy with my uniform, I was only a little boy, dressing up. When I was happy with my engineering, I was only a little boy playing with his bucket and shovel by the beach. I believe in the bucket and the shovel and the uniform. But I don't believe that fighting for the Union was any better than fighting against the Union.

ROBERT-OWEN (*drawn in*): And how does this affect the Bridge?

BAUMGARTEN: Bridge building *ist grosses Kinderspiel.* But the things that make people build bridges are stupid. Once I thought that Manhattan and Brooklyn ought to be joined together. Why should they? Just as much bad as good will come of it. Will it raise land values? That means the poor man won't be able to afford a house. Will it give more people a chance to work in Manhattan and live in Brooklyn? That means they will waste a great deal of time on El trains and trolley cars. All the reasons for building the Bridge can be demolished: they wouldn't satisfy the brains of a nightwatchman.

JEFFERSON: Building bridges is one of the ways of being a man. Father, you mustn't desert me now because you are drawn back to your books.

BAUMGARTEN (*gently*): You can do without me.

ROBERT-OWEN: There are a hundred ways of being a man. Fighting battles is one of the brutal and obstructive ways. So is much of your engineering. All your games are children's games until you learn the man's game: *Why* are you playing!

BAUMGARTEN: You will never know that.

ELIZABETH: You can make a game of knowing it, perhaps.

ROBERT-OWEN: That's quite true: but that's another kind of game.

LOLO: Will you teach it to me?

ROBERT-OWEN: You don't want to leave your dolls too soon.

LOLO: Oh, you are horrid.

ELIZABETH: He said it was a man's game. That lets you out, you *female.*

LOLO: Miss Blue-stocking! I suppose you know a lot about it.

BAUMGARTEN: Come, come: one is not seventy every day. Let us have a little Schnapps before the coffee party.

BASTIAN (*in the next room—triumphantly jumping his king*): So: and so: and so: that makes a game.

GOEBEL: I haven't played checkers for five years.

BASTIAN (*getting up*): Edgar Poe says that it is the scientific game. Chess is complicated. Checkers is abstract and *mathematisch.*

BAUMGARTEN (*affectionately clapping Bastian on the back*): *Ach! du Alte. Spielst du noch mit der Philosophie?*

BASTIAN: *Nein: ich lese nur George Sand. Sie ist doch wunderbar: die ganze Revolution lebt zwar in ihren Buechern.*

(*Hicks goes over to join the older ladies. Mrs. Baumgarten gets up and excuses herself to go out and tend to the glasses.*)

JEFFERSON (*taking Lolo's arm*): If Benns won't teach you what the man's game is, I'll teach you all about the bridge game, Lolo. Come out with me someday and I'll show you a great sight: we'll go to the top.

LOLO (*immediately taking to him*): Will you? You're a nice brother-in-law to have. Everybody else tries to treat me as if I were a little child still.

JEFFERSON: To tell the truth: I think I fell in love with the whole family. I like Margaret because she is Margaret; Elizabeth because she has a mind; and I like you because—

LOLO (*flirting*): Oh do you like me? You never said that before!

JEFFERSON: Of course I do: I can tell you now, since you are wearing long dresses, and do your hair up.

LOLO (*drawing him over to the window*): Will you show me what you're working on now?

JEFFERSON (*aside to Margaret*): See Margaret: I'm glad there's one member of the family that takes a little interest in the Bridge. Elizabeth prefers to copy legal rigamarole. You make me feel that every minute I spend on the Bridge is a disloyalty to you: you couldn't behave any worse if I kept a mistress.

MARGARET (*stiffly*): Don't let your tongue run away with you.

JEFFERSON: Oh Lolo? She's grown up.

LOLO (*who, a little excitedly, has a notion that mistresses must be even more wicked than they seem, or why should all the fuss be made about them?*): Of course I'm grown up. But nobody in the family will realize it.

JEFFERSON: Come over to this window: we can get a good view from here.

ELIZABETH (*in a corner, to Robert-Owen*): Religion isn't modern. I have stopped going to Church; and I'm neither better nor worse for it. I can't say my prayers any more. It isn't real. Even if we don't know why the winds blow, we don't have to pretend it's an unexplorable mystery. Someday geography will tell us.

ROBERT-OWEN: By religion you mean ceremonies or ritual or Christianity. But that isn't what is real in religion. What is real is the conviction that there is something at the heart of life that matters —something that makes war an ignoble kind of game; something that makes the losing of one's life in rescuing a child, for example, a fine and necessary act—necessary if one is to be a man.

ELIZABETH: But most of life falls in between: it's neither brutal nor heroic.

ROBERT-OWEN: We have stopped thinking heroically: that's why it seems so. All that our generation seeks is comfort: upholstered chairs and plenty of food and padded coffins. When life stands for something, the means of living don't matter. I visited Renan in Paris: he lives with his sister in a little attic flat: I stayed to dinner and we had onion soup, an omelet and coffee—and no apologies. He is a great scholar, a cosmopolitan spirit; and he lives like a monk in a cell. That's the religious tradition: where the spirit burns brightly it supplies its own warmth.

ELIZABETH: How you've changed since you left America: you were quite a dandy then. I don't know if I agree with you. I believe in everyone's having a job and doing a great deal: but I don't know that I want to do without a comfortable bed and a warm house.

ROBERT-OWEN: I visited Millet, too. He is an old man now. He lives like a peasant: sleeps on straw: he has meat once a week: bread and butter and milk twice a day.

ELIZABETH: What is the virtue of all that?

ROBERT-OWEN: The virtue is that something grows and stirs inside of one: something we stifle and stultify with comfort.

ELIZABETH: Perhaps when we have comfort enough we will go on to something else.

ROBERT-OWEN: That's our delusion. The true doctrine is: seek first the Kingdom of Heaven, and then everything else will be added. Our method is to seek everything else first: but we don't seriously believe in the Kingdom of Heaven, and can't by this method possibly find it.

ELIZABETH: You've become a Christian, then? I thought you were a follower of Draper when you went away.

ROBERT-OWEN: I'm not an ecclesiastical Christian. I'm a Buddhist or a Confucian or a Mohammedan just as much as I am a Christian. The religions of our time are none of these things. But they stand for a great and important part of man's life. If we are not to remain a lot of raw adolescents we must understand the things they strive to understand: the cosmos man himself helps to create.

ELIZABETH: Doesn't science do that?

ROBERT-OWEN: Renan thinks that science is the answer. I am not sure of that. I don't know. The great men of science, like Clerk Maxwell and Faraday are beyond my reach; the lesser ones are too dogmatic and cocksure to convince me that their spirit is any different from that of the mummified theologies that they defy.

ELIZABETH: I had everything stowed away very tidily in my mind. Religion was dead. Science was here. Comfort was good. Why did you have to disturb it? I'm not sure you are right; but now I'm not sure I am either.

ROBERT-OWEN: I can take nothing for granted any longer. (*Puckishly, quite aware of what he is doing*): There are cookies in the dining room: let's help ourselves to some.

ELIZABETH: You are either a hypocrite or a skeptic. The cookies will give me indigestion if I listen to you.

(*They go out together. In the meanwhile, Mrs. Baumgarten comes back with a tray of cordial glasses; while the General pours the brandy.*)

BASTIAN (*gleefully, to Goebel, who is thoroughly bored*): And George Sand *sagte*: M. de Musset: "I hear you have been boasting that you are one of my lovers." Hee! Hee! De Musset *antwortete*: *Nein*: "No: on the contrary, I have been boasting that I was *not* one of your lovers." Hee! Hee! Hee!

BAUMGARTEN: I have not read a novel since I was in Germany. I read *Die Leiden des Jungen Werthers* and Ekkehard and Walter Scott. In America life has been a novel. I owed my father-in-law three thousand marks when I came here. He got all of that back and more before he died. I have been too busy to read novels.

MRS. BAUMGARTEN: If the Revolution of Forty-eight had been successful, you might have been a *docent* in Jena. Just think! Life is much the same wherever one lives. One enjoys adventure when one is young; I also enjoyed balls and party dresses and moonlight drives along the Rhine. Later on one enjoys babies and responsibility. Now I am a grandmother. If we were young again I should want to go to California.

GOEBEL (*to Bastian*): And the young Kaiser will say to Bismarck: "You are an old man; but I am the German Emperor!" Mark my words!

BAUMGARTEN (*courteously passing around the brandy*): Germany before Forty-eight was a great country. Today, I had rather be in America. A thorough nincompoop like the Kaiser may become President in America; but he doesn't remain there for the rest of his life.

GOEBEL: Presidents are all right in America; but *unser Deutsches Volk*—

BASTIAN: *Na, na*: Germany will be a republic, too. You cannot halt the wheels of Progress.

MRS. GOEBEL (*to Margaret*): In Germany, you know, I would be Frau Tax Commissioner Goebel. I sometimes think that would be very nice, especially before the servants.

MARGARET (*with half an eye upon Jefferson, by the window*): Yes:

262

I suppose so. (*Baumgarten doesn't notice Jefferson and Lolo. Margaret, with a slight note of stress, addresses her husband*): Don't you want to drink the General's health, Jefferson?

BAUMGARTEN: Come, *mein Kind*: Lolo too: she is quite a young woman now.

(*There is a pause of embarrassed respect while everyone fingers his glass.*) Lolo (*breaking the silence with the brashness of youth*): Here's to Father Baumgarten: may he live as long as his Bridge!

MRS. BAUMGARTEN (*looking around*): Where are Elizabeth and Mr. Benns?

(*Elizabeth and Robert-Owen come in rather bashfully and take their places with glasses in the circle, somewhat spoiling Lolo's declaration.*)

BASTIAN (*as the oldest man*): *Also! Prosit! Lebt wohl! Lebt lang!*

(*They all drink, or sip, or gulp, each after his fashion and degree of appreciation.*)

BAUMGARTEN: Ladies and Gentlemen: you do me a great honor. If I lived to be a hundred and seventy-six I couldn't be any happier. I have been a student, a revolutionist, a general, an engineer. It is good to be all of these things; but the best of all is to be a husband— (*he takes Mrs. Baumgarten affectionately by the waist*) —a father— (*he clasps his hand on Jefferson's shoulder*) —and a friend. (*He holds out his hands to the whole company; and they all impulsively gather around him to formally shake hands, all the women kissing his cheek, Mrs. Baumgarten last of all kissing him on the mouth.*)

LOLO (*aside, excitedly, to Robert-Owen*): I will never marry anyone but an old man. Old men are splendid. They have seen life. They understand one.

(*Robert-Owen raises his eyebrows ironically, with a smile quivering around his mouth.*)

LOLO: Oh I know what you think. Don't be a beast.

ELIZABETH (*with the cold implacable enmity of an independent woman and an older sister*): Last week it was the dancing master.

ROBERT-OWEN (*banteringly*): Are none of us safe from you, Lolo?

LOLO: I gave *you* up a long time ago.

ROBERT-OWEN (*more ironically, turning to Elizabeth*): You see? I am a free man.

LOLO: She is a free woman: that lets you out.

ELIZABETH: It is a vulgar little brute, Robert. Perhaps it will grow up.

ROBERT-OWEN: Oh, I hope not! Out of the mouths of babes and suck-lings—

JEFFERSON (*watching the baiting*): Leave Lolo alone. She has her own personality: why shouldn't she keep it?

ELIZABETH: If I had her sort of personality, I'd try to lose it somewhere!

ROBERT-OWEN (*remorsefully*): That's unkind. You are right, Jefferson. Let's form a society for the preservation of Lolo's personality. President, Jefferson Baumgarten: Vice President and Secretary, Robert-Owen Benns. Main Office: 11 Fulton Street. Subscriptions invited; no donation is too small.

LOLO (*almost in tears, holding on to Jefferson's sleeve*): I won't have anything to do with them. You are my Galahad: you must protect me.

JEFFERSON: My father has a spyglass here. Let's take a look at the Bridge through that.

LOLO: Oh good! Let's do it. (*Jefferson goes out of the room. Lolo turns to Elizabeth*): You and Margaret think I'm only interested in men. That isn't true. I am interested in Work and Personalities and Ideas!

ELIZABETH: Was I very unkind, Lolo? I didn't mean to be. You're a little spitfire. You'd better powder your nose.

LOLO (*spontaneously kissing her*): Do you like Robert?

(*Elizabeth looks around annoyed, to be sure that Robert hasn't heard, and doesn't answer.*)

LOLO (*delighted*): You do! Good-bye independence!

(*Jefferson comes back with the spyglass. Baumgarten notices it.*)

BAUMGARTEN: What are you going to do, my boy?

JEFFERSON: Lolo wants to take a look at the Bridge from here.

MRS. BAUMGARTEN: The piers are beautiful at sunset, with New York behind them.

BAUMGARTEN: Perhaps everybody would like a look.

JEFFERSON (*adjusting the spyglass*): Just let me get an approximate focus. There: she's a stunner against the evening light.

LOLO (*excitedly taking the telescope from his hand*): It's the eighth wonder of the world!

(*Everyone begins to draw toward the window: grouping around Jefferson and Lolo.*)

GOEBEL (*in the far corner, to Bastian*): At the last meeting of the Verein they elected me President.

BASTIAN: So!

MARGARET (*to Colonel Hicks*): Yes: but I should be a happier woman if that Bridge were built.

HICKS: You have your children, ma'am.

MARGARET (*bitterly*): But I might as well be a widow. He lives with the Bridge morning, noon, and night.

HICKS (*getting up and bowing*): I have never seen the Bridge from here; do you mind?

(*Margaret nods her assent, and Hicks goes over to the window.*)

MRS. BAUMGARTEN: Did you ever see such a sunset!

BAUMGARTEN (*affectionately swinging an arm around his wife*): Or such a birthday!

JEFFERSON (*excitedly*): Or such a Bridge! Who wants to look at it next?

(*Curtain*)

Scene Seven

The field of the spyglass. The bay window is replaced by a subjective screen whose images reflect the personality that views it. At one corner of it is a dark blur, representing the knob at the end of the window-shade string. One is conscious slightly of the black rim that rounds off the field.

LOLO: Would you like to see it, Mrs. Goebel?

MRS. GOEBEL: Thank you. Where do I look? (*There is a tremendous blurred magnification of a nearby house*) I don't see anything at all. Oh: thank you: yes: yes: it's very nice. (*The piers of the Bridge appear, but dimly: they never get in focus. In the front of one of them appears Mr. Goebel: very stiff and important. He wears a badge and shows it to people who approach: they all turn back.*) Would you like to see it, Mrs. Baumgarten?

MRS. BAUMGARTEN: Thank you: I have watched it nearly every day. Perhaps Colonel Hicks would like—

HICKS: Thank you, ma'am. Ladies first.

ELIZABETH AND MARGARET: Do take a look.

> (*The Bridge, without being structurally complete, appears: very firm in outline. A military body of men is marching over it: they break step. There is a puff of smoke and an explosion: the piers remain but a mass of writhing iron work falls into the water. The great Bridge suddenly dwindles to a real bridge across a small river: Hicks is standing on a mound, directing the fire of a battery: there is an explosion, and the main part of the Bridge drops.*)

HICKS: A great bridge General: a great bridge. It would take quite a few mortars and howitzers to destroy communications between Long Island and the mainland.

BAUMGARTEN: Not a chance in the world. The enemy would never get near enough. They have ten inch guns at Sandy Hook now.

BASTIAN: Thank you, Miss Mills. Age before beauty, *nicht wahr?* (*The Bridge, with the addition of a few Gothic pinnacles, comes into view.*) So! Prachtvoll! Kollossal! (*A green park appears at the Brooklyn approach; the framework of the Bridge becomes cov-*

266

ered with ivy: the park and the ivy turn into a country scene, by a small river: with a young man and a young lady standing on a bridge, throwing crumbs over the parapet to a few swans.) It's not the sort of bridge one would take a young lady courting on. *(The Bridge reappears in full scale, with more fantastic pinnacles, and little boxes or arbors all the way across the Bridge with lovers spooning in them: flowers and box trees line the footpath.)* So. *Alles hier in Amerika ist zu praktisch.* When I was young, young men committed suicide when young ladies didn't respond to their advances. *So. (Twenty young men suddenly rush out of the arbors and throw themselves into the water. Twenty young women look over the side with horror and throw out life lines: the young men climb up the life lines and embrace them.)* We always went spooning on bridges, so that we could threaten suicide more easily. Those were romantic days. *(He sighs deeply: and the gay piers of the Bridge turn into gaunt factory chimneys.)* Yes: yes: this is *Amerika! Herr Goebel: möchten Sie?*

GOEBEL: If you please. *(The piers glimmer into existence for a second: then become sign posts: This way to Floral Gardens: ten minutes' walk from the railroad station. Then a vast sign: Auction of choice real estate. Millions to be made on Long Island. Goebel suddenly is in the midst of a counting room, counting coins that he pours out of vast bags of Money. Another sign: elegant rural villas. A whole street of turreted, bayed, scroll-sawed, balconied villas, with stained glass bathroom windows, appears.)* The Bridge is wonderful: the Bridge will do a great deal for real estate. We should have had it long ago. *(The interior of a bank)* Where do you think is a good place to buy lots now? Flatbush? Canarsie? Oyster Bay? Bay Ridge? Coney Island?

MARGARET'S VOICE: May I now? I see it every day; but do you know, I've never really looked at the Bridge? *(The pier of the Bridge, high above the waterfront. Jefferson's figure appears. A great beam swings around and sweeps him off the Bridge. Margaret stands below in a house dress and apron: Jefferson falls into it: he is a little baby. She holds him to her bosom: she is alone with him in the Columbia Street back yard: it is surrounded by a wire fence a hundred feet high: she murmurs):* You must not try to climb out of here.

JEFFERSON *(jocosely)*: You've had that glass five minutes, Margaret. Are you dreaming, my dear?

LOLO: May I have it again?

MARGARET *(wearily)*: Take it. I wish the Bridge were all built.

LOLO: The Bridge is like a man: it is firm and strong: it has no frills. *(The piers of the Bridge appear in their lean reality: Jefferson appears acrobatically suspended between the two piers: the Bridge disappears: he is an acrobat: Lolo and Jefferson are on a trapeze: he swings her through the air: she lands gracefully on the parapet of the pier and curtsies and throws kisses to a great multitude of people descended below. Jefferson appears alongside her, bows, holding her hand: he throws a rope up in the air: it stays there: she mounts to his back and he begins to climb the rope.*)

ELIZABETH (*tartly*): Are you going to hold it all day? I haven't had my turn yet.

LOLO: Oh, I forgot. The masonry is wonderful: so solid: so firm: up and up and up!

ELIZABETH: Isn't it a pity that it's Sunday. I should like to see the people working on it. (*The Bridge, in tremendous bustle and activity: gangs of workers are busy on every part of it: they are all women, except a few men who are carrying the water and distributing sandwiches, like super-busboys. A fat genial woman smoking a heavy black cigar, is foreman. Elizabeth is dressed like a surveyor, with high boots and open-fronted shirt: she is giving orders. Jefferson approaches with a baby-carriage and three children: Margaret orders him off. A gang of men approach: they begin throwing missiles: the women pick up their tools and charge them: the men run away and the women follow them. The Bridge reappears in focus: then Elizabeth is seated at a desk, dictating to a male stenographer in a sissified dress. The Bridge again appears.*) Bridges are neuter, aren't they?

JEFFERSON: On the contrary, there is a man and a woman in all good things. The piers are he's: the suspensions are she's. What is neutral is something less than a man or a woman: a bridge is something more. A piece of scientific research is something more. A good marriage is at the bottom of everything.

MARGARET: I wish you realized that for yourself, Jefferson.

JEFFERSON: I do: you are in the Bridge, too, Margaret.

MARGARET (*quietly bitter*): Buried there.

BAUMGARTEN: We shall all be buried there, perhaps. But it will be our monument. If I had to choose between going to the Pantheon in Paris or being remembered by this Bridge, I'd take my chances on the Bridge. May I have a look? (*He focuses sharply on the donkey engine at the bottom of the pier*): Jefferson, they haven't covered up the machinery on the Brooklyn pier. Carelessness.

JEFFERSON: The devil. I'll send a note over to the nightwatchman.

BAUMGARTEN: You think the Bridge is interesting now, when you see just the piers. In another three years, you will see something different. Yes: that will be a bridge. (*The completed Bridge, thronging with passengers and traffic, suddenly floats majestically into view.*) The city will change. (*Towers begin to appear on the Manhattan side: first the New York World dome, then the Sun*

*tower, then the St. Paul building, then the horizon fairly heaves
with towers.)* But the Bridge will remain. *(Its clear, lithe outlines
become a beautiful purple: it suddenly mists into obscurity
through the drop of a tear. Baumgarten's voice shows emotion).*
I was once a boy and now I am an old man. I have changed. The
world changes. When a husband loves his wife and a wife loves
her husband, no other change matters. One sees the beginning and
end of many things in one's lifetime. There is no beginning or
end to love. It is a great blessing. Nothing else matters, my children. You think that it is great to build bridges? I will tell you
something greater than that: I have loved, and been loved by
one woman. There: there: forgive me. I feel too happy. Let us
all sit down and eat. We will drink champagne and enjoy all the
day gives us.

ELIZABETH: How does that affect your philosophy, Robert?

ROBERT-OWEN: Jesus felt at home at the Marriage at Cana. Why
shouldn't poverty know champagne occasionally? A naked man
doesn't spurn the sunlight. How does it affect your philosophy,
Elizabeth?

ELIZABETH: I feel that I haven't any.

LOLO: Oh, look at the Bridge now!

*(Everyone's eye takes in the Bridge and the housetops transformed
against a gold and salmon and lemon glow, topped by a turquoise
sky: exhilarating and unbelievable. The field of the telescope and
the film images disappear. The group turns away from the window, in pairs, as the sunlight streams in, following the General,
who gallantly escorts his wife: her arm locked in his and his free
hand patting her hand tenderly.)*

(Curtain)

Scene Eight

The top of the pier at a point below the coping which has not been laid on. The vast blocks of granite form a flat surface, broken only by a deep depression into which the cradle, a great iron cushion which carries the cables still to be wound through the piers, is being lowered, with the aid of a small derrick and skids. High above the water, with the sun fading through an April haze into the Jersey meadows that spread out into the distant background, the bodies of the men, the cradle, and the donkey engine look sharp and diminished, as if seen through the wrong end of an opera glass. A wooden scaffolding connects the top of the pier with the base. Standing on the base of the elevated donkey engine, Jefferson is following every move of the gang with intense but reserved interest: Powers, moving from one part of the cradle to another, like an agile terrier, is bossing the job.

POWERS: Now thin: wan: two: HEAVE!

GANG: Hi!

(The cradle edges down a little deeper in the trough. Powers raises his hand to the engine man: the engine puffs and tugs at the cable from which the cradle is suspended.)

POWERS: Slip it under her waist. You on the left. *(Shouting to the engine man)*: Give it another lift, Mike! All together: shove.

TONY THE DAGO: Jesus Christ!

BILL THE SWEDE: Poosh!

POWERS: Ease off: ye'll break the cable! *(The cable holding the cradle collapses into limpness.)*

JEFFERSON *(calling)*: John!

POWERS *(with the consciousness that Jefferson isn't needed)*: What in hell do ye want?

JEFFERSON: We need a bigger engine and derrick.

POWERS: Arrah! It's a waste of time. The men can do it.

JEFFERSON *(hurriedly, as if he were an impertinent outsider)*: All right, all right: go ahead.

270

POWERS: Now thin boys. It's almost launched she is. Give her a long shove in the behind. (*He signals to Mike*): Lift! Hi! Wan, two: heave! Wan, two: heave. And a wan, two.

GANG: Hi!

POWERS: That's a daisy. One more push and she'll be in Donegal. A little guts is better than all the derricks in the world.

PAT (*under his breath*): The little bastard's going to break our backs.

TONY THE DAGO: Watsa deef. Worka today. Next day Saturday night. Then we do the poosh wid da bigga stick.

GROGAN: Is there anny water in the bucket?

FRED (*the wit—pointing down to the river*): Lean over here and take a drink. There's all you want. (*Grogan looks over the side: Fred gives his head a ducking which almost sends him off the pier*).

POWERS: None of yer skylarkin' there. Git to yer places. Bill, Grogan, Tony, Fred, over on this side. (*To the other men*): You push. (*To this gang*): You shove under with the derrick and give her an extry lift. Two foot more and it'll be a goal!

BILL THE SWEDE: Poosh: poosh like she never been screwed before!

PAT: We'll split a gut before we're through with this damned baby!

GROGAN (*singing*): O Casey he danced wid a strawberry blonde and the band played on . . .

POWERS: Shut up the lot of yez. Ye'd think this was a fireman's picnic. Now then: all together. Ready Mike? One two:

(*They push: but immediately become aware that they are not having any effect: the derrick doesn't work. Jefferson turns around impatiently to Mike: there is the faint sound of five o'clock whistle from below and from various factories in the distance.*)

POWERS (*surprisingly lenient*):Now thin, are ye sleeping Mike?

MIKE: There's the five o'clock whistle.

POWERS (*taking a few steps toward the engine*): What's that ye say! Say it again to me face. Wake up ye goddamn son of a bitch. Say another word and I'll make ye stay up here till the rising of the moon.

MIKE (*doggedly*): Sure: it's five o'clock. I said it.

POWERS (*turning a nasty red and becoming on fire with rage*): You chicken-livered dirty black dog of a son-of-a-bitching Orangeman: don't give me any of your lip. It ain't five o'clock up here till we finish with this cradle if we stay till midnight.

MIKE (*taking comfort in the sheer weight of physical superiority*): I'm a union man. I say it's five o'clock.

POWERS: Will ye work or won't ye?

MIKE: How long are you goin' to keep us up here?

POWERS: That's none of your goddamn business, so long as you get paid for it. (*Using sarcasm*) The dirty white-collared dude wants

271

to call on Miss Flossie Astorbilt to take her to the opery and sit among the Four Hundred.

VOICES FROM THE GANG: Come on Mike. Can that stuff. Let's go. What the hell's the difference. It's only twelve o'clock in Frisco.

MIKE: I ain't said nothin' about not workin'.

POWERS: Arrah! Then shut up. Give us a little steam when we want it, instead of leaving us with the cramps in the belly.

MIKE: All right: all right: I'll give you your steam.

BILL THE SWEDE: You ain't never bane a sailor. They'd knock you into the river for saying less than that on a ship.

POWERS (*using his victory boldly*): Now thin: all the gentlemen that has dates for the opery, the theayter, the horse-show, and Mrs. Astorbilt's dinner party kin leave immediately to get into their glad rags. The rest of yez will stay and get double for overtime.

GROGAN: My stomach is achin' like a maiden's heart it is for a can of beer.

JEFFERSON: Come on, men: all together: and when the cradle is set, the treat's on me.

GANG: All right sir. That's telling. Here we go. Give the word, Powers.

POWERS: All set? (*He turns around significantly to Mike*): Now thin: wan: two: wan two: wan— (*The cable holding the cradle breaks with a loud crack, releasing the cradle and staggering the men at the skids*). Damn it and to hell!

JEFFERSON (*running over*): We need a bigger cable.

FRED (*reflectively*): I'm glad my foot wasn't under that: my corns have begun to ache at the thought of it.

POWERS: Bigger cable nawthin': that bloody Belfast gosthoon didn't put the power on till the boys had her up: he snapped the cable, he did. Lay hold there: slip the old cable off. Hold on! It wasn't the cable: it was the chain. One of the links is gone.

JEFFERSON: That's all right then.

FRED (*rising to the occasion*): I can lend you my new cuff links if that will be any use.

POWERS (*impatiently waving him off*): Arrah: this ain't the time for foolin'.

JEFFERSON: Look here: we can hitch it on directly.

GROGAN (*lunging with his elbow into Pat's ribs*): Did you hear what Fred was afther saying? Cuff links! Hah! hah!

PAT: Sit down: watcha standin' up for. Let the little bastard do the work himself. Him and the old man think they're building the Bridge between them.

TONY THE DAGO (*curiously*): You no like work? Me have helluva good time. Bigga de muscles: bigga appetite: plenty nice wine and garlic. Strong. My girl worka in de factory: we save money get married: plenty children. Children eat garlic: getta strong: go to

272

factory too: me old man have nicea garden: many children: plenty wine: no worka at all. Jesus Christ!

PAT: Yer heathen.

TONY THE DAGO: Me Catholic: samea Pope as you.

PAT (*turning aside contemptuously*): You're a Dago. That's different.

JEFFERSON (*holding the limp hook and cable to keep it connected with the cradle, and looking back toward the engine*): Now then: Just make it tight.

(*Nothing happens.*)

POWERS: Mike: wake up there Mike. (*He looks at the engine*): Where the hell has Mike gone to?

(*The gang is sheepishly silent. Fred goes to the edge of the pier.*)

FRED (*with serious waggery*): He musta fallen over. Poor fella: he had everything to live for.

GROGAN (*looking over the scaffolding*): It's down the bottom of the pier he must be by now.

POWERS (*leaning over the ladder down the scaffolding*): Yer dirty lazy black good for nawthing scut of a sea-pirate: yer Fired! Don't let me lay eyes on yer again. I hope yer break yer lazy coward's neck before ye hit the bottom. (*Rising*): The dommed dog: did ye ever see the like of that! (*Examining the cradle more closely*): and she's almost in position.

JEFFERSON (*decisively*): Never mind Mike!

POWERS: I'm afraid to have a try wid the boys without the engine. We might give her a shift out of position.

JEFFERSON: That's all right. Take hold of the hook: all right? I'll take the engine.

POWERS (*obediently*): All right, sir. Left is up: right is down.

JEFFERSON: I know.

POWERS: Now thin, boys!

(*They all jump with alacrity into positions. Fred alone breaks out.*)

FRED: I'll bet a pint of Jersey Lightning against a trip to Coney Island that the old man snaps the cable himself.

GANG (*unanimously*): Shut up!

POWERS: Ready sir?

JEFFERSON: Ready!

POWERS: All together boys: one: two—

GANG: Hi!

POWERS: One: two—

GANG: Hi!

JEFFERSON and POWERS together: One: two: one: two: one: two—

POWERS (*crescendo*): and a *wan, two!*

GANG: Hi!

POWERS (*to Jefferson*): Ease off! There she floats!

GANG: Hoorah!

JEFFERSON (*coming over to examine it*): Fits like a glove!

BILL THE SWEDE: That's the way to fill the old hole!

FRED: Let's call it a day's work.

JEFFERSON (*to Powers*): I don't think we need a bigger engine, John.

POWERS (*drily, wiping the perspiration off his face*): I don't think we do sir!

JEFFERSON (*turning to the gang*): All right: the drinks are on me.

GANG: Let's go!

(*Curtain*)

Scene Nine

A long worker's shed at the bottom of the Brooklyn pier: bare boarded walls, with a row of nails running all the way along the walls, the place being lighted by day through a window at each end, and through the open doors. It is now five o'clock on a December day, almost dark outside, and the dreary smokey flames of two swinging oil lamps, the kind used by signalmen, are the only source of light. In one corner Flanagan, a nightwatchman, is filling a whole row of red glazed lamps near an antiquated stove. On a bench near him Grogan is amateurishly tying up his hand, which has been ripped by a nail and is bleeding profusely. There is a single tap with running water, and a trough beneath it, in the right hand corner of the shed.

FLANAGAN (*looking up*): Have ye washed yer paw?

GROGAN: What do I wanta be washing it for? I washed it this morning.

FLANAGAN: Yer binding it up with all the dirt in it. It's the lockjaw ye'll have before ye know it, and the Mother of Heaven herself won't keep ye from it. Wash it off and I'll bind it up for ye meself when I get the lamps filled.

GROGAN: It's only a scratch. I wouldn't a come down atall but it's being almost five o'clock anyway—though it's bleedin' like a damned monthly, it is. It ain't more than skin deep.

FLANAGAN: There's them that have died from a pimple let alone a scratch in the fist. Have ye got any whiskey on yet?

GROGAN (*reaching with his uninjured hand to the back pocket on the opposite side*): There's a flask in me pocket but I can't reach it. Ye can have a drop if ye'll take it. It's a freezin' cold day; and many's the nip I've had against the cold lest the cold have a nip at me.

FLANAGAN: Kape yer whiskey. When we wash yer hand I'll sponge it with whiskey before I put the bandage on. That will kape it clean.

GROGAN: Whiskey was meant for the stomach, not for the skin. I seen a man pour some whiskey oncet on the back of his hand and it ate all the hair offen it. It's no good for the externals: God meant it to be drunk.

FLANAGAN: Ye'll do what I say or it's in the morgue they'll be putting yer body, ye big stiff, before the chickens are roosting tomorrow night.

GROGAN (*going over to the tap, putting his wounded hand under it, and then dancing around in anguish*): Jesus Christ: Mother of Mercy: St. Patrick and St. Thomas and all the angels above. The cold water burns like pitchforks in hell!

FLANAGAN: Lave it under a second, ye big baby, and get it clane. Now then. (*He counts over the lamps*) Wan for the footway: three for the street: wan for the dock is five: wan for the dump is six: wan for the tracks is seven, and wan for the toolshed is eight. (*He stands up and goes over to Grogan, grabbing his hand as one might a child's*).

GROGAN: I reached up for me hammer, and there was that dirty nail poking its nose out of the shoring.

FLANAGAN: 'Tis a nasty scratch; it might be the tooth of a tormented woman, it might. D'ye call that clean? Put yer hand in the water. Stand still ye big baby. There: that's better. Now where's the whiskey?

GROGAN (*coaxingly*): It's frozen I am with the water and the pain. Take the cork off and give me a swig, will ye?

FLANAGAN (*taking the bottle out of Grogan's pocket and measuring it against the light*): Take a swig of it nothing! There's just enough left to soak the bandage in. Now where's a piece of cloth?

GROGAN (*pointing to a soiled handkerchief*): This is what I had on.

FLANAGAN: That thing? With the snot lyin' heavy in the creases? Where was yer born, yer greenhorn? Here's me own handkerchief which the old woman put in me pocket the night. Take it and mind yer bring it back the morrer.

GROGAN: Is it a doctor or a nightwatchman ye are?

(*Flanagan pours some whiskey on the middle of the handkerchief, which he has folded into a diaper, and begins to adjust it deliberately on Grogan's hand.*)

FLANAGAN: Never mind: I seen a thing or two in my day. I was an orderly in the hospitals during the war. This isn't the first time I've put on a bandage.

GROGAN (*in pain*): Holy St. Peter and all the Popes and Cardinals.

FLANAGAN: It'll burn for a minute.

GROGAN: It is burning the minute.

FLANAGAN (*giving the bandage a final knot*): There: that's tight. Sit down to get yer breath and in a minute ye can go home.

(*He picks up four of the lamps and opens the door. The whistle blows. One by one dark forms loom out of the darkness under the pier outside, and stumble into the shed, sometimes remembering to shut the door and sometimes not.*)

276

GROGAN (*moaning to himself*): Dear Mother of God: it's burning for fair: he's poisoned me hand altogether.

PAT (*entering and talking to Fred*): I sez to the old man: You fathead, if you can do the job better than I can, why don't you do it?

FRED: If he heard you, you'd a been fired. When you stand up to the old man your voice is so loud it would hush a baby to sleep.

PAT: Do you think I'm afraid of him?

FRED (*getting down on his hands and knees and snapping like a dog at Pat's trousers*): Woof! Woof! Woof! When Little John snaps at your breeches, you'll run away.

PAT: Git out!

FRED: Woof! woof! (*He adroitly reaches up and gives Pat a hard pinch in the buttocks.*)

PAT: Leave off, ye clown. If ye do that again I'll fart in yer face.

FRED (*getting up*): When I want to commit suicide I'll turn on the gas myself, thank you.

(*Fred goes over to the tap to wash up. Pat takes a long draft of whiskey from his pocket-flask.*)

PAT (*noticing Grogan*): Want a drink?

GROGAN (*nursing his hand*): That divil Flanagan murdered me with his ice water and his bandage. Put it up to me mouth, will yer?

PAT (*putting the bottle reluctantly up to Grogan's mouth*): I showed that little divil, the old man, where he got off today. He sez to me: Is that a crowbar or a toothpick yer handlin'? And I sez to him, sez I, I sez—

FRED (*drying his face on the roller*): Sez he, he sez—

PAT: Shut up!

MAGONIGLE (*coming in with Murphy and Ahearn*): We've got to organize everybody on the job, from the waterboy to the superintendent.

MURPHY: Yer going too fast. One thing at a time. The riveters come first: we got our own union to begin with, and we ain't going to mess the whole business up with the stone masons and the carpenters and the laborers and the hod carriers. Let each craft mind its own business.

MAGONIGLE: In the long run we'll stand or fall together. There are four unskilled workers to every craftsman on the job. If we could organize them to begin with the rest would be easy.

AHEARN: The initiation is a hundred dollars. They couldn't pay it.

MAGONIGLE: That means we got to lower the fee.

AHEARN: We don't want to lower it. If there's too many riveters there won't be enough work to go round.

MAGONIGLE: There's plenty of time to face that when the day comes.

MURPHY: One thing at a time, I say. We're a skilled craft and we're entitled to a raise in pay if we can get it. I don't mind the helpers being included: but we can't wait until every damned wop and Dago and greenhorn joins his own union.

MAGONIGLE: What we need is one big union.

AHEARN: Everybody?

MAGONIGLE: Everybody!

AHEARN: I'm agin it.

MURPHY: And so am I. If we're all organized there's no sense in any of us being organized. Before you know it, the hod carriers and the spade men will be wanting the same wages as the skilled workers.

MAGONIGLE: Why shouldn't they?

AHEARN: Don't be jokin'.

MURPHY: What would be the good of learnin' a trade and spendin' all the time on the apprenticeship if it didn't get you nothin'?

AHEARN: The Dagoes don't deserve more than they're gettin'. They live on spaghetti and save all their money.

MAGONIGLE: The capitalist class all pulls together. They try to help each other out: they compete between themselves, but when it comes to fighting us, they're as solid as a dutch wall. The only way we can beat them is to stand together too.

AHEARN: Standing together is one thing: and letting all the wops and Dagoes and swedes in is another. Number one comes first in this world. Steam riveter's local number 17 is all I care about. If the sandhogs and the hodmen want to organize, who's preventing them?

MAGONIGLE: Suppose you're a hundred per cent organized: suppose you strike. Baumgarten can just thumb his nose at you for six months: there's work enough at both ends to keep the rest of the gang busy without the riveters; in six months he can get all the riveters he needs from other parts of the country. But if we were all in one union, and we all struck, he'd be in the soup. You can't organize two hundred men and have them getting used to the job and get the hang of it without missing them when they lay off. He'd whistle hard before he got another man like Powers. He'd go three quarters of the way to meet our demands. He couldn't do anything less.

MURPHY: When a man doesn't have to learn his trade ye can't organize him. Don't ye suppose we learned our lesson already? A man who's so thick and ignorant he ain't ever mastered a craft, is ready to snatch the first job that's low enough for his intelligence, and damn all the rest of us. No thank you. Let the riveters keep to themselves.

MAGONIGLE: That's all very well now, but—

AHEARN: It's now we're talking about.

MAGONIGLE: If the Union gave me a couple of organizers, I could get the whole bridge gang in the union this side of six months.

AHEARN (*astounded*): The riveters organize the rest of the bridge at Local No. 17's expense? Are you crazy? That's bloody socialism, it is.

MURPHY (*reassuringly*): That's one way of looking at it, Magonigle: but it won't go down with the boys, and you know it. We ain't runnin' a United Orphans Workers Benefit Lodge. Now Casey has the right idea: he says that the riveters ought to strike for more money before any of the other crafts do. If anybody gets a raise, we will then.

AHEARN: That's right: we ain't a charity organizations society. We got to strike the first begorra and get while the gettin's good.

MAGONIGLE: Do we want more money, or do we want justice?

AHEARN (*sapiently*): When the riveters get more money, it's justice: if they don't, it's neglecting the widders and orphans and grinding the face of the poor.

MAGONIGLE: If I didn't think that a little victory over the capitalist classes by the Riveters' Local was part of the big victory by the workers of the world, the Union could go to hell and find another president.

MURPHY (*placatingly*): Don't talk about leaving the Union, Magonigle. We need an honest man and a good talker like you.

AHEARN (*following the lead*): That's right, Magonigle: we need an honest man. No hard feelings. You're a loyal man and we're loyal men. You call a strike and we'll follow you till the last penny goes out of the till. We're for the rest of the working class, too, so long as you don't forget Local No. 17.

MURPHY: We'd better have a talk with Casey tonight. The time's coming to do something. We've got to prepare our demands.

MAGONIGLE: That's just what I wanted to talk to you about . . .

AHEARN (*noticing that four men are entering the door, carrying a limp figure*): And who's this poor slob?

POWERS (*coming in and bossing the proceedings*): Here yez: draw that bench over to the fire, will yer: and put him down here. Fred: you'd better run for the doctor: quick.

GROGAN: Is it dead he is?

MURPHY: He's more dead than alive.

TONY: What's happened da bigga steef?

FRED (*tossing a comb he has been using over to the workers clustered around the prostrate man*): Comb his hair while I'm gone. That bird has a date tonight at the Pearly Gate. Dress him up nice. If the doctor isn't home I'll bring back the undertaker.

POWERS (*tensely*): Begone you damned sluggard. Or the undertaker will have two jobs on his hands.

(In fact: Fred has lost no time and is out of the door before Powers' words can follow him.)

GROGAN: It's a priest he needs and not a doctor. I'll go for Father de la Salle. *(He makes the sign of the cross over the man.)* Bless you and keep you and may the saints intercede for you, Amen.

POWERS *(with his head to the man's chest)*: Thanks be to God: his heart is beating. He only fell a matter of twenty feet.

FLANAGAN *(coming in)*: I seen him fall. He landed on his head: It's a wonder it didn't crack his skull open.

PAT: There's a big bump comin'.

MURPHY: Give him some whiskey: 'twill keep the heart going.

POWERS: Has anyone got a decent drop on him?

(Ahearn offers his flask and Powers gently puts it to the man's lips.)

AHEARN: It's what's coming to all of us one of these days. A bridge worker doesn't last. Ten years of it and it's time to say yer prayers and kiss the childher good-bye.

MURPHY: That's what the saying is. There's a corpse in every truss.

POWERS: Shut up yer pack of bloody ravens. Take off Bill's shoes and rub his feet some of ye. He's almost ice. Flanagan: you know how to treat a man: pour some of this down his throat, will yer, whilst I chafe his hands. The poor devil.

PAT: It's waking a corpse we'll be.

AHEARN: His eye twitched: did ye see it twitch?

MAGONIGLE *(who is tenderly chafing the hand on the opposite side of Powers)*: This sort of thing is happening every day now. If the capitalists had to pay a man's sickness and accident, and his widows and orphans if he died, there wouldn't be so much of it.

POWERS: Capitalists be damned. It's the carelessness of the gang. He was on the pier, and some damned scoundrel took away the ladder that leads from the platform to the bottom: it was so dark he didn't see it was gone.

MAGONIGLE: It's easy to blame everything on us. Why shouldn't there be a permanent ladder there?

POWERS: Why shouldn't ye all have nursemaids with a snot-rag to blow your noses, too. If it isn't wan thing its another. I suppose when Brown and O'Rourke both fell into the water last summer wid sky-larkin' the management was to blame, too.

MAGONIGLE *(shifting his line)*: If a man had something to live for he'd be more careful.

POWERS *(dourly)*: What have we all got to live for?—six foot of ground in the end, the same for the rich man as for the poor. Woodlawn is no better than Potter's Field.

(The man gives a feeble groan.)

FLANAGAN: There's still life in him. If there ain't any bones broken he may get off easy wid con-cussion of the brain.

PAT (*naïvely*): A con-cushion is it?

FLANAGAN: I seen 'em many a time that way. They get laid out like a corpse for a matter of two days, or maybe a week; and then they're all right again, all but feelin' a little light in the upper story maybe every once in a while.

MAGONIGLE: If this was our bridge and we were running things, there wouldn't be so many accidents. The capitalists don't care when a worker dies. There are plenty more where they came from.

POWERS: Don't talk like a black, blitherin' fool. Do ye think the capitalists grind the dead workers up into sausages? If it wasn't for me keepin' a watch on the practical jokes and the skylarkin' there'd be a dozen killed and injured for every one that gets it in the neck now.

MAGONIGLE: You're all right Powers. I ain't saying anything against you, except that you're always ratting the men.

POWERS: Bridge building isn't a game for children. If it's afraid of a little danger and hardship y'are, ye'd better be a letter carrier or a grocer.

MAGONIGLE: We can face danger as well as the next man. It's the unnecessary waste of life that's a crime and an injustice.

PAT: There's warmth in his soles: if I rub any harder twill raise a blister: but his calf is like a sheet of ice.

POWERS: Poke the fire up.

MAGONIGLE: It'll be different someday.

POWERS: Maybe it will and maybe it won't. When you can get justice in the courts or charity in an orphan asylum or religion in a church, you'll be able to get an honest day's work out of a gang of men without someone to drive them and keep them going. I'm not saying it won't come, and I'm not saying it will come. But you nor I will never see it, Brother Magonigle.

MAGONIGLE (*confidently*): Our children will see it!

POWERS: I'm a childless man; I buried me hope when I buried me wife; and I gave up me faith in the Church when I gave her body to the earth.

GROGAN (*coming in excitedly*): He can die in peace, he can. Here comes Fader de la Salle with the Holy Ointment.

(*The man gives a much louder groan.*)

POWERS: Die nawthin'. The color's coming back to his lips. Where the hell is the doctor?

(*Curtain*)

Scene Ten

Below the arch of the bridge pier: the shaded side with its back to New York: through the opening a July moon is beginning to rise over the housetops which are already edged with a greenish white anticipatory light. With the exception of one or two solitary apartment houses, all the buildings one sees through the vast aperture are low: here and there a green light glimmers dimly in one of them. From the suspended cable of the Bridge, now hangs a narrow footway which connects it with the shore, and is the first indication of the permanent span. A solitary excursion boat, with a searchlight, lights up the pier for a minute, and then passes up the East River, with a minor hum of waltz music faintly drifting through the moist warm air: in the distance, the mild whistles of lazy ferryboats: below every once in a while the gruff hoot of the Fulton Ferry, which has a short run and won't stand any nonsense.

A little shriek of terrified laughter comes from the narrow footway, which sways like an Alpine suspension bridge and is a hundred times as long. The shriek comes from Lolo, who has paused for a second: behind her is a darker figure whose voice rings clearly through the evening. As they draw nearer, Jefferson Baumgarten's sunburned face and crisp beard emerge from the shade: with one hand on the handrail on his left, he is steadying Lolo with his right hand.

JEFFERSON: Don't stop! What did I tell you? Don't you dare stop. Steady. Go on!

LOLO: Don't hold me. I'm all right.

JEFFERSON: Always look fifty feet ahead of you. Never mind looking what you're stepping on. The boards are there.

LOLO: I know. I know.

JEFFERSON: If you can do this, you can do anything in the Alps. I told you what fun it was.

LOLO: Do we climb up that ladder? It *is* fun. I think I'd dare to go anywhere with you. (*They are both now directly under the arch, but below the masonry on to which they are about to climb; and so cannot be seen. Helplessly*): It doesn't reach the top. How shall I get up?

JEFFERSON: I forgot about that. Come down then: I'll get up to the top and pull you. (*Jefferson presently hoists himself with the energy of a schoolboy, leans down, and pulls Lolo up after him.*)

LOLO: It takes one's breath away!

JEFFERSON: Good heavens: I've ruined your dress. I should have been more careful.

LOLO: That's nothing. It was an old dress. Did we come all that distance on that little footway? Do we have to go back the same way?

JEFFERSON: No: there are a series of ladders from the scaffolding from this pier. (*He takes her by the waist and leads her over to the side of the pier*). We can go down that way, if you'd like.

LOLO (*leaning over the edge and shuddering*): Oh! What a drop! I could never do that.

JEFFERSON: You're caught between the devil and the deep sea.

LOLO: I don't care: so long as you are here. It was nice of you to take me over.

JEFFERSON: You're the first woman to set foot on the Bridge.

LOLO: Hasn't Margaret ever come with you?

JEFFERSON: Margaret and I once climbed in the Austrian Alps together; but since the children came, she won't climb anywhere. Her nerve has somehow left her.

LOLO: I don't see how anybody could be afraid if you were there. Do you suppose the others will go back?

JEFFERSON (*a little gruffly*): Let's forget about the others. Sit down. If you weren't just a little girl scarcely out of your pinafore, and if I weren't your esteemed brother-in-law, Lolo, I'd tell you you were very beautiful.

LOLO (*delighted*): Let's pretend we aren't. What did you say?

(*She sits down on a coping: he joins her.*)

JEFFERSON: The moon is rising.

LOLO: We are all alone. Nobody could ever reach us. Do you really think I'm beautiful? I didn't think you noticed such things. You always seem to be bound up with the Bridge.

JEFFERSON: Isn't the Bridge magnificent? It's like the Alps. But you are wonderful. You're like the Alpine flowers in May. There's perfume in your hair: there's starlight in your eyes.

LOLO (*putting him off a little*): See the lights in the excursion boat up the river. Ssh! I can hear the waltz they're playing.

JEFFERSON: I suppose you have a string of admirers already. Yes: I know you have. I dropped into your parlor one Sunday afternoon.

LOLO (*contemptuously*): They're all *boys*. They're timid and silly: they're all afraid of me. They sit around all evening with their eyes popping out of their heads; and whatever they say, I contradict them, just to be nasty, and they never say Boo!

JEFFERSON: We're all boys. I suddenly feel very boyish and young again.

LOLO (*incredulous*): You? You're not a boy: you're a big strong handsome man.

JEFFERSON: That is the mask, Lolo. That is my beard; that is my name: that's my professional status: Jefferson Baumgarten, engineer, builder of bridges, faithful husband, dutiful father. It's years since I've been alone in the moonlight with a beautiful girl. The mask has fallen. I am a boy again!

LOLO: I don't believe it!

JEFFERSON: I shall make you believe it. I am not a builder of bridges but a designer of fairy castles: that's my real vocation. And you are my captured princess. (*He bends down swiftly and kisses her hand.*)

LOLO (*springing up with her eyes all a-dare*): Not captured yet!

JEFFERSON (*snatching after her dress*): There is no escape!

LOLO (*swishing away, leaving a piece of torn lace in his hand*): Get me if you can. (*She runs to the other side of the pier, and as he almost reaches her, doubles, and flings herself over the ladder, holding on to the top with her hands.*)

JEFFERSON (*excitedly running over*): I've got you!

LOLO: Take me if you can!

JEFFERSON (*pulling her up by holding her shoulders, and suddenly lifting her on high*): You are mine!

LOLO: Let me down!

JEFFERSON: You are a goblet of wine. (*He raises her higher.*) I am drunk with the bouquet of you.

LOLO: Jefferson!

JEFFERSON (*lowering her till her face is opposite his: then crushing her against him*): Prosit—and eternal youth! (*Her face is tense and drained with a painful ecstasy: their lips meet and do not easily part.*)

LOLO (*softly*): Dear!

JEFFERSON (*panting*): Where are we? This is summer madness.

LOLO: It's wonderful. This is a fairy castle in the middle of the world. You are a fairy prince. The moonlight is a lamp in our garden.

JEFFERSON: You are a dream! your eyes are diamonds: your hair is spun gold. (*Taking her hands and holding her off at a distance*): You are Lo-lo-lo-lo-lolo!

LOLO: You are a dream, too. We have dreamed the same dream.

JEFFERSON: You are a witch: you have robbed me of my mask.

LOLO: You are a wizard: you make me feel naked. I am afraid of you! Listen: a boat is coming up the river. Do you hear the waltz? (*An old-fashioned band sends soft swoony notes up through the air.*)

JEFFERSON (*embracing her, and then seizing her around the waist*): My lovely hussy: I kiss your unseen nakedness: you are mine!

LOLO (*very softly*): Dear—dear—dear!

(*Without another word, they dance together, as the music draws nearer, dance as it grows fainter, continue dancing, Lolo humming to herself in a sort of swoon, until from sheer exhaustion, they drop, by a common movement, on to the coping. They are both warm— warm and panting: he draws away from her for coolness, and holds her hand with a sort of aloof tenderness. Her eyes are closed: a smile of languid satisfaction plays about her mouth.*)

JEFFERSON: It is a very hot night. You must rest. You are exhausted.

LOLO (*closing her eyes, as if clinging to something, and waving her hand in a negative*): Shh! (*There is a long pause.*)

JEFFERSON: The moon is high now. It must be ten o'clock. (*He takes out his watch and strains to look at it. From the distance come the clanking ten beats of the church bell. To himself*): And there's a delegation from the City Council coming tomorrow morning.

LOLO (*opening her eyes with a smile*): Where am I?

JEFFERSON (*soberly*): On the Bridge.

LOLO: Has the fairy castle vanished?

JEFFERSON: Fairy castle? Yes: it's all gone. The Bridge is the Bridge. You are Miss Lois Mills, my wife's youngest sister. I am your esteemed and respected brother-in-law.

LOLO: Just that?

JEFFERSON: Just that.

LOLO: And the fairy prince?

JEFFERSON: The fairy prince designs bridges, bosses men, argues with the City Council, buys life insurance, plays soldiers with his children, and always comes home by eleven to his wife! He has forgotten how to waltz! When he sees a witch he crosses himself three times!

LOLO: I'm sure there are no witches around here.

JEFFERSON (*wearily*): What has happened has happened. If I knew what I was leading you into I wouldn't have taken your dare to bring you across.

LOLO: Don't apologize; I led you!

JEFFERSON: I wouldn't change a thing that has happened. But I am sorry if you would.

LOLO: Not a thing: except the waking up.

JEFFERSON: The end of all memories is that we must leave them behind us: the end of all dreams is that we must wake up. If this was a dream, I remember it too clearly: if it was a memory, I dreamed it too well!

LOLO: I shall never have a nicer brother-in-law than you: not even if Elizabeth marries Robert-Owen. (*With decision*) I am glad you took me over the Bridge. Now I know what the difference between a boy's love and a man's love is.

JEFFERSON: Nonsense! I was never so much a boy as I've been tonight. I don't love you: the moonlight and the perfume of your hair bewitched me.

LOLO: There are all kinds of love. (*Cryptically*) Has Margaret ever known that kind of love?

JEFFERSON (*stiffly*): Yes. There are things one doesn't talk about, Lolo. You've only seen one side of me. Margaret has seen that; she has seen a hundred other sides, too. There's nothing so monotonous as what's called an adventure. If you wish to know all that love is capable of you must be married: take the stormy days with the calm: July madness with November frosts.

LOLO (*hastily*): Let's not talk about Margaret now.

JEFFERSON (*looking anxiously at his watch*): Good Lord: the time is flying. Margaret will dread that something has happened to us. We must go back right away.

LOLO (*ruefully*): My dress is all smudged and creased.

JEFFERSON (*impatiently*): That's all right. Come along!

LOLO: How are we going back?

JEFFERSON: I'll lead this time: you can steady yourself on my shoulder. Remember to look up and ahead of you. It will be after eleven before we're home again. Why the devil did we come out?

LOLO: Don't be cranky. (*He goes over the edge; and she poises herself, to drop onto the ladder*). Catch me if I fall.

JEFFERSON: Come! Come! it's only a six inch drop to the top rung. You've got quite as steady a head as I have.

LOLO (*threatening*): Jefferson: if you're cross and sullen I'll tell Margaret everything! One would think you had seduced me and were afraid to face the consequences.

JEFFERSON: I'll tell her myself. Or rather: I won't have to. She will know everything in five minutes better than I can tell her.

LOLO: You should have thought of that before you began building fairy castles.

JEFFERSON: If we were lovers, we couldn't quarrel more about nothing.

LOLO: Forgive me. It was my fault. You shouldn't have come back to earth so suddenly: I was halfway between. I shall always remember tonight. And always be happy about it.

JEFFERSON: Forgive me Margaret—Lolo. Forgive me Lolo. It has been a glorious night. I'll always remember it, too. Damnation! (*His figure appears in the full moonlight, jerkily recovering himself.*) That might have been a nasty slip then. Let's walk a little faster.

LOLO: I'm not afraid now. I could walk all alone I think.

JEFFERSON: If I make any more missteps you may have to.

LOLO: Be careful, Jefferson.

JEFFERSON: Mind your own feet, Lolo. I hope Margaret has some sandwiches and beer ready for us when we get back. Isn't it a hot night? Do you know: three of our men had to be taken to the hospital today: one of them had a sunstroke. So it goes. I'm getting older myself, with all the worry.

LOLO (*anxiously*): Did you slip again? Are you all right?

JEFFERSON: Quite all right. (*Voice loses itself in the distance*) Quite all right!

(*Curtain*)

Scene Eleven

Robert-Owen's studio on Poplar Street: a night in early September, with a touch of a cool land breeze coming over from the mainland of New Jersey. The studio windows which make up most of the rear wall are clear part of the way up, and then frosted: through them one can see distant rooftops, and, more dimly, the apparently completed outlines of the Bridge.

In one corner, on the right, there is a small model's platform, with an easel, holding a picture turned to the wall, and a small table on which lies a clean palette, a closed box of oils, a palette knife, a jar of modelling clay, an unopened box of twenty-five cigars. Against the opposite wall is a stout oak table on which is a pile of sandwiches, to which Miriam and Elizabeth, who are seated at the table, are adding more. Right under the studio window there is a large divan, big enough for three to sleep on without knocking elbows; and around it are grouped a few miscellaneous chairs: a Morris chair, almost new, covered with a Morris print, two painted kitchen chairs, a box covered with baize, and a low chest, draped with a cheap Persian cotton, and covered with pillows. On the walls are, without any particular effort at spotting, the following pictures: a pastoral by Corot, a sketch by J. F. Millet, a large preliminary sketch by W. H. Hunt for one of his figures at the Albany State Capitol, a little oil by Monet in his earliest manner, a panel of one of William Morris's bird wall papers, two Daumier lithographs, one of 'The Philanthropist,' the other of 'The Connoisseur,' these last being Robert-Owen's two largest aversions, his father, and his lower self! Interspersed among these are some of Robert-Owen's own sketches, chiefly of bridgeworkers, longshoremen, mothers and children, broken old men, done with some of the strength and care of Thomas Eakins, but more exaggerated, with more love of line and less concern for chiaroscuro.

Robert-Owen is restlessly hovering over the table, with a pretence of helping; but to tell the truth he is doing very little work. His sister Miriam, a large, slightly stout girl, who resembles Robert-Owen only in her somewhat sensitive mouth, is actively taking charge of affairs. She is an early prototype of that new species in

*human natural history, the social worker, with a narrow intelli-
gence, positive views, restrained sympathies, an unflagging sense
of superiority bolstered up by her efficiency and her powers as
an inquisitor, and her belief that poor people would be justified
of their Maker if they resembled her in every respect: morals,
manners, taste, efficiency, tidiness, and complete lack of scruple in
seeing that Number One got everything she wanted before Number Two was tended to at all. Since poor people can only exist as
a race by forgetting Number One and sharing their last crust with
Number Two, Miriam's principal duties consist in making her
self-appointed charges as uncomfortable as possible without doing
a single thing to positively relieve their condition. She feels very
warm and magnanimous about the 'sacrifice' she is making. In her
attitude toward her brother she feels much the way she does to
the poor: she sees in him the same improvidence and lack of ambition and self-respect: but since he belongs to her by class and kin,
she is good humored about it, and tolerantly superior.*

ELIZABETH: Do you think there are enough sandwiches, Robert?

MIRIAM (*interposing firmly*): Not half enough, my dear. I am almost
afraid we need an extra loaf of bread.

ROBERT-OWEN: I can run down and get another if you think so.

MIRIAM (*judicially*): Well, with the cake, perhaps we have enough.
That will be enough sardine sandwiches, I think. If we have too
many of them people will get thirsty.

ELIZABETH: My dear, you are dreadfully efficient. I wasn't meant to
be a housewife. I can't even make sandwiches.

MIRIAM: One must be efficient, Beth, if one is always dealing with
poor people. You've no idea how slack they are. I always think
there'd be no poverty if the poor were more efficient. It isn't that
they don't earn money, you know; but they don't know how to
keep it. As soon as they get a little they blow it in. The first
thing I do now when I want to rehabilitate a family is to open
a bank account. It doesn't matter how little it is, it's something
to get a start. If they haven't any money, I put in ten cents myself
to begin with, and when they get a dollar, they can pay me back.

ROBERT-OWEN: Don't preach that doctrine around here, Miriam old girl.
The poor know the proper value of money: which is to spend
it quickly so one won't fall in love with it. That's what I'm doing
now. If I hadn't sold a picture the other day, I wouldn't have had
a party tonight.

ELIZABETH: Is that what this is about?

ROBERT-OWEN: Yes, my first picture. And (*to Miriam*) not a silly red
cent of it is going into a bank account.

MIRIAM (*reproachfully*): You learned bad habits in Paris, I'm afraid.

If you're content to live on bread and cheese, I suppose one will never be able to make you look ahead a little.

ROBERT-OWEN (*picking up a sandwich and munching*): Bread and cheese when one has to, and no cheese in a pinch: nothing, with a little water and a pleasant smile when the wolf really begins to snap at one's ankles, and (*picking up another sandwich*) cakes and ale when the sun shines again.

MIRIAM (*repulsed*): I simply couldn't live that way. I am like Father. I don't want a great deal of money for myself: we live quite simply you know: just the two maids and only one pair of horses: but I do like to know that the money is coming in regularly; and that there's plenty in the bank to tide one over emergencies.

ELIZABETH: That's what I used to think. That's why I wanted to earn my own living.

MIRIAM (*with a complete sense of righteousness*): Every sensible person *must* think that way.

ELIZABETH: I'm not so sure about that now. The first year I was in the office, I was entranced. It was all very exciting: meeting men in a business way, having one's own job, doing one's own work. No silly social calls and that sort of thing. No cards and no gossip. It's begun to wear off now: the hundredth time one makes out a deed isn't as exciting as the first.

ROBERT-OWEN (*keenly*): Are you tired of eating?

ELIZABETH (*taking up a sandwich and holding it up to him, smiling*): Not in the least.

ROBERT-OWEN: Are you tired of sleeping?

ELIZABETH: No, I enjoy it.

ROBERT-OWEN: Are you bored to death by a good talk?

ELIZABETH (*flirting*): Not with you, Robert.

MIRIAM: What is he driving at?

ROBERT-OWEN: Do you dislike walking in the country in September?

ELIZABETH: No, again, Robert.

ROBERT-OWEN (*triumphantly*): Of course not. You can repeat a vital activity a hundred times and it is just as fresh and delightful as the first time. If you are tired and bored by office work, that's proof enough that it isn't a vital activity.

MIRIAM: But *I* don't get tired with my work!

ROBERT-OWEN: Bossing other people and minding other people's business, my dear sister, is a vital activity for you. It is regrettable for the rest of us, but you seem to thrive on it.

MIRIAM: Stop joking, Robert, when you talk that way to me people often think you are serious. (*Robert-Owen opens his eyes wide and starts to say something, but he decides not to.*)

ROBERT-OWEN (*following it up*): If you don't live in your job and through your job, you won't live very much outside of it.

ELIZABETH (*irrelevantly*): Is Jefferson coming this evening?

ROBERT-OWEN: I don't know. I've invited everybody. The General is ill still and can't come.

ELIZABETH: Jefferson lives in his job, doesn't he?

ROBERT-OWEN: He is as absorbed in it as a child. I tremble to think what will happen when the Bridge is finally built.

ELIZABETH: It will be a great achievement.

ROBERT-OWEN: Ah! but the wonderful thing is to have a goal that can't be achieved. The greatest artists are those who know how to fail: that is why Michelangelo stands head and shoulders above all the other men of the Renascence, with the exception of Leonardo. His goal always lay beyond. What one achieves belittles one: it is almost comic. What one strives for and fails to achieve is a greater thing. The essence of tragedy lies precisely in that failure.

ELIZABETH: I don't believe in tragedy. I don't see that there's anything essentially beautiful or necessary in frustration and death. It is better to hit the mark than to aim at such a distant target that one must fall short of it.

ROBERT-OWEN: What sort of creature hits the mark? In painting it is the Bougereaus and the Carolus Durans. In business it is men like Astor and Vanderbilt and Carnegie—or like my father: proud of his model flats: Benns' model flats! In life generally, it is the busy nonentities and mediocrities, the people who are bound to hit the mark because they keep to the iron track and refuse to think of any destination that lies off the track. Who was the greater man?— Pericles, who exploited Athens' allies to build the Parthenon or Plato, who wrote 'The Republic' and denounced the Athens that he knew?

MIRIAM (*incontinently interrupting the conversation*): The bell rang then.

ROBERT-OWEN (*under his breath*): The downstairs door is open. Life knows something better than a great achievement: it is the failure to encompass something beyond one's powers, but not beyond one's conception.

ELIZABETH: Why should one aim at failure?

MIRIAM (*inexorably*): The bell rang again.

ROBERT-OWEN: One doesn't aim at failure: one aims at something great and godlike and one knows if one has aimed high enough failure will be one's reward.

ELIZABETH: And isn't that tragedy?

MIRIAM: I can hear them on the stairs. Please open the door, Robert.

ROBERT-OWEN: Yes. That is Tragedy! Life's ultimate encounter with reality.

(*He goes over to the door on the left and steps out into the hall.*)

291

MIRIAM: It's very early for anyone to be coming, isn't it?

ELIZABETH: Where do you want to put the rest of these sandwiches?

MIRIAM: We'd better have an extra plate for them.

ROBERT-OWEN: That's quite all right, Jefferson. Come right in. The girls are making sandwiches. You know my sister of course?

(*Jefferson enters the room with Robert-Owen. He looks a little wilted: some of his buoyancy has disappeared: lines have begun to draw around his mouth: the whites of his eyes are cloudy with strain.*)

JEFFERSON: Is this a party? I'm sorry, I'd better not stay.

ROBERT-OWEN: It's just an impromptu thing. I tried to reach you at the office, but they said you had to attend a stockholder's meeting in Manhattan.

ELIZABETH: You look tired, Jefferson.

JEFFERSON: I *am* tired. I had rather work twenty hours on the Bridge than spend twenty minutes at a stockholder's meeting.

MIRIAM: Stockholders are necessary evils, aren't they, Mr. Baumgarten?

JEFFERSON: I suppose all evils are necessary: at least they hurt less if we think they are. The only thing these fat gentlemen with the white waistcoats think about is when their investment is going to pay dividends. There wasn't a single human being there who realized that the Bridge was a bridge, and not just a way of multiplying the number of figures on a green certificate.

MIRIAM: I am sure my father understood.

JEFFERSON (*surly*): He was just as bad as the rest of them. He wants to get large dividends so that he may build more model flats and have the pleasure of being a philanthropist as well as a financier.

ROBERT-OWEN: Don't talk about the model flats in this company, Miriam. It's a little *de trop*. I happen to have a friend who lives in one of them—Shane Magonigle, the labor leader.

MIRIAM (*proudly*): They are clean and decent and inexpensive: there aren't drunken people in them, and there is a big court in the center.

ROBERT-OWEN: The less said about my father's philanthropies the better. The chief difference between his flats and those of the ordinary landlord is that under the guise of philanthropy he is able to institute a set of police regulations for running the flats which protect his property from misuse, and enable him to earn as much on his investment as the ordinary slum landlord without letting his property deteriorate.

MIRIAM: Father had better not hear of you talking that way, Robert.

ROBERT-OWEN (*calmly*): Father forgets that I don't accept any of his money now; and he can't cut me off from his property any more completely than I have cut myself.

MIRIAM: Oh! If you *will* be stubborn. . . .

ROBERT-OWEN: You began it, Miriam: so let's call it quits. Father is a philanthropist: he wants to do good to his fellow men. (*Pointing to Daumier's Philanthropist*): See, there's his picture on the wall.

MIRIAM (*eagerly*): You've done father's portrait?

ROBERT-OWEN (*grimly*): No: Daumier did it thirty years ago.

MIRIAM (*angry at being caught*): Ohh!

JEFFERSON: Mr. Benns is making plans to build more model flats around here—on the other side of Atlantic Avenue. He thinks that the Bridge will give the people on the East Side the opportunity to clear out of the slums.

ELIZABETH: I had never thought of that. The Bridge is bound to have all sorts of effects, isn't it?

JEFFERSON (*moodily*): I'm not concerned with them.

ROBERT-OWEN: What! Don't you believe in doing good to your fellow men? Don't you believe that the Bridge is an epoch-making stride in the march of humanity towards the peaks of progress? Don't you believe that the Bridge is going to lower taxes, purify politics, increase the mobility of labor, lower the birthrate among the poor, improve property values, and aid in the dissemination of Christian principles? You are a renegade to your class, Jefferson!

JEFFERSON: The General often says that building bridges is like warfare: the honest men do the fighting, run the risks, and lose their lives in battle. But neither side gains a victory, since the people who actually come out on top are the non-combatants who stay behind and grab the plunder when the fighting men on both sides are exhausted. I stand responsible for the Bridge itself: the piers are solid: the spans will bear the maximum standing load demanded: cable cars and elevateds will be able to run back and forth, day and night, between Manhattan and Long Island. That's all that I am concerned with. The Bridge hasn't altered the proportion of rogues and honest men in the world.

ROBERT-OWEN: You're exhausted tonight, Jefferson. You'll never get another bridge to build if that's the way you feel about it. Don't you realize that since steam engines and suspension bridges and electric telegraphs have come into the world everything is different? (*With savage irony*) The ladies are more virtuous: business men are more honest: workers are more sober: we are in every way more moral and virtuous than any nation that has ever existed on the planet before. Have a sandwich! Let me pour you a little port wine: we don't have to wait for the rest of the company to begin.

ELIZABETH: Don't you think we are—more—moral?

JEFFERSON: Not a bit of it. Robert is right on that score. Read the police reports: violent assaults, murders, suicides, rapes. . . .

293

MIRIAM (*indignantly*): But that's among the poor. What do you expect? They are ignorant and brutal.

ROBERT-OWEN: The century of progress seems to have increased the number of the poor on the face of the earth; and in spite of free education, it has extended the sphere of the ignorant and widened the scope of ugly bestiality. The wars and massacres of this century compare favorably with any other.

MIRIAM (*with the fervency of a High Churchwoman repeating the first words of the Apostles' Creed*): I believe in machinery and progress!

JEFFERSON: Words: words: words. I don't believe in any of your words: I believe in deeds. I don't know whether the Bridge is good or bad: I don't know whether it will help a single human being to be better or wiser or saner or sounder. But the Bridge is a deed: a great deed. When Powers works on the Bridge, there is a demon at work in him: he is alive. When the men finished winding the first span of cable there was a demon in them: they were alive. When I designed the caissons—brought the men together and set them to work—when I raised the flag on top of the first pier—when I throw myself every morning into some new task that presents itself—well, I have a demon, too: I am alive. That is what matters: not what comes of the Bridge. They can scrap it tomorrow, for all I care, if someone can design a better one. It's the work that counts and not the reward. The same reward is coming to all of us, as Powers says: six feet of earth.

ROBERT-OWEN: These are words, too. There are different ways of being alive: Miriam has her way: my father has his: Baxter the politician has his. When Baxter has clinched a beautiful piece of bribery or graft he feels just as happy as you do, no doubt, when you finish a pier. If being alive is all that counts, they are all justified.

JEFFERSON: I have more respect for Baxter, with all his lowness, than for the delicate ladies and gentlemen who do nothing because they are afraid to soil their gloves or their conscience. It took a grafter like Tweed to build the Broadway Boulevard: all the honest people in the city had neither the foresight nor the energy, nor the self-interest, to work for a decent city improvement.

ROBERT-OWEN: You don't believe more than half of that, Baumgarten.

JEFFERSON: Not more than half, perhaps: but at least half. It's better that people should be alive, than that they should all dry up with prudence and delicacy like the Shakers at New Lebanon, who are withering away because they will not risk their seats in heaven by succumbing to the necessary lusts of the flesh.

ROBERT-OWEN: For an animal to be alive, health and activity are enough. We are all animals; and that is the minimum that a human being

294

requires. But to be a human animal one needs more: to be alive means to recognize the difference between good and bad, truth and error, beauty and deformity, destruction and creation and to choose the things that confirm and intensify one's humanity.

JEFFERSON: The Bridge stands above those distinctions.

ROBERT-OWEN: No: it embodies them. It's not because you've had animal ecstasy in the building of the Bridge that it satisfies: you delude yourself there. On the contrary: it's called out every particle of truth in you: your science, your mechanical skill, your judgement: it's moralized you: you've worked with a great company of men and you know your place with them, as they do with you. You don't know anything about painting or sculpture, but the Bridge has brought out your love of beauty, too. Your original design for the piers and coping was hideous, but by altering their proportions you've made something of it. You are getting worn and tired over it, Jefferson—do have another drink!—but you are becoming more alive as a man. Your philosophy of work is just a trumpery excuse for something that is much deeper than your philosophy.

JEFFERSON: I don't altogether understand you, Robert. I thought you painted pictures. My father is the philosopher of the family: he was brought up on Hegel. I read Mills' logic and threw it in the wastebasket. I've never read any more philosophy. What I have is my own.

ROBERT-OWEN: One discovers things with one's brush before one can with any other instrument of the mind. Rembrandt painted the modern novel long before anyone wrote it.

JEFFERSON: Thanks, that's plenty of wine. I mustn't drink any more. You are too much for me tonight, Robert. I don't quite follow you.

MIRIAM (*decisively, as if summing up and settling the whole argument*): It's what I say: work is our salvation.

(*There is a knock at the door and before anyone can answer it Lolo thrusts her head impishly in.*)

LOLO: I hope I'm not too early.

ROBERT-OWEN: Come in, Lolo. It's too late to make the sandwiches; but you can begin to eat 'em if you're hungry.

LOLO: Thank you: Good evening! (*To Miriam*): Isn't it dreadfully exciting: it's my first studio party. I feel awfully wicked. (*To Elizabeth*): I might have known you'd be here. (*To Jefferson*): Oh! You too? (*She goes over to him in a rather self-possessed way and kisses him on the forehead, with almost a touch of malice.*)

ELIZABETH: Did you want to see Robert without a chaperone?

ROBERT-OWEN (*alarmed*): No! No! No!

LOLO (*to Elizabeth*): Cat! Pussy! Meow! (*To Robert-Owen*): Don't be afraid.

JEFFERSON: I am not up to Lois tonight, Robert. Give her something to subdue the animal.

LOLO: I thought you respected my personality.

ROBERT-OWEN (*bowing in mockery*): We all do.

(*Lolo sees a brilliant scarf on a chair by the model stand, goes over, throws it on her shoulders, takes what she fancies is a very daring and sophisticated pose.*)

JEFFERSON: We respect the personality of the tiger, too: but not by remaining in the same room. (*To Robert-Owen*): Too much animal, too little truth, beauty, and morals!

LOLO (*plucking a rose from a bowl and putting it between her teeth*): Senorita Carmencita! Will you paint me sometime, Robert?

ROBERT-OWEN: I never do costume figures. But you give me a notion: let's make this fancy dress. I've a lot of old shawls and peasant clothes in my chest.

LOLO (*screaming*): Ooh! Are we going to dance, too?

JEFFERSON: I'd better go: there isn't any animal left in me tonight. Between the stockholders and you—Robert-Owen!

ROBERT-OWEN: Don't think of going. Two of my friends from Montparnasse are coming in with a mandolin and a guitar. We'll have music and dancing and costume.

ELIZABETH: You perplex me more than ever, Robert: how does this fit in with your philosophy?

ROBERT-OWEN: Dance, Elizabeth, and find out! (*He goes over to the chest and picks out a bundle of shawls, smocks, and ribbons*): There are more things in my philosophy than are dreamed of on heaven or earth, Horatio!

MIRIAM: I'll put on this blue smock and be Little Bo-Peep.

ROBERT-OWEN (*gaily*): Little Bo-peep had lost her sheep
And didn't know where to find them:
They drank charity soup
And they died in a group
And left Miss Bo-peep behind them.

JEFFERSON: You make me feel like an old man, all of you. I haven't danced in years. It seems as though my whole life had got submerged in the Bridge. I wish Margaret were home from the country. She'd like this sort of thing.

ELIZABETH (*tying some shawls in turn over her shoulders*): You'd learn again quickly. Dancing is like swimming.

LOLO (*coming over to Jefferson and staring impolitely in his face*): You haven't danced in years?

JEFFERSON (*firmly*): No. (*Then he suddenly becomes abashed*): Not that I remember!

LOLO (*startled and affronted*): Oh! . . . You'd better stay then: I am sure that Elizabeth or Miss Benns will teach you.

MIRIAM: There goes the bell.

ROBERT-OWEN: I've answered it already.

(*Lolo, pirouetting around, humming the same waltz that she danced with Jefferson on the bridge pier*).

MIRIAM (*to Jefferson*): You ought to dance. I am sure a little relaxation is good for everybody. You can work much better next day.

JEFFERSON: My head aches. I'll go home before people begin to come.

LOLO (*taunting him*): Margaret isn't home, Jefferson.

JEFFERSON: If I weren't your brother-in-law I'd wring your neck, Lolo.

LOLO: If you weren't my brother-in-law you mightn't want to. Go home, why don't you? Who is keeping you?

JEFFERSON: Little creatures like you shouldn't be allowed at large in society.

LOLO (*going over to him, and very serious for a second*): I shall always remember that night. Don't pretend to me that you've forgotten it.

JEFFERSON: No, that's the worst of it: I haven't. Whenever I feel foolish and feeble I remember it.

LOLO: I don't know whether I ought to hate you or not. But I'll tell you a secret. (*She bends his head down and whispers to him*).

JEFFERSON: Married? Why you're only a girl.

LOLO: He's only a man—a nice strong one, too. . . . Mind, don't tell anybody.

(*Curtain*)

Scene Twelve

About seven-thirty on a March night which has left dim masses of torn windy clouds in the western sky. Jefferson's bedroom: a large walnut double bed, placed along the wall, with the head pointing toward a door and the opening that leads to the washroom in the middle: the foot pointing toward the window, the curtains of which are still drawn back. There is a night lamp on the table by the bed; it lights up a little patch directly beneath it, and throws the rest of the room in a murky green pallor, in the midst of which Jefferson's face stands out, thin, jagged, white. There are two vast vases of flowers on the dresser. The carpet is a black ground filled with tiny rosebuds, which, like everything else, seem green in this sickly light.

Elizabeth is seated on a low rocker at the foot of the bed, gazing intently at Jefferson.

ELIZABETH (*reciting very softly*):

> Here where the world is quiet
> Here where all trouble seems
> Dead waves' and spent winds' riot
> In doubtful dreams of dreams . . .

(Her voice grows softer and she finally stops.)

JEFFERSON: Go on. I just closed my eyes. I'm listening.

ELIZABETH: I really think you've had enough, Jefferson. This is your first day up. Don't you want to nap a little now?

JEFFERSON: No. I don't want to sleep. I'm slept out. (*With the childish assumption of command natural to one who has spent three weeks in bed*): Talk to me then.

ELIZABETH: What shall I talk about? Powers came to leave his respects while you were having your supper.

JEFFERSON: Is everything going all right?

ELIZABETH: Like clockwork. He says not to worry.

JEFFERSON: That's good.

ELIZABETH: The men have sent you a big bouquet of flowers, again.

298

JEFFERSON: They shouldn't do it. (*His eyes fill with tears*): Why should I get the flowers? I'm not the only one to get pneumonia working on the Bridge.

ELIZABETH: Poor people are always doing nice things they can't really afford to.

JEFFERSON: We're a big family now. With all the fight and strain of it, it's funny how we grow to like each other!

ELIZABETH: I forgot to tell you that Father de la Salle came this afternoon. Delia asked him to sprinkle some holy water on you. Margaret told him to do it while you were asleep.

JEFFERSON (*smiling feebly*): It will make Delia feel better. I guess I can stand it.

ELIZABETH: Well, that's all the news I think.

JEFFERSON: Talk to me!

ELIZABETH: Oh, Lolo is engaged to be married again.

JEFFERSON: She ought to be vaccinated against it. If she comes in tonight, please shoo her away: she has so much vitality she is discouraging.

ELIZABETH: I will.

JEFFERSON (*suddenly*): Are you going to marry Robert-Owen?

ELIZABETH: No.

JEFFERSON: I thought you two got along well together.

ELIZABETH: We do. I like him very much.

JEFFERSON: Marry him!

ELIZABETH (*smiling*): No: not even for you, Jefferson.

JEFFERSON: You're both intelligent people.

ELIZABETH: Perhaps that's why.

JEFFERSON: You prefer a dead job to a live man I suppose.

ELIZABETH: No: I've chucked that, too.

JEFFERSON: Chucked it? You never told me.

ELIZABETH: How do you suppose I spent so much time around here?

JEFFERSON: You don't mean—

ELIZABETH: Margaret needed someone to look after the household and the children while she was nursing you.

JEFFERSON (*irritated*): The devil! I wasn't so sick as all that. That was a sacrifice unbecoming an independent woman.

ELIZABETH: It wasn't such a sacrifice. I'd been realizing all along that I wasn't getting all I wanted to out of the job. Your being sick was an opportunity.

JEFFERSON: What will you do when I'm better?

ELIZABETH: Find something more amusing.

JEFFERSON: I wasn't as sick as all that.

ELIZABETH: It's a good thing you didn't realize it at the time. When the crisis came the doctor was ready to give you up.

JEFFERSON: Hah! Death's door.

ELIZABETH: Come: you're getting better. Let's not dwell on that.

JEFFERSON: I've discovered something, Elizabeth. (*Very confidentially*): Death is a blind alley. When all the paths of life are shut, death is what remains!

ELIZABETH: There's nothing beyond?

JEFFERSON: What was there before? One's ancestors. What is there beyond? One's children. That's all. I've faced it.

ELIZABETH: Why do we want something more then?

JEFFERSON: I don't. I could die happily anytime. If the Bridge were finished, I could die very happily.

ELIZABETH: Intellectually, I agree with you: but it is a cold agreement. I want more.

JEFFERSON: You want children.

ELIZABETH: No.

JEFFERSON: Yes! Children! Heaven was invented by spinsters and bachelors who denied themselves the legitimate means of becoming immortal.

ELIZABETH (*turning the subject away*): I mustn't let you talk so much, Jefferson. I'm sure you ought to sleep now.

JEFFERSON: If I sleep I'll dream about the Bridge. I won't be happy till it's done. It's like an unfinished organ of the body which somehow must knit together.

ELIZABETH: It's an hour after your supper. It's time to take your tonic.

(*She goes over to his bedtable, mixes him a dose of tonic, and then holds his head efficiently whilst he swallows it. She then beats up his pillow.*)

JEFFERSON: Thanks, Elizabeth. I hate to be such a trouble.

ELIZABETH: That's all right; I'm going to leave you now. If you want anything, just ring the bell. I'll be in the front room.

(*She leaves the room. Jefferson stares ahead of him a little while in silent meditation; then he slumps down a little further in the bed and draws the covers up to his neck and closes his eyes. Presently Margaret comes in very silently and sits down quietly in the chair Elizabeth has occupied. The strain has taken away the slight roundness of her face, and she is now beautiful in a tense exalted way. She has been buoyed up by the crisis; it has taken away the sting of a thousand little daily unnoticed sacrifices.*)

JEFFERSON: Margaret?

MARGARET: I am here, dear.

JEFFERSON (*opening his eyes*): I knew you were here. I didn't hear you come in, but I felt you here.

MARGARET: Shut your eyes again, darling.

JEFFERSON (*reaching out for her with his hand*): I want to talk to you.

MARGARET: Just a little. You ought to go to sleep soon. Tomorrow, the doctor said, you might stay up for ten minutes if it was sunny.

JEFFERSON: Margaret: I am always a bother to you: and I give you nothing in return.

MARGARET: You mustn't say that! You've given me everything.

JEFFERSON: How are the boys?

MARGARET: Tom and Charles have had colds; so I didn't want to let them up. Peter came in to say good night to you, but you were asleep.

JEFFERSON: Nothing serious?

MARGARET: No: almost everybody has a cold. Charles has won the first prize in his class.

JEFFERSON: Tom has a better mind, I think.

MARGARET: So do I. He's more like you.

JEFFERSON: Nonsense: if he takes after anybody, he takes after his grandfather. I must spend more time with them when I am well again.

MARGARET: They'd love it if you took them on long walks the way you used to.

JEFFERSON: Will you come along, too, Margaret?

MARGARET: I'd be in the way.

JEFFERSON: Do you remember when we went climbing in the Alps?

MARGARET: Do I?

JEFFERSON: You could climb like a mountain goat then!

MARGARET: Remember the goat that poked his head in our bedroom window in that little inn in the Schneebergertaal?

JEFFERSON: And the towel he chewed before we could rescue it?

MARGARET: No, it was a nightgown!

JEFFERSON: Sure it wasn't a towel?

MARGARET: Positively: don't you remember I bought a flannel peasant's nightgown in the next Dorf?

JEFFERSON: Red flannel. It was as beautiful as a ball dress.

MARGARET: You used to pay a lot of attention to my dresses then.

JEFFERSON: Darling!

MARGARET: Darling!

JEFFERSON: They are nice boys, aren't they?

MARGARET (*nodding*): They are.

JEFFERSON (*with tears in his eyes*): You are very beautiful. I don't know how you keep so beautiful.

MARGARET: Don't be foolish. No one else thinks so.

JEFFERSON: Nonsense: there is nobody like you! (*He kisses her hand*): I don't deserve half of you. When I am better we must go off somewhere together.

MARGARET: That would be wonderful.

JEFFERSON: Why haven't we seen more of each other these last years,

Margaret? Sometimes it almost seems as though we had drifted apart.

MARGARET (*quietly, without bitterness*): You have been building the Bridge.

JEFFERSON: That damned Bridge! It has come between us.

MARGARET: And I have been minding the household and the children.

JEFFERSON: Yes: the children come between us, too!

MARGARET: I suppose it couldn't be different.

JEFFERSON: No: but somehow, it ought to be different, at least better. The Bridge has been a great thing for me: but it isn't everything in life. I'm forty-five already: you are thirty-seven. No: that can't be. You don't look more than twenty-five.

MARGARET (*tenderly*): You look even younger now, Jefferson. You are thin and wan now, like a young poet.

JEFFERSON: I wish I could write verses to you. You will always be young and always beautiful. And you're the mother of three children, too.

MARGARET: Sometimes it doesn't seem that either of us has grown up a bit. It's wicked of me, I suppose, but when you're feeling like this, I almost feel as if Charles and Peter and Tom were just strangers who've intruded on us.

JEFFERSON: Do you? I always hesitated to say that for fear you'd think I was jealous of the care you gave them.

MARGARET: Oh, one must look after them of course. They are very precious. But you are even more precious, darling. You have been everything.

JEFFERSON: I'm falling in love with you all over again, Margaret. I am dizzy. You are a miracle. I married many women when I married you; and I have fallen in love with them many times. Do you love me?

MARGARET: I love you, dear.

JEFFERSON: And I love you. I wish the Bridge were out of the way. I want to begin our life all over again. Let's see: in another year Tom will be in college. Peter might go to boarding school; it would make him more independent; and maybe Elizabeth would look after Charles.

MARGARET: At least the Bridge will be finished.

JEFFERSON: Yes: if nothing happens. I must get back on the job and push it through.

MARGARET: We'll have a second honeymoon.

JEFFERSON: Our second? Our thousandth. We must go away all alone, and not let anybody know where we are, except in case of emergency.

MARGARET: I've dreamed of doing that.

JEFFERSON: We'll do it.

MARGARET: Dear! ... (*She suddenly becomes conscience-stricken*): But you must rest: I mustn't let you get so excited. You have made me very happy.

JEFFERSON: Don't go away. Just lie down here beside me and hold my hand. I won't say another word. Please lie down.

MARGARET: Promise! Not a word!

JEFFERSON: Not a word!

(*He moves over to make room for her. She lies down tenderly alongside him. Her eyes are brimming with joy and gratitude.*)

JEFFERSON: You're not crying, Margaret?

MARGARET: I am so happy. So happy. I must cry.

(*Curtain*)

Scene Thirteen

The Plaza at the Brooklyn end of the Bridge. The gala day of the open-
ing has filled it with a mob of excited people whose warmth takes
away a little of the cool autumn smell that is already in the Sep-
tember air. At the farthest end, near the Bridge, a big band has been
braying periodically, like a hundred brass jackasses. Back of the
speakers' platform, which is the present foreground, a section has
been roped off for the bridgeworkers, who can thus be near the
oratory, without taking up any of the precious space in the grand-
stand devoted to stockholders, politicians, financiers, owners of
racing stables and gaming houses, and respectable nonentities, to-
gether with their wives, daughters, mothers, and mistresses.

The occasion has been celebrated in the best bourgeois style:
angular, self-conscious, flatulent, and without the faintest spark of
decent ceremonial. To make up for the lack of beautiful costume,
or special music, and to punctuate the opening with the proper
sense of solemnity, there have already been two and a half hours
of unremitting oratory broken by a trumpet solo of The Star-
Spangled Banner, and it is still almost an hour from the end. The
workers are restless. A number of vacant places in their enclosure
testify to their impatience and their thirst.

GROGAN (*suddenly waking up*): Is it over yet?

PAT: Over? It's been over a dozen times, and each time somebody winds
the organ up again and it plays the same tune.

AHEARN: Shh: I can't hear what he's saying.

FRED (*leaning over confidentially*): I'll tell you.

AHEARN: What was that?

FRED: Let me whistle it for you. (*He makes whistling and farting*
noises.)

BILL THE SWEDE: Choost keep quiet. I want to hear the name of the next
speaker. I tank he bane countryman of mine.

(*The band across the Plaza strikes up a medley of patriotic tunes,*
consisting principally of Dixie, Old Kentucky Home, Marching
through Georgia, and Where Is My Wandering Boy Tonight?)

304

MACKAYE: When do they pass around the whusky, mon?

FRED: See that saloon over there on the corner? They're serving drinks free this morning. Just sneak over.

MACKAYE (*suspiciously*): Why aren't ye there yerself?

FRED: I promised my mother never to drink on holidays.

GROGAN: What's that he says about drinking?

MACKAYE: This mon says they're setting up the drinks on the house over there in that saloon.

PAT: And if it's on the house, they put knockout drops in for good measure and shanghai you away to sea before you can say Jack Robinson, I'm thinking.

AHEARN: Shut up: listen what he is saying.

FRED (*holding his nose and affecting to be prostrated*): Somebody let something loose around there. Was that you, Grogan?

BILL THE SWEDE: Choost be quiet. Ay! He bane a fine man. He bane inventor from Stockholm: I bane Stockholm man, too. My brudder almost married a girl that worked in kitchen in the house next door to him.

AHEARN (*to Fred*): Are you an American?

FRED: I'm not a Castle Garden American. I come from the back country.

AHEARN: Well then: why can't you keep quiet?

FRED: Most of the people where I come from are quiet: they're lying in the cemetery.

GROGAN: Ye'll be there yerself next if this big Mick lays you out.

FRED: Attenshun, children! The class will kindly come to order. Miss Grogan; where did you get that spot on your pinafore? Don't let me see you lying on the grass with Patsy Flanagan again.

PAT: Keep your dirty mouth clean one day in the week, can't you! This is the opening of the Bridge.

FRED (*promptly*): Well: now she's opened let's all have a try at her.

ALL (*in ragged unison*): Shut up! The police will put you out.

A POLICEMAN (*reluctantly sauntering up*): Stop the gabbin' boys: it'll soon be over.

PAT: Kin we go now?

GROGAN: What do ye want to go for? This is the last time you'll have anything to do with the Bridge.

AHEARN: She was a bird to work on: many's the boy that's taken an express train to heaven without bargaining for the ride.

MACKAYE: It's a guid bridge: but the bridge across the Firth of Forth is the bridge, mon. This is just a wee Tom Thumb sort of bridge. The viaducts across the hills of Edinburgh are almost as big: at any rate, the principle is the same. If ye know the principle ye can build a bridge anywhere.

PAT: Well, we're all here.

GROGAN: Them that *is* here. I'm thinkin' we ought to have a drink for them as isn't.

AHEARN: Do ye remember Jim O'Connell?

GROGAN: A riveter was he?

MACKAYE: Ay.

GROGAN: I don't remember him.

PAT: I do: he was before your time. Do ye remember Karl the Dutchman?

GROGAN: The Karl that broke his neck?

PAT: The same.

GROGAN: He was a good man.

AHEARN: He was stringin' the cable, wasn't he?

PAT: He was: and the car got stuck; and he climbed out on her.

GROGAN: And then she slipped.

PAT: And the brakes didn't work.

AHEARN: And it knocked his hand loose and sent him for a gool.

PAT: He was breathin' when the Father gave him the last rites. May the saints take him!

AHEARN: Amen.

FRED: Karl was a funny feller. He liked machinery the same as you and me would like a girl. I bet when he got to heaven the first thing he did was to oil the hinges of the Gates and try the locks.

MACKAYE: Ye'd better provide yerself with a suit of asbestos when ye leave this worldly domain.

FRED: If there are ladies in hell, I'll take it in the altogether.

PAT: Will ye be quiet. The next speaker is Baxter.

AHEARN: Yes: and that's Casey alongside him; Casey that used to be in Riveter's Local No. 17. It's now up in Albany he is.

GROGAN: Trust Casey to find a soft job.

AHEARN: If Magonigle was as practical as Casey, the Union wouldn't be busted.

MACKAYE: Ay, mon; and if Brother Magonigle was as practical as Casey he'd own lots in Flatbush, too.

FRED: What's happened to Magonigle?

AHEARN: He's all over the country now, trying to build up a National Organization.

PAT: I've heard that Casey played the Steam Riveter's local dirt.

AHEARN: Ye'll hear a lot of things if ye keep the flaps on your ears open.

GROGAN: Well none of us own any lots in Flatbush from building the Bridge or managing the funds of the Union.

AHEARN: Don't be blackguardin' the Union. If Casey took anything we'd better shut up, or the foes av labor will hear ye and say I told you so.

MACKAYE: Ay, and when ye protect the rascals that way, ye give them a free hand to prey upon yourself. If ye hold that every union man is an angel, ye'll have nothing but pickpockets and cutthroats and traitors running your unions before you know it.

AHEARN: I won't argue with you.

PAT (*ecstatically*): It's a grand speaker he is. Will ye listen to him.

GROGAN: That ain't Baxter.

FRED: Do you want to hear one of Baxter's speeches? This is his Fourth of July oration; he also uses it on St. Patrick's Day and Thanksgiving. (*Fred hiccoughs and belches in various fashions*): Hic!—Me Friends: I—hic—thank you!

(*While the men keep on talking, the voice of an orator, his portly figure seen only from the rear, drowns them out, in tones ranging from an orotund shout to a hoarse whisper, in the fashion of the day.*)

ORATOR: I find it difficult to improve upon the remarks of the last speaker, who justly compared the technical genius of the two Baumgartens, Father and Son, to that of Leonardo da Vinci. Where our friend has done such ample justice to those whose devoted efforts made this great span possible, I can only say: Amen. This is a great day. As citizens of this great city we have reason to be proud of all the builders of this bridge, from the far-seeing merchants and business men who sponsored this project to the Mayors and City Fathers of the two boroughs that are now united for all time by these spidery steel cables. Their zeal and vision have brought forth the mighty metropolis of Greater New York, the Empire City, foremost among the cities of the world with respect to property values, taxes and assessments, elevated railroads, docks, and ship tonnage. The great emporium of commerce and industry is now married in holy wedlock with the City of Homes and—yes—the City of Churches, which has more miles of paved streets and more Protestant Churches than any other city in these United States. We live in a great city. We live in a great country. We live in a great age. (*The orator drones on in an undertone through an endless mass of statistics, intermingling with the voices of the gang, which slowly become fully audible.*) We have girdled the earth with railroads and anointed its fair bosom with factories; we have extracted from the bowels of the earth that which is more precious than rubies—coal!—and we have harnessed the lightning to do our daily work. When we talk our words echo to the ends of the earth, via the telegraph and the cable, a thousand times faster than that famous shot at Concord which was heard round the world. Behold this mighty Bridge, the Eighth Wonder of the World, worthy to stand beside the great pyramids of Egypt. (*A burst of applause.*)

307

GROGAN (*suddenly waking up*): What's he saying?

PAT: The same old chune on the same old organ.

FRED: He said if your mother was a lady you wouldn't have been a son
of a bitch.

(*Curtain*)

Scene Fourteen

The garden of Jefferson's home. Facing north one has on the right the door to the wash-house, which leads into the kitchen; in front of one, part of the way, is a wooden fence, spiked at the top for the annoyance of alley cats and second-story men; beyond that, the fence is an iron picket one, showing other gardens, with lilac bushes and rustic arbors beyond. On the West is the waterfront, with the masts of a few schooners lying against the tops of the warehouses in the foreground, and in the distance one gets still another aspect of the Bridge.

The afternoon of the same day as the opening ceremony. The Bridge itself is hung with American flags: a few easy chairs are scattered around on the lawn, along with a kitchen table, improvised for the occasion as a tea-table and covered almost to the ground with a table cloth. Jefferson, Margaret, Elizabeth, Mrs. Baumgarten, and Robert-Owen are seated around the table drinking coffee and eating coffee cake with chopped almonds and a sugar-and-cinnamon crust.

MRS. BAUMGARTEN: It is too bad your father didn't live to see this. It would have made him happy.

JEFFERSON: I don't think the actual opening would have added much to his happiness. He would have been planning a new job by now: and it probably wouldn't have been a bridge.

MRS. BAUMGARTEN: He had a great deal to live for; but he died with a smile. I hope I shall smile, too, when my time comes.

MARGARET: He never seemed to be vexed with people. Jefferson is always upset by people: if he can't love them or cajole them he must bully them or command them or change them. Father Baumgarten always seemed to keep them a little apart from him . . .

ELIZABETH: It was almost as if he didn't see them as people: as if they were ideas or representations.

MARGARET: Yes: people and things always seemed to be shadows to him, I think: perhaps that's why he took them so easily.

MRS. BAUMGARTEN: He had friends everywhere: he used to drink wine with the Catholic priest in this parish; and he never passed Baxter's saloon without having a chat or a drink with that dreadful old man.

JEFFERSON: Did I ever tell you the story of how Baxter got the Sand Street property and made us pay rent on it when the General had commandeered it?

ROBERT-OWEN: Was that when—?

DELIA (*at the door of the wash-house*): There's a delegation from the Brooklyn Property Owners Association. They want to congratulate you and present you with a memorial . . .

JEFFERSON: And deliver another speech? No thank you! I've had enough. Tell them that I've been exhausted by the reception and have been put to bed by the doctor's orders and can't be disturbed on any account for a week.

MARGARET: Do you think that will keep them away? Say that Mr. Baumgarten has left the city on an important business matter and will not return for a fortnight.

DELIA (*sharply*): Well: what *am* I to say?

MARGARET: Say nothing: I'll go out myself and tell them. (*Delia goes out.*)

JEFFERSON: Good heavens: this is the fifth delegation or committee that's come this afternoon. I should have thought that four hours of oratory this morning was enough for them.

ELIZABETH: I caught you yawning shamelessly, Jefferson.

JEFFERSON: I wouldn't have stayed to yawn if I could have broken through the crowd. Did you ever listen to such gas and wind before! (*Imitating*) This greaaaat peepul—this greaaat city—these greeeat financiers and far-sighted business men!!

ELIZABETH: Yes: and scarcely a word about you or about Father Baumgarten or the Bridge. That's the gratitude you get. That's what you've given your life and your best years for.

JEFFERSON: I didn't care about myself; but they might have said something about the men. Every man who worked on that Bridge was as much a hero as if he had fought a dozen battles: every day was a battle, and more than one man bears the wounds of it still—or came to worse. But the way those windjammers talked you'd think that stock certificates wound the cable and greenbacks hammered in the rivets. There wasn't a single lawyer or politician there who knows what a day's work is outside of assorting papers or counting bills.

ROBERT-OWEN: They didn't wish to sully the bright occasion by mentioning the killed and the wounded.

ELIZABETH: Do you suppose that was it?

JEFFERSON (*crossly*): Oh: don't talk to me about it. If ever there was an anti-climax that ceremony was.

310

DELIA (*poking her head through the door again*): The Fulton Street Shopkeepers Benefit Association would like—

JEFFERSON: That's enough. Turn them out: and if any more of them come, tell them that I've retired from public life.

MARGARET: Let me tend to them, Jefferson. (*She rises firmly and goes out with Delia.*)

ELIZABETH: Perhaps we'd all better leave and give you a little solitude. It's been an awful strain.

JEFFERSON: Don't go. I am a little dazed by it all. I never bothered to think what I'd do when the Bridge was finished; and now it's all done and it's out of my hands, I feel empty.

ROBERT-OWEN: Sit back, Jefferson, and look at the Bridge.

JEFFERSON: I've been looking at it and thinking about it all day. Why does a thing that's done suddenly seem so stale and useless?

ROBERT-OWEN: All day! You haven't begun to look at it. Fold your hands and spend a whole year looking at it.

JEFFERSON: I can't fold my hands: what would be the good of it?

ROBERT-OWEN: Try it and find out.

JEFFERSON: I must have my work to do.

ROBERT-OWEN: Your work will always feel incomplete if the action alone is all that matters to you.

JEFFERSON: What does matter?

ROBERT-OWEN: What matters are the meanings that come out of the action.

JEFFERSON (*beginning to pace up and down*): I must work. I can't sit crosslegged and look at the end of my nose.

ROBERT-OWEN: You are hiding your emptiness.

JEFFERSON: This isn't the only bridge in the world. There are plenty more to build: and I'd like to try my hand at a great dam and waterworks system, too—to irrigate the dry lands of Arizona for instance.

MARGARET (*coming back*): They've gone.

JEFFERSON: That's good. Are the boys back yet?

MARGARET: No: they can't keep away from the Bridge today. They're so proud of you!

JEFFERSON: Happy the prophet who's honored in his own household. (*Turning to Elizabeth*) What do you think, Elizabeth?

ELIZABETH (*simply*): I envy you. Some day a girl may have that sort of career, I hope.

JEFFERSON (*turning to his mother*): What do you say, mother?

MRS. BAUMGARTEN: There is a boy in you, Jefferson, that wants to build bridges. If the boy is happy, let him go on.

JEFFERSON: That's just it. I don't know whether the boy is happy or not. I ought to be happy. The Bridge is done: our sons are growing into manhood. I have Margaret. But when I stop and think

311

about it, it is all a little empty. (*Hastily, noting a change on Margaret's face*) Not marriage, Margaret: one's career, one's work. I almost killed myself working on this Bridge—and what for? So that property values might go up around Borough Hall? So that Baxter and Co. might graft more extensively?

ROBERT-OWEN: Doesn't the Bridge itself satisfy you?

JEFFERSON: The Bridge: yes. But it's done: don't you see, it's done!

ROBERT-OWEN: No: it's just begun.

JEFFERSON: But my part is done. And here I am—I suppose you don't feel that way?

ROBERT-OWEN: Try again, Jefferson. You reached your goal this time. Next time try something you can't reach!

JEFFERSON: But that would mean failure.

ROBERT-OWEN: Are you satisfied with your success?

JEFFERSON: No.

ROBERT-OWEN: Then change your goal.

JEFFERSON: I don't see what you are driving at!

ROBERT-OWEN: We'll talk about it some other day. Your Bridge is stunning in this light. I will have to paint it.

MRS. BAUMGARTEN: But the afternoon is chilly already. Don't you think we had better go in?

JEFFERSON (*going to the front of the garden and muttering to himself*): By God: it *was* worth while!

(*Margaret comes over to him silently and lays her hand on his shoulder.*)

JEFFERSON: I am. You are. The Bridge is. I am sure of these things. (*A long brooding pause.*) Or am I?

(*Curtain*)

(signed) Lewis Mumford
Aug. 30, 1927

312

Part Four

1932-1936

What I Believe

At the age of eight I believed in the omniscience of my teachers and the power and glory of the United States. When I learned that Brazil had a greater area than my own country, I felt that geography was an indignity, and if the facts could not be disputed, we ought to annex Brazil.

At fourteen, I believed in a very personal God who helped me usually to get good marks in my examinations, and in the offices of the Protestant Episcopal Church of America. This belief remained with me at least two years, until I discovered to my horror that the priest had a way of going through the prayers rapidly, as if he wished to get the day's job done. In an excess of piety, I left the church and fell into the arms of Spinoza. God was in me and I was in God, but the sky from that time on was empty!

When Europe went to war, I was eighteen, and I believed in the revolution. Living in a world choked with injustice and poverty and class strife, I looked forward to an uprising on the part of the down-trodden, who would overthrow the master class and bring about a regime of equality and brotherhood. In the subsequent years I learned the difference between a mass uprising and the prolonged spiritual travail and creation of a revolution; politically, I am no longer naïve enough to believe that an uprising can change the face of the world. But I have never been a Liberal, nor do I subscribe to the notion that justice and liberty are best achieved in homeopathic doses. If I cannot call myself a revolutionist now, it is not because the current programs for change seem to me to go too far: the reason is rather because they are superficial and do not go far enough.

My principal quarrel with the Russian communists, for example, is not over their ruthlessness in achieving the new order, but over their acceptance of half the fallacies of the mechanistic system of thought which happened to be dominant when Marx formulated his revolutionary dogmas. This system subordinates all human values to a narrow utilitarian scheme, as if production had no other end than production, and the result is a caricature of both society and the human personality. The orthodox communist has not escaped the mechanistic prison by taking possession of it and assuming the duties of jailer; nor does the jail look more inviting when it is called a Proletarian Palace.

It is a new life I would aim at, not simply a new balance of power. Such a life would leave less of the present world standing than Soviet Russia has left.

These original beliefs in one's country as the sole home of the saintly and the elect, in some institutional embodiment of Christianity, and in a dramatic transformation of a sordid present into a beatific future were common, in various proportions, to most members of my generation. They constituted our system of working values through the greater part of childhood and adolescence.

Some of us have remained fixed in these attitudes: manhood finds them still measuring the size of the United States Navy against that of its nearest rival, or, in more refined moments, comparing the value of our poetry or technology to that of some other country—as if there existed any rational purpose today which was not common to men of different regions and did not depend upon their continuous coöperation and intercourse. Some of us still talk about revolution, without altering our interests or occupations in the smallest way to accomplish it; while others of us are still seeking, in psychoanalysis or the latest reports of molecular physics, our God.

What has happened to my original belief in 'my country'? What remains of it is no longer a disguise for my childish egotism. To enjoy one's own region, to feel attachment to some particular landscape and way of life does not demand that inverted form of patriotism which consists in a blind resentment against what is foreign and an intense desire to extirpate it. As a New Yorker—aware of the procession of ships up and down the Bay, seeing strange faces, hearing strange voices almost every hour—I am much closer to Europe than to Oregon. This is natural and seemly. What is unnatural is the political theory which would disregard these real loyalties and attachments in an effort to create a uniform grade of cannon fodder for the next war.

To confine human association to the political state, or to make membership in that state the highest good, is like trying to put an actual landscape that stretches many miles toward the horizon into a wooden picture frame. Cultures cannot be isolated; they grow by perpetual intercourse across the boundaries of time and space; without cross-fertilization they are sterile—sterile and sour.

As an expression of the will to power, the sovereign state is an enemy of culture: its only significant purpose is to preserve justice and liberty among its constituent cities, regions, associations, corporations. This purpose is not furthered by patriotic taboos, fortifications, tariffs, frontiers, and an everlasting parade of the instruments of war. 'My country' is the common territory of all men of good will. As for the actual soil, I agree with Nathaniel Hawthorne when he said that New

England was about as large a patch of earth as he could feel any natural affection for.

Well, just as my childish pride in the United States has been transformed into a more comprehensive grasp of society and culture, so my parochial religion and my sanguine social faith have, without disappearing as a nucleus, undergone a profound change. How shall I describe the results? One's deepest faith cannot be expressed. As Walt Whitman put it, the best cannot be said; the best is that which must be left unsaid. Whatever I can say will be only a faint symbol of that deeper urge of life, that rationality beneath all reasons, which bottoms one's existence.

An adequate faith ought to harmonize one's actual scheme of living, one's conscious reflections, and the inner go of the self; while it faces the evils of existence, it should recognize and consciously multiply the goods. What are these goods? Where does one find them? What attitude must one bring toward them?

Most of the ethical philosophies of the past have sought to isolate the prime goods of life, making pleasure or efficiency or duty or imperturbability the chief end of the disciplined and cultivated mind. Since no one goes through the world unhurt, and since violence and injustice often have the upper hand, many of these systems have sought by a sort of supernatural bookkeeping to redress the evils of existence in another sphere. To seek pleasure, or happiness, or immortality, has been the goal of these faiths; if not now, then hereafter.

No such single goal seems to me legitimate or even desirable. The fact that sunshine is good does not make the Sahara an ideal place to live in. Instead of beginning with such factitious ends, and reproaching the universe because it does not fully serve them, let us rather begin with the nature of life itself.

One begins with life; and one knows life, not as a fact in the raw, but only as we are conscious of human society and use the tools and instruments society has developed through history—words, symbols, grammar, logic, science, art. Life considered apart from this milieu is merely an abstraction of thought. One begins with a world of values and only as a result of persistent inquiry and experiment does one reach such a useful concept as that of a physical universe, considered as self-existent and separate from these organic values.

The vague stir and strength within us, which we associate with the beat of our hearts or the expansion of our lungs, requires for sustenance a whole solar system, merely to maintain such elementary conditions as the heat of our blood. And similarly, the crudest social existence implies the effort of untold generations of men to differentiate foods from poisons, invent tools, create symbols and expressive gestures. Individualism in the sense of isolation is merely a spatial illusion. The more self-sufficient an individual seems to be, the more sure it is that, like Thoreau at Walden Pond, he carries a whole society in his bosom. This fact applies equally to nations. Both physically and spiritually we are members one of another; and we have never been anything else, although the callosities of ignorance and egotism have sometimes made us insensitive to this condition.

Life, then, implies these manifold coöperations, and the finer life becomes, the more complicated is this network, and the more highly conscious does one become of it. Goethe once declared that the sources of his thought were so numerous that one who traced them out would find it difficult to attribute any originality to him; and since Goethe's honesty was equaled only by his pride, one may take his witness as final. The business man who fancies he has made his own fortune, or the inventor who imagines he has the sole right to his invention, is merely ignorant of his sources. The individual contribution, the work of any single generation, is infinitesimal: the power and glory belong to human society at large and are the long result of time.

This is the philosophic justification for communism, and since it coincides with the practical reason for communism—namely, that every human being requires approximately the same amount of air, water, clothing, food, shelter, with small differences to allow for climate and the type of work—the political institutions of society should be arranged to establish this minimum basis of life, differentiation and preference and special incentive being taken into account only after the security and continuity of life itself is assured. This is my elementary political faith; it corresponds roughly to Plato's.

The task of organizing a basic communism is not an easy one. Special societies, like monasteries and armies, have often achieved a rough measure of it; but the real difficulty is to apply it to the community at large and still preserve those delicate volitions and those intense individual interests which are an incentive to creative activity. One of the first moves in this direction is obviously to alter by example and education the current scheme of values. In our present society, pecuniary prestige comes first; life and the values derived from living exist on sufferance.

While a basic economic communism, which would extend to the whole community the decent practices of the household, seems to me a necessary measure of justice and practical statesmanship, one need not therefore hold, with an older school of revolutionary thinkers, that the evils of life are solely the work of an ominous capitalist class, or that they are entirely economic in origin and would be abolished under a more humane regime.

On the contrary, I have no more notion of abolishing evil than I have of abolishing shadow in the world of light. Fourier's crazy belief that the ocean itself under a harmonized social order would turn into lemonade, and Spencer's picture of the future society as a sort of polite eternal Sunday afternoon, are merely exhibitions, as it were, of an unfathomable shallowness. Evil and good are phases in the process of human growth; and who shall say which is the better teacher? Illness, error, defeat, frustration, disintegration, malicious accident, all these elements are as much in the process of life as waste, nutrition, and repair. The very forces which, if triumphant, would destroy life are needful to season experience and deepen understanding.

Observing this, the popular religions of the past have celebrated almost solely the negative aspects of existence. But, in release from their superstitions, one must not commit the opposite error of neglecting the role of evil and forgetting its value. Customs and actions we habitually call good have large capacities for mischief: who does not know the charity that poisons the giver and the purity that offends common decency?

Similarly, the evils of life have a certain capacity for good; and the mature person knows that they must be faced, embraced, assimilated, and that to shun them, or innocently hope to eliminate them forever is to cling to an existence without perspective or depth—a child's picture done in pretty chalks, charming perhaps, but only that. Like arsenic, evil is a tonic in grains and a poison in ounces. The real problem of evil, the problem that justifies every assault upon war and poverty and disease, is to reduce it to amounts that can be spiritually assimilated.

This doctrine is just the opposite of certain 'optimistic,' life-denying attitudes and habits of mind that have become popular during the last three centuries: particularly, the notion that comfort and safety and physical ease are the greatest blessings of civilization, and that every other human interest—religion, art, friendship, family, love, adventure—must be subordinated to the production of an increasing amount of 'comforts' and 'luxuries.' Believing this, the utilitarian has turned an elementary condition of existence into an end. Avaricious of power and riches and goods, he has summoned to his aid the resources of modern science and technology. As a result, we are oriented to 'things,' and have every sort of possession except self-possession.

Today it is only a fortunate minority of wealthy people, together with a handful of "the undeserving poor" (to use Doolittle's epithet in 'Pygmalion') who have any notion of the true uses of leisure and who are not bored or frightened by the mere prospect of achieving it. By putting business before every other manifestation of life, our mechanical and financial civilization has forgotten the chief business of life: namely, growth, reproduction, development. It pays infinite attention to the incubator—and it forgets the egg!

Now the end of all practical activity is culture: a maturing mind, a ripening character, an increasing sense of mastery and fulfillment, a higher integration of all one's powers in a social personality; a larger capacity for intellectual interests and emotional enjoyments, for more complex and subtle states of mind. Arrested personalities look back with regret to some temporary fulfillment in youth, as Mark Twain looked back to the happy adventures of Huckleberry Finn. Developing personalities accept, without impatience or regret, the next stage in their growth; by the time they are mature, they have no difficulty in putting away childish things.

Growth and culture imply activity and periods of leisure sufficient to absorb the results of this activity, using it to enrich art and manners and personality. The Athenians were quite right in believing that these things could not be achieved by anyone who was forced to spend the entire day in some spiritually deadening or physically exhausting task in the shop or the countinghouse. Jesus-ben-Sirach came to the same conclusion, and Emerson finally gave up long hours of work in the garden because the toil robbed him of ideas. Most of us who have enjoyed both manual work and contemplation would agree with Patrick Geddes when he says that two hours of physical activity are all one can profitably use in a day devoted to intellectual interests, and that the hard-working laborer who has any mental life left at the end of his day is nothing less than a prodigy.

The practical moral to be drawn from this is that servile labor—even if it produces 'comforts'—should be minimized to the utmost, and that leisure must be distributed more universally in the form of a shorter working day, instead of being permitted to exist as the penalizing burden of 'unemployment.' Without leisure there can be neither art nor science nor fine conversation, nor any ceremonious performance of the offices of love and friendship. If our Machine Age has any promise for culture, it is not in the actual multiplication of motor cars and vacuum cleaners, but in the potential creation of leisure. But so long as 'comfort' and not life is our standard, the Machine Age will be impotent.

All our higher activities are curbed by the present alternations of excessive toil and short periods of sodden release. The fact that the majority of people go to the theater, for example, at the end of a long working day explains in good part the quality of the drama they demand; in a state of physical fatigue, they are unable to experience the deep or subtle emotions that the great dramatists or composers call forth. Except for an occasional musical festival for the leisured, like those at Salzburg or Glastonbury or Bethlehem, there has been little opportunity in our civilization to experience art under conditions which permit sensitive enjoyment, to say nothing of complete rapture.

And if painting and poetry have so meager a role in the life of modern people, one might sufficiently account for it by the fact that they demand responses which few people are able to give at the end of a working day—or for that matter, a working week. There is no proof whatever that the capacity for art and thought is smaller today than in the thirteenth century or the fifteenth; but the conditions favorable to this capacity belong to only a handful of specialists and dilettantes.

What applies to the contemplative arts, applies equally to the arts of action: the dance, gymnastics, and above all, perhaps, to sexual intercourse. Without leisure, freshness, energy, they lose their inner impetus, and must be excited to activity by the rivalry of athletic matches, by the negative stimulus of ill health, or by preliminary bouts of strong liquor. Yet all these arts are quite as central to life as the most beneficent instrumental activity. In so far as many primitive communities have maintained the arts of action in a more consistent and whole-hearted way than our Western civilization, we need not boast too loudly about our advantages; for our 'progress' has not been unmixed with lapses and regressions in matters that are far more important to our welfare than the production of cheap pig iron.

Instead of the one-sided practical activity fostered by the ideals of the utilitarians and the working out of modern technology, with its intense specialization, I believe in a rounded, symmetrical development of both the human personality and the community itself. Economics would play a part in that development, but it would not dominate it.

The two ages of human achievement that stand out for me are those of fifth century Athens and fifteenth century Florence; and both of them were, effectively speaking, the work of amateurs, who, by a symmetrical development, gave to each aptitude a quality which years of separate specialization would in all likelihood never have produced. That specialization leads inevitably to efficiency is a specious argument; for as there is, in Ruskin's words, no wealth but life, so there is no efficiency except that which furthers life. Moreover, this argument takes no account of the mountains of useless, arid work that are accumulated under our present habits of specialization; and it gives to this practice the sole credit for gains which are due to quite another modern technique, namely, cooperative intercourse and association.

The metaphysical case against specialization is even more overwhelming. We live in a world where no single event exists by itself, but, on the contrary, is organically conditioned by its entire environment, physical and human. If one attempts to deal with any little segment in isolation, one is dealing with a figment; and one begins to know a little about the things which are closest to one's interest only when one traces out their interrelationships with that which may, apparently, lie far beyond. While abstract analytical thinking is one of the great practical achievements of the race, it is misleading and mischievous unless it takes place in a life directed environment.

How are we to achieve this? By heaping together in a vast mechanical accumulation all of our specialized researches? By attempting to boil all knowledge and practice down into popular outlines? Alas! no: the result of such an arithmetical addition of specialisms would merely be another specialism. While a schematic synthesis may be a help to orderly thinking, the place to achieve organic unity primarily is in living itself, in encompassing all the activities that make a full life.

We must experience at first hand manual toil and aesthetic ecstasy, periods of routine and periods of adventure, intellectual concentration and animal relaxation. We must know what it is to be a cook, a tramp, a lover, a digger of ditches, a parent, a responsible worker. In this way we shall be exploring our environment and exploring the possibilities of ourselves in relation to the personalities around us—instead of shrinking, after a preliminary skirmish or two, into a sort of war of attrition with life, seeking to achieve a maximum of safety and comfort in the dugout of some specialized interest, and viewing the horizon with the aid of a periscope.

Such a complete mode of living must inevitably carry over into each special situation: only a vicious system of mis-education can prevent it. By ceasing to live in isolated compartments, one avoids the delusive habit of treating the world in this manner, and one approaches each event with an intuition of its wholeness—as not primarily physical or biological or economic or aesthetic, but as all of these things together in a certain unique combination. Temporarily, as a practical convenience, one will not be afraid to use the method of analysis to the utmost; but, weighing, measuring, calculating, decomposing, we shall still be aware of the organic whole in space and time with which we started, and to which, enriched by the process of analysis, we must ultimately return.

My faith, for its full consummation, must be embodied in a community. But how shall I describe it? This life does not exist in the past, although every great civilization in its best moments gives more than a hint of it and plenty of guarantee against its being fantastic and beyond reach. Here and there it may be said to exist in some living person, or to be embodied symbolically in a poem or a novel, such as 'Moby-Dick,' 'War and Peace,' or 'The Magic Mountain.' If one were founding a church, instead of summing up one's intuition of life, one would include in the calendar of saints a Blake, a Goethe, a Whitman. And while among men of science this faith has cohered more slowly, partly because the pattern of research has been set by seventeenth century physics, it gets rational support from science and today would include scientists like A. N. Whitehead, J. S. Haldane, C. G. Jung.

For me the confirmation of my intuitions came through acquaintance with Patrick Geddes, whose long life spans the service of many sciences, from biology to sociology, and many types of activity, from that of the speculative philosopher to the planner of cities. Geddes showed that a conception of life, unified at the center and ramifying in many inter-relations and comprehensions at the periphery, could be rationally lived; that it had not been outmoded by the age of specialization but was actually a mode that might, through its superior vitality and efficiency, supplant this age; that one could practice in one's own person, in the germ, a type of thinking and feeling and acting which might ultimately be embodied, with fuller, deeper effect, in the whole community; that, even on the crude test of survival, a life that was organically grounded and pursued with a little courage and audacity had perhaps a better chance than the narrow goals and diminished possibilities of our dominant civilization. My utopia is such a life, writ large.

To be alive, to act, to embody significance and value, to be fully human, are goals that are difficult of achievement. Who has not his dead hours, his moments of apathy or disintegration—and who persists, for any long period, in being half the man he is capable of being? These goals are none the worse for being difficult. They come at least within the realm of possibility; and, pursuing them, one arises early and smells the dew of morning, or, at night, one sinks with a good conscience into one's bed, as one may hope to sink, without bitterness or a vain sense of disappointment, into one's grave.

If a religion be that which gives one a sense of the things that are worth dying for, this community with all life, this sense of a central purpose in oneself, inextricably bound up with the nature of things, even those accidents and brutal mischances that are so hard to assimilate —this faith may be called a religion. For a good lover knows when to conquer and when to renounce; and he who loves life well will not grudge the surrender or fail to recognize the appropriate moment for it. Life is measured by the capacity for significant experience, and not by power or riches or length of days.   —The Forum. November 1930

OBSERVATIONS ON KARL MARX.   Marx deserves more discussion. His metaphysics and his logic were entirely in opposition to his vital instincts, and unfortunately, like a good Jew, he trusted his head and did violence to his guts. He knew, for example, that the ruling classes in Greek or early Roman times were different from those in Victorian England. He knew that they lived to do something else than to accumulate surplus value for themselves by a process of driving their slaves brutally, and that this value—I am using his terms for convenience —was not the object of their system of industry. If that was so, there was nothing to prevent modern capitalism from being modified or changed; for it was not ingrained in human nature. Unfortunately it was necessary for Marx's dialectic to make the capitalist entirely a product of the technological process, and the process entirely a product of a narrow rapacious kind of creature: so the whole structure was dialectically watertight. But it began to be punched with holes even in Marx's day, when, thanks to the landed classes, the bureaucracy, and the better capitalists themselves, the meanest and most ferocious forms of exploitation were abolished. Marx's sound instincts made him respect Robert Horner, the factory inspector who did so much to mitigate the cruelties practiced on the textile workers; but if a single man could do so much, and if a whole class could ameliorate its methods within thirty years, the doctrine of increasing misery and increasing suffering and hopelessness was already in limbo while he was writing 'Das Kapital.'

Marx's system was watertight only in terms of the actual methods of production in the 1820's, and in terms of the Ricardian economics which were formulated upon that foundation. His other weakness was likewise that of his opponents: he assumed a cosmopolitan development of industrialism with a therefore united working class. He did not foresee the possibility of machine industry being integrated on a more local basis, or of finding that basis *just because* it was integrated. Hence the doctrine of World Revolution. In terms of Cobden and Marx, Trotsky was right in holding that the only revolution possible was a world one: but Lenin was right in beginning at once in Russia without waiting for the world outbreak, and Stalin, stupid pig though he is, was equally right in holding that Russia could uphold the revolution within her own borders even if the rest of the world remained capitalist. (See Keynes on that point). Resources are still on a worldwide basis and they demand internationalism; and we shall never have a peaceful world or a workable one until they are rationed out all over the planet. But the machine itself, just because the knowledge and technics have spread so rapidly, needs no longer be on a worldwide basis for either production or trade. So you are right: Marx was a visionary, a Jewish visionary: an inspired Rabbi correcting an inspired stock broker (Ricardo). . . .
—Letter to C.K.B. July 4, 1933

. . . The real weakness of the Marx-Engels analysis is that it was too narrowly an analysis of profits rather than products: the whole theory of surplus value assumes that the critical damage comes from taking an undue share of the value produced from the worker, instead of producing the wrong products and thus creating the wrong values. Marx wanted a revolutionary overturn in order to change the bookkeeping: he had no notion whatever of altering the technology: for that part of industrial society just unfolded itself *dialectically!* But a thoroughly automatic machine technology with the worker completely displaced— therefore producing no value at all, surplus or otherwise!—is not in the Marxian picture. Hence the mischief of keeping communism chained to that particular chariot. . . .   —Letter to C.K.B. September 11, 1932

We must meet this week, with Wilson, dear Waldo, and discuss the Call for a Writer's Congress you sent me: meanwhile I want to tell you briefly why I will not sign it. To me it is a pretty sad document: as dead and uncreative as the radical movement itself in America has been these last ten years, and beneath this deadness and uncreativeness is a laziness in thinking that amounts to dishonesty. The program that is offered is based upon six points, all of them negative: beginning first of all with an injunction to fight against imperialist war and defend the Soviet Union! In the name of what is the fighting to be done? Answer: in the name of an incipient proletarian revolution. In the form that this revolution has taken in Russia, and that it takes even more in the stale formulae derived from that revolution, I do not believe in it. Too many mistakes were made in the course of that revolution, and later incorporated as a form of orthodoxy, to be of service in an American movement. At the present moment, a revolutionary movement does not have to protect Russia against the capitalist nations: it has to protect itself equally against the tactics and the assumptions, against the forms of autocracy that have been developed there—and against the notion of creating by force alone what cannot be produced by intelligence and persuasion. Except by physical means, you cannot fight fascism in terms of the Russian Revolution: Their social and political tactics are now identical, even though their class and economic bases are dissimilar. Beneath both movements is a profound disrespect for human life, for the autonomy of the personality and the group, and for the basic liberties of civilized existence. . . .   —Letter to W.F. January 6, 1935

THE 1933 BRANCUSI EXHIBITION.   Here is the Brancusi of old, the Brancusi whose newborn child and whose head of Mlle. Pogany once seemed so startling; and here is the new Brancusi, demonstrating that his secret lay not in the newness or unexpectedness of his forms but in his essential capacity as a sculptor to conceive new molds for our own experience. For he has continued his explorations of time and space and movement, of materials and textures and surfaces, and like some ancient deity he creates plastic forms—a rooster or a blonde metallic Negress—which have the effect of being new biological species.

If you can imagine a geometrical theorem that produces a smile, a machine shop that has become introspective, a lump of clay that displays adolescent ambitions to become a crystal, or two lovers who have dissolved into stone—if you can imagine any of these things, you are ready for Brancusi. If you cannot, you had better confine your explorations of the new world of form to the latest plumbing fixtures and electric gadgets; they are not so subtle and so human as Brancusi's sculptures, but they are a step in the right direction. "It's pure joy I'm giving you," says Brancusi in his brief introduction to the catalogue. "Don't look for obscure formulas nor for mysteries." The counsel is excellent. For the first effect of the show should be to make one clap one's hands and turn a few handsprings; the existence of so much pure imagination makes one feel young and innocent again. And part of Brancusi's own pleasure, I am sure, is a counterpart to that which one felt as a child on the beach when one finally succeeded in turning out a pail of wet sand in such a fashion that it would stand up and show no flaw. This elementary feeling for clean form and for the material in itself is one that we have almost lost today. Brancusi restores it to us, as he restores so many other parts of our deserted heritage. . . .

Craftsmanship and pure mathematics, the natural and the artificial, the living and the mechanical, the spontaneous and the calculated, primitivism as deep as a jungle fetish wedded to a rationality as coldly elegant and abstract as a demonstration in mathematics by the late Henri Poincaré—these are the ingredients of Brancusi's art. But heed him well! Do not look for mystery; look for joy and humor and the delight of being equally at home in every part of the world.

—The New Yorker. 1933

. . . Apart from writing my book I have no events to record, no adventures, even in the mind; although after years of delicious effort, years which I would not for anything have shortened, I have finished 'The Guermantes Way'; and in less time than it takes me usually to read the Sunday newspaper, or so it seemed, I finished the now current volume of Jules Romains, who still maintains himself in my esteem, partly no doubt because he condenses the contents of so many hundred Sunday newspapers for me, but partly, also, because after the sociologist has returned with his report, and duly analyzed it, for the benefit of the busier members of the class who keep notebooks, the poet suddenly awakes and in the course of a brief chapter sets all the dry paper aflame, proving that the real use for all these paperoid preparations is after all to provide light for the eyes, warmth for the heart—those neglected organs.   —Letter to B.D. August 6, 1936

The Barlach war memorial is alone worth a visit to Hamburg: a flat shaft that rises from a base below one of the most frequently used bridges. The German Ku Klux Klansmen have objected to the mother and child rendered in low relief on one side; their ground is that the figures look Slavic, a criticism even more absurd than the pious English outrage over the fact that Epstein's Madonna looked Oriental. What really troubles the Nazis is that the whole monument is so free from

Bismarckian pomp and bluster; freer even than Tessenow's excellent interior of the war memorial in Berlin, with its metallic wreath and its top open to the sky. Barlach is a real *Nordgotiker*, essentially a hermit-artist, produced by what is still living in North Germany of the Middle Ages. In Lübeck, an hour away from Hamburg by train, one can see the first three figures of a series Barlach is doing; they occupy a special space in the old Katharinenkirche, now used as a museum. The strong Gothic interior, doubly strong by reason of the fact that it is painted a cold white, is just the right setting for Barlach's art; it needs the echo of that background to hold its reality, and to make one see that Barlach has not copied Gothic but *is* Gothic, perhaps one of the last creatures produced by that vanished world.

—The New Yorker. October 8, 1932

In the nineteen-hundreds, two influences seeped into the American home and altered the attitude toward pictures. One of them was that of William Morris, who had observed that no one should ever possess anything he did not know to be useful or believe to be beautiful—a principle that obviously left most reproductions in limbo on both scores. The other crept in subtly at the very moment that the Kaiser was shouting about the Yellow Peril: the Japanese influence, brought to these shores by La Farge, Whistler, Fenollosa, and the French impressionists. It may also be, as a writer in 'Camera Work' once suggested, that the photograph, with its austere mountings, set an example for the style of decoration in other departments. One by one reproductions left the walls of the American home, sometimes to be replaced by original paintings, sometimes leaving behind a blank spot.

The same quality of mind that made the Japanese house anticipate in its method of design almost all that is best in modern architecture enabled the Japanese to develop a fine ritual for showing and enjoying pictures. Both Japanese precedents are, by some accident, closer to the practical needs and psychological insight of the modern man than anything the Occident can show by way of precedent. One may sum up the Japanese practice in three simple injunctions: Do not use pictures as permanent wall decorations. Look at one picture at a time. (If it won't stand up under this scrutiny, throw it out!) Change your pictures frequently. If these principles were generally observed, the presses of America might turn out millions of reproductions without hurting anyone; and until they do become popular, even original pictures should be kept in museums, if only to keep their owners from becoming weary of them.   —The New Yorker. December 12, 1936

Thirty Years
Before McLuhan

Communication between human beings begins with the immediate physiological expressions of personal contact, from the howlings and cooings and head-turnings of the infant to the more abstract gestures and signs and sounds out of which language, in its fullness, develops. With hieroglyphics, painting, drawing, the written alphabet, there grew up during the historic period a series of abstract forms of expression which deepened and made more reflective and pregnant the intercourse of men. The lapse of time between expression and reception had something of the effect that the arrest of action produced in making thought itself possible.

With the invention of the telegraph a series of inventions began to bridge the gap in time between communication and response despite the handicaps of space: first the telegraph, then the telephone, then the wireless telegraph, then the wireless telephone, and finally television. As a result, communication is now on the point of returning, with the aid of mechanical devices, to that instantaneous reaction of person to person with which it began; but the possibilities of this immediate meeting, instead of being limited by space and time, will be limited only by the amount of energy available and the mechanical perfection and accessibility of the apparatus. When the radio telephone is supplemented by television, communication will differ from direct intercourse only to the extent that immediate physical contact will be impossible: the hand of sympathy will not actually grasp the recipient's hand, nor the raised fist fall upon the provoking head.

What will be the outcome? Obviously a widened range of intercourse: more numerous contacts: more numerous demands on attention and time. But unfortunately the possibility of this type of immediate intercourse on a worldwide basis does not necessarily mean a less trivial or a less parochial personality. For over against the convenience of instantaneous communication is the fact that the great economical abstractions of writing, reading, and drawing, the media of reflective thought and deliberate action, will be weakened. Men often tend to be more socialized at a distance than they are in their immediate, limited, and local selves: their intercourse sometimes proceeds best, like barter among savage peoples, when neither group is visible to the other. That the breadth and too-frequent repetition of personal intercourse may be socially inefficient is already plain through the abuse of the telephone: a dozen five minute conversations can frequently be reduced in essentials to a dozen notes whose reading, writing, and answering takes less time and effort and nervous energy than the more personal calls. With the telephone the flow of interest and attention, instead of being self-directed, is at the mercy of any strange person who seeks to divert it to his own purposes.

One is faced here with a magnified form of a danger common to all inventions: a tendency to use them whether or not the occasion demands.* Thus our forefathers used iron sheets for the fronts of buildings, despite the fact that iron is a notorious conductor of heat: thus people gave up learning the violin, the guitar, and the piano when the phonograph was introduced, despite the fact that the passive listening to records is not the equivalent of participating in an active performance; thus the introduction of anesthetics increased fatalities from superfluous operations. The lifting of restrictions upon close human intercourse has been, in its first stages, as dangerous as the flow of populations into new lands; it has increased the areas of friction. Similarly, it has mobilized and hastened mass-reactions, like those which occur on the eve of a war, and it has increased the dangers of international conflict. To ignore these facts would be to paint a falsely over-optimistic picture of the present economy.

Nevertheless, instantaneous personal communication over long distances is one of the outstanding marks of the neotechnic phase: it is the mechanical symbol of those worldwide coöperations of thought and feeling which must emerge, finally, if our whole civilization is not to sink into ruin. The new avenues of communication have the characteristic features and advantages of the new technics; for they imply, among other things, the use of mechanical apparatus to duplicate and further organic operations: in the long run they promise not to displace the human being but to re-focus him and enlarge his capacities. But there is a proviso attached to this promise: namely, that the culture of the personality shall parallel in refinement the mechanical development of the machine.

Perhaps the greatest social effect of radio-communication, so far, has been a political one: the restoration of direct contact between the leader and the group. Plato defined the limits of the size of a city as the number of people who could hear the voice of a single orator: today those limits do not define a city but a civilization. Wherever neotechnic instruments exist and a common language is used there are now

* *"Permissions become compulsions." See 'The Pentagon of Power,' 1970.*

the elements of almost as close a political unity as that which once was possible in the tiniest cities of Attica. The possibilities here for good and evil are immense: the secondary personal contact with voice and image may increase the amount of mass regimentation, all the more because the opportunity for individual members reacting directly upon the leader himself, as in a local meeting, becomes farther and farther removed. At the present moment, as with so many other neotechnic benefits, the danger of the radio and the talking picture seem greater than the benefits. *As with all instruments of multiplication the critical question is as to the function and quality of the object one is multiplying.* There is no satisfactory answer to this on the basis of technics alone: certainly nothing to indicate, as the earlier exponents of instantaneous communication seem pretty uniformly to have thought, that the results will automatically be favorable to the community. —From 'Technics and Civilization.' 1934

. . . As for the Book,* it still goes: indeed "goes" is little better than Ogden's Basic English, for pours, thunders, avalanches, tramples, and billows, knocking its poor author against the rocks as if he were shooting the Niagara, dragging him down to depths he had never suspected, whirling him through caverns measureless to man, scraping his buttocks against flinty facts and even more jagged theories, and in general knocking both wind and sense out of him, but at least leaving him with no doubt about the fact that he is living: for if Dr. Johnson vindicated reality by knocking his stick against the railing, how much more does one establish the fact of life by taking such a Niagara rapids journey! At the moment, I am just in the midst of proving, as an appendix to some remarks about War as a compensatory mechanism in an industrialized society, that the Class War, while real as a fact, is equally illusory and mischievous as a substitute for the realities of a genuine revolution: a point which will be misunderstood completely by Messrs. Calverton and Joe Freeman, but which is established, so far as I am concerned, by both logic and history—and what other props has man's judgement than those two? . .   —Letter to B.D. August 3, 1933

If one wishes to make the parallel between Roman civilization and our own gripping nightmare, one need only read Gibbon and then turn one's eyes from the pages of the book to the street outside. As Rome's civilizing energy went downhill, power came more and more to rest, not on intelligence and consensus, but on the force of arms and threat of murder. Already we of the Western world have seen the

* *Technics and Civilization, 1934.*

330

spectacle of a handful of gangsters, armed with machine guns, terrorizing and exacting tribute from a whole industry, in broad daylight and in the midst of populous cities—whose officers the gangsters themselves partly control. So, too, we have seen political parties, organized on gangster principles, paralyzing a modern state in a fashion that recalls the early work of the Vandals: again we have seen these parties attempting to terrorize by swagger and promise of unlimited brutality the somewhat more civil polities in Western Europe that surround them.

These are all plainly the phenomena of degradation and decay: physical power and fear become the sole binding forces of a society when it loses the last remnants of a more human religion and more rational collective goals. But against these forces we have powerful energies at work that move in the opposite direction: energy and intelligence for which one can find no counterpart in the Rome of the fifth century A.D. For one thing, we have deeper stores of sheer biological vitality; for another we have a body of socialized knowledge and able technical practice, and all that further skill in social cooperation for which our scientific and industrial achievements have set a pattern, whilst the Romans, to the end, were hopeless empirics, who attempted to run a fast empire with a system of accountancy whose mathematics were so clumsy they could not be applied to the management of a country store.   —The New Republic. November 27, 1935

The World of Goya
and Picasso

As with Delacroix, one may look upon Goya as either the last of the
princely line of Renaissance painters or the first of the new republican
succession that otherwise began with Manet. In any case, he was a
giant. How many painters after Goya had so many important things
to say and so many effective ways of saying them? Daumier and Van
Gogh are perhaps his nearest rivals, yet neither of them quite had his
immense technical span. . . .

In a sense, there is no Goya style; but there is Goya in all his styles;
no other artist knew better how to adapt his method and his point of
view to the subject. The result is that ultimate style in which the
painter's individuality is so completely blended with the subject that
it cannot be extracted as a separate mark. There are, of course, great
painters whose style is easy to identify as soon as they appear on the
scene; but there is a handful of even more consummate stylists whose
individuality is too finely disciplined to leave such a coarse trail on the
canvas: Tintoretto and Giovanni Bellini, for example. Goya belongs
with the second group. One does not recognize his tricks first and then
enjoy the painting; one enjoys the painting and then recognizes that
only Goya could have painted it.

Marvellous as Goya's paintings are in range of expression, his drawings and prints are no less remarkable. The sepia washes, represented
here by specimens from the Metropolitan's recently acquired album,
are worthy to rank near Rembrandt's drawings. As for the etchings,
in particular the 'Disasters of the War' series, the quality that made
them odious to nineteenth century collectors only brings him closer
to sound contemporary taste. Goya respected the reproductive process,
and maintained the same even level in his first impression as in his last.
He did not achieve a few good prints by way of a series of messy approximations. His combination of aquatint and etching gave him the
same range in prints as in an original pen-and-brush drawing; and
when lithography was invented, he quickly applied himself to it and
demonstrated its serious possibilities. If only a few drawings, such as
'Crowd in a Park' or 'Foul Night' were left, one would still be assured
of his power and reach.

The change in taste that has taken place during the last generation has given us a new insight into Goya's aesthetic achievements, but the revival of Goya's fame is also due to the fact that our knowledge of the human personality and our experience of the series of catastrophes and mass brutalities that began with the World War have given us a new insight into his message. Brutality is no longer for us, as it was for the Victorians, something that exists on the edge of the jungle; it is something that may break at any moment into the parlor, in the form of a fascist squad or an aerial torpedo. What is peculiarly 'modern' in Goya is his combination of an intense realism and a high regard for fact on one hand, with an imagination that stops at nothing, and understands that nightmares can be realities and realities can be nightmares.

The Goya who drew the 'Caprices' and the 'Disparates' did not have much to learn about the murkier sides of the personality from Dr. Freud; he understood the character of our present psychoses—the fears, hatred, obsessions that keep men from being sane and magnanimous and human. Only the most courageous of spirits could have faced both the terrors he found in his own consciousness and the brutalities he found in the world outside. 'God Spare Us Such Bitter Fortune' is the title of his drawing of a man showing a dagger to his wife and child. What the alternative was shows in the print called 'You Can't Look'—a group of victims shrinking before the points of massed bayonets, driven toward them by unseen soldiers. "The man," wrote Goya, "who shuts his eyes to the unsteadiness of fortune sleeps soundly amid danger. He can neither dodge impending harm nor make ready for calamity." Goya sought to open the eyes.

Love of life, love of women, love of the day's drama, all plainly vibrate through the work of this stormy, passionate, and tremendously intelligent man. During the latter part of his life, the catastrophes of war turned this love into an equally passionate hatred for all manner of frustration and cruelty and evil; instead of the Duchess of Alba, he shows us the butchered naked bodies of women, sprawling not in wantonness but in a last spasm of agony. One can say of Goya, as one can say of few painters, *he told the whole story*. And his horror and hatred are all the more terrible because none knew better than he how deliriously good life could be.   —The New Yorker. February 8, 1936

THE NEW GROPPER SHOW.   It has left me with a desire to write him an Open Letter. It would go like this: "Dear William Gropper: Where have you been keeping this talent of yours all these years, and why have you not shown it more freely? When I put that question to you the other night, you said something about your skepticism about the value of painting under the present capitalistic order of society. I understand that feeling. For a while William Morris could be the idle singer of an empty day, but toward the end of his life his gorge rose. Today art is neither the honest day's work it was during the Renaissance nor the elegant, self-disciplined play that it might be in a society that knew how to extract leisure from the slavery of machines. Almost the only people who look upon painting as more important than a bathing-beauty contest or a cocktail party are those who would exterminate it altogether because they do not find the American flag in the right-hand corner of every canvas. So far, your skepticism and your scorn are both understandable.

"But if you mean that you can't take painting seriously so long as the state of the world is rotten, I think you are wrong. The world would long ago have become depopulated if lovers had acted on that premise. And Breughel the elder might well have stopped painting had he realized that the century he lived in was ushering in that first development of large-scale finance capitalism, mechanized warfare, and militarized industry which was to sound the doom of the ways of life he depicted with so much spirit. No. The fact is that painting is as natural to man as the more primitive biological acts that preserve his existence. It began in the Aurignacian caves, and it will outlast the subway and the bomb shelter. Yes, the machine age itself.

"To create images, to play with images, to contemplate images, to share images are part of what it means to be human. Painting today, by reason of what it stands for, is both an act of protest and an affirmation. A protest against fear, routine, dullness, meaningless restriction— in short, the defeat of life—and an affirmation of what it means to be truly alive. Your own paintings have this quality of affirmation in a very high degree, the more because you have not kept your eyes off the vindictive realities that surround us. People cannot rebuild a rotten world unless they have a sounder and richer one inside themselves. Whatever exemplifies life assists in this process of growth and renewal. And those who have your gifts must have the confidence to use them."   —The New Yorker. February 15, 1936

STORY OF AN ACROBAT.   When the great Picasso show was assembled at the Galeries Georges Petit in Paris in 1932, one naturally supposed that New York would see it soon thereafter. But the next opening was in Zurich, where Dr. Jung beheld it and wrote a learned and amiable paper on its psychological significance: typical schizophrenic symptoms. After that Picasso came to Hartford, probably in search of the ghost of Mark Twain—who was also pretty schizophrenic—or the no less elusive corporeal self of the lawyer who wrote 'Le Monocle de Mon Oncle.' At all events, New York was treated like a tank town. It is only now, with two handsome and fairly exhaustive exhibitions on view, that Picasso and New York are on even terms.

Sooner or later, everyone will have to make a reckoning with Pablo Picasso, which means, in fact, that everyone will have to figure out for himself what the meaning of modern civilization was between 1900 and 1935. The man has not merely been a great artist; he has been a barometer, sensitively recording in advance the state of the cosmic weather. The symbols he used were not, perhaps, quite as clear as those on the dial, but even scientific barometers require interpretation.

From moment to moment, Picasso has recorded the go of things: sentiment, humanitarianism, primitivism, constructivist architecture, mechanization, the nightmare of war, the unreality of peace and sanity, above all the racked and divided minds of all sensitive men. These things occur successively in Picasso's paintings. Part of his paintings will survive as art, great art; the rest will survive as history. Rarely does one find an artist of Picasso's dimensions who is so much both the victim and the master of fashion. His invention has been copious, wild, outrageous, and yet somehow inevitable. He has all the characteristics of a major artist except the capacity for consecutive growth. He has had many clever imitators and loyal followers, but the only person of talent in his generation in Paris who refused to be drawn into the Picasso circle was Pablo Picasso, his most envious rival, his most treasonable disciple. Most of his life has been spent escaping from his latest self.

It is customary to associate the experiments of the post-impressionists with the constructive theories of Cézanne—attempts to reconstruct order on a more logical basis. But this element played a small part in Picasso's early development. Picasso's first paintings, at the Seligmann exhibition, show something strikingly different; he began, as a serious artist, at the point where Van Gogh left off when darkness gathered about him and the black crows flew over the dark-blue cornfields at Auvers. The Blue Period was a period of deep emotional response to the blues of life: poverty, wretchedness, chills and weariness and starvation. The 'Woman Seated with Fichu,' the 'Old Guitar Player,' and the 'Woman Crouching' are paintings to be hung in the same gallery with Van Gogh's 'Potato Eaters.'

A terrible sincerity, a deep sympathy, characterize most of the paintings of the Blue Period. This sympathy united him not only with the miserable waifs and wastrels he portrayed but with those other painters of the meek and the humble—Daumier and Goya, painters who were to be restored, at this very moment in history, partly because their images had at last bitten, like an acid, through the solid armor of the proud and the righteous. In this group of paintings, the 'Woman with a Crow,' done in 1904, strikes me as one of the supreme examples; the drawing of the elongated hand here is quite unsurpassable. In 1905, this note of despair, which could have led only to suicide, lifted. Picasso's palette changed, as browns and roses succeeded the blues, and his mastery of line disclosed itself in a series of nudes and harlequins whose beauty equals and sometimes, possibly, surpasses Degas. For a moment, Picasso was in poise. Note the 'Woman with the Loaves,' in which the bread she carries on her head rhythmically balances her breasts. Picasso's humanity was perhaps succored by gaiety and love—the charms of the body, the tender forms of children, the dream world of Harlequin and Columbine and the acrobats. Such nudes as 'The Toilette' and 'The Coiffure' are infinitely better than the ponderous vacuity of the columnar neoclassic matrons that ushered in Picasso's postwar phase.

After 1905 came the period of experiment; the 'Corsage Jaune,' begun in 1907, presents a new palette for Picasso, a palette composed of ashen grays and acidulous yellows and unrelenting blacks; and for the world it presents a new type of imagery. Art from the time of the Renaissance had rested on two important assumptions. If you knew enough about the appearance of an object, you would finally be able to embody its reality; hence measurement, hence perspective, hence natural color scales, and finally the movement from the studio to the open air. Likewise, if you knew enough about the physical reality, about the anatomical or constructive form, you would eventually arrive at a true order of appearances. Picasso renounced these assumptions. The inner and the outer world had for him no such connections as the classic painters assumed; to deform the image, to decompose the human body, to suppress external shapes—these were other paths to reality, a reality more akin to the physicist's or engineer's world than to that of naïve humanity.

After 1910 Picasso became a byword, among collectors, for the audacious and the original and, above all, the incomprehensible; and perhaps Picasso was tempted to justify his reputation, or at least to live up to it—all the more because it may perhaps have touched his mordant Spanish sense of humor. At all events, Picasso became an international performer, a man whose gestures became fashions. His infinite variety of technical resources served only to set off the emptiness of his later development; there is a close parallel here between the development of

Picasso and that of James Joyce. The further he went away from the Blue Period, the more fashionable his tricks became, the more obvious it was that—as Hawthorne once said of another—he had cut himself off from the magnetic chain of humanity.

In some ways, there was genuine development—mastery of fresh realms of color. But among the audacious and amusing paintings of the last few years—the 'Nature Morte' and the 'Dame Ecrivante,' and vital, luscious paintings they are—there is nothing that I would place beside the 'Blue Boy' or the 'Femme au Peigne.' At the top, sheer genius; at the bottom, emptiness, sterility, a failure to find material sufficient to justify that genius. If this is a true picture of the man, it should be obvious why his paintings are, in their good and bad qualities, a portrait of our civilization. Another case of poverty in the midst of potential abundance.   —The New Yorker. November 14, 1936

DARTMOUTH JOTTINGS.   How John Stearn became professor George Lord's best pupil. Lord when Stearn was a promising young student, gave him an inscription to decipher. It was a pretty hard one, and Stearn was muffing and guessing, and getting discouraged. Lord came around and stood over him while he was working. Stearn's muffs got worse and he was ready to give up. Finally, Lord could stand it no longer and gave Stearn a clout on the head. When Stearn looked up, horrified and surprised, he saw Lord standing over him, the tears rolling down his cheeks. From that time on Stearn applied himself seriously to Greek scholarship. This year he was appointed to the American School at Athens, taking Lord's place on the American Committee.
                                                                                    —RN. 1934

All talking about oneself, all strict accounting of one's motives and impulses and actions, even if set down in a diary, sounds priggish. I have been doing a lot of this lately, and I know. Very well: but one must go ahead and do it just the same—not as a habit, but in times of doubt, conflict, fresh decisions.   —RN. 1930

After a talk by Charles Beard at Dartmouth, Professor George Lord [Greek Scholar] said to me: "We must help create the intellectual atmosphere Dr. Beard demands."

"You are doing more," I said. "You carry it around with you." Lord: "No: I am weak, weak and old. (To President Hopkins) We are all weak: we fail to do our share toward bringing the necessary changes about, because we are lazy; we won't apply our intelligences, and we are too polite. Each one of us has failed to make some essential contribution because we were too damned polite to the person we should have enlightened."   —RN. 1930

Dartmouth. A talk by Charles Beard at the Graduates Club on the need for national planning. Two things remain in my mind: he pleaded for a grand conception of civilization, based on the ethical belief in the good life. He looked for some new Aristotle to frame the tasks of planning in synthetic terms, working toward this end. I felt more keenly than ever before the need for 'Form' and my duty to put my utmost into it.*   —RN. November 21, 1931

Being again in Hanover seems like a dream. Not the fact that you and I thickfeelingly, warmdizzily love each other: that is rock and cement and reality. I mean the trip up here: the same wait at the station: the same Pullman car with the same crack in the linoleum of the men's room: the same shuffling porter who always forgets somebody's bag; the same scenery dun, sober, a little *dirty*, the same steward and the same lamb chop special with the same taste, at the same price, plus the same tip, giving the same feeling of repletion which doesn't wear off until one comes within sight of the same crazy railroad station and climbs into the same bus. Have I been doing this a million times? I could do it blindfolded, the way that an insect builds its nest; indeed, if one part of the chain were missing, if for example it were a veal chop special, I would probably, like the insect, have to go back to New York and begin it all over again, before I could set foot in White River Junction. A month hence, in a fit of momentary forgetfulness, I may find myself on the same train, and only remember, when I reach for a book in my bag, that I have no business then going up to Dartmouth at all! And then where will I be? Probably, I fear, between Stamford and Bridgeport. And here I am in the same room at the same Inn, writing—alas! alas!—the same letter. The only happy thing I can extract from all this sameness is that the letter is still to the same wife.   —Letter to S.W.M. January 13, 1932

* *'Form' was the abbreviated title of a book I had written in 1930, putting together my key ideas on Architecture, Cities, the Machine, Regionalism, and even on Sex and Marriage. Alfred Harcourt wisely suggested that I do a more thorough job; and the four volumes of the 'Renewal of Life' series followed.*

338

Random Notes

VISIT TO ALEXANDER FARQUHARSON: A thin drizzle, London gray and bleak once more, and my feet walk automatically along the gray Victorian street to Le Play House. The once bright black letters on the pillar of the porch have been rubbed out. The same bleak buildings, crumbling black on the outside: within, the same dark brown woodwork and uncarpeted wooden stairs I first climbed a dozen years ago. The stenographer, rather plumper than the angular female clerk who used to do duty there, announced me to Farquharson. There he was! The frail, waxen-white wisp of a man had become round and solid and red-faced: Shelley into John Bull. We talked together in Branford's room, now pale gray with cherry-red woodwork; I seated on the one comfortable chair, Farquharson's Morris chair; and then we went to lunch and came back and talked again. A dozen years rolled away. Our minds met and clashed and drew fire, one from the other, as they used to do when Branford was alive. There we were, in Branford's room, discussing his bequests, considering the best manner of making his work permanent. Farquharson had replaced him, I felt, as certain worms displace a dead snail and live within its shell. There was nothing dishonorable about this, but here he was, in Branford's place, and Branford was gone.   —RN. 1932

The porter at Basel, learning that we were going on to Zurich, put us quickly through the customs and the Kontrol and told us we could take the new Reingold Schnellzug for a small supplement. We waited for the train to come while he praised it and talked about the world. I asked him about the great concrete structures one saw a little way before one reached Basel. He said they were the new electric works, built jointly by the Germans and the French. Then we talked about politics. I said: "The war is not over." "Of course," he said, "there is no peace yet. With the tariff wars now it is worse than if they were actually at war. If this goes on, everything will go *kaput*."

—RN. May 1932

In München, when I voiced my doubts to Karl Vossler about breaking in on Thomas Mann he replied: "But he is a writer, and if I tell him that you are an American and have read 'The Magic Mountain' four times and wish to pay your respects to him, he will be delighted. Every writer likes to hear praise of his works." When Vossler phoned, Mann said I might come for half an hour; but when I started to leave at the appointed time, he kept me for another half hour, discussing not Mann but Rudyard Kipling and Ernest Hemingway, both of whom Mann had been reading with keen appreciation for their prose style.

—RN. 1932

... The book [Technics and Civilization] has become gigantic, but the more one puts into it, the more empty somehow it gets: or rather the holes become more visible, as when one blows up a child's balloon the flaws in the rubber become clearer with every extra inch it is distended. This monstrous work is but the sketch of the book I want to write: the very touch of failure that already hangs on my words as they reach and snatch after the thoughts that elude me is perhaps in another sense the best pledge of success. When at last one knows anything well one realizes how vastly one is ignorant and how "life is not long enough to know antimony." [Robert Boyle, 'The Skeptical Chymist.'] As one really gets on with one's knowing one leaves one's little limitations and one's easy acceptances, and begins to touch the bottom of things—as one becomes, if in minute amounts—godlike, one realizes that one lacks alas! the most important qualification for godlike knowledge—namely, an eternity to acquire it in! ...   —Letter to C.K.B. June 4, 1933

The efficiency of an economic system depends upon the adjustment of the means of living to the needs of life: it is not a quantity but a ratio, and there is no indication at all that the amount of work or goods can be expanded without limit as capitalist economics proposes. In terms of life, a social scheme that produces a handful of olives and dates and bread may be more effective than one rich enough to produce a Roman banquet and a special chamber called a vomitorium to take care of the results of gluttony.   —RN. October 1933

Friedrich Engels wrote a whole series of papers on housing a couple of generations ago in which the only positive housing program he could visualize when the revolution should take place was the expropriation of the bourgeois quarters by the proletariat, who would divide them up into apartments and move in. This is what actually took place in Russia; but so far from being a mark of the revolution, it is an indication that the revolution has not yet taken place. For a genuine revolution involves a recognition of the fact that the quarters of the rich, so far from being desirable, are not fit to live in: these houses and apartments represent wealth only in the bourgeois sense of being costly.   —RN. October 1933

THE BUFFALO WATERFRONT.   Long tongues of water between wastes of open grass, with the grain-boats and the ore-boats adroitly maneuvered into the thin passages. These boats have clean decks, with the smokestacks in the extreme stern. Around the harbor stand the white grain-elevators, classic in their main forms, with fantastic chutes and passageways thrown across from one part to another high in the air. Nothing in the city except Wright's Larkin Building compares with them in simplicity and dignity. Beyond lie the steel works, with the iron ore and limestone in mountains around them. The furnaces rusty and full of 'pathos.' Only two of them smoking.

On the other side of the avenue, parallel to the steel works which close off the lake-front, are the workers' houses, some of them standing isolated in the filthy cindery ground, others in even dingier rows: not a tree or a patch of vegetation anywhere. The whole effect is one of raw horror, accentuated by the flat waste of the landscape itself. (Different here from Homestead.) Wright's Larkin Building is superb: red brick, like his other Buffalo houses, with a handsome entrance. A reddish brownstone used for low ornament on upper stories. The interior white brick, fresh and spotless. Metal desks, designed by Wright; also badly designed metal chairs, painted. An absurd fireplace in the Reception Hall. A superb piece of monumental architecture— but now an empty temple to a dead god, doomed to sink into the industrial swamp around it.   —RN. November 10, 1934

The fact that two events are contemporary does not establish a connection between them or make them part of the same social milieu. Thus the mechanistic conception of the universe, with its dead, imageless, inorganic world, and Baroque painting, with its great images and its powerful sense of the organic, in line as well as in symbol, were both visible in the same century. They were the products of different components in the social heritage; one was rising and the other was falling. The effects of the mechanistic conception were not fully visible until the nineteenth century; but the existence of Baroque art is no disproof whatever of the anti-visual, anti-organic results of mechanistic abstractions. To interpret any given stretch of history as all of one piece seems to me basically false. Every period has its historic dominants, so to say, and its historic recessives, to say nothing of its still active survivals. That is why a cross-section of society—such as is implied in contemporary views—is always historically inadequate, because in the nature of things it centers attention upon the dominants, and like any cross-section halts the flow of time.   —RN. 1934

Architecture is either the prophecy of an unformed society or the tomb of a finished one.   —RN. 1934

. . . I trust you are back in stride with more to show for the last few months than I can. At least you have not been spending your time in aimless Pullman cars, like a Thomas Wolfe hero, have not been dispersing yourself in unimportant lectures to vacuous people, have not been showing, as I have, latent capacities for mob oratory in addressing groups on War and Fascism. One is damned in one's work, not by the cohorts of Satan, against whom one is on one's guard; but by all the little Children of Light who bait one with their good intentions and make one surrender one's proper virtue in the interests of *their* virtue, as if, in the long run, that could be more important. Henceforward, I shout to the heavens, I shall deliver no more lectures on behalf of good causes: I am the good cause that denies the need for such lectures. Avaunt! importuning world! Back to my cell. . . .
—Letter to V.W.B. April 12, 1935

. . . My own philosophy could be treated as a modification of Bergson's, for whereas he draws a distinction between intuition, which is vital, and reason, which is mechanical, and lets it go at that, I go on to point out that the mechanical itself is a creation of life, and only when it is perversely divorced from all our experiences, including our feeling and intuition does it become dangerous, that is, anti-vital.
                    —Letter to V.W.B. August 17, 1935

As city life develops the ratio of creation to consumption increases: likewise the ratio of consumption and creation to conversion and production. The latter must remain crude at an early stage for lack of an incentive to develop: it takes culture to utilize any degree of energy. Failing culture, energy dissipates itself on the barbarian ritual of conspicuous waste.   —RN. 1935

342

I was talking to Waldo Frank about President Hopkins of Dartmouth. "He is not so much a Liberal," I explained, "as a wise Tory." "That," he exclaimed, "is almost the perfect definition of a Liberal." Later Waldo asked: "Would you call Franklin Roosevelt a wise Tory?" "No," I answered. "He is only a wily Tory."   —RN. 1936

Chaos, if it does not harden into a pattern of disorder, may be more fruitful than a regularity too easily accepted and a success too easily achieved.   —RN. 1936

New York and Alfred Stieglitz

In all my vivid adolescent experiences of the city I was keeping company, without knowing it, with an older contemporary, Alfred Stieglitz, who during my college days was holding forth at his first gallery, '291,' where he introduced Cézanne, Picasso, Braque, along with his own photographs to the more alert spirits of my generation. Had I known his work, my own appreciation of contemporary art would have come earlier; but my real awakening came from beholding the first large Brancusi exhibition in 1920, in a made-over stable on East Fortieth Street.

Though in time Stieglitz and I got to know each other, I never became an intimate of the 'Stieglitz group,' who were mainly painters and critics, or photographers like Steichen and Strand. By the time I encountered him in person at his first big exhibition at the Anderson Galleries in 1921, I had already drawn too much from Patrick Geddes to transfer my allegiance to another master, still less to become a close and loyal disciple, as Waldo Frank and Paul Rosenfeld were in their younger days. But I felt with Stieglitz the sort of underlying kinship and sympathy I was to feel later with some of my Tammany colleagues on the Board of Higher Education, like Maurice Deiches. Had I not as a boy gone regularly to the horse races he loved? Did I not share at least in memory his love of that sport, with all its kinesthetic tensions and esthetic delights? Did we not fasten on the same images of the city's daily life: the horses that drew the old horse-cars, the railroad yards with their puffing engines and interlacing tracks, the ferryboats on the Hudson? Had we both not gone to the City College? Were we not both in fact dyed-in-the-wool New Yorkers?

For all that I missed coming closer to Stieglitz in those early years as he himself, he confessed to me, had missed the one poet whose vision of life was nearest to his own, Walt Whitman. But Stieglitz fortunately remained alive through the span of my young manhood and middle age, long enough for him to have read the appreciation of the man and the city I contributed to 'America and Alfred Stieglitz.'

Yet these sentimental affiliations between Stieglitz, myself, and our common mistress, Mannahatta, form only a small part of the impression Stieglitz made upon me. What made him stand out among all of his contemporaries was something that he first expressed in his photography, and eventually in his life: a sense of unswerving devotion to the higher realities the arts seek to translate. In a world moved by meretricious fashions and publicity-directed novelties, he served art with a kind of monastic devotion: integrity personified. In his personal relation Stieglitz was far from being a spotless saint: he could on occasion be preachy, bitter, ungenerous to those who did not accept his own values —sometimes very private ones—as ultimate. But he was not afraid to stand alone; and day after day at An American Place he kept vigil over the works of the artists on whom he had staked his whole later career: Dove, Marin, Hartley, O'Keeffe. One such life in every generation, the life of a Whitman, a Ryder, a Melville, a Stieglitz, might redeem even Sodom and Gomorrah. And who could doubt that New York needed such redemption?

When I first met Alfred Stieglitz half a century ago, he was saying and doing the same things that I found him saying and doing the day we said good-bye for the last time. That fact is more important than the outer changes that came over him, the changes that turned the demonic man of sixty, with his Pan-like face, the hair sprouting from his ears, the red vest worn almost like a banner, into the ethereal figure with the wispy white hair, the dark eyes of indrawn pain, and the black cape—more saint than satyr in appearance—who remained at the end. Stieglitz transcended such outward changes: he lived in a perpetual present, and the quickest wink of his camera shutter could give him a glimpse of eternity.

Unlike his contemporaries, Stieglitz was concerned with being, not becoming: each moment was good for what it was, not because it had its origin in something more primitive and inchoate and was leading into something more highly developed and more fully organized. Big and little, near and far, now and eternity, were all one to Stieglitz: in a world of being they were reduced to the same measure. Being itself was good: a child's being, a lover's being, an old man's being: these held all of life's essence. Stieglitz valued the beautiful products of art, but even more he reverenced its inscrutability and its inviolability: his own. He dared to remain himself, whilst the world around him changed, fashions came and went, reputations burgeoned and wilted. That self-centeredness gave Stieglitz a wider periphery than most of his contemporaries; perhaps it was his best gift to them; for it was what they lacked.
—Unpublished ms. 1936–1965

The Course of Abstraction

Before going over The Museum of Modern Art's Exhibition of Abstract Art, we might clear our minds if we faced the fact that the abstractions of the present generation of painters offer no essentially new elements in art. To begin with, all painting and sculpture is abstract; even at its most realistic, it is a displacement of something that exists in life with a symbol that has only a limited number of points of resemblance. A sculptured head can smile, but it cannot wink; it can also live without the aid of a body and the usual apparatus for breathing and for digesting food. Every work of art is an abstraction from time; it denies the reality of change and decay and death. Only on a Grecian urn can a lover console himself over his inability to catch his mistress with the reflection that beauty and love will remain permanent.

Visual art, again, demands an abstraction from the four other senses. It belongs to a world where taste and smell and sound are absent, where touch exists by means of a visual counterfeit, and where (at least in painting) the movement of the observer and the many-sidedness of things are lost in a static image. The truth is that almost all that we call culture is based upon a system of abstractions; the signs of language and the symbols of art and religion are mere shorthand curlicues for the reality they indicate or express. The most fulsomely realistic genre picture of a country grocer's store in Kansas is closer to a geometrical form by Ozenfant than it is to the patch of life it seeks to imitate. The man in the street has been looking at abstract art all his life without realizing it. What he falsely calls realism is only a more familiar series of abstractions.

By nature, any single work of art is a thinning down of concrete experience. If this were its only characteristic, one would have to reject art as a weak surrogate for life, as the Philistine does—a tepid beverage, for people who are not strong enough to take life neat. But art makes up for its limitations by a series of special advantages. By means of abstractions, certain qualities of experience can be intensified. Divorced from immediate practical necessities, art can respond to experiences our daily duties usually shut away from us, and it can rearrange our perceptions and feelings in new patterns, more significant for us than life as we have actually lived it. In a period of social development, art can make us anticipate new experiences, and put us in a frame of mind to welcome them, as the sharp eye of a good hunter will pick out a bird in a faint stir of leaves, before it takes wing. It was in this fashion that the Renaissance painters, who invented deep-space perspective, and built it up on a strict mathematical basis, prepared us for the visual background for our new conquest of space through maps and ships and rapid means of locomotion.

How does this apply to the development of abstract art during the last thirty years? As Mr. Alfred Barr has well shown in arranging the exhibition, that movement had many aspects, and the new abstractions pointed to many different modes of experience. But surely one of its main expressions was an attempt to symbolize in new forms the world in which we actually live, to call attention to those particular experiences that alter our spatial relations and feelings, and to represent, by means of the image, the same attitudes and perceptions that were being expressed in the physical sciences, in psychology, in literature, and finally in all the mechanical arts. So, far from being divorced from the currents of life, the abstract artists were closer to the vital experiences of their period than were the painters who kept to more traditional forms. The meaning of any particular painting was not always clear, nor were the efforts at expression always successful. But the connection between the image and contemporary reality was close.

The facts about abstract art have been obscure partly for the reason that artists, and the few critics who understood their aims, were more concerned with the formal and technical problems raised by these new abstractions than with their underlying content. In fact, in a revolt against banal illustration, the abstractionists even claimed that their art had no contents, except lines, surfaces, and volumes, duly organized; they attributed to paintings and sculptures the characteristics of architecture, without being able to supply either the rational uses of a building or the symbolic uses of a monument to justify their new organizations of form. They deceived themselves, these critics and artists. Their forms were sometimes undecipherable, but our initial inability to read their unknown language was no proof that it would remain meaningless once we had a clue to its word forms and vocabulary.

Take the derivation of the early Cubist forms from African sculptures. Is it not absurd here to overemphasize the form and forget the social milieu? This drawing upon Negro art for a fresh impulse was a sign of a new respect for primitive races and cultures that came in with the twentieth century. People began to realize that although the primitive African had not invented the steam engine, he had successfully expressed in his art certain primal feelings evoked by fear and death; likewise, he knew a great deal of essential lore about the erotic life, which the 'civilized' white had emptied out of himself, as Havelock Ellis's contemporary treatises on the psychology of sex were demonstrating. Remember, too, the impending fear of war that ran in successive spasms through the peoples of Europe. In his admirable essay on Strauss's 'Elektra,' Mr. Paul Rosenfeld has pointed out how these terrorized mass feelings expressed themselves in Strauss's music, prophecy of the catastrophe to come. So with the rigid shapes, the barbarous heads, the deformed fragmentary images in the early Cubist paintings— the human body exploded on the canvas. Half a dozen years later, the war came, and those shattered forms were 'realized' on the battlefield.

I do not say that this is the whole story, for one may look at the Cubist's analytic dismemberment of form in still another way. The disappearance of the realistic image and the building up of a picture from a series of separate points of view have a scientific reference. This side of abstract art connects closely with Einstein's first theory of relativity, published in 1905: an announcement of a fresh way of looking at the world, in which the fixed station of the observer was no longer, as in Renaissance painting, taken as one of the main elements that determine all the lines in the picture. Do not misunderstand. Einstein did not produce Cubism any more than Cubism produced Einstein. They were, rather, both contemporary formulations of the same common facts of modern experience. Looking at it in this fashion, one may better appreciate Marcel Duchamp's original painting, 'Nude Descending a Staircase.' Plainly, it was an attempt to incorporate time and movement in a single structure. That picture is one of the masterpieces of the Cubist movement, although once it was one of the chief targets for mockery. Patently, such symbolism often failed to come off. Witness the comically feeble and pathetic painting 'Dog on a Leash' by the Italian Futurist, Giacomo Balla.

The next great contribution of the abstract painters was to prepare the eye more acutely for the new rhythms and the new spatial arrangements and the new tactile qualities of an environment that had been radically transformed by the machine. The engineer, in the course of the previous century, had often dealt with aesthetic problems accidentally; occasionally he would even make aesthetic decisions. But in the paintings of Léger, the sculptures of Brancusi, Lipchitz, Duchamp-Villon, and Gabo, there was a recognition of the fact that the machine had by itself profoundly altered our feeling for form. We liked hard things, finished things, accurate things, required less assurance of solidity, of static balance, and of symmetry, and found a fresh use for glass to symbolize that new world in which electric waves and light rays could pass through 'solid' bodies. The language of these new symbols has scarcely been worked out even now, but one cannot doubt its importance in projecting the new facts of our experience.

This aspect of abstract art led directly into the new machine arts and crafts, and one of the best features of the present exhibition is its demonstration of the effects of these new symbols upon typography, poster art, stage design, architecture, and furniture.

—The New Yorker. March 21, 1936

NOT SINCE ALBERT PINKHAM RYDER'S WORK WAS SHOWN   at the Metropolitan Museum in 1918 have we had a better opportunity to see his paintings than this season. Farewell to the notion that Ryder was a painter with a single style or a single fixed technique. Here is pretty much the entire range and development of the man, or at least a synopsis of it: one passes from thin pigment to thick pigment and varnish, from the rapid brush strokes of 'Holland' to the sometimes miraculous, even enamel of the final period. And the change of interest and subject matter is equally remarkable.

Sweet adolescent commonplaces, done in soft autumnal coloring, are the marks of Ryder's earliest work. He begins with such feeble paintings as Christ walking with a shepherd's crook in the Garden of Gethsemane, or the 'Wayside Forge,' a reddish composition, marred by age and fire, that slightly recalls an inferior Blakelock. There is little in these early pictures save a certain delicacy of feeling, a certain timidity that keeps him from making gross and pretentious blunders. Such paintings somewhat excuse the judgement of Ryder's aunt, the good lady who advised the young aspirant to give up any hopes of being a painter. If that advice does not altogether damn her as an art critic, it shows that she was a poor psychologist. She did not know enough about her nephew to appreciate the depth and intensity of his feeling. So she could not guess that he would persevere with his art until his feelings became perfectly articulate, until it reached a pitch of perfection at which every stroke would reflect the quiet harmony and the deepening insight of his own life. . . .

There were weaknesses in Ryder's original equipment, and if those of technique diminished with time, others, derived from nature, like his festering eyes, which dreaded sunlight, remained. But no painter could have been less handicapped by the frailty of his natural endowments; he used every grain of his talents, and he knew how to harmonize what he was with what he might be. Ryder could not for his life have turned out a popular illustration of bathing or skating for 'Harper's Weekly,' as Winslow Homer did, nor could he have engraved a banknote with classic goddesses, like Walter Shirlaw. But he had qualities that more than made up for lack of the superficial brilliance one finds even in the juvenilia of Homer: he had an extraordinary persistence, and a no less extraordinary capacity for growth.

One finds Ryder at the beginning of this series of paintings little more than a child who has aspirations to be a great painter. One finds him at the end, after years of unfaltering discipline and devotion, a painter who, without losing the simplicity of a child, has actually attained maturity and greatness. His paintings belong to the nineteenth century; they belong to it like the tales of Hawthorne or Poe, the music of Wagner, or the poems of Baudelaire; and yet as paintings they are dateless: they are as far from the literalism of the realists, or the externality of the impressionists, as they are from the vapid sermonizings of the Watts and the Böcklins. Originality does not consist in avoiding the influences of history, tradition, and contemporary life, but in completely assimilating them and making them into new flesh and blood; and in this sense Ryder was surely one of the great originals of the nineteenth century.

Of all the paintings in the present show, perhaps the most precious to lovers of Ryder is his self-portrait. It is a small painting, glazed and reglazed without damage to the brilliant colors that glow under the surface, and the finish is remarkably without flaw. Here is Ryder in early middle life: fresh, sweet, even-eyed. Like so many other paintings of his, it has a lesson to teach our generation: the lesson that importance is not measurable in mere space—not in space in the headlines and not space occupied by the canvas on the wall. What counts in a little painting by Ryder is something which I trust I do not make more obscure by giving it a name: spiritual pressure, an unwillingness to be satisfied by the second-best, the half-finished, the unrealized. In the service of an ill-balanced personality, the pressure and grip and intensity one finds in Ryder's work would have made a financial Napoleon or a crazy political dictator; in the case of this harmonious soul, it made a great artist.   —The New Yorker. November 2, 1935

What a fine opportunity to know men and cities—or rather *my* city— this appointment to the Board of Higher Education has given me. My milieu, this last five years, had gotten too narrow: my contacts with practical life were becoming feeble. And now I am in the thick of it: observing the members of my City College committee—the strait-laced, capable, 'patriotic' Charles Tuttle, the conscientious well-to-do accountant, Klein; the puerile but decent Tammany appointee, Judge Dyer; the kindly bloated bullfrog, Maurice Deiches; and the rest of them. And not least, getting fresh glimpses of my New York: the harbor from the window of Tuttle's office near the Battery, with the ferryboats and barges darkening the waters with their curving wakes as the haze thickens in the late afternoon sun—or the deserted streets of Madison Avenue at two in the morning, after a long meeting of the Board—or the Boardroom where this small fragment of the city detaches itself from the whole and guides in a fumbling, contradictory, but certainly conscientious way, the destinies of perhaps 50,000 professors and students. Administratively this Board must be a psychological replica of a thousand other boards, boards that declare dividends, run horse shows, govern clubs, conduct asylums and hospitals. The life of the city quickens in one's pulses.　　—RN. 1936

The other day, while I was prowling through the exhibition of the New York realists at the Whitney Museum—it was not the critics' preview—I became suddenly conscious of the other visitors. They were the sort of people you might expect to find at a fire, but never at an art gallery. There were groups of crisp, black-haired men, with cheeks like Westphalian hams, whom you might see dining at Cavanagh's or at Joe's in Brooklyn; there were shrewd horsey-faced fellows you'd more likely meet in the paddocks or the prize ring, judging limbs and shoulders, than in the midst of a collection of paintings. Politicians, real-estate brokers, contractors, lawyers—what were they doing here? My guess is that they were New Yorkers, pulled into the gallery by that dark, secret love for the city that New Yorkers hide from the world even when they brag about the city's wonders. And they had come to the right place, for the nine artists who are represented in this show,* through the work they did between 1900 and 1914, loved the city too; not less, perhaps, because five of them came from the dingy, unexciting, provincial streets of Philadelphia as it was at the beginning of the century.

To their contemporaries these artists were tough babies. Four of them had got their training after art school doing sketches for the Philadelphia Press, and they all had the journalist's eye for news and human interest, and they weren't afraid of going off the old beats to find them. There had been genre painters of New York life before: men like J. G. Brown, who had painted bootblacks and gamins. But these figures had no more aesthetic importance than a Horatio Alger hero, whose precise counterpart they, in fact, were. When Luks caught two little urchins dancing wildly, he didn't bother to change their clothes or wash their faces; he slashed their figures onto the canvas with a vigor begotten of his own delight. When in the 'Wake of the Ferry,' Sloan shows a lonely figure of a woman, standing partly exposed to the rain, looking out over the gray waters, he symbolizes forever the intense loneliness, as final as that of a deserted hermit on a Himalayan peak, almost everyone has known in the midst of crowded Manhattan.

—The New Yorker. February 27, 1937

* Henri, Luks, Sloan, Glackens, Bellows, Coleman, Lawson, Shinn, and Du Bois.

A Scramble of Letters to C. K. B.

ON AMATORY AMBIVALENCE.   It's such a relief to me . . .
to have admitted at last to myself that it's painful, but possible, to love
two girls at one time—and to do injustice to them equally. It's only
through being separated from both of you, at equal distances, for six
weeks, that I have been able to discover for myself how curiously little
sexual excitement has to do with it—except as a natural ingredient like
conversation or any other medium of intimacy.   —July 1930

Why News from Nowhere Ought to Remain There.

Utopias rest on the fallacy that perfection is a legitimate goal of human existence. They mistake the points of the compass for alternative
destinations and real cities, forgetting that North and South point to
equally barren wastes, and that East and West inevitably meet. In
fact, fixed points and ideal directions are of practical use only because
they cannot be achieved. Humanity would starve in utopia as it would
starve at the Poles; for a good spiritual diet must contain a certain
amount of phosphorous, iodine, and arsenic, although they are poisonous if taken in large quantities. The problem of evil is to distribute
the poison in assimilable amounts.

When I was younger neither evil nor ugliness had any part in my
view of a desirable world: I conceived that the mission of intelligence
was to stamp them out. I sought perfection and without knowing it
accepted death. If my search had been a little more effective I would
have killed myself through an excess of virtue: for the virtuous son
would have strangled the faithful lover: the faithful lover would have
strangled the growing man: the growing man would have been stunted
by his inhibitions and would have shot himself or written 'The Modern Temper.' I was saved, if indeed I am saved, by the immitigable
presence of error and vice, by sufficient amounts of miscalculation,
self-deception, and blackguardism. As soon as I was strong enough to
take an honest look at myself I discovered that I was neither so vir-

tuous, so faithful, nor so inhibited as I had made myself out to be. Conclusion? Damn utopias! Life is better than utopia. . . .*

–Letter to C.K.B. July 1930

* *This conviction, already latent in 'The Story of Utopias,' thenceforth threads through all my writings: indeed a whole chapter, 'Life is Better than Utopia,' has a crucial place in 'Faith for Living' (1940). Despite this evidence many people persist in calling me a Utopian.*

ON A TONSILLECTOMY.   . . . I have written this letter to you so often in my mind that it is already stale, like a manuscript that has been revised too often, however lovingly; and I shan't be able to give you half the sense of adventure and horror. The sticky New York days before the operation: the increasing sense of calm and relief when the day finally came: the amusement of lying in a hospital bed, quite healthy and ruddy-brown, and of seeing how easy it was to accept all the little details, the winding sheet, the turban, and that sort of thing: then alone in the operating room for five minutes, blankly looking with a blank mind at a blank ceiling: the appearance of a lovely blonde nurse, sweating like a waterfall under her costume and one's sense of delight at finding the right level with her in the first thrust: watching oneself go under the ether, feeling the numbness, looking up at the doctor, hearing the nurse say: "Are you putting him under so soon, doctor? We were just beginning to get acquainted," (Nice girl!), and so, here it comes . . . But I see that I haven't given you half the fun of it. There was Sophia, for example, with her experiences of being curetted, [after a miscarriage] if that's how one spells it, wondering when the nurse was coming in to *shave* me; and then there was the dim, muzzy state of awakening, when I was sweet and impish, and asked Sophie if I had called her by the right name. But what is the use of having a highly disciplined imagination? I had anticipated a dozen different eventualities: a hemorrhage, post-operative pneumonia, choking, a blood transfusion, a funeral in Woodlawn, even going so far as to picture a highly touching meeting of you and Sophie, each of you being for the moment very much of a gentleman and trying to conceal from the other how much I loved her. I thought in fact that I had canvassed all possible misfortunes and catastrophes, and that nothing could surprise me; but I had forgotten one thing: one's throat for almost five days actually hurts. That was a surprise, and I felt like a little child who discovers for the first time that he lives in a cruel universe, where candy melts and fire is hot. . . .

But there were so many things I wanted to tell you about the hospital, and most of them alas! have almost vanished, but I recall the fact that the nurses, for one, had very trim buttocks and were younger and fresher than I remembered them from previous visits, and very prompt and efficient, too: that is, prompt always, and efficient up to the point of not losing their modesty; for who could predict, in this modern and rationalized age, that the technique of giving a male patient a bath and an alcohol rub should—shades of Odysseus and Nausicaa!—include every necessary part of his body except his genitals—with the result after four days of heat that I acquired some nameless and fortunately only temporary itch, all for lack of soap and water and a woman's soothing touch!   —September 28, 1930

POST-TONSILLECTOMY FANTASIES.   At one period in bed, being very dull and having no one to amuse me, stirred by a smugly self-righteous advertisement of a sanitary toilet paper, I began to compose a series of howlingly good contraceptive advertisements, anticipations of the day when they should come forth, like Kotex and Sani-tissue, from their devious concealment. If only I could remember all those ads! One of them was for Puella Pessaries, by the makers of Kleinert's Dress Shields (the House that has Protected Women for Half a Century); and another was a historical ad, with a picture of Monsieur le Colonel Condom, Comte de Roquefort, pacing up and down the terrace of the Chateau Roquefort, and deciding that he must preserve the honor of the woman he loved. But how? Then the great idea comes! He calls for his housekeeper . . . and so on. Then there was the solid middle class ad, very practical, of a father and a mother and two children: a balanced family seated in front of a very bad three-colored fire. "Do not endanger their safety and comfort: take no chances! In case of failure, we pay the Hospital bills." And then there were the diaphragms in five colors, to match Milady's underthings; and much, much more, all the details of which—and it was all in the details of course—I have unhappily forgotten.   —September 25, 1930

THOUGH WHEN WE MET   I was concerned far more with letters and philosophy than with housing and architecture, I did, consciously or not, have something to do with your descent into social statistics, figures, responsibilities, housing research, and political propaganda; and now that you are up to your neck in it, hating figures, hating housing, hating me, it is only too obvious that this is the last thing I had in heart or mind when we met. What was your attraction? Why, naturally, the fact that you were so coldly and completely indifferent, so wayward, so irresponsible, so unconcerned with the weal of the world, so completely egoistic and self-absorbed, such a monster of aloofness and such a mistress of playful irresponsible aestheticism. Even your amorous responses had the cool disengagement of a spectator, viewing a new artist with an open mind.   —Letter to C.K.B. June 7, 1933

"I have been becoming American this last year," said Catherine Bauer last night, "and I don't like it. When I was in Europe it was only an accident that made me return to America instead of becoming a Russian or a German or a Frenchwoman. I might have made my life anywhere, become anything." "That," I said, "is an idea that could have occurred only to an American."   —RN. May 16, 1930

. . . Eleanor Brooks very decently read off the palm of my hand the night before last. Looking at my right hand, which represents the original endowment, she said: "It is the hand of a man with modest talents who, if he followed the lines here indicated would have had a smooth and happy life. And here," she said, turning to the left hand, "are lines that show that you have sacrificed your happiness by erecting a series of purposes and goals, which will give you a more interesting life, but a more difficult one. In early middle age there is a serious break: maybe jealous cliques work against you, maybe a woman enters, I can't say: but after a period you go beyond it. This line indicates the affections: there are various women in your life; but although they mean something to you, they do not mean enough to deflect you from your purpose."

To this I add: Eleanor knows too little about me, and seems too lacking in intuitive flashes to make me believe she invented this out of her head or out of hearsay. And of course it is all 'superstition'! Still, it may happen that this superstition is exactly the same as the old-wives' interpretation of dreams seemed, until the subject was reopened by Freud. But how remarkably correct both as biography and character analysis!
—July 25, 1934

YESTERDAY GEORGIA O'KEEFFE'S EXHIBITION OPENED.
Cary Ross eyed me suspiciously in the hall and said ominously: "You'll have a surprise." (Has he a suspicious eye? Does he always look ominous?) But the only surprise of it was to find how good she was originally; for one of her first two drawings—not the one Stieglitz regards as Sacred, but the other—was in some ways as good as anything she has done since. Although Stieglitz put a few of the weaker and more metallic

355

paintings on the walls, the show is strong: one long, loud blast of sex, sex in youth, sex in adolescence, sex in maturity, sex as gaudy as 'Ten Nights in a Whorehouse' and sex as pure as the vigils of the vestal virgins, sex bulging, sex opening, sex tumescent, sex deflated. After this description you'd better not visit the show: inevitably you'll be a *little* disappointed. For perhaps only half the sex is on the walls: the rest is probably in me. . . .   —Letter to C.K.B. January 30, 1934

. . . A last I have read Colette. Just the sort of novel for either of us to read: an egotistic male, a playwright, who takes his little girls as they go but still loves his wife: also his secretary, who is witty and sophisticated and intelligent. Like you she is an ashen blonde, too; and his wife, an older woman, who is large and dark-skinned, doesn't mind his trifling love affairs, but resents the secretary, whom she really likes. I shall burn the book in the furnace! But I have discovered the secret of Colette's power and influence. Instead of saying: "She had an impulse to embrace him and he fondled her," she says: "She drew his arm around her waist and he played with her breasts." Always the exact physical description instead of the abstract bowdlerized image. The other secret, the thing that makes American best-sellers every year, from 'The Bridge of San Luis Rey' onwards, is that various characters drop enigmatic and 'profound' remarks on life and character, which sound exciting and mean exactly nothing. . . .   —Letter to C.K.B. 1934

A JUNGIAN ANALYSIS.   Coming from Jung's privately published talks in one of his seminars, full of interesting self-revelations and exposures, I have the best example in the world before me to think clearly about us and our little difficulties: all the more because I almost howled with delight, again and again, at finding that Jung and I had reached by different paths a very similar philosophy, so that sections of my essay in 'Living Philosophies' might have been inserted in Jung's talks, and no one have been the wiser. It all began with this long quotation from Jung . . .

"Just so with a man about his books. He does not want to tell of the secret alliances, the *faux pas* of his mind. This is what makes most autobiographies lies. Just as sexuality is in women largely unconscious, so is this inferior side of his thinking largely unconscious in a man. And just as a woman erects her stronghold of power in sexuality, and will not give away any of the secrets of its weak side, so a man centers his power in his thinking and proposes to hold it as a solid front against the public, particularly against other men. He thinks if he tells the truth in this field

356

it is the equivalent to turning over the keys of his citadel to the enemy. But this other side of his thinking is not repellant to a woman, and therefore a man can usually speak of women as belonging in general to two types, the mother and the hetaira. The hetaira acts as the mother for the other side of men's thinking. The very fact of its being a weak and helpless sort of thinking appeals to this sort of woman; she thinks of it as something embryonic which she helps to develop. Paradoxical as it may seem, even a cocotte may at times know more about the spiritual growth of a man than his own wife."

This gave me, to begin with, a very sharp image of you and me: you, the only one to whom I have ever shown the very first draft of anything I have written, the only one to whom I have completely let down my intellectual as well as my emotional barriers. I had seized you and appropriated you in just this relation: and you had accepted the seizure and appropriation because it fitted the person you had been and wanted to be; for it was not entirely as a jest—was it?—that you have accepted the label of the 'Mistress type' from that girl at college.   —July 25, 1931

To return to us: six relations will not cover everything. You forget the relation of the feminine part of my ego to your intellect: it is a pure mother relation, and I can watch this development with a pride and selflessness which would make the great abnegators of fiction seem ruthless ideologists. The test of this was really my reaction to your winning the 'Fortune' prize: there wasn't, so far as I could touch bottom at all, the faintest grain of jealousy in my feelings, nothing more than a wisp of regret at not having my summer handsomely solved by the possession of an unexpected thousand dollars; and that had nothing to do with you. But of course there is a danger in that very mother relation . . . As long as I can remain to a certain degree aloof, I cannot merely give you all I have, but I can face with a certain nonchalance the day when, if you are intellectually worth your salt, you will leave me: when you will have taken from me all that can nourish you and when, in order fully to break away, you will have to slay me and turn your back on me. The instrument of this release and this reintegration will almost certainly be another man: and no matter what the extent of your emotional and physical attachments to him might be, the affair, or the series of affairs, might easily prove disastrous to the rest of our relationship. If I did not respect your mind it wouldn't matter: or rather it would be legitimate for me to play upon the feminine side of you as hard as I know how, and to keep you and win you back by those sure and dastardly methods. That would be the natural masculine response. But there is the mother side of me that wants to see you grow, that knows that my part in your growth will not be fully successful until the painful moment when you rise up and leave me finally comes: that realizes, in addition, that you must sow your intellectual wild oats all over the place, and that if you were content with less you would not be worth as much attention and effort as I have actually given. —July 28, 1931

POSTSCRIPT TO A PARTING.   . . . Ever since getting your letter Wednesday I have been living in a different world. It is like waking up on a battlefield on a clear morning in spring: there is a corpse hooked over a fence and half an arm with a clenched fist is lying next to one's coat, and there are a couple of burned holes in one's pants: so that there is no doubt that something ghastly has really happened; but this fact only increases by contrast the intense innocence of the blue sky and the sound of a song sparrow bursting in the thicket. One's throat is sore, too, so probably one shouted a great deal during the battle, and one can scarcely move one's right leg. And yet the mere fact that one can call out "Hello" and move one's left leg becomes, on this spring battlefield, an astonishing blessing. And that is how I feel now. . . .

P.S. Since the smoke of battle is clearing, I may tell you, mayn't I? how *much* I enjoyed that letter of yours in which you said I was the cream in your coffee. It was a perfect declaration of love. I remembered that you never took cream in your coffee, and that you always said that it spoiled it for you . . .   —July 29, 1934

Note on Character. Sophia to me: "In some ways you are the most exasperating man—because you are so sweet and good—and so absolutely ruthless."   —RN. 1936

BETWEEN FRIENDS.   . . . Queerly, in the midst of these last terrible five months, the most sinister in some respects that I have lived through, part of me has remained completely unscathed: I have been conscious of a happiness and a satisfaction in all that makes domestic life sweet that I had never experienced in any such fullness before. What complex brutes we are! No mere stream of consciousness method will ever quite depict the co-existence of incompatible layers of self, and the changes that take place in their position and involvement as

358

one keeps on living. One thinks of oneself as a country under a firm monarchy, dominated by a single set of laws, where the only events that matter happen in the capital: whereas actually we are a federation in which a bandit chief may temporarily exercize more power than the throne, in which different races live side by side, sometimes quarreling, sometimes in amity, and in which extremes of prosperity and poverty, of happiness and sordid disorder, may co-exist even more flagrantly than they do in the streets of New York and London . . .

—Letter to B.D. May 31, 1936

Surrealism and Civilization

Surrealism. Is it a passing fashion or a new sphere of painting? Is it a variety of art or a metaphysical theory of the universe or a subversive political weapon or a series of practical jokes? Is it a meaningless revolt or a revolt against meaning? Or merely paranoia become playful? All these are weighty questions. One or two of them, incidentally, have something to do with art.

Usually, one of the easiest ways to place a movement is to ask where it began and who started it. Some say surrealism began with a group of young European exiles who sat in a café in Zurich in 1916, concocting a revolution in art called Dada (the art to end all art) at the very moment that Nikolai Lenin, a lover of the classics, was planning a revolution in politics. The two revolutions split at that point, but both were deeply in revolt against the heavy platitudes, the unctuous moralities, and the drab acceptances of the world of 'reality,' and they came together again in 1925, when everything fashionable had suddenly to prove its right to exist by showing that it was connected with Marxism. Most of the books and manifestoes that have been written on surrealism confine themselves to these Continental origins. They therefore neglect the wild surrealist element that has been present in American art and in American humor from the very beginning.

One of the great merits of the Modern Museum show is that it presents the immediate origins and achievements of surrealism against a broad background of fantastic and irrational art that goes back to the Middle Ages. Scarcely anything that has conceivably paralleled the present movement or contributed anything to it has been neglected by Mr. Alfred Barr: now a painting by Hieronymus Bosch, now a photomontage from the New York 'Evening Graphic.' The final result of such inclusiveness and exhaustiveness is that one begins to find surrealist images sticking out of every hole and cranny, and one loses sight of two or three of the great landmarks in painting that lead up to surrealism. These landmarks, though included in the show, are swamped in the weltering, dreamlike confusion of it. If I single them out, it may make the going a little easier.

The main divisions of surrealist art are distinct, but have a common foundation in the mind: the pathologically irrational, the comic, and the random unconscious. Each of these sides is in opposition to the conceptions and practical needs of everyday life; each of them stresses the private and the subjective and the whimsical, and belittles the public and the objective and the dutiful. The first, and at the moment the most engrossing, side of surrealist art begins with Goya. He etched a whole series of prints, called 'Caprices,' which for more than a century seemed only a perverse mystery to most lovers of art, prints with strange demonic figures leering savagely or obscenely at the spectator, or with natural figures in crazy attitudes, committing obscure follies. These prints seem to rise, like a miasma, from the murder and torture Goya depicted in the plates on the Horrors of War. Today, Goya's images recur too frequently in the photographic sections of the newspapers to be dismissed as 'unreal,' and it is perhaps no accident that a country that has known brutal irrationality in so many forms should have contributed so many leaders to the surrealist movement today—Picasso, Dali, Miró. If this were all there is to surrealism, one might justify Mr. David Gascoyne's beginning his 'Brief Survey' with Gilles de Retz and the Marquis de Sade.

The comic side of surrealism is familiar to the English-speaking world from 'Mother Goose' onward. "Hey-diddle-diddle, the cat and the fiddle," the Jabberwocky, the Yonghy-Bonghy-Bò, and the folk tales of Munchausen and Paul Bunyan have had their counterparts in an equally crazy folk art, like the china cat decorated with flowers in the present show. This part of surrealist art flourishes on the incongruous and the unexpected. It is at its best, in painting, in Dali's picture of the wilted watches, in those curious collections of objects that Roy assembles in his canvases, or in those marvellous montages of old woodcuts that Max Ernst has put together with such loving patience. One does not have to read Bergson's disquisition on the significance of laughter to enjoy this part of surrealism. Surely, the very worst compliment one can pay it, even when it is savage or sinister, is to greet it with a respectfully solemn face. If Goya contributed the sadistic nightmare, Edward Lear discovered the magical release of nonsense. (But surrealism has its practical side, too. It was a surrealist experimenter who had the courage to put sugar into a concrete mix to make it stronger.)

The last ingredient in surrealism is the unconscious. Ever since the Renaissance, painters have conscientiously been painting only what they could see with their eyes. "I don't paint angels," said Courbet, "because I have never seen one." But images of all sorts are perpetually welling up out of the unconscious: modern man, concentrated upon conquering Nature and piling up riches, penalizes daydreaming and forces these 'irrelevant' images back or keeps them from germinating; he has invented a score of contraceptives for the imagination, and then is surprised to find his life has become a sterile one. At night, however, the repressed images spring up again. These products of the unconscious are not necessarily sinister or macabre. In a more benign form, they took shape in the paintings and prints of Odilon Redon, as they had done in those of William Blake before him, and though Redon has had very little influence over the French, German, or Catalonian surrealists, the benigner unconscious activity he exhibited can be seen in the works of modern Americans like O'Keeffe and Dove.

If one judges surrealism by the aesthetic and human values that lie outside it, a good part of it is rubbish; its value lies not in what it so far has found but in the fact that it has opened up the gallery of a mine which may, with more adequate tools, be exploited for more precious ore than that which has so far been brought to the surface. One of the most powerful and inventive of the European surrealists, Max Ernst, is only a moderately good painter; and if the earlier surrealist paintings of Chirico, spacious and noble in composition, still remain very fine, if Roy is always an admirable craftsman, and if Masson and Miró both have a graceful and deft touch, the quality of the paintings remains an incidental if not a negligible part of the whole movement. To judge the art fairly, one must realize that it is a symptom—a symptom of the disorder and brutality and chaos of the 'real' world; an attempt through disintegration—as in a Freudian analysis—to dig down to a point solid enough to serve as a fresh foundation. With all its praise of the irrational, there is method in the surrealist madness.

Until a generation ago, only soothsayers and ignorant folks believed in dreams. It took the genius of Freud to combine the ordinary consciousness of the neurotic with the ordinary dreams of the normal man, and to see that there was an underlying identity; *dreams meant something*, and in a sense, the more irrational they were, the more they meant. We can no longer go around pretending that the world is the same world it was before Freud gave us this clue. What we can see and measure and count is only a part of the picture. The complete picture is not so clear and not so orderly as the mind, for practical purposes, would like to have it.

This is one of the great commonplaces of our generation; and the proof is that it has made its way into literature so thoroughly that no one bothers there to call it surrealist. In Virginia Woolf's 'Mrs. Dalloway' the returned soldier, Septimus, is suffering from a psychoneurosis, and this is the way she describes his feelings: "He lay very high, on the back of the world. The earth thrilled beneath him. Red flowers grew through his flesh; their stiff leaves rustled by his head. Music began clanging against the rocks up here. . . . It cannoned from rock to rock, divided, met in shocks of sound which rose in smooth columns (that music should be visible was a discovery) and became an anthem, an anthem twined round now by a shepherd piping." Need I point out that one has only to transfer these images onto canvas to have a complete surrealist painting?

Anything that can be imagined is real, and nothing is so real as an obsession. In those words one might sum up the present attitude of the surrealists. Like every new school, they have wilfully lost sight of the historic reality which they wish to supplement or replace; they deny the orderly, the rational, the coherent, the visible. But what they are doing in fact is to widen the scope of reality. They are exploring foul underground caverns where one hears only the whir and whistle of invisible bats; they are holding the manacled hands of the prisoners in moldy dungeons; they are making their way, by touch rather than by sight, through slimy passageways that may bring them up to the surface of 'normal' life with a better comprehension of what lies beneath. Like the modern psychoanalysts, the surrealists have approached the normal by way of the pathological. That follows inevitably from the fact that the willing, wishing, urging, passionate part of man's life has been slighted, stifled, and even banished altogether in favor of practical routines. Distrusting the imagination, we let it sneak back into life only in the guise of fancy dress or an even fancier disease—just as many of us never get a real opportunity for pleasurable idleness until we find ourselves on our backs in a hospital, recovering from the birth of a baby or an operation for appendicitis.

But it would be absurd to dismiss surrealism as crazy. Maybe it is our civilization that is crazy. Has it not used all the powers of the rational intellect, all the hard discipline of the practical will, to universalize the empire of meaningless war and to turn whole states into fascist madhouses? There is more here than meets the eye. Demons, for the modern man, are no less real than electrons; we see the shadow of both flitting across the screen of visible reality. Surrealism makes us conscious of this fact, it arranges the necessary apparatus. Before we can become sane again, we must remove the greatest of hallucinations—the belief that we are sane now. Here surrealism, with its encouraging infantile gestures, its deliberately humiliating antics, helps break down our insulating and self-defeating pride. Even in perverse or sinister or silly forms, the surrealists are restoring the autonomy of the imagination.   —The New Yorker. December 19, 1936

363

Premonitions of War

. . . Little Geddes has had a good winter so far. I must tell you the latest story about him. Sophie found him one afternoon dancing up and down, his face distorted, and she asked him, a little frightened, what on earth was the matter with him? "I am a soldier," he explained, "and when soldiers can't go to war, they dance madly!" . . .

—Letter to P.G. January 27, 1930

Young Geddes kept his temper for a long week at a time, and thereby earned (for the household) a twenty-two calibre rifle: we went on our first murderous expedition against nature today, taking pot-shots at derisive crows and finally—thanks to Geddes's good eye—intercepted a woodchuck, that grubby little vegetarian Cain, in an effort to reach home plate. Some lurking savage in me shrinks at nothing about this but the final scene of slaughter; as for Geddes, the savage in that hardy bosom dances rather than lurks: and I try to keep myself from wondering openly whether this innocent rapine is but the preparation for such strife as is taking place in Spain—which at least has an element of human reason in it—or perhaps for the emptier and more dastardly strife that would mark another world war.

Really: you and I grew up in an innocent world. Soldiers then were all of the tin variety: they liked drums and music and such innocent displays of brass buttons as colored people used to like in a cakewalk: they still thought of war in terms of manly encounters on galloping horses, indeed, only as a more spectacular exhibition than a hunt or a horseshow. Now war is as grim as the assembly line of a Ford factory and as relentless as a financier: the morals of the rattlesnake are everywhere. Sometimes I am tempted to stand up on my two legs and preach: one last desperate sermon to my friends and brothers: one frantic gesticulation toward safety before some putrid fool touches off the dynamite. When we were young we could ask ourselves: What can we conquer? Now we can only ask: What can we save? That shrinkage of ambition is not due to age but to the times we live in.   —Letter to V.W.B. July 24, 1936

364

SYMPOSIUM ON WAR.   Question: *What will you do when America goes to War?* This question is too abstract to permit a clean answer. What war? When? For What purposes? Between the passive phase of war, under which we now live, and its active phase, I recognize only a difference of degree. In general, I oppose war because of its imbecility, its absence of human purpose, its brutalization of life, its abject failure to achieve reasonable goods, and its futile simplification of all the conflicts and real issues involved in life in communities. In so-called times of peace I fight this war animus; and I shall continue to fight it when war breaks out—even if the war itself be the less of two evils, and even if the issues compel me, momentarily, to participate in the war. But I am no absolute pacifist: it is neither the waste of war nor its toll of death that appals me, but the fact that this waste and these deaths come to no purpose, by reason of the very technique of fighting and its special behavior patterns—no matter how just and rational the cause seems at the outset. War is always a losing fight even when it is a just one.

Question: *Would a prospective victory by Hitler over most of Europe move you to urge U. S. participation in opposition to Germany in order to prevent such a catastrophe?* Certainly I would favor United States participation; indeed the menace seems to me great enough at the present moment to warrant the collective institution of a blockade on all war material and on all raw materials indispensable for armament. This would take the guts out of Germany's present bellicoseness before Hitler is sufficiently armed to fight. A preventive international blockade—not of course including foodstuffs—would probably save millions of lives within the next decade. The failure to apply it is due to the fact that all the other big states of the world differ from Nazi Germany only in degree: they are unwilling to face applying a measure which might—as in the case of Italy with Abyssinia—be applied against them.

—When America Goes to War: A Symposium.
Modern Monthly, June 1935.

365

POSTLUDE

1895-1975

Prologue to Our Time

I was born in October 1895, five years before the turn of the century, and the trumpet fanfare on which that wonderful and terrible century died still echoes faintly in my ears. But though, with the aid of family photographs, I can fish up from the depths of infancy sights and smells and fears and dreams, my conscious life dates from the twentieth century. Being a child of my time, I expected much of the new century. This period was destined, almost everyone then confidently supposed, to produce even greater wonders than the steam engine, the electric telegraph, the Hoe printing press, the dynamo, for daring inventors and even more daring prophets, such as H. G. Wells, were already proclaiming that the airplane, the ancient dream of Flying Man, was just around the corner. And, indeed, these one-eyed prophecies came true.

Things of another kind, unfortunately, were also lurking in the same dark alleys of the future. For in the year after my birth Antoine Henri Becquerel, by a happy accident—or was it really so happy?—discovered the radioactive rays emanating from uranium, which were named after him, and when I was three years old the Curies, following his trail, had isolated the first particles of that active but so long unnoticed element—radium. This was but one of many shattering transformations. The very December of the year of my birth, Roentgen had announced his discovery of X-rays, which, penetrating once seemingly impenetrable objects, broke down the wall between the inside and the outside of 'solid' bodies. We had begun, whether we liked it or not, to live in a porous, permeable, increasingly translucent world, whose walls and boundaries, if not altogether illusions, existed mostly in the mind.

But at the turn of the century, everyone still hoped for the best; only benighted souls or disturbed minds furtively suspected the worst. Even a child of five, thanks to his insecurities and anxieties and confusions, was better prepared—had he only remained young—than was any adult for the events that would follow in his own lifetime; witches, ogres, malignant demons, imbecile giants were still real to him, and when, in the pride of adolescence, he would learn to dismiss these frightening images, along with Santa Claus, fairies, and angels, he would deprive himself for much of his life of any clue to the satanic realities that already threatened him.

In most departments, and not least in science, a certain blind assurance prevailed, distorting observation and undermining judgment. The physicists, the guild whose later discoveries would shake the foundations of civilization, were wide of the mark in their neat assumptions about the nature of the physical world: they did not, as Henry Adams soon discovered, accept radium easily. Having forgotten the enlightening intuitions of Michael Faraday, who from the beginning had rejected their too tidy conception of atomism, the exponents of the exact sciences were convinced that they had already staked out the ultimate boundaries of the material universe and that no new discoveries of radical importance would be made; their ideology found no place for invisible internal activities or unfathomable depths. The physicists' chief anxiety before Haber discovered how to extract nitrogen from the air was that our planet's wheat supply might fall short. The fabric of nineteenth century thought seemed so tightly woven and so durable that the editors of the British periodical 'The Nineteenth Century' refused to change its name to honor the new century: they bowed to the calendar only to the extent of retitling their magazine 'The Nineteenth Century and After.'

Now we know better. We have found out what "and After" means. So far from having reached their ultimate goal, the physical sciences were preparing for a gigantic leap forward, and comparable advances would shortly be made in the life sciences. But meanwhile those aspects of civilization which most closely reflected the human condition and carried with them all the tragic decisions and defeats of history would, for lack of any self-alerting sense of danger, experience a sudden jolt and shudder. In time, we would find that an ancient geological fault which runs through every stratum of recorded history had opened, sending great nations and empires hurtling backward—backward and downward—into an abyss of barbarism that the nineteenth century could not even imagine. But the Industrial Revolution—or, at least, the Scientific Revolution—had changed all that, had it not? When people were faced with any unpleasant contradictory evidence, they refuted it decisively, as one of the characters in Wilkie Collins' 'The Moonstone' did, with *"But this is the Nineteenth Century!"* Only a few desolate men, such as Jakob Burckhardt, Herman Melville, and the even more sinister Dostoevski, had been prescient enough to glimpse even a fraction of the evils that the First World War would disclose. While at its end most of the superstructure of civilization was left standing, somewhat battered but repairable, the foundations that had long been crumbling were visibly sinking—and kept on sinking.

At the dawn of the twentieth century, the illusion of stability and solidity still prevailed. And yet, and yet . . . Am I not playing down the underlying anxiety? More than once, H. G. Wells, in the midst of his exuberant scientific fantasies about the future, expressed forebodings of disaster. While it was typical of the period that as late as 1919 the historian F. S. Marvin could call the passing era the Century of Hope, Wells as early as 1895, in 'The Time Machine,' saw in the growing pile of civilization "a foolish heaping that must inevitably fall back upon and destroy its makers in the end." Yet his conclusion was even more typical—and irrational—than anything Marvin had to say. "If that is so," Wells wrote, "*it remains for us to live as though it were not so.*" Was that security blanket what the cold, unblinking rationality of modern science actually shivered under?

"Ta-ra-ra-boom-de-ay: did you see my wife today? No, I saw her yesterday: ta-ra-ra-boom-de-ay." That seemed the smartest and naughtiest of retorts when it was sung in the music halls of London and New York, but one now finds a curious innocence about its sophistication. My infant ears also heard another song, even more innocent in content, which now has a somewhat more ominous sound than anyone who heard it then could have guessed: "There'll be a hot time in the old town tonight!"

Even yesterday—that is, two generations ago—the events that were to divorce the twentieth century from the glories and triumphs of the nineteenth were visible in cautionary samples. The convulsive weakness of imperialism as it was practiced by the greatest of the colonial powers, England, was disclosed in the fumbling, amateurish conduct of the Boer War, in which, incidentally, the presumably civilized British leaders employed that instrument of massive political coercion, the civilian concentration camp, and almost at the same moment treason and anti-Semitism joined hands in the French Dreyfus case. Thus, Nazism and Stalinism and Nixonism, as one may now call the corresponding American mode—indeed, all the variants of an oppressive totalitarianism—were already being incubated. Yes, political botulism was spreading, and my country's soil was not immune. At the beginning of the new century, the systematic infliction of torture upon war prisoners, in what was politely termed the 'water cure,' by the American Army in the Philippines, and the wanton sacking of Peking by the combined international forces that put down the Boxer Rebellion set the stage for the epoch we now confront, with its steadily augmenting horrors, from Buchenwald to Vietnam. All the historic collective evils—war, genocide, lawless government—that went into mass production after 1914 a knowing eye might have detected much earlier in these samples.

Had I known the state of the historical weather at the time I emerged from the womb, I might well have been tempted, like a prudent woodchuck in February, to return to my tunnel and await a

371

change of season. But I should have had to wait a long time; in fact, I would still be waiting. As for interpreting those high, thin streaks of cloud which indicate to the weather-wise eye that a great storm is coming, to herald, in turn, a cyclic change in the climate itself, only a handful of those who were then alive could have been capable of it. The majority, whether in Europe or America, were encased in bulletproof ideological vests, which protected them not merely against other systems of ideas but against the direct impact of their own contradictory experiences. And that was even worse, for those experiences might have led them to modify the premise underlying this whole age: the doctrine of Progress.

This doctrine reflected the high humanitarian hopes of the eighteenth century philosophers—impulses that eventually brought about happy political and social innovations, among them constitutional government, universal suffrage, and free public education. But the even more rapid advances in exploiting coal and steam and automatic machines overshadowed these human gains, for they conveyed the notion that mankind's improvement could be brought about by the continued invention of ever more powerful man-displacing mechanisms. This belief was reinforced by the Darwinian interpretation of biological evolution through 'natural selection'—fostering the "preservation of Favored Races in the Struggle for Life" (Darwin's words). This curious reading of the fight for existence applied not merely to races and species but to nations and classes, and embellished the brute fact of survival with a smug eulogy of the survivors. What self-flattery for the ruling classes! What consolation for their predestined victims!

On this theory of human development, Progress meant man's increasing success in overcoming his physical limitations so as to impose his own machine-conditioned fantasies upon nature. By definition, technological change and human improvement were now coupled together, and, also by definition, the forces that made for progress were inevitable, inviolable, irresistible. The latest discovery, the latest invention, the latest fashion was *ipso facto* the best, and the more ruthlessly our industrial advances erased the monuments, and even the happy memories, of the past, the more acceptable (progressive) were the results. Thus, even Modern Man would become "obsolete," one American contemporary observed when the first atomic bomb was exploded. On the same progressive principle, democracy must yield place to totalitarianism, for, as Anne Lindbergh remarked, Nazism was "the Wave of the Future."

'Good' and 'bad' had nothing at all to do with Progress, for they belonged to the platonic world of values, which science had flatly excluded from the area of verifiable knowledge. No longer were self-knowledge, and discrimination between good and evil, the beginning of wisdom. This bias is still known in the scientific world as 'objectivity.' These battered clichés also linger today along with others based on scientific and technological notions, in the slogans of the ad writer, the industrial designer, the avant-garde artist, and the go-go professors—all shining brightly against their 'up-to-date' Jules Verne background. If this conception of Progress had any substance, no part of man's past experience was worth examining or evaluating for preservation and possible future use on a higher level of culture ("history is bunk"). Progress was a tractor that laid its own roadbed and left no permanent imprint of its own tracks, nor did it move toward an imaginable or a humanly desirable destination. "The going is the goal," a pragmatic philosopher said; past and future had both been swallowed in the void of a meaningless now.

Such are still the pious beliefs of the futurologist, whose inflated expectations, like the inflated values of our dubious financial-credit system, are based on the supposition that the day for casting up a balance between assets and liabilities can be indefinitely postponed. Are not the losses in fact gains, he asks, like his predecessors, since only through constant waste and war can the megamachine keep on expanding. That this limitless mechanical progress carried with it the possibility of an equally indefinite human regression did not occur, as late as the nineteen-sixties, to the faithful disciples of Marshall McLuhan, Daniel Bell, or Arthur Clarke—those giant minds whose private dreams all too quickly turned into public nightmares.

Progress indeed! That the March of Progress would in fact lead to worldwide calamity and catastrophe was something the Age of Confidence never saw as the most remote eventuality. Even while the bridge to the Brave New World of technology was visibly buckling and breaking apart, my friend Van Wyck Brooks, steeped in humane tradition as he was, clung to the comforting dogma of Progress and reproved me for not bowing to the idols he and Charles Beard accepted. In this one respect, the Old Guard and the Advance Guard were almost indistinguishable. A century earlier, Emerson himself had shared with Mark Twain the belief that the great mechanical inventions, from the cotton mill to the electric telegraph, had decisively established the reality of human progress. And those who march to this tune are, alas, still in fashion. Did not the president of a great university the other day publicly salute Buckminster Fuller, that interminable tape recorder of 'salvation by technology,' as another Leonardo da Vinci, another Freud, another Einstein?

This popular conception of Progress dismissed as unreal the possibility of arrest, reversal, discontinuity, or regression, no matter how often history had demonstrated the occurrence of all four. Yet the physical world itself, for all its regularities and uniformities, has its ups and downs, its contractions and expansions, even its total extinctions. Indeed, the entire universe, astronomers now darkly suspect, may someday coalesce into a ponderous, impenetrable mass, as hostile to all dynamic and dispersed forms of 'matter' as to life itself. At all events, nothing is more certain about our earthly habitat and its denizens than the fact that the processes of building up and breaking down continue, at varying rates of speed, in every organism, in every ecological group, in every society. As long as the tissue-building, self-regenerating, growth-promoting functions provide a margin of free energy, life goes on. But what monsters would walk the streets—what stumbling giants, what mountains of obesity—if organic vitality meant limitless growth!

I find it hard to believe, I confess, that for more than a century some of the best minds of the West could have operated so long on that faulty premise of Progress. Meanwhile, during this last half century we have seen that the most startling advances in scientific technology have by their very success hurled great nations and empires into a morass of political and moral depravity. For have not supposedly civilized governments countenanced or committed scientifically organized tortures and massacres indistinguishable from the unbridled collective sadism of an Ashurbanipal or a Genghis Khan?

The age of "the men who are ten years old," long ago predicted in the Pali Buddhist texts, had arrived before my adolescence ended: ten-year-old minds enclosed in a ten-year-old culture with only a ten-year future—if that. In an editorial in 'The Freeman' in 1921, I described my generation's fate as 'The Collapse of Tomorrow.' But the Buddhists had peered deeper into the future, for they said of "the men who are ten years old" that "their violent hatred against each other will predominate, with violent enmity, violent malevolence, violent lust for wholesale killing." A world picture that omitted all values except those fostered by science and technology was left with only a blank (nihilism) in our proper human realm. Homer, Herodotus, and Shakespeare were far better equipped to interpret man's condition and arm him to face the future than the latest clutch of futurologists.

Even now, perhaps a majority of our countrymen still believe that science and technics can solve all human problems. They have no suspicion that our runaway science and technics themselves have come to constitute the main problem the human race has to overcome. Only a handful of sensitive scientists, such as Max Born, were ready to admit that this lay at the bottom of our difficulties. Strangely, the palpable rationality of the scientific method within its own accredited area gave rise in the great majority of its practitioners to a compulsive irrationality—an uncritical faith in science's godlike power to control the destinies of the human race. Those who have studied the ancient Mesopotamian and Egyptian religious texts know how cruel, destructive, and inhumane man's godlike faculties actually can be. Only mammalian tenderness and human love have saved mankind from the demented gods that rise up from the unconscious when man cuts himself off from the cosmic and earthly sources of his life.

Very late in my own development, I discovered what any number of more gifted minds should have discovered long before; namely, that the basic ideology which pervaded the Western mind at the beginning of the century was only a scientifically dressed-up justification for the immemorial practices of the ruling classes—historically attested in Egypt, Babylonia, Assyria, Peru, and, indeed, wherever the archetypal megamachine was in control. The dominant institutions of our time, far from being new, were all in the thrall of a myth that was at least five thousand years old. Only one value was acknowledged, and that one was taken for granted: the reality of power in all its forms, from sun power to military power, from manpower to steam power, from cannon power to money power, from machine power and computer power to sex power.

This simplistic formula for Progress created the overriding imperative that the very victims of the power complex meekly accepted: one must go with the tide, ride the wave of the future—or, more vulgarly, keep moving. The meaning of life was reduced to accelerating movement and change, and nothing else remained. Behold the ultimate religion of our seemingly rational age—the Myth of the Machine! Bigger and bigger, more and more, farther and farther, faster and faster became ends in themselves, as expressions of godlike power; and empires, nations, trusts, corporations, institutions, and power-hungry individuals were all directed to the same blank destination. The going was the goal—a defensible doctrine for colliding atoms or falling bodies, but not for men.

Half a century before my own time, Tennyson, in 'Locksley Hall,' had captured the Victorian faith in Progress, with all its comforting emptiness, in "Let the great world spin forever down the ringing grooves of change." For most people, to increase the pace of change by every kind of invention and innovation became nothing less than the whole duty of man. At least, it was the duty of the New Man, and, of course, of the New Woman. Implicitly, the progressives followed the reactionary principle of Jean-Jacques Rousseau: "Reverse all that is now done and you will be right." Particularly if the people who had been doing it were one's elders, one's parents, those in authority.

And now I smile a wintry smile. That was the doctrine I grew up on, and my earliest patron saints were Bernard Shaw and H. G. Wells. Even the master of my youth, Patrick Geddes, who now seems to many people one of the great minds of the period, would write me, "It is time to be getting on with our ideas," and, despite his warm relations with the poet Rabindranath Tagore and the physicist Jagadis

Chandra Bose, he criticized Gandhi's program for achieving freedom from Britain and its machine-driven capitalism on the ground that Gandhi's belief in spinning by hand, without even the use of an electric motor, was only Ruskin, 1850; that his belief in passive political resistance was Thoreau, also 1850; and that his militant nationalism was Mazzini, 1848—just as if these dates deprived similar later proposals of validity. Still, what was Geddes's own belief in "getting on" but the progressive ideas of Condorcet, 1789; of Auguste Comte, 1840; and of Frédéric Le Play, circa 1870? By now, they are all just as dust-covered by the March of Progress as those of Gandhi himself. So even Geddes' understanding of biological time in Bergson's sense— as duration in a present that could not even exist in the mind without a bonding together of the past and the future—was tarnished by the fallacious doctrine common to the whole age. At bottom, when he was immersed in the actualities of contemporary history, Geddes himself knew better; his lapses only show what a hold the doctrine of Progress had maintained.

For the first twenty years of my life, or even longer, I shared most of the naïve hopes of these leaders and rallied to the movements and projects that promoted them; in fact, my first definite inclination to a vocation was to that of an engineer, and the most progressive kind of engineer, too—an electrical engineer. I need not apologize for that part of my past, and I am not sorry about it, for this early acceptance of—indeed, high excitement over—the doctrine of Progress has given me a vivid understanding of my 'progressive,' power-infatuated contemporaries. But this early commitment had likewise enabled me to winnow out what was valid in the concept of human progress from the purely mechanical metaphors that so largely had been motivated by the man-devouring ambitions of Bronze Age gods, and incited further by the demented fantasies of absolute rulers.

For all this, there actually was a vital human core in the doctrine of Progress which those who prated most about Progress had lost. What was significant—more than that, sacred and forever memorable —was the slow accretion, though unsteady and intermittent, of meanings and forms and values, those tiny radioactive particles that each generation separates from the gross ore of human experience. To the extent that this precious residue has been extracted and treasured, every part of life—every constructive or creative achievement, every active expression of love—has the aura, however faint, of divinity. To mine and crush tons of pitchblende so that a few grams of radium may become available, metaphorically speaking, is the worthiest conceivable task for mankind, no matter what the penalties and sacrifices: a true fulfillment of emergent evolution and human destiny, though there is no quantitative measure for this kind of creativity or this kind of achievement. But, in a strict sense, this is transcendence, not progress—a change of levels from the human to the divine.

Even when viewed from a less exalted position, there was something to be said for the belief in Progress as it suddenly bloomed in the eighteenth century: the Age of Enlightenment confidently proposed to achieve on earth the equality and justice and love that the Christian Church had dared to promise only in Heaven—and then, quaintly, only after the righteous were segregated from the sinners. As Albert Schweitzer pointed out, Western civilization in the eighteenth century honorably, if belatedly, began to carry out the more universal ethical precepts of Christianity. As a result of this newly affirmed faith in the natural goodness of man, sundry improvements were actually made. Here and there, imprisoned people were treated with more humanity and kept in more sanitary quarters; the insane were no longer shackled and whipped; little children were treated with more understanding and valued in their own right; and for the first time the deplorable condition of the great mass of workers became a matter of open public concern and, fitfully, of amelioration. Many of these departures were pushed further in the nineteenth century. Rousseau's and Froebel's new principles for educating the child and Diderot's acute observations on aiding the deaf, dumb, and blind carried into the daily life of millions the basic precepts of the New Testament, and effected miracles, too: witness Helen Keller. But none of the great projects of the eighteenth century were pushed far enough to alter radically the basis of civilization; and when they went furthest—as with the egalitarian programs of Socialism—they disclosed unsuspected flaws in their conception.

If I have mocked the doctrine of Progress, I have done so only to attack the simpleminded notion that human improvements are guaranteed by purely scientific and technological advances—that they are the predictable outcome of today's panacea, 'research and development.' The genuine improvements, however fragile or fitful, do not deserve to be ignored. Nor have I any notion of belittling these generous visions of human improvement because they were so easily mistaken for the dawn of even better days. The fault was that those who regarded faith in Progress as a moral imperative mistakenly assumed, on the basis of only a century's experience, that the forward movement was continuous, inevitable, and in most respects benign, and, as well, that it could not be retarded, much less opposed or reversed.

"You can't turn the hands of the clock back," people would say, with an owlish air of finality. As if society were not as much of a human artifact as the clock, as if anyone would harbor a clock whose mechanism made no provision for turning its hands forward or backward so that it would keep correct time, as if clocks and communities were as immune to human regulation as the solar system! On the same principle, one might design motorcars whose speed could not be regulated, whose destination could not be altered, cars that lacked brakes to halt them when there was danger of collision. People should talk more carefully about machines, for machines wouldn't be of much use if they did not embody many organic principles unrecognized by the doctrine of automatic Progress.

Yet all things considered, it was to my advantage that the hopes and expectations of the Enlightenment were still vivid in the days of my youth. Those cheerful thoughts entered my bloodstream and today, in whatever dilution, continue to circulate through my body. Indeed, they provide a certain almost physiological sustenance, which those who were born even half a generation later fatally lack. Without that deep animal faith, I could not now review the events of my life and times.

Fortunately, the clouds that soon began to efface all color and light from our sky did not also remove the sun. Some of us still have minds sufficiently immersed in the living stream of human history, and buoyed up by its accumulation of values and meanings in language, art, religion, and science ever since the emergence of man as a recognizable species, to enable us to retain some measure of the emotional energy that has kept the human race alive through an endless series of frustrations, crippling injuries, and disasters—not only natural disasters but even more disheartening man-made ones. Those whose minds were formed in that better day still do not regard all human communication as gibberish, all beautiful form as no better than a child's mud pie.

Even as I put this contrast into words, the reader will mark my hostility to the fashionable nihilist doctrine of our day: the cult of anti-life, with all its psychotic violence and its infantile debasements. That hostility applies equally, of course, to those who seek salvation by giving their energies to quickening, through science and technics, the destructive forces that are now released from their natural limitations and cultural restraints, and are overrunning the habitat and degrading it. I have not lived for three-quarters of a century without some understanding of both aggression and regression—for the irrational avant-garde of the arts and the meticulously 'rational' avant-garde of computerdom are heading toward the same goal. They reinforce each other and converge upon a zero point, where their juncture will signal a self-obliterating explosion.

Plainly, this hostility of mine marks me as still a child of an earlier period, who is increasingly at odds with the world he has faced as an adult, and is even more remote from the world his grandchildren may have to face.

Yes, at the turn of the century the climate of the world was changing; and part of my vocation was to interpret that change, to become acutely aware of its menacing possibilities while I worked, within my range, to forfend them. For those of us who have been awake to realities, this has been a lonely role. But more than half of my life went by before I realized how lonely. There are plenty of people today who view what has been happening in the twentieth century as an entirely normal manifestation of man's nature and destiny. They have no notion of how many dearly bought achievements of human culture (those particles of radium!) have now been buried in irredeemable rubbish heaps or swept out to sea in violent floods.

Most of our contemporaries, perhaps, still see only the endless bounties and benefits resulting from that part of our culture which has been changing most rapidly, and have closed their eyes to the varieties of dehumanization and extermination that twentieth century men—not just the Nazis and the Stalinists—have practiced on a colossal scale. They prefer not to think about the millions who met premature death in war or were gassed in extermination camps, or the countless men, women, and children who are being killed or maimed for life in automobile accidents, week after week, year after year. Even if our contemporaries hide these facts from themselves, there are others, too palpable to be overlooked, in "great" cities, where horrors in the form of mugging, rape, murder, and torture are practiced alike by criminals and by putative guardians of the law. Inoculated against any evidence that is contrary to their basic assumptions, these desensitized minds still believe that "science will find the answer," or that if worst comes to worst, a saving minority of mankind will escape to some other planet in a spaceship. This, incidentally, was the scenario of a play I outlined in 1914 or 1915—only in my version, I am proud to record, the more human residue of mankind remained behind.

By now, the myth of the machine, the basic religion of our present culture, has so captured the modern mind that no human sacrifice seems too great provided it is offered up to the insolent Marduks and Molochs of science and technology. Those who are in the grip of this myth imagine that with an increasing budget for scientific R. and D., with a more voluminous productivity, augmented by almost omniscient computers and a wider range of antibiotics and inoculations, with a greater control over our genetic inheritance, with more complex surgical operations and transplants, with an extension of automation to every form of human activity, mankind will achieve—what? "Happiness," people used to say, wistfully. But do they now not mean anesthesia? These processes are being directed by those who conceive happiness purely in terms of their ability to foster their own favored activities, and to execute plans that would, with the aid of sufficient Foundation grants, give them almost complete authority over the destiny of the human race. Life so misconceived and so misdirected can produce only mindless nonentities, incapable of performing as autonomous beings any organic or human functions.

One dare not smile in reflecting what happened to these soaring post-nineteenth century hopes at the very blast-off. The best one can say about them is that most of the scientifically organized imbecilities predicted by Aldous Huxley for the Brave New World in "the Seventh Century After Ford" have already become realities. But in my youth, as a zealous reader of Hugo Gernsback's monthly 'Modern Electrics,' I shared my generation's pious belief in our future; and I still look forward to the valid possibility of a slowing down of the pace of automation and depersonalization great enough to permit us to safeguard the immense treasuries of knowledge and technical facility now at our command. There is hardly an invention, a method, or a process produced by the institutions that now work in such a dismally negative fashion which might not in future prove humanly valuable, sometimes highly desirable, if it were applied at the right moment, in the right quantity, for the right purpose—that is, if it were under constant human evaluation and control, if it were directed to higher goals than the expansion of the megamachine and the exaltation of those who command it and profit by a virtual monopoly of its rewards.

But even at their best all these improvements, however helpful, remain peripheral: they fail to do justice to man's central concern, his own humanization. In letting depersonalized organizations and automatic contraptions take charge of our lives, we have been forfeiting the only qualities that could justify our existence: sensitiveness, consciousness, responsiveness, expressive intelligence, human-heartedness, and (alas, one cannot use this word now without wincing) creativity. And love! Yes, love above all. When, more than a century ago, Emerson observed that "things are in the saddle and ride mankind," he identified the conditions we now face in their full-grown form. And as man himself, he who was once—in all his self-sustaining racial, tribal, regional, national, civic, and ultimately personal varieties—potentially an autonomous being, shrinks and disappears, a new kind of creature, infra-human, fabricated to make our complex megamachine workable, has come into existence: the bureaucratic personality, punched and coded for the machine. As Max Weber predicted over fifty years ago, that under-dimensioned personality has become the all but universal type.

Now this inexorable regimentation, in its fabrication of such a rigid and sterile personality, has given rise to a counter-adaptation, for the bureaucratic type has been compensated for and secretly aided by its negative counterpart: the beatnik, the hippie, the gangster, and their later underground successors, who have rejected the dehumanized order of bureaucratic automation by rejecting as well those humanized modes of behavior by means of which man emerged from his original animal limitations. Indeed, they reject even such orderly routines, such life-sustaining activities, as animals themselves exhibit in acts of grooming, mating, food gathering, and nurturing of the young; and, in order to live at their chosen subanimal level, they destroy their minds and do violence to their bodies with drugs. Year by year, they ingeniously invent more sophisticated modes of disorder and perpetrate them on defenseless communities.

On the bureaucratic side, Adolf Eichmann, the man who faithfully carried out orders from above, is the veritable Hero of Our Time; and a thousand other Eichmanns stand ready to wipe out not just the Jews but the larger part of the human race as soon as the order comes through from the Pentagon or the Kremlin. There are Hitlers in every war office, and Eichmanns in every rocket center, in every aircraft carrier and submarine, in every nuclear and chemical and bacterial laboratory, as the consistently atrocious practices of the American military forces in Vietnam demonstrated.

Those of us who have lived to see this last transformation know the worst about our own countrymen—and so about the human race. The better world my generation grew up in was not wholly a complacent illusion, but we were scarcely equipped to reckon with the massive potentialities for evil that civilization, by its own dynamism and cold audacity, had expanded. Yet did not Giovanni Battista Vico warn us at the beginning of the enlightened eighteenth century that there was no barbarism more savage than that of 'civilized' man? Now 'The Age of Monsters' is here.

Obviously, I have, not without inner resistance, come to a vision of the world different from that which comforts—or, at best, only slightly discomforts—many of my contemporaries. It seems to me that, on the basis of rational calculations, derived from what must admittedly be incomplete evidence, *if the forces that now dominate us continue on their present path* they must lead to collapse of the whole historical fabric, not just this or that great nation or empire. Unfortunately, if we continue to act upon the premises that have increasingly automated all human activities, there will be no stopping point before the ultimate terminus: total destruction. Already, languages show signs of slithering into incoherence and confusion, with vocabularies so limited and a semantic structure so primitive that beside them the most elementary tribal language must count as a delicate work of art. H. G. Wells' dire prediction that "mind is at the end of its tether" can no longer be lightly dismissed as mere senile despair, as it could be in 1945.

To flinch now from facing these realities and evaluating them is to me an act of intellectual cowardice. But because I have dared to face and evaluate them I have often been dismissed as a 'prophet of doom.'

This is no more intelligent than to say of a physician who diagnoses a possibly fatal disease and applies his skill to curing it that he is a willing ally of the undertaker. On the contrary, every fibre of my being revolts against the fate that threatens our civilization, and revolts almost equally against those supine minds that accept it as inevitable, or, even worse, seek treasonably to justify its 'inevitability.'

From first to last, my own beliefs challenge those who think there is no turning back on the road that mankind is now travelling, no possibility of changing our minds or altering our course, no way of arresting or redirecting the forces that, if they are not subdued, will bring about the annihilation of man. For the last thirty years, then, I have been forced, much against my native interests and talents, to confront the suicidal nihilism of our civilization, for I believe that only those who are sufficiently awake to the forces that menace us and who have taken the full measure of their probable consequences will be able to overcome them. It is not as a prophet of doom but as an exponent of the Renewal of Life that I have faced the future: not by accident do the books I wrote between 1930 and 1950 bear that phrase for their common title. That title may seem, in the light of what has followed since, almost wantonly hopeful; certainly it did not spring from discouragement or despair. For those who share this vision, life itself is the central good and the source of all other goods: life in all its organic manifestations, and even in its dismaying contradictions, its ultimate tragedies—life embracing not alone love, courage, human-heartedness, and joy but alienation, frustration, and pain.

Now, what I mean by "life" cannot be packed into a single sentence or even a single page. Jeffery Smith, my onetime professorial colleague at Stanford, used to tell of a simple farmhand who had battled against odds all his life, raising a large family while barely able to keep his head above water. If any man had a right to be disheartened or bitter over his fate, it would seem to have been that man, yet he had never despaired. Then, a little while before he died, a visitor found him in a grievous condition, with an ailment that could no longer be fought off or grimly concealed. "Yes, my boy," he said. "My time has come. The feast of life will soon be over."

The feast of life! This phrase, uttered by a man who had faced more than his share of the burdens and miseries of life and seemed to have had too little of its rewards, is an affirmation that should confound a thousand nihilisms. The spirit is at one with the faith Whitman proclaimed, in his acceptance of evil as well as good, in his readiness to count no aspect of life too mean, too vile, too repulsive to be reckoned as part of its meaning and value. And did not Plotinus say that it was better for even an animal to have lived and suffered than never to have lived at all? This, I take it, is what a contemporary witness, Solzhenitzyn, has declared, with equal conviction, about his own experience of cancer, made doubly unbearable by his harsh imprisonment.

In the Second World War, "the feast of life" was snatched from our son at the age of nineteen—all too soon. But when, a little earlier, he was recalling with his sweetheart some of the most disruptive episodes in their association at school, he remarked, "I'm damned if it wasn't fun." Grievous though such an early death was, he had nevertheless known many moments of fulfillment. Far more lamentable is the kind of mental decomposition that takes place in those who have never consciously savored life's feast, for their unlived life takes its revenge, now sinking into docile acceptance of their prisonlike routine, now erupting in fantasies and acts of insensate violence. These victims are the real proponents of doom.

As the twentieth century approached, there was some popular debate as to when the old one came to an end, many holding that 1900 was the veritable beginning, in the face of those who could prove by the calendar that January 1, 1901, marked the true turning point, since the next century was not in existence until the nineteenth had completed its course. Little children are just as puzzled by the fact that when they are five years old they are in their sixth year. My wife remembers that as a child she always resented this premature advance of her age. But this debate is about an abstraction. In terms of events, the nineteenth century began in 1815, as my history teacher, Professor Salwyn Schapiro, used to point out, for it was then that the Napoleonic Wars came to an end; and the nineteenth century terminated in 1914, when the cycle of conflicts and calamities through which we are now living began.

Assuredly there were many signs that were a good augury for the twentieth century. In an effort to head off the coming war, the czar of Russia, no less an advocate of peace (and no more!) than his latter-day successors Khrushchev and Brezhnev, had in 1899 convoked the first great international peace conference, at The Hague; and even before that, at the World's Columbian Exposition, in Chicago, in 1893, an equally remarkable World Congress of Religions and their churches— bodies harder to disarm and unite than the more openly belligerent nations—had taken place. One might multiply these favorable instances. When the Paris Universal Exposition of 1900 opened, one of its features was the Rue des Nations, an effort (promoted by Patrick Geddes, who was an indefatigable internationalist) to give a concrete expression to the ideas of peace and coöperation by getting each nation to contribute a building in its own characteristic style, as an integral part of the larger whole, safeguarding variety while promoting the unity that the railroad, the steamship, the telegraph, and the telephone had already made possible—indeed, almost imperative. Such, at least, was the intention of this symbolism. Geddes was unable to get backing for his proposal to make this demonstration a permanent one, but, as it happened, the idea was carried out in Paris only a generation later, in the new students' quarter, the Cité Universitaire.

All over the planet, national barriers were breaking down. The risks on a fire-insurance policy in Chicago might be covered by organizations in London, Budapest, and Hamburg, just as Lloyd's still breaks up such risks among its share-takers. Banditry and piracy had ceased everywhere, except in petty strongholds like Sicily, and only a token force of soldiers and battleships was needed to hold vast empires in Africa and Asia, thus supplying at least outward order and security in partial atonement for the malign and callous exploitation that Joseph Conrad was soon to portray in his classic story 'Heart of Darkness.' For the first time in history, as the Italian historian Guglielmo Ferrero pointed out, "the freedom of the seas" actually prevailed throughout the world. Something better than the ancient Pax Romana seemed definitely established. Such conflicts as the Boer War and the Spanish-American War and the Balkan Wars appeared to be little more than a final trickle of bellicosity and savagery, dripping from a faucet that had been turned off.

There was further room for hope because more people than ever, beginning with the socialists and communists, were conscious of the many measures that needed to be taken to repair the inequities and injustices left over from the past. The democratic, egalitarian spirit seemed on the march everywhere: did not the liberal British Prime Minister Sir Henry Campbell-Bannerman proclaim that "good government" was no satisfactory substitute for self-government? And yet one must never forget that there remained a deep morass of human misery, for the margin of capitalist profits was still widened by the ancient method of grinding the face of the poor and calling in the police or the soldiery when the working class or the conquered tribes staged a rebellion. That underlying poverty remains today in supposedly affluent countries, such as the United States, and it is accentuated, rather than lessened, by doles, not to mention corruption, theft, and other impromptu modes of equalization.

Yet even the working class had a freedom then that no one now confidently enjoys. At the beginning of the twentieth century, anyone could travel anywhere he wished, except in Turkey and Russia, without a passport. Workers could move about freely on this planet if they were willing to face the hardships of steerage transportation. They sometimes moved seasonally from one country to another—say, from Italy to the Argentine. My wife's father and mother, thanks to such bribes as even poor people could bestow on the official wretches who guarded the frontiers, escaped from Russia early in the nineties, in order to avoid the long separation that military service would have imposed upon this just married Jewish couple. They had it hard when they reached America, but they stayed; even anti-Semitism was a little less virulent here. As for the proliferating middle classes, never before had such an abundance of material goods and so much cheap human service been at their disposal. For the first time in history, the whole planet was well policed—a precondition for any other kind of comity and unity. And the old moralities were still so studiously respected that—to take a trivial but significant example—newsstands were left unguarded in New York, permitting the buyers to make their own change.

It is only now, when these conditions have ceased to exist, that we can fully realize how much had actually been accomplished in establishing a more benign law and order, in lessening the more outrageous forms of injustice and violence. In many areas, there had been genuine improvements, so the representative figures of the Victorian Age had a right to crow loudly over their political achievements. But there were even surer signs that the tides of life were running high again. Auguste Rodin, the greatest sculptor of his time—probably the greatest since Michelangelo—became a commanding symbol of this vitality. He towered above his contemporaries almost as much because of his feeling for life as for his translation of that feeling into the animated forms, the fluent solids, of his sculptures. A benign deity was he, half Pan, half Jove, whose dancing bodies and passion-entwined lovers celebrated all the qualities left out of the cold Newtonian world picture that had fostered only science and technics. Ranged alongside Rodin were the many mighty spirits of the nineteenth century—scientists no less than artists—who were equally exalted by a fresh vision of life emerging from the primordial slime to dominate the planet and leave the imprint of organic form over every part of the environment, while the inner life of man had been animated and intensified by the works of Delacroix and Van Gogh and Cézanne, of Goethe and Tolstoi and Dostoevski, of Herman Melville and Walt Whitman.

Quite aside from the two-faced triumphs of technology, there was a great outpouring of energy in all the arts, first expressed in music, from the eighteenth century of Haydn and Mozart on, and this ultimately found its way into the remotest channels. To forget all these positive manifestations would be to repeat the howler made by Mark Twain when, on Whitman's seventieth birthday, in 1879, he congratulated Whitman on having lived long enough to behold the invention of the steam engine and the printing press, and thereby to have had a glimpse of man "at his full stature at last." If all the technical triumphs since 1815 had been wiped out the instant they occurred, the exuberant creativity of the Western mind would still have made this one of the most notable moments in human culture. The outlines of man's life were being redrawn, and large segments of his past, which had left only a faint impression on his customs and traditions, and a still fainter one on the written record, became visible. The discovery of man's origins, as archeologists raked among the bones and the stones buried in ancient geological strata, threw a fresh light on the human psyche. And when Picasso and his fellow-artists came into contact with primitive art they recognized vitalities that spoke directly to them. The rediscovery of the meaning of African and Polynesian art was also a rediscovery, parallel with Freud's 'Interpretation of Dreams,' of the dark continent of the psyche, and a recognition of the fact that no part of man's nature or his history could be buried or ignored without reducing his potentialities.

For those of us who came to maturity at the end of this period, Isadora Duncan, creating an imaginary Greek world out of our own twentieth century consciousness, more primitive than archaic, more archaic than archeological, will always remain a symbol of these ideal potentialities. Let us spare ourselves any ironic afterthoughts we might have today, for we might realize how little she represented anything that could now be called Greek—as little as Winckelmann's white plaster cast admiration for Hellenistic sculpture. What mattered in Isadora's Hellenic dances and dramatic presentations was not the Greek themes or the gauzy costumes but the uninhibited vitality, the sense of a glorious nakedness about to be affirmed, not only in the rituals of lovers but in every part of life. That illusion threw a veil over the more sordid aspects of the period that followed.

This upsurge of living ideas, this embrace of living organisms, this realization of life itself flowing through time, continuous but never more capturable than water is in a net, was expressed to perfection in the metaphysics of Henri Bergson. At the beginning of the twentieth century, he replaced the grim Malthusian picture of life as a lethal struggle for domination and survival with the picture of creative evolution, forever inventing new organs, building new forms, exploring new possibilities, intuitively finding new meanings, to be understood only by further acts of living. This was the underlying faith of the best minds of the period; and, allowing for differences of method and temperament, this is what links me to Bergson, to Kropotkin and Whitehead, and to my own master, Patrick Geddes. For all of them life, human life, and the highest product of human life, the increasingly conscious mind, widening and deepening, conscious even of its unconscious treasure hoard, came first.

Some of this vitality was an integral part—often a major part—of the inheritance of my generation, and for a while it tided us over the most threatening moments of the new century. For, as a healthy body does not usually register the first symptoms of a disease except in some purely local manifestation, so we did not recognize the more insidious forces within our culture that were attacking us. And when we finally became aware of our actual state, we fastened all too easily upon one single manifestation, war, as if it were not a symptom but the main cause. This sense of abundant vitality belonged to our youth; it was the reservoir upon which the prewar generation continued to draw; and even in old age some of us, having sufficient memory of that primordial energy, still derive from it courage in Shelley's words to "wage contention, with the times' decay"—no matter how impossible the odds.

By altering the angle of vision, by turning away from our knowledge of the pustulating evils of the last half century and dwelling only on the goods that still beckoned the Western World in the year I was born, I could, I realize, draw another picture, equally true—to the point where it became smudged and then obliterated by our actual experience. To draw that hopeful picture, I need only suppose that the First World War did not in fact break out—that instead there was a postponement, and that all the tensions and hostilities that brought it about dissolved themselves in a gale of cosmic laughter, while all the instruments of war passed into obsolescence in a double sense, never to be replaced, never to be improved. The world we would be facing now would still not be any blithering utopia, but the meaning of life would no longer be reduced to the evasion of premature death, and we could cultivate new flowers without augmenting the crop of nettles. But such happy endings cannot be faked.

Both the highest creative possibilities of the twentieth century and its tragic eventualities emerged symbolically in the life and thought of Dr. Sigmund Freud. His career tells both the best and the worst about the period we are now living in. It was Freud who reintroduced, in the guise of science, the very world that science had turned its back on at the beginning of the modern period: the world of dreams, of potentialities and ideal goals, if also the world of repressed desires and demonic impulses, often too morbid to be exposed to view and too life-threatening or life-debasing to be translated directly into action. This was a darker continent than Africa, and one penetrated it at one's peril, on the heels of this daring explorer. Freud, by uncovering the unconscious, had enlarged the boundaries of man's conscious life; and, much against his own medical training and expertness, he had given man's teeming fantasies, rejected by exact science, a status and a function equal to those of the objective world. To forget that man is a dreaming animal, who had perhaps dreamed himself into consciousness, was to ignore the very conditions of his emergence from animalhood.

This radical insight into the nature of man's whole inner life, as symbolized by but not restricted to his dreams, has not yet been generally accepted, since it challenges more primitive notions about the nature of the external world—views no less naïve than the wanton subjectivity of earlier religions. Yet 'The Interpretation of Dreams' opened up theretofore impenetrable areas of reality as decisively as radium and the other invisible rays had done in physics. Freud himself was too much a man of the nineteenth century to throw off its own materialistic premises; on that score, Jung, with a more adequate metaphysical background, went deeper than Freud, and remained closer to the sources of man's actual development. Though Freud in the end was to speak for disintegration and death more than for life, as the cancer that killed him penetrated every part of his being, he deepened our sense of reality and unwittingly prepared our minds for the dire events that were to follow. Ironically, when the First World War came, Freud's fine analytic intelligence, so sensitive and so subtle, was overlaid by uncritical hatred of The Enemy, which was supported by a pathetically puerile emotional identification with his own Germanic tribe. He who spoke so contemptuously of the irrationality of early religions bowed to the no less primitive idols of Nationalism. So if in his younger days Freud had helped to liberate the forces of life, he later, in turning from Eros to Thanatos, and thus canonizing the death 'instinct,' helped to undermine resistance to the forces of disintegration; in effect, he enfeebled us and disarmed us. When Albert Einstein consulted Freud about the nature of man, as bearing upon the possibility of eventually eliminating war, Freud spoke with the same naïve confidence in his competence to give an answer that he did when he dismissed religion as an obsolete illusion close to the classic manifestation of a neurosis.

That Black Hole of Freud's ultimate pessimism anticipated the scientific theory of the Black Hole in the universe—the Black Hole that astrophysicists now interpret as the fateful implosion and recoalescence of all the stars and planets and asteroids of the currently expanding universe into a solid, impenetrable lump, duplicating one whose explosion, perhaps tens of billions of years ago, created the starry sky itself and ultimately all the little pockets of life that possibly found a niche on this or that remote planet. The coincidence of these two varieties of Black Hole is of course an accident, indeed only an accident of metaphor, and the metaphor in both cases may be as willfully subjective as the visions of archangels and seraphim and thrones which buoyed up the waning energies of earlier ages. Yet no matter how these Black Holes are read, they remain an awful challenge; and at a lively luncheon of astrophysicists which I attended at M.I.T. one of their number irritably wondered how anyone could go on living from day to day without exhibiting any concern over this astronomical prospect, more lethal than the Black Hole of Calcutta, which threatens to bring an end to all cosmic existence—at least for the time being.

But are we sure that we are looking at the universe? Or is this ultimate black lump, like Freud's final orientation toward death, an image we find in our own demonic mirror, by closing our eyes and reading only what we see within? The astrophysicists are daringly open-minded fellows, and, like the good mathematicians they are, they must reckon with the paradox of the Möbius ring, and the possibility that their outer world is only our inner world turned inside out. So, perhaps, with a further twist of the ring, the impenetrable Black Hole might prove the shadow of a brighter sun. Even the notion of an Explosion and an Implosion, a 'beginning' and an 'ending,' may be only a very human metaphor, which the universe, for reasons of its own, neither recognizes nor exhibits. On that ultimate skepticism my own faith blithely flourishes. Let the curtain rise on the twenty-first century—*and After!*

IDENTIFICATIONS

A.Y.	Avrahm Yarmolinsky
B.D.	Babette Deutsch
C.K.B.	Catherine Kraus Bauer
D.C.L.	Dorothy Cecilia Loch (Delilah)
J.L.	Jerome Lachenbruch
J.S.	Josephine Strongin
P.G.	Patrick Geddes
S.W.	Sophia Wittenberg
S.W.M.	Sophia Wittenberg Mumford
V.B.	Victor Branford
V.W.B.	Van Wyck Brooks
W.F.	Waldo Frank

NOTE ON THE TEXT

In preparing these manuscripts for the press I have made only the most minor deletions and corrections, though my notes and letters are all first drafts which I never took the pains to rephrase. Even in the most minor corrections I have not been tempted to alter the meaning or make the text conform to my present views. In my rare departures from this rule I have put the additional words in brackets.

Index